perspectives
Online Journalism

edited by
Kathleen Wickham
Department of Journalism
The University of Memphis

Boulder • Bellevue • Dubuque • Madison

Our mission at CourseWise is to help students make connections—linking theory to practice and the classroom to the outside world. Learners are motivated to synthesize ideas when course materials are placed in a context they recognize. By providing gateways to contemporary and enduring issues, CourseWise publications will expand students' awareness of and context for the course subject.

For more information on CourseWise visit us at our Web site: www.coursewise.com

CourseWise Publishing Editorial Staff

Thomas Doran, ceo/publisher: Journalism/Marketing/Speech
Edgar Laube, publisher: Geography/Political Science/Psychology/Sociology
Linda Meehan Avenarius, publisher: CourseLinks
Sue Pulvermacher-Alt, publisher: Education/Health/Gender Studies
Victoria Putman, publisher: Anthropology/Philosophy/Religion
Tom Romaniak, publisher: Business/Criminal Justice/Economics

Other CourseWise Journalism publications
Journalism 2001 by Christopher Harper and the Indiana Group
Walking the HighWire: Effective Public Relations by Merry Clare Shelburne

Cover photo: Copyright © 1997 T. Teshigawara/Panoramic Images, Chicago, All rights reserved.

Interior design and cover design by Jeff Storm

Copyright © 1998 by CourseWise Publishing, Inc. All rights reserved

Library of Congress Catalog Card Number: 97-075311

ISBN 0-395-902266

No part of this publication may be reproduced, stored in a retrieval system, or transmitted, in any form or by any means, electronic, mechanical, photocopying, recording, or otherwise, without the prior written permission of the publisher.

Printed in the United States of America by CourseWise Publishing, Inc.
1379 Lodge Lane, Boulder, CO 80303

10 9 8 7 6 5 4 3 2 1

from the Publisher

CourseWise Publishing
Tom Doran

"You spliced it. You plug it in."—A weekend electrician to a colleague

Image having the choice of publishing for any academic discipline. Imagine selecting from such diverse and interesting fields as psychology, music and biology. Or journalism. Would you choose journalism? If you did choose journalism, what course would you choose to introduce the *first* publication in a new reader series? Intro to Mass Media? Media Law? Media and Society?

Yours truly faced just these choices when launching our new publishing company this past spring. Five other seasoned publishers and I divided editorial responsibilities by academic disciplines. As CEO, I had first choice. And I picked journalism. Furthermore, following the "lead by example" maxim, I was to publish our first reader. Our investors—and my colleagues—preferred a high-profile, sure-thing topic for this critically important first reader.

And so, when I confidently announced this past March that our first **PERSPECTIVES** would be for the Online Journalism course, support for this decision matched that of the weekend electrician. There were three concerns: the course was relatively new, it was being taught in a variety of ways and the subject matter made it a moving target. These concerns were the reasons I thought it would be the perfect place to start.

The Online Journalism course is an exciting development for the discipline of journalism. The fact that it is relatively new presents an opportunity to grow with and, hopefully, help share this important course. The fact that a variety of learning tools are used to teach this course makes it a perfect candidate for a reader. The fact that the subject matter is changing almost overnight makes our CourseLink Web Resources a perfect companion. And, on a selfish note, working with the instructors who teach this course is teaching me to be a smarter publisher.

One such instructor is Kathleen Woodruff Wickham. Kathleen is a practicing journalist who's been teaching journalism courses at The University of Memphis for 14 years and launched the computer-assisted reporting course at Memphis a few years back. A colleague recommended Kathleen knowing that, as investigative reporter, she had written investigative stories about organized crime. "She's tough enough to pull it off" was part of the endorsement.

And tough she's had to be. Our crackerjack editorial board didn't pull punches. The organization and article selections have been through a number of iterations. Through long, hot summer days and nights, Kathleen hammered away until we agreed she had crafted a R.E.A.L. learning tool: **R**elevant, **E**xciting, **A**pproved, **L**inked. My thanks to Kathleen and each member of the editorial board.

So now I get to plug it in. CourseWise is proud to introduce our first reader in the **PERSPECTIVES** Series—***PERSPECTIVES**: Online Journalism*. Good luck with this exciting course! Let us know how we did. Write me: tdoran@coursewise.com

from the
Academic Editor

Kathleen Woodruff Wickham
The University of Memphis

Online Journalism has a heart and a soul. Technical skills are the heart. The following readings portray its soul. They examine the powers and responsibilities of the media; the joy, excitement and romance of the profession and the traditions, concepts and beliefs that form news values in today's world.

For more than 14 years I have tried to convey these concepts to my students at The University of Memphis. I learned them during the 10 years I spent as a newspaper reporter in New Jersey. But it wasn't until I attended a conference sponsored by Investigative Reporters and Editors, Inc., that I realized how much the field had changed. I recognized college journalism had to adapt to meet the needs of the students or our students would be left behind. I left the conference with a mission: convince my colleagues that we needed to take a leadership role in teaching our students the basics of computer-assisted reporting. I was successful in launching the department's computer-assisted reporting course. And readings have been a part of the course from Day 1.

Some readings in this book came from my dog-eared binders. Members of the editorial board recommended others. The editorial board members are journalists and academics I have known professionally or have met at journalism conferences. These readings have depth and breadth. My goal was to select readings that will prepare students to become effective and successful journalists in the online world.

Over the years, I have found that when I digress from the formal language of a lecture to my real-life experiences, students' eyes light up, their backs are straighter and their attention sharper. Through anecdotes, they gain understanding. I would like these readings to function as anecdotes, to get the students' attention, to serve as a window on the larger picture.

All too often students decide to major in journalism because they like to write. They don't realize that is only part of the job. They need to be a curious observer of the world around them. Some writers have argued that such curiosity cannot be taught. I think it can be cultivated. These readings are intended to help with that process. My hope is that these articles help students see the range of possibilities in the online world and prepare for the challenges and hurdles this kind of journalism offers.

The Internet has traveled from the research center, to the newsroom and on into studies, libraries and dorm rooms across the world. And as it travels it creates change. Student journalists have to be prepared for these changes. This reader will set them on that path by challenging them to think critically about this new world of online journalism, and their role in its continued evolution and development.

Editorial Board

James J. Brodell
Assistant professor of journalism at Metropolitan State College of Denver. He's worked at a variety of newspapers including *The Sun Bulletin*, Binghamton, N.Y.; *The Daily Journal*, Caracas, Venezuela; *The Daily Advance*, Dover, N.J.; *The Home News*, New Brunswick, N.J., and *The Daily Sentinel*, Grand Junction, CO. He's also been the editor/owner of *The Citizen Newspaper*, Clifton, Colo. He brokered newspaper properties in four western states and is the author of *How to Purchase a Newspaper and Succeed*, the authoritative book on newspaper acquisitions.

Rose Ciotta
Computer-assisted reporting editor at *The Buffalo News* and teaches at the State University of New York–Buffalo. She chairs the education committee for Investigative Reporters and Editors Inc.

Sarah Cohen
Training director for the National Institute for Computer-Assisted Reporting. Before that position, she worked as a reporter in Florida at the *St. Petersburg Times* and *The Tampa Tribune*.

Anders Gyllenhaal
Executive editor of *The News & Observer*, in Raleigh, N.C., where he has also worked as managing editor and metro editor. He has been in the newspaper business for two decades, working as a reporter and editor at the Harrisonburg (Va.) *Daily News Record*, the *Atlantic City Press* and the *Miami Herald* before moving to The N&O in 1990.

Christopher Harper
Park Distinguished Professor in the School of Communications at Ithaca College. Before joining the academic world, Harper worked in a variety of capacities for the Associated Press, *Newsweek Magazine*, ABC News and ABC 20/20. His articles on digital journalism have appeared in various publications, including *American Journalism Review, Editor & Publisher Interactive* and the *Newspaper Research Journal*. He is the lead author of a new book for the news reporting course: *Journalism: 2001* (from CourseWise, Inc.) and a new book on digital journalism to be published in 1998 (from The New York University Press).

Penny Loeb
Senior editor on *U.S. News & World Report's* investigative reporting team and teaches at the University of Maryland. She previously worked at *New York Newsday*.

Eric Meyer
Managing partner of NewsLinks Associates, an independent research, consulting and publishing firm specializing in online and visual journalism, and serves on the journalism faculty at the University of Illinois where he teaches courses in information design and online publishing.

Stephen C. Miller
Assistant to the technology editor at *The New York Times*, and oversees the training of reporters and editors on using new technologies and writes on computer issues for the paper. Miller previously worked for CBS News, was a contributing editor for *Seybold's Outlook on Professional Computing and Home Office Computing*. He has written for numerous other consumer and trade magazines. Miller is currently on leave as a Professional in Residence at the Freedom Forum and is researching his book, *While Our Backs Were Turned: How Computers Changed Journalism*.

Neil Reisner
Computer-assisted reporting specialist at *The Miami Herald*. A reporter for nearly two decades, he served as training director with the National Institute for Computer-Assisted Reporting. He has taught journalism at Rutgers and Columbia universities. Reisner started his career as government reporter and computer-assisted reporting specialist for daily newspapers in New Jersey.

Steven S. Ross
Associate Professor of Professional Practice at Columbia University's Graduate School of Journalism. He has co-authored the largest studies of media use of cyberspace and has run Columbia's new media workshop. He has written 18 books, including many on computer technology.

Kathleen Woodruff Wickham
Newspaper reporter for 10 years in New Jersey at *The Star-Ledger*, in Newark, *The Press of Atlantic City* and *The Daily Advance in Dover*. She has been teaching journalism at The University of Memphis since 1983 and initiated the department's computer-assisted reporting course in 1994. She has freelanced for local and national publications, including *The New York Times*.

WiseGuide Introduction

Critical Thinking and Bumper Stickers

Let's start with bumper stickers. Why? WiseGuides thinks there's a particular bumper sticker that goes to the heart of critical thinking: Question Authority. The issue is not "authority" as right or wrong, but the questioning itself. It helps develop awareness and a clearer sense of what you yourself think. That's critical thinking.

Question Authority

Critical thinking is a new label for an old approach to learning: that any idea, hypothesis or assumption should not go unchallenged. The physical and life sciences use systematic questioning and testing methods known as the scientific method, which rests on the notion that all information must be verified. Objectivity is the benchmark on which all knowledge is to be pursued. In the social sciences, however, where the goal is to study people and their behavior, either individually or in groups, things get fuzzy. It's one thing for the chemistry experiment to work out as predicted, or for the petri dish to yield a certain result. It's quite another matter, however, in the social sciences. The subject is ourselves, and objectivity is harder to achieve.

Although you'll hear critical thinking defined in many different ways, it really boils down to analyzing the ideas and messages that you receive. What are you being asked to think or believe? Does it make sense, objectively? Using the same facts and considerations, could you reasonably come up with a different conclusion? And, why does this matter in the first place? As the bumper sticker urges, question authority. "Authority" can be a textbook, a politician, a boss, a big sister, or an ad on television. Whatever the message, learning to question it appropriately is a habit that will serve you well for a lifetime. And in the meantime, thinking critically will certainly help you be course wise.

Getting R.E.A.L.

This reader is one of our *R.E.A.L. learning tools.*™ That means that the readings and the other learning aids explained below are **R**elevant, **E**xciting, **A**pproved and **L**inked. Our Academic Editor and our Editorial Board developed these tools to assist you in thinking critically about the important issues of the course. CourseWise then tested these tools by putting them through our R.E.A.L. filter—a development model that includes feedback from both instructors and students. From that process, we developed the following suggestions on how to wisely use *R.E.A.L. learning tools.*™

Explanation of WiseGuide Pedagogy

WiseGuide Intro

A wise reader is better able to be a critical reader. Therefore, we want to help you get wise about the articles in this reader. For each section of *Perspectives* you'll find tools to help you be a wise reader. The first tool is the WiseGuide Intro. The Academic Editor and the Publisher teamed up to introduce the section and give you an **overview of topics** covered in the section, explaining why particular articles were selected, and what's important about these articles.

Next you'll find several bulleted points. They're either **learning objectives** (what you should learn from the section) or **key points** (what are the most important things to remember from this section). The bullets will help you focus your study of the topics covered in the section.

Finally, you'll see **questions** that introduce each article. These are designed to stimulate some critical thinking. Wise students will read an article keeping these questions in mind (we'll repeat the question at the start of the article as a reminder). When you finish the article, check your understanding. Can you answer the question? If not, go back and reread the article. For many of the questions we've included **sample responses** online at CourseLinks.com. Log on and check your understanding against some sample responses written for you by the Academic Editor.

WiseGuide Wrap-Up

Be course wise and develop a thorough understanding of the topics covered in this course. At the end of each section we'll give help to you to do just that with **summary points**—succinct phrases that summarize what you just read. Whether a concluding comment about one of the articles or a key point summarizing the section as a whole, *these* bullets reiterate what's most important to understand from the section you just read.

Finally, WiseGuides end with our effort to get you wired up. We will help you connect with **select Internet resources** and integrate them into your understanding of the subject and the course. At the end of every section we offer R.E.A.L. Sites that will enhance your understanding of a topic (remember to start at *courselinks.com* so that if any of these sites have changed you'll have the latest link).

The CourseLinks™ Site

The CourseLinks web site links these readings and the key course topics to an exciting and integrated array of online learning tools. Each site features carefully selected readings, links, quizzes and worksheets—tailored to your specific course and approved as *R.E.A.L. learning tools.*™ Always fresh and ever-changing, The CourseLinks™ Site provides you with new and evolving resources that have been recommended and approved by the Academic Editor and our Editorial Board of instructors who teach this course regularly. This is not a hodge-podge of web sites better suited for surfing than studying. The CourseLinks web site features carefully integrated resources designed to help you be course wise.

How to Use The CourseLinks™ Site:

Begin with the **Editor's Choice** page. Here you'll find updates on news related to your course, with links to the actual online source. In this column, we'll also tell you about changes to the site and online events, like guest speakers in the **CourseWise Auditorium.**

The next step is to gain a perspective on your course. Visit the **Course Overview.** This combination syllabus-and-topic-guide helps you prepare for the semester by putting the course in a context you recognize. It also provides a baseline for connecting the R.E.A.L. Sites to your course content.

At the core of a CourseLinks site is the list of <u>R.E.A.L.</u> **Sites.** Like the readings in this book, these sites have been selected, reviewed, and approved by the Academic Editor and our Editorial Board. These CourseLink sites, just like the readings in this book, are arranged by topic, and are annotated with short descriptions and key words. This way they'll be easier to use for reference or for research.

Next stop should be the **WWW.orksheet**. This quiz tests your knowledge of specific web sites. You'll be asked key questions about the content of a R.E.A.L. site or two. You can submit your answers to your professor—to show that you really DID visit the site—or yourself, to keep as a reference.

Another popular learning tool is the **Course Quiz.** The questions on this self-scoring quiz are related to articles in the reader, R.E.A.L. Sites and other course topics. To answer them, you'll need to have done a bit of exploring. It's a fun way to be course wise.

If you're new to the Net or want to brush up, stop by **The Web Savvy Student** site. This online publication is a unique supplement to The CourseLinks™ Site. **The Web Savvy Student** provides basic information on using the Internet, creating a web page, communicating on the web, and more. Quizzes and Web Savvy Worksheets are provided to test your knowledge. And you'll find Web Savvy R.E.A.L. sites that will further enhance your understanding of the Web. **The Web Savvy Student** site is a bonus supplement that's included with all CourseLinks sites!

Finally, drop by the **Student Lounge** to chat with other students taking the same course, or learn more about careers in your major. We've also added a list of sites that you might find interesting—some are serious, some are off-the-wall. Take a look around the Lounge and give us your feedback. We're open to remodeling the Lounge per your suggestions.

Some House Keeping Notes

"Putting it in Perspectives" Review Form

At the end of the book CourseWise provides the "Putting it in Perspectives" review form. This form can be used by faculty for assignments or by students for self-paced study or extra credit. Feel free to copy this form and distribute as needed.

Building Better Perspectives!

Students and Faculty: please help us build better *Perspectives*. Tell us what you think of this *Perspectives* volume so we can improve the next one. It's quick and easy. Here's how you can help:

1. Visit our CourseLinks site: *www.courselinks.com*
2. Go to the specific bulletin board for this Perspectives and click on "Building Better Perspectives."
3. Instructions for submission and forms will be available online.

At the web site, you can help determine which articles are **R.E.A.L.** learning tools™ (**R**elevant, **E**xciting and **A**ppropriate for **L**earning) by giving a √ to the articles that *have* the **R.E.A.L.** attributes and an **X** to articles that *lack* the **R.E.A.L.** attributes. That's all there is to it.

We encourage you to provide feedback after reading each article. We'll provide a gentle reminder with prompts at the end of each reading in this book. Thanks in advance for helping us build better *Perspectives*.

Student Internships

Note to students: if you enjoy evaluating these articles or would like to help us evaluate the CourseLinks™ for this course, check out **The CourseWise Student Internship Program.** For more information visit http://www.coursewise.com

Contents

section 1

A Better Hybrid: Trends from Changing Technologies

"By juxtaposing the best of the new model—computerized access, delivery, and a packaging of information—with the best of the old model—insightful reporting in a well written story—a better hybrid model that combines the best of both is created." From "The Evolution of the Newspaper in the Future" by Chris Lapham

Using the Internet, readers and viewers can directly sample events and locate sources of information vital to their lives without journalistic gatekeepers. What does this mean for journalism? What challenges and opportunities do emerging technologies present for the craft of journalism and the business of media communications?

1. **Ambrose, S. "When Was the Real Techno-Revolution?" A Forbes online article.** Available at http://www.forbes.com/asap/120296/html/stephenambrose.htm Traces the speed of the communication age. Solid background for discussions about on-line journalism. Starts with Jefferson and moves forward at a nice clip. **3**

2. **Wright, R. "The Man Who Invented the Web" Time, May 19, 1997, p. 64-68.** A profile of Tim Berners-Lee, the man who invented the world wide web. **5**

3. **Pavlik, J.V. "The Future of Online Journalism" Columbia Journalism Review, July/August 1997, p. 30-36. D. Caruso and A. Tucher ("Why Web Warriors Might Worry" p. 35), ("Show Me the Money" p. 32)** Deals with how online media connects with its readers, discusses push technologies and how news is packaged for online readers. The sidebars deal with the issue of online papers loosing money and why publishing organizations are subsidizing online media. **10, 14, 16**

4. **Harper, C. "The Daily Me" American Journalism Review, April 1997, p. 40-44.** Discusses customized news services at MIT and other "push" services. **20**

5. **Gunther, M. "News You Can Choose" American Journalism Review, November 1995, p. 35-38.** Deals with the issue of television and online news. Relates to customized news. **25**

6. **Lapham, C. "The Evolution of the Newspaper of the Future" CMC Magazine, July 1, 1995, p. 7+.** An essay on how technological change is changing mass media forms. With a call to action for newspapers interested in meeting the challenge. **30**

7. **Shaw, D. "Can Newspapers Find Their Niche in the Internet Age" Los Angeles Times, June 16, 1997.** Unless they combine the strengths of print and cyberspace, traditional media may have trouble surviving. **35**

8. **Biggs, Brooke Shelby. Stealth Sidewalk. Available online at http://www.packet.com/packet/biggs/nc_today.html** Questions the traditional media's reaction to MicroSoft's Sidewalk publication. **42**

9. **Harper, C. "The Haves and Have Nots" Editor & Publisher Interactive, May 16, 1997.** Explores computer/Internet usage patterns, noting that national demographics are followed on the Internet. The figures are important. They also speak to the issue of recruiting minorities to newspaper jobs. **44**

10. **Mendels, P. "Minorities Seek Online Identities" The New York Times Cybertimes, June 16, 1997.** A look at minority usage of the Net, both as consumers and as producers. **47**

11. **Shaw, D. "Internet Gold Rush Hasn't Panned Out Yet for Most" Los Angeles Times, June 19, 1997.** A look at the shakeout period, advertising issues, issues of free access and security concerns. **49**

section 2

On the E-Beat: Moving to the Center of the Newsroom

"Computer-assisted reporting has now moved from the computer nerd in the corner to the center of the newsroom." From "Baby You Should Drive This Car" by Rose Ciotta

This section explores different perspectives on the new and emerging field of online journalism. We'll examine how both the business and jobs within the business are changing as a result of new technologies. These readings explore the range of "beat possibilities," ranging from productivity gains through computer-assisted reporting to the changing expectations of the online public.

12. Fulton, K. "Future Tense: The Anxious Journey of a Technophobe" Columbia Journalism Review, Nov/Dec. 1993, p. 29-33. A first-person account of a journalist's acceptance of the Internet and related technologies. With a discussion of its impact on the field. **60**

13. Ciotta, R. "Baby You Should Drive This CAR" American Journalism Review, March 1996, p. 34-39. How reporters are using CAR in the newsroom and why some are not. **65**

14. Reisner, N. "On the Beat" American Journalism Review, March 1995, p. 44-47. How CAR techniques improved newsroom coverage of everything from local to major stories. **71**

15. Sullivan, D. "Building Your Own Local Hall of Records" The IRE Journal, March/April 1997, p. 10-11. Through electronic databases of local public records journalists can build the electronic version of their local hall of records in an easy-to-use format.. **76**

16. Williams, P. "Database Dangers" Quill, July/August 1994, p. 37-3. Computer-assisted research can have a downside. Examines the five common pitfalls of online research and how to avoid them. **79**

17. Horton, S. "The Widest Possible Access" Popular Government, Winter 1993, p. 11-16. Written by a staff member of the Wake County manager's office, the article gives a view of how government views the information explosion. **82**

18. Shaw, D. "Newspapers Take Different Paths to Online Publishing" Los Angeles Times, June 17, 1997. Shaw contends most newspapers repackage their paper without taking full advantage of the Web's unique capabilities. **88**

section 3

Online Careers: A Specialty or Recasting the Mold?

"No one can forecast whether multimedia journalism will become just one more specialty, or fundamentally remake the mold. But for newspaper people restless about the future, taking a taste of new media seems wise." From "The New Journalist" by Charles Stepp

What will be expected of entry-level journalists by the time this year's freshmen enter the work force? In this section we'll take a look at journalists who have left traditional journalism jobs for jobs in new media. We'll look at newspapers where online journalism occurs daily. And, we'll explore what job skills are needed in the exploding online world. Articles under consideration for this unit include:

19. Stepp, C. "The New Journalist" American Journalism Review, April 1996, p. 19-23. Online era demands added skills and innovative ways of looking at the profession. Editors are looking for people with a blend of traditional and futuristic skills. **97**

20. Moeller, P. "The Digitized Newsroom" American Journalism Review, Jan/Feb. 1995, p. 42-47. The Raleigh News & Observer uses powerful databases, online research and new approaches to reporting and writing to become a leader in computer-assisted reporting. **103**

21. **Landau, G. "Quantum Leaps: Computer Journalism Takes Off" Columbia Journalism Review, May/June 1992, p. 61.** Starting with Elliot Jaspin, Landau traces the growth of computer-assisted journalism with a brief look at the people and a longer look at the stories. **108**

22. **Harper, C. "Doing It All" American Journalism Review, Dec. 1996, p.24-29.** The Chicago Tribune is one of the few papers with reporters devoted exclusively to its online version. A look at how it all works, from the reporter's viewpoint. **112**

23. **Ianzito, C. "It's a Job but Is It Journalism?" Columbia Journalism Review, Nov/Dec. 1996, p. 31-35.** First-generation Web content-providers provide a view of the field while editors provide their views as well. **118**

24. **Shepard, A. "Webward Ho!" American Journalism Review, March 1997, p. 33-38.** The chance to be a pioneer in the new medium of the Web is luring traditional print and broadcast journalists. At MSNBC. **124**

25. **Morgan, H. "Doing It in Dayton" Quill, May 1994, p. 29-33.** The Dayton Daily News incorporated major changes into its newsroom structure—all at once. These included computer-assisted reporting and new writing styles. **129**

26. **Pogash, C. "Cyberspace Journalism" American Journalism Review, June 1996, p. 26-31.** A look at online 'zines and the people who work for them. A lively look at the topic. **134**

27. **Weeks, L. "Baron of Business News" The Washington Post, Dec. 8, 1996, p. H01.** A lengthy article on media mongrel Michael Bloomberg. Known best for his information-service terminals, he also owns a Wall Street magazine, TV network and radio station. **136**

section 4

A New Wild West: Where's the Law? Whose Ethics?

"It's really the Wild West out there," says one New York advertising executive. "I don't have to really worry about truth in advertising on the Internet. I just have to worry about kiddie porn." From "Bad Law, Tough Issues; The Internet, Free Speech and the CDA" by Christopher Harper

Is it true that the first defense against unethical, inaccurate or unfair journalism really starts with the individual reporter? If so, is the online legal and ethical arena that different from its print counterpart? If not, what then? This unit looks at what rules and regulations have been applied to the new Wild West and the debates generated from recent court rulings.

28. **Harmon, A. "Internet Tests Boundaries of Decency—and Nations" Los Angeles Times, March 19, 1997.** Written the day the Supreme Court heard arguments relating to the Communications Decency Act, it dissects the issues in light of the global nature of the Internet. **144**

29. **Harper, C. "Bad Law, Tough Issues: The Internet, Free Speech and the CDA" Editor & Publisher Interactive, March 18, 1997.** A look at CDA prior to the Supreme Court's ruling and how libraries, universities and government are dealing with the issues in three cases. Short article. **147**

30. **Labriola, D. "Getting Through the Maze" Presentation, Sept. 1994.** Usage of Internet clips, audio and video to create multimedia products—the legal hazards. **150**

31. **Penchina, R. "Venturing Online: Protecting You and Your Product in Cyberspace" Editor & Publisher, June 24, 1995, p. 15, 16, 123.** Discuss what materials can be republished on the Internet. **154**

32. **Levinson, N. and Demac, D. "The Cutting Edge: New Media Bring New Problems to Copyright Arena" Los Angeles Times, Sept. 2, 1996, Business section, p. 1.** Story on the status of intellectual property in the electronic marketplace and how developers of electronic material should be compensated. **156**

33. **Mann, F. "Moving Beyond 'Code First, Ask Questions Later'."** Examines ethical issues surrounding online newspapers. **159**

section 5

Digging Behind the Screen: Two Cases

"Every news organization ought to be digging beneath surface events on local, national and international issues." From "Drawing Conclusions from Investigative Reporting" by Steve Weinberg

Computers are only a tool in the arsenal of good reporting. While articles in this section deal with controversies surrounding investigative journalism online, they also examine fundamental questions pertaining to the craft of journalism—no matter the medium.

Case 1: *The San Jose Mercury News*

34. **Hinkle, P. "Soul Searching in San Jose" Columbia Journalism Review, July/August 1997, p. 38-43.** A look at the controversial series after the editor of the Mercury News said he felt there were flaws. **166**

35. **Kornbluh, P. "The Storm Over 'Dark Alliance'" Columbia Journalism Review, Jan/Feb. 1997, p. 32-39.** An examination of the controversial series and the impact of the Web in spreading the story. **172**

36. **Weinberg, S. "Drawing Conclusions from Investigative Reporting" The IRE Journal, Nov/Dec. 1996, p. 4-7.** An examination of the controversies over several major investigative stories that utilized online journalism reporting techniques. Takes a look at some of the projects and the people who write them. **180**

Case 2: Timothy McVeigh and *The Dallas Morning News*

From five stories that appeared in Quill, April 1997 **185**

37. **Langer, R. "Our Story, Process Correct"** The editor of the Dallas Morning News defends his decision to run the story on the Web site prior to print publication. **185**

38. **Buser, P. J. "Fair Trial vs. Free Press"** A look at McVeigh trial coverage and other famous trials. Considerations that might be a factor in publishing different facets of a highly public trial. **187**

39. **Sanford, B. "Openness Benefits All"** Discussion about pre-trial publicity. **191**

40. **Buser, P. J. "Legal Ethics Issues"** What guides attorneys in their decisions re: leaks. **193**

41. **Steele, B. "Until We Know, Let Us Challenge"** An ethical discussion relating to the whole incident. **196**

Index **201**

Topic Key

This Topic Key is an important tool for learning. The Topic Key will help you integrate this reader into your course studies. Listed below, in alphabetical order, are important topics covered in this volume. Below each topic you'll find the article or articles relating to that topic. Note that the Topic Key might not include every topic your instructor chooses to emphasize. If you don't find the topic you're looking for in the Topic Key, check the index or the OnLine Topic Key at the **courselinks**™ Site.

Access Issues
  The Widest Possible Access

Advertising
  The Future of Online Journalism
    Show Me the Money
    Why Web Warriors Worry
  Can Newspapers Find Their Niche
  Newspapers Take Different Paths

Broadcast News
  News You Can Choose
  The Future of Online Journalism
  The Digitized Newsroom
  The New Journalist
  Webward Ho
  It's a Job, But Is It Journalism
  Doing It All
  Baron of Business News

Careers
  It's a Job, But Is It Journalism
  Webward Ho
  The New Journalist
  Doing It in Dayton
  Baby You Should Drive This CAR
  On the Beat
  The Digitized Newsroom
  The Daily Me

Community Journalism
  Doing It in Dayton
  The Digitized Newsroom

Computer-Assisted Reporting
  Baby You Should Drive This CAR
  On the Beat
  Building Your Own Hall of Records
  The Digitized Newsroom
  Database Dangers
  Quantum Leaps
  The Man Who Invented the Web
  Soul Searching
  Drawing Conclusions

Copyright
  Getting Through the Maze
  Venturing Online
  The Cutting Edge: New Media

Current Issues
  Our Story, Our Process Correct
  Fair Trial vs. Free Press
  Openess Benefits All
  Legal Ethics Issues

  Until We Know, Let Us Challenge
  Soul Searching
  The Storm Over "Dark Alliance"
  Drawing Conclusions

Database Searching
  Database Dangers
  Baby You Should Drive This CAR
  On the Beat
  The Digitized Newsroom
  The Widest Possible Access
  Doing It in Dayton
  The Man Who Invented the Web

Decency
  Bad Law, Tough Issues
  Internet Tests Boundaries of Decency

Demographics
  The Haves and the Have Nots
  Minorities Seek Online Identity
  Internet Gold Rush
  Future of On-line Journalism

Diversity
  The Haves and the Have Nots
  Minorities Seek Online identity

Desktop Journalism
  When Was the Real Techno-Revolution
  Stealth Sidewalk
  The Man Who Invented the Web
  Baron of Business

Economic Models
  Internet Gold Rush
  The Future of Online Journalism

Ethics
  Fair Trial vs. Free Press
  Openess Benefits All
  Our Story, Our Process
  Legal Ethics Issues
  Until We Know, Let Us Challenge

Features
  Baby You Should Drive This CAR
  On the Beat
  The Digitized Newsroom
  The New Journalist
  Baron of Business

Freelance Issues
  The Cutting Edge: New Media

Future Trends
  Future Tense

  The Evolution of the Newspaper
  The Future of Online Journalism
  Can Newspapers Find Their Niche
  Newspapers Take Different Paths
  Internet Gold Rush Hasn't Panned Out

History
  When Was the Real Techno-Revolution
  The Man Who Invented the Web

Information Retrieval
  Database Dangers
  Baby You Should Drive This CAR
  On the Beat
  The Digitized Newsroom
  The Widest Possible Access
  Doing It in Dayton
  The Man Who Invented the Web

Internet Usage
  The Future of Online Journalism
    Show Me the Money
    Why Web Warriors Worry
  Can Newspapers Find Their Niche
  Newspapers Take Different Paths
  Internet Gold Rush

Legal Issues
  Getting Through the Maze
  Venturing Online
  The Cutting Edge: New Media
  The Widest Possible Access
  Fair Trial vs. Free Press
  Openess Benefits All
  Legal Ethics Issues

Marketing
  Can Newspapers Find Their Niche
  Newspapers Take Different Paths
  Internet Gold Rush
  The Haves and the Have Nots
  Minorities Seek Online Identity
  The Future of Online Journalism
    Show Me the Money
    Why Web Warriors Worry
  The Evolution of the Newspaper
  Stealth Sidewalk

Mass Communication
  The Future of Online Journalism
    Show Me the Money
    Why Web Warriors Worry

xiii

The Evolution of the Newspaper
Stealth Sidewalk
Can Newspapers Find Their Niche
Newspapers Take Different Paths
Internet Gold Rush
News You Can Choose
Doing It in Dayton
The Digitized Newsroom
The Man Who Invented the Web
When Was the Real Techno-Revolution
Stealth Sidewalk
Baron of Business
The Haves and the Have Nots
Minorities Seek Online Identity

Media Writing
The Daily Me
News You Can Choose
It's a Job, But Is It Journalism
The Digitized Newsroom
Doing It All
Doing It in Dayton
Cyberspace Journalism
Webward Ho!

Minority Issues
The Haves and the Have Nots
Minorities Seek Online Identities

Multimedia Issues
Getting Through the Maze
Venturing Online

Online Access
The Widest Possible Access

Online Magazines
Cyberspace Journalism

Online Newspapers
The Evolution of the Newspaper
Can Newspapers Find Their Niche
Newspapers Take Different Paths
Internet Gold Rush
Baby You Should Drive This CAR
On the Beat

The Digitized Newsroom
Future Tense
The Future of Online Journalism
The Haves and the Have Nots
Minorities Seek Online Identity
Doing It in Dayton
The Daily Me
News You Can Chose
Show Me the Money

Online Searching
Database Dangers
Baby You Should Drive This CAR
On the Beat
The Digitized Newsroom
The Widest Possible Access
Doing It in Dayton
The Man Who Invented the Web

Personalized News Services
The Daily Me
News You Can Choose
Stealth Sidewalk

Pornography
Internet Tests Boundaries of Decency
Bad Law, Tough Issues

Profiles
Baron of Business
Quantum Leaps
The Man Who Invented the Web

Push Technologies
The Daily Me

Regulation
Internet Gold Rush
Internet Tests Boundaries
Bad Law, Tough Issues

Reporting
On the Beat
Baby You Should Drive This CAR
The Daily Me
Doing It in Dayton

Research
When Was the Real Techno-Revolution
The Man Who Invented the Web

Security Issues
Internet Gold Rush

Skills
The Future of Online Journalism
On the Beat
Building Your Own Hall of Records
Database Dangers
Baby You Should Drive This CAR
The Daily Me
The New Journalist
Doing It in Dayton
It's a Job, But Is It Journalism
Webward Ho
Digitized Newsroom

Story Strategies
On the Beat
Building Your Own Hall of Records
Database Dangers
Baby You Should Drive This CAR
The Daily Me

Webcasting
Can Newspapers Find Their Niche
Newspapers Take Different Paths
Internet Gold Rush

Writing Online
The Daily Me
News You Can Choose
It's a Job, But Is It Journalism
The Digitized Newsroom
Doing It All
Doing It in Dayton
Cyberspace Journalism
Webward Ho

'zines
Cyberspace Journalism

section 1

A Better Hybrid: Trends from Changing Technologies

Key Points

- Identify the major technology trends that are impacting online journalism.
- Recognize the opportunities and challenges these trends present to online and traditional publishers.
- Explore your opinions about how these technologies should be used. As a journalist, what developments will you want?

"By juxtaposing the best of the new model—computerized access, delivery, and a packaging of information—with the best of the old model—insightful reporting in a well written story—a better hybrid model that combines the best of both is created."
—Chris Lapham

WiseGuide Intro

Journalism's basic values consist of a commitment to readers and viewers to inform, explain and analyze local, national and world events. Online media technologies have affected these values to a significant degree. Because of the Internet, readers and viewers can directly sample events and locate sources of information vital to their lives without journalistic gatekeepers. Furthermore, they can communicate with the larger world at minimal cost. Because so much information is readily available, the public is quick to question editors' decisions and to make their own news judgments. And, with push technology, web pages and customized news services, readers and viewers can create personal news sources and eliminate the traditional journalistic filters.

In this section, we'll explore the trends in online journalism that present both enormous challenges and wonderful opportunities for traditional and nontraditional publishers alike. We'll see that, indeed, a new hybrid appears to be emerging. We'll explore this dynamic and its impact on journalism and the reader.

One such impact is that online opportunities have already begun to shrink the power of institutional voices. Another is that the Internet has created new opportunities for diverse members of the community to be heard and to be informed. A bottomless news hole is another piece of the new hybrid. To take advantage of these trends, online publishers are deploying different tactics ranging from providing hourly news updates to posting news stories on Web sites before they appear in print.

Publishers, however, are still in search of the right hybrid, experimenting with what to offer on their Web sites while conducting extensive customer research. Options include expanding the depth of traditional coverage of news stories, restaurant and movie reviews, sports scores, classified ads, business news, and public records through the use of multimedia. Providing links to related material is one popular trend. Another trend seems to be expanding nontraditional features such as archives, specialized updates and interactive reports.

There is a downside. Online publications run the risk of resembling all-news radio, with an emphasis on immediacy over depth and context. With push technology, readers can restrict the information flow, narrow their view of the world and limit their exposure to the world beyond the borders they select. While the end user's ability to access and customize information online does not spell doom for journalists, it will certainly present challenges and force change.

> **Questions**
>
> 1. Does delivering a story online change how the story is developed? Presented? If so, what's changed?
>
> 2. What do customized news and push technologies mean for online journalism? What are the pros and cons of this kind of technology? How should publishers incorporate these technologies?
>
> 3. Will the demographics for online publishers be similar to or radically different from those of more traditional publications?

The result is that, in the future, editors also may have to consider the best medium for presenting the news. Will it be print, audio, video or a combination? The gulf between print skills and broadcast skills is narrowing as online technologies develop. But, in reality, most journalists are going to need multimedia skills in the future. An individual journalist might not work in all areas, but journalists will need to understand the needs of the field to produce credible online news and related editorial content.

Traditional journalism is undergoing tremendous shifts, upheavals and changes—but not to worry. Radio, and then television, required a different skill set for delivering the news. Cable was another challenge. In each case, journalists adapted and can be expected to do so in the future. The demand for journalistic skills will continue no matter how the field evolves. As you'll read in the Perspectives within, the options are increasing, and a new hybrid is emerging. But the need for the basic values of journalism remains.

A historical look is required to understand better the impact technology has had, and continues to have, on society. In the following article, Stephen Ambrose traces the impact of technology on American society, beginning with Thomas Jefferson and ending with a look toward the next century. How do you think Thomas Jefferson would have reacted to the idea of online journalism? What do you think Samuel Morse's role might have been had he been born a century later? What tools will journalists be using in the year 2099?

When Was the Real Techno-Revolution?

Stephen Ambrose

Stephen Ambrose's big break came when Dwight Eisenhower asked him to be his biographer. He has been among the most eclectic of American historians, with bestselling books on Richard Nixon, D Day, and most recently, Lewis and Clark.

We live in an age in which rapid change is certain. We have lived in a century that has experienced more change than any other. Or so we believe. In fact, the generation that had to deal with the greatest changes in business, commerce, war, and all other aspects of human life lived in the first half of the nineteenth century, not the second half of the twentieth.

In 1810, nothing moved faster than the speed of a horse. Nothing ever had moved any faster and, so far as the people of 1810 were aware, nothing ever would. Trade goods or information, news of any kind, and armies all moved by either muscle power, wind in the sails, or falling water. When Thomas Jefferson left the White House in 1809, it took him ten days of hard riding to get to Monticello. Had a Roman legion set off up the Missouri River in 1804, except for the rifle and sextant, its equipment would have been the same as Lewis and Clark's, and it would have moved at the same pace. Writing in the last decade of the nineteenth century about conditions in the year of Jefferson's inaugural, Henry Adams put it perfectly: "Great as were the material obstacles in the path of the United States, the greatest obstacle of all was in the human mind. Experience forced on men's minds the conviction that what had ever been must ever be."

Jefferson was an exception. In 1793 he saw a hot-air balloon ascent. He wrote his daughter, "The security of the thing appeared so great that I wish for one sincerely, to travel in, as instead of ten days, I should be within five hours of home." He was attracted to the idea of using steam power to move carriages. In 1802 he predicted, "The introduction of so powerful an agent as steam to a carriage on wheels will make a great change in the situation of man."

But not even Jefferson could imagine the impact of the invention that did the most to change the world, the telegraph. In 1844, twenty years after Jefferson's death, Samuel Morse sent the first message over an electric wire. It was not perfected in time for the Mexican War, the last one fought by the United States in which the War Department could not communicate with its generals in the field. In the Civil War, the telegraph allowed the two presidents instant contact with the generals (in 1942, when General Eisenhower in North Africa was being pestered by Washington, he groaned that he wished they were back in the days of the sailing ships).

Before Morse, and before the train (which was dependent on the telegraph for safe, efficient operation), it took a month to get information from Chicago to New York. By the 1850s, information moved all but instantly. That changed everyone's lives. It unified the nation. It made the stock market possible. Its impact on commerce and trade was beyond description. It immediately opened the opportunity for military and commercial espionage; during the Civil War, each side tapped into the other guy's lines, which led to encoding messages, which led to code breaking and thus to the first signal intelligence.

Thanks to trains and steamships when Abraham Lincoln became president, Americans could move bulky items in great quantity farther in an hour than they could when Jefferson left office, when such a move might take a day. This great leap forward in transportation in so short a time was, along with the telegraph, the most unexpected and consequential technological revolution of all.

In dealing with the changes in the digital revolution that are sure to come in the twenty-first century, we have an advantage over the men who led the divided nation during the Civil War. Jefferson Davis and Abraham Lincoln were born when Jefferson was president. When they were growing up, no one imagined the telegraph or the train. As presidents, the very life of their nation depended on how well they utilized the telegraph and the trains. For us, even though we cannot always imagine *what* technological changes will be made, we do expect their occurrence. The challenge of adjusting to change cannot be what it was to Davis and Lincoln.

But as with them, as with their successors, so with us today—technology has advanced very much faster than politics, meaning that we know how to work miracles in electronics, but we have not learned how to prevent war. And here the lesson of history is clear: The side that gets ahead and stays ahead in technology, especially electronics, will win, as happened in the Civil War, World Wars I and II, Korea, and the Persian Gulf. Vietnam is the apparent exception, but in Vietnam the United States chose not to use its technological advantages to their fullest.

So my prediction is that if the United States stays ahead of the world in electronics and electronics-dependent weapons, in the year 2099 she still will be a democracy, proud and independent. The leading journals of the day will be carrying think pieces about how quaint we of 1996 were, with our inability to even begin to anticipate what actually happened.*

 **Article Review Form at end of book.**

Available at http://www.forbes.com/asap/120296/html/stephen_ambrose.htm

Tim Berners-Lee created the computer programming that led to the development of the World Wide Web. In the following article by Robert Wright, you get to meet Berners-Lee and discover why he is not as well known as Bill Gates of Microsoft Inc. When was hypertext first conceived? Why was hypertext not initially developed? What three developments are credited to Berners-Lee?

The Man Who Invented the Web

Tim Berners-Lee started a revolution, but it didn't go exactly as planned

Robert Wright

You might think that someone who invented a giant electronic brain for Planet Earth would have a pretty impressive brain of his own. And Tim Berners-Lee, 41, the creator of the World Wide Web, no doubt does. But his brain also has one shortcoming, and, by his own account, this neural glitch may have been the key to the Web's inception.

Berners-Lee isn't good at "random connections," he says. "I'm certainly terrible at names and faces." (No kidding. He asked me my name twice during our first two hours of conversation.) Back in 1980 he wrote some software to help keep track of such links—"a memory substitute." The rest is history. This prosthetic extension of his mind took a vast evolutionary leap a decade later, and then grew to encompass the world. It is the reason that today you can be online looking at a photo, then mouse-click on the photographer's name to learn about her, then click on "Nikon" to see the camera she uses—traveling from computers in one end of the world to those in another with no sense of motion.

Berners-Lee is the unsung—or at least undersung—hero of the information age. Even by some of the less breathless accounts, the World Wide Web could prove as important as the printing press. That would make Berners-Lee comparable to, well, Gutenberg, more or less. Yet so far, most of the wealth and fame emanating from the Web have gone to people other than him. Marc-Andreessen, co-founder of Netscape, drives a Mercedes-Benz and has graced the cover of several major magazines. Berners-Lee has graced the cover of none, and he drives a 13-year-old Volkswagen Rabbit. He has a smallish, barren office at M.I.T., where his nonprofit group, the World Wide Web Consortium, helps set technical standards for the Web, guarding its coherence against the potentially deranging forces of the market.

Is Berners-Lee's Volkswagen poisoning his brain with carbon monoxide? He wonders about this by way of apologizing for the diffuseness of his answers. "I'm not good at sound bites," he observes. True, alas. But what he lacks in snappiness he makes up in peppiness. Spouting acronyms while standing at a blackboard, he approaches the energy level of Robin Williams. He is British (an Oxford physics major), but to watch only his hands as he talks, you'd guess Italian. Five, six years ago, during his "evangelizing" phase, this relentless enthusiasm was what pushed the Web beyond critical mass.

The breathtaking growth of the Web has been "an incredibly

Copyright © 1997 Time, Inc. Reprinted by permission.

good feeling," he says, and is "a lesson for all dreamers . . . that you can have a dream and it can come true." But Berners-Lee's story has more facets than simple triumph. It is in part a story about the road not taken—in this case the road to riches, which in 1992 he pondered taking, and which he still speaks of with seemingly mixed emotions. His is also a story about the difficulty of controlling our progeny, about the risky business of creating momentous things, unleashing epic social forces. For Berners-Lee isn't altogether happy with how the World Wide Web has turned out.

He says he'd give the Web a B-plus, even an A-minus, that on balance it is a force for good. Yet an "accident of fate" has compromised its goodness. And that accident is intertwined with—perhaps, perversely, even caused by—his decision back in 1992 to take the road less traveled. The question that fascinates people who have heard of Berners-Lee—Why isn't he rich?—may turn out to have the same answer as the question that fascinates him: Why isn't the World Wide Web better than it is?

Berners-Lee comes by his vocation naturally. His parents helped design the world's first commercially available computer, the Ferranti Mark I. "The family level of excitement about mathematics was high," he says, recalling the breakfast-table teasing of his younger brother, then in primary school, who has having touble fathoming the square root of negative four.

In adolescence Berners-Lee read science fiction, including Arthur C. Clarke's short story *Dial F for Frankenstein*. It is, he recalls, about "crossing the critical threshold of number of neurons," about "the point where enough computers get connected together" that the whole system "started to breathe, think, react autonomously." Could the World Wide Web actually realize Clarke's prophecy? No—and yes. Berners-Lee warns against thinking of the Web as truly alive, as a literal global brain, but he does expect it to evince "emergent properties" that will transform society. Such as? Well, if he could tell you, they wouldn't be emergent, would they?

But making them as benign as possible is what gives his current job meaning. Even if the Web's most epic effects can't be anticipated or controlled, maybe they can be given some minimal degree of order. As director of the Web consortium, he brings together its members—Microsoft, Netscape, Sun, Apple, IBM and 155 others—and tries to broker agreement on technical standards even as the software underlying the Web rapidly evolves. His nightmare is a Web that "becomes more than one Web, so that you need 16 different browsers, depending on what you're looking at." He especially loathes those BEST VIEWED WITH ACME BROWSER signs on Web sites.

Most of the consortium's achievements to date are, if important, arcane. (You probably don't care that HTML 3.2 is a widely respected standard, even though that fact greatly eases your travel on the Web.) But some are more high profile. PICS, the Platform for Internet Content Selection, is a proposed standard that would let parents filter out offending Web sites. It's a kind of V chip, except with no government involvement; you subscribe to the rating service of your choice.

It is for "random reasons" that Berners-Lee is known as the inventor of the World Wide Web, he says. "I happened to be in the right place at the right time, and I happened to have the right combination of background." The place was CERN, the European physics laboratory that straddles the Swiss-French border, and he was there twice. The first time, in 1980, he had to master its labyrinthine information system in the course of a six-month consultancy. That was when he created his personal memory substitute, a program called Enquire. It allowed him to fill a document with words that, when clicked, would lead to other documents for elaboration.

This is "hypertext," and it was hardly new. The idea was outlined by Vannevar Bush in 1945 and envisioned as an appendage to the brain. Berners-Lee explains the brainlike structure of hypertext by reference to his cup of coffee. "If instead of coffee I'd brought in lilac," he says, sitting in a conference room in M.I.T.'s computer-science lab, "you'd have a strong association between the laboratory for computer science and lilac. You could walk by a lilac bush and be brought back to the laboratory." My brain would do this transporting via interlinked neurons, and hypertext does it via interlinked documents. A single click from lilacs to lab.

The trouble with most hypertext systems, as of the late 1980s, was that they were in one sense unlike the brain. They had a centralized database that kept track of all the links so that if a document was deleted, all links to it from other documents could be erased; that way there are no "dangling links"—no arrows pointing to nothing, no mouse-clicks leading nowhere. When Berners-Lee attended hypertext exhibits and asked designers whether they could make their systems worldwide, they often said no, citing this need for a clearinghouse. Finally, "I realized that this dangling-link thing may be a problem, but you have to accept it." You have to let somebody in Tokyo remove a document without informing everyone in the world whose documents may point to it. So those frustrating WEB SITE NOT FOUND messages delivered by today's browsers are the price we pay for having a Web in the first place.

In between the birth of Enquire and the birth of the Web a decade later, the world had changed. The Internet, though still unknown to the public, was now firmly rooted. It was essentially a bare-bones infrastructure, a trellis of empty pipes. There were ways to retrieve data, but no really easy ways, and certainly nothing with the intuitive, neural structure of hypertext.

To Berners-Lee, now back at CERN, one attraction of the Internet was that it encompassed not just CERN but CERN's far-flung collaborators at labs around the world. "In 1989, I thought, look, it would be so much easier if everybody asking me questions all the time could just read my database, and it would be so much nicer if I could find out what these guys are doing by just jumping into a similar database of information for them." In other words: give everyone the power to Enquire.

Berners-Lee wrote a proposal to link CERN's resources by hypertext. He noted that in principle, these resources could be text, graphics, video, anything—a "hypermedia" system—and that eventually the system could go global. "This initial document didn't go down well," says Berners-Lee. But he persisted and won the indulgence of his boss, who okayed the purchase of a NeXT computer. Sitting on Berners-Lee's desk, it would become the first Web content "server," the first node in this global brain. In collaboration with colleagues, Berners-Lee developed the three technical keystones of the Web: the language for encoding documents (HTML, hypertext markup language); the system for linking documents (HTTP, hypertext transfer protocol); and the *www.whatever* system for addressing documents (URL, universal resource locator).

Berners-Lee also wrote the first server software. And, contrary to the mythology surrounding Netscape, it was he, not Andreessen, who wrote the first "graphical user interface" Web browser. (Nor was Andreessen's browser the first to feature pictures; but it was the first to put pictures and text in the same window, a key innovation.)

The idea of a global hypertext system had been championed since the 1960s by a visionary named Ted Nelson, who had pursued it as the "Xanadu" project. But Nelson wanted Xanadu to make a profit, and this vastly complicated the system, which never got off the ground. Berners-Lee, in contrast, persuaded CERN to let go of intellectual property to get the Web airborne. A no-frills browser was put in the public domain—downloadable to all comers, who could use it, love it, send it to friends and even improve on it.

But what should he name his creation? Infomesh? No, that sounded like Infomess. The Information Mine? No, the acronym—TIM—would seem "egocentric." How about World Wide Web, or "www" for short? Hmm. He discussed it with his wife and colleagues and was informed that it was "really stupid," since "www" takes longer to say than "the World Wide Web."

There was no single moment when the magnitude of Berners-Lee's creation hit home with thunderous force. But there have been moments of sudden reckoning. Two years ago, Berners-Lee still had pictures of his two young children on his Web site. Then someone pointed out that there were enough data there for "strange people" to locate them, and that there were strange people on the Web. "You have to think like that more as the thing scales up," he acknowledges.

The Web's growing lack of intimacy, in a way, symbolizes his one big disappointment with it. It was meant to be a social place. "The original goal was working together with others," he says. "The Web was supposed to be a creative tool, an expressive tool." He had imagined, say, a worker posting a memo on a Web site accessible only to colleagues and having them react by embedding hyperlinks that led to their comments or to other relevant documents; or a bicoastal family similarly planning its annual reunion on the family site.

But the Web turned out otherwise. Robert Cailliau of CERN, Berners-Lee's earliest collaborator on the project, describes the Web's prevailing top-down structure: "There's one point that puts the data out, and you're just a consumer." He finds this model—whose zenith is the coming wave of so-called

A Better Hybrid: Trends from Changing Technologies 7

push technology—an "absolute, utter disaster."

Berners-Lee is more diplomatic. He has no gripe about commerce on the Web. (He buys CDs there.) And it was inevitable, in retrospect, that much Web activity would be, well, passive, with people absorbing content from high-volume sites. But he'd hoped the ratio of active to passive would be higher. It irks him that most Web site-editing software is so cumbersome. Even the software that spares you the drudgery of actually looking at HTML code calls for some heavy lifting. You chisel your text in granite and then upload the slab, after which changes are difficult. "The Web," he complains, "is this thing where you click around to read," but if you want to write, "you have to go through this *procedure*." As Cailliau puts it, people have come to view the Web as "just another publishing medium. That was definitely not our intention." Berners-Lee, it turns out, is a kind of accidental Gutenberg.

Berners-Lee considers the Web an example of how early, random forces are amplified through time. "It was an accident of fate that all the first [commercially successful] programs were browsers and not editors," he says. To see how different things might have been, you have to watch him gleefully wield his original browser—a browser *and* editor—at his desk. He's working on one document and—flash—in a few user-friendly keystrokes, it is linked to another document. One document can be on his computer "desktop"—for his eyes only—another can be accessible to his colleagues or his family, and another can be public. A seamless neural connection between his brain and the social brain.

What if the "accident of fate" hadn't happened? What if Berners-Lee's browser-editor, or some further evolution of it, had become the Web tool that first reached the masses? The world almost found out. In 1992, two years after he created his browser, and before Andreessen's Mosaic browser existed, he and Cailliau consulted a lawyer about starting a company called Websoft (the name has since been taken). But the project held risks, and besides, Berners-Lee envisioned competitors springing up, creating incompatible browsers and balkanizing the Web. He thought it better to stay above the fray and try to bring technical harmony. "Tim's not after the money," says Cailliau in a tone of admiration perhaps tinged with regret. "He accepts a much wider range of hotel-room facilities than a CEO would."

Berners-Lee admits to no regrets at having taken the high-minded, low-profit route. He says he is grateful that Andreessen co-authored a user-friendly browser and thus brought the Web to the public, even if in non-ideal form. Yet it can't have been easy watching Andreessen become the darling of the media after writing a third-generation browser that lacked basic editing capabilities. When I ask, "So there was a moment when you might have been Marc Andreessen?" Berners-Lee says, "I suppose so," and then smiles in a slightly stiff, even frosty, way. "The world is full of moments when one might be other things," he says. "One is the decisions one's taken." File closed.

Berners-Lee is not easy to read, not prone to self-disclosure. Ask him if he's a sociable guy, and he tells you that on the Myers-Briggs test, "I rate pretty much in the middle of introversion vs. extroversion." Ask about his wife, and he'll tell you that she is an American he met in Europe while she was working for the World Health Organization, after which details get sketchy. "Work is work, and home is home," he says. And when you cross the border between them, his turbocharged gesticulation subsides.

Other sources volunteer that Berners-Lee met his wife Nancy Carlson at an acting workshop; he turns out to have an artistic, piano-playing, festive side. "He is both British and the life of the party, and that's not a contradiction," says Rohit Khare, who recently left the Web consortium. "He can be the life of the party without making the party about him."

Berners-Lee, standing at a blackboard, draws a graph, as he's prone to do. It arrays social groups by size. Families, workplace groups, schools, towns, companies, the nation, the planet. The Web could in theory make things work smoothly at all of these levels, as well as between them. That, indeed, was the original idea—an organic expanse of collaboration. But the Web can pull the other way. And Berners-Lee worries about whether it will "allow cranks and nut cases to find in the world 20 or 30 other cranks and nut cases who are absolutely convinced of the same things. Allow them to set up filters around themselves . . . and develop a pothole of culture out of which they can't climb." Will we "end up with a world which is full of very, very disparate cultures which don't talk to each other?"

Berners-Lee doesn't kid himself. Even if the Web had followed the technological lines he envisioned (which it is finally starting to do, as software evolves), it couldn't force people to nurture the global interest, or even their neighborhood's interest. Technology can't make us good. "At the end of the day, it's up to us: how we actually react, and how we teach our children, and the values we instill." He points back to the graph. "I believe we and our children should be active at all points along this."

On Sundays Berners-Lee packs his family into the car and heads for a Unitarian-Universalist church. As a teenager he rejected the Anglican teachings of his parents; he can't bring himself to worship a particular prophet, a particular book. But "I do in fact believe that people's spiritual side is very important," and that it's "more than just biology."

He likes the minimalist Unitarian dogma—theologically vague but believing in "the inherent dignity of people and in working together to achieve harmony and understanding." He can accept the notion of divinity so long as it is couched abstractly—as the "asymptote" of goodness that we strive toward—and doesn't involve "characters with beards." He hopes the Web will move the world closer to the divine asymptote.

Berners-Lee is sitting at his desk, in front of bookshelves that are bare, devoid of books and other old-fashioned forms of data. A few sheet-metal bookends stand there with nothing to do, and nearby are pictures of his family. He concentrates, trying to put a finger point on his notion of divinity. A verse he's heard in church comes to mind, but all he can remember are fragments. "All souls may . . ." his voice trails off ". . . to seek the truth in love . . ." He is silent for a moment. His brain has failed him. The inspiration strikes. "Maybe I can pick it up from the Web." In a single motion, he swivels his chair 180° and makes fluid contact with his IBM Thinkpad.

 **Article Review Form at end of book.**

Online journalism offers opportunities for the media to provide greater depth of coverage to wider audiences. But, as Denise Caruso and Andie Tucher note in the sidebars to John Pavlik's article, there are several areas of concern. What are their concerns? Why are there questions about financing?

The Future of OnLine Journalism

Bonanza or black hole?

John V. Pavlik

John V. Pavlik is executive director of The Center for New Media at Columbia University's Graduate School of Journalism. He is a senior fellow at the San Diego Supercomputer Center, one of four such centers funded by the National Science Foundation.

If you build it they will come—at least some of them. Imagine a library that carries the equivalent of 1,600 daily newspapers from all over the globe. Now stop imagining. It's here: the Internet provides more news content than that every day, most of it free. So it's not surprising that increasing numbers of the world's forty million to fifty million Internet users are going online for their news.

The wild Internet provides a lot of information of dubious value, of course, which is part of what makes going online an adventure. But the digitally up-to-date also know that the quality of much of the news online is as high as that of leading newspapers or newsmagazines or TV or radio outlets, because much of it comes from those media.

Yet that fact leads to a question: If online journalism is little more than another delivery system for "old" media—even if it's a potentially better delivery system—what's all the fuss about? In terms of journalism, what's the point?

For many of us in this field, the point is to engage the unengaged. Some of us envision a kind of news that, as it upholds the highest journalistic standards, will allow news consumers to understand the meaning of the day's events in a personalized context that makes better sense to them than traditional media do now.

Since networked new media can be interactive, on-demand, customizable; since it can incorporate new combinations of text, images, moving images, and sound; since it can build new communities based on shared interests and concerns; and since it has the almost unlimited space to offer levels of reportorial depth, texture, and context that are impossible in any other medium—new media can transform journalism.

An example from MSNBC on the Internet nicely illustrates the potential. On February 21, NBC's *Dateline* ran a piece about dangerous roads in America, zeroing in on three particularly treacherous thoroughfares. The program invited viewers to log onto the MSNBC site to learn about roads in their community. Those who did so could enter their zip code and, within seconds, based on federal data, find out how many fatal accidents had occurred in that community between 1992 and 1995 and on which roads. Within twelve hours MSNBC logged 68,000 visitors to that feature.

Money magazine's Money Online—which won the 1997 National Magazine Award for new media, the first time such an online award has been given—provides another example. Back when Steve Forbes was pushing the flat-tax concept in his presidential campaign, a Money Online feature allowed people to key in their earnings profile and see how the proposed tax would affect them.

Yes, the potential to customize content also means readers may select only what appeals to their narrowest interests. This

---

Reprinted from *Columbia Journalism Review*, July/August 1997. Copyright © 1997 by Columbia Journalism Review.

"You News" kind of journalism could thus become a force for atomization, for further civic decay.

But the optimists, and I am one of them, don't believe it. Research for half a century indicates that people use media, new or old, to connect to society, not separate. People go online primarily to connect with the news of their community, whether a geographical community or one formed around some other common bond. They use customization features to supplement their general news appetites, following their particular interests in finance, travel, education, the environment, or any number of things. So, rather than fracturing society, new media—with online journalism at its core—can help to keep us connected.

Must publishers participate? Will readers and/or advertisers ever pay for it? My own sense is that if we make the journalism engaging enough, it will gain financial support. Already, we can see glimmers of a transformed journalism in some of the good online work that is out there now.

News Online: A 1997 Baedeker

Think of the online news world as a vast virtual newspaper divided into sections—national, regional, business, technology, politics/culture/opinion, and sports. (There is an international section—a variety of notable online journalism offerings from outside the U.S., such as the Spanish-language La Nacion Online of Costa Rica or the Jerusalem Post Daily Internet Edition—but I'll focus on domestic news here.)

Within these sections, who is doing the job well? Which sites are beginning to produce a new kind of journalism? Here are some of them.

National News

The best national news sites are those that, along with repackaging or "repurposing" their regular print content, offer original material designed specifically for the Web. The CyberTimes section of The New York Times on the Web, for example, provides extensive original coverage of new media. The *Times* online version also publishes photojournalism, such as a photo essay by Sebastião Salgado documenting the plight of Brazil's "Landless Workers' Movement"—forty-two images, accompanied by audio captions from Salgado, news reports, a map, and various archival materials.

Many national sites also cover breaking news, and the better ones use their reservoirs of space to add depth and texture. The Washington Post's web site, for instance, offered thorough online coverage of the surprising recent Iranian presidential election, adding news that did not appear in the printed *Post*, reference material, and other resources. The site showed the capability to do some original reporting recently by supplementing a special *Post* report—titled D.C. SCHOOLS: A SYSTEM IN CRISIS—about that education system's collapsing infrastructure, bloated bureaucracy, and failing special-education programs. The web site's report added a comparison of 1996 SAT scores between D.C. and suburban schools, profiled the Board of Trustees, and invited online reader discussions.

Time Online impressively covered the Heaven's Gate tragedy—offering detailed reporting from the magazine's online staff as well as the print side, extensive photo coverage, and even an electronic link to Heaven's Gate's own web site, which allowed visitors to learn about the cult from its members' words. *Time*'s site became an important historical record, with layers of content that the printed magazine couldn't accommodate.

Similarly, CNN Interactive—which is one of the world's busiest news web sites with some 3.5 million "page views" a day—features extensive original coverage of the environment and ecological issues. And CNN Interactive goes into considerable depth on all kinds of stories that get only a minute or two on TV.

Regional News

Mercury Center, Website of the *San Jose Mercury News*, is known recently for increasing the impact of the paper's widely debated "Dark Alliance" series partly by spreading the series way beyond the paper's circulation area and partly by adding original documents (court transcripts, search warrant documents, and so forth), along with photos and even sounds (including a section of a wiretap of a drug dealer), to the basic story. But the site is famous for such use of layered publishing on many stories.

Mercury Center features simple and easy-to-use navigational tools that allow the reader access to every section and service in the site. The top of the page offers an index of sections, from Asia Report to Talent Scout, and services, from the Mercury Mall to the Yellow Pages. The Yellow Pages gives readers access to Zip2, an electronic directory of more than 16 million businesses nationwide, fully searchable, all for free—a capability no print outlet can match.

The site also offers Good Morning Silicon Valley, special online coverage of the high-tech industry. Another feature is the digital News Library, where readers can call up more than a million articles, including all stories in the *Merc* published since 1985 plus the archives of nineteen other Knight-Ridder papers. Readers can run free searches that return a list of headlines and the first graf of every story. Beyond that, only subscribers can get full stories, paying a minimum of twenty-five cents apiece.

As an example of how journalists can employ the near limitless space of the Web to add depth and context, consider how the *Chicago Tribune* used its web site to memorialize Mike Royko after he died April 29. The interactive tribute includes fourteen news stories about Royko, an electronic message board where some 700 readers had posted messages by the end of May, and an archive of dozens of Royko's best columns.

Tribune Company is a partner in an interactive feature called Digital City, which offers entertainment, lifestyle, and community information at the local web sites of newspapers in its chain, such as *The Orlando Sentinel*. Digital City is a direct competitor with Microsoft's online city-based service, Sidewalk, which gives readers similar community information, including movie and restaurant reviews, and theater guides.

Boston.com has set the standard for convergence—the coming together of once separate media, print and electronic, in a digital, networked environment. The site provides not only an electronic window into Boston's arts, weather, and commerce, but also gives you access to the online content of eighteen local media, including *The Boston Globe, Banker & Tradesman* (Massachusetts business news), and WGBH, Boston's celebrated public broadcaster.

For quality original online news content, The Nando Times—the technologically innovative web site affiliated with *The Raleigh News & Observer,* a McClatchy paper—has helped set the standard. One of the site's hallmarks is its interactive Nando News Watcher, which uses "push" Internet broadcasting technology to broadcast, or "push," content to the user. The News Watcher continuously feeds customized local, regional, national, and international news to your computer screen, where it retreats to a small window when you are using another application.

Among small-city papers distinguishing themselves in the online arena is the flood-battling *Grand Forks Herald* in North Dakota. The 38,000-circulation daily has used its Northscape web site to serve its beleaguered community. A number of news web sites include access to The Wire, the site introduced in 1996 by The Associated Press that provides continuously updated breaking news. New Jersey Online and *The Dallas Morning News* were the first to run The Wire, but they've been followed by many others.

Business and Financial

The best offer a combination of straight reporting and analysis, plus features not possible in print or broadcast media. Bloomberg Personal, Reuters, The Wall Street Journal Interactive Edition, and CNNfn all provide near-real-time stock quotes updated regularly, as well as financial research tools, such as company profiles. CNNcq also offers an interactive mortgage calculator for people trying to figure how much house they can pay for. Rich Zahradnik, vice-president of CNNcq Interactive, says "page views"—a more conservative and accurate count than "hits"—at the site have increased from about five million a month in 1996 to some thirty-six million a month. And Lou Dobbs, anchor of CNNcq and executive vice-president of CNNcq, contends that the interactive capabilities keep people lingering at the site, a challenge for new media publishers, who find the Net-surfer attention span is short.

Business Week Online, a finalist for the National Magazine Award for new media this year, also has services and material to hold the user's interest. Bob Arnold, its editor, notes that Business Week Online includes every work printed by the magazine and its international sisters, as well as a daily briefing culled from Standard & Poor's and from news items filed by the *Business Week* staff around the world—primarily reporting that might not find its way into the magazine because of space or timing. The site also offers a searchable electronic archive of *Business Week* dating to 1991 and expanded coverage of one of its franchises, the ranking and evaluation of business schools. Since technology is an important subject in the magazine, Business Week Online offers "Maven," a computer buying guide produced in conjunction with National Software Testing Laboratories, another McGraw-Hill property. The site has been host to more than 300 online conference and chat sessions on America Online.

Technology

The most popular online news is about information technology. CNET: The Computer Network, is a combination of web sites, and it publishes perhaps the premier web site on computer developments for the general consumer audience at its News.com site.

Ziff Davis's ZDNet publishes infotech news and product reviews geared for professionals. A recent special report, for example, reviews CD-Rom drives of every speed and type. Readers can customize the report, requesting a graphical display of the drives, say, from best to worst in terms of a variety of characteristics such as speed, performance, or ease of installation. The site also offers downloads of more than 1,000 software packages. And it provides news, which readers can customize for six subjects, issues, or companies. All free.

Culture, Opinion, and Politics

The Web has produced a set of chic and well-traveled distinctions for the digital literati, the best of which engage readers in discussions and push the storytelling envelope. Some are connected to print publications. One of the most visited sites is HotWired, the online cousin of *Wired* magazine, which features commentary on new media issues.

The recently renamed Atlantic Unbound, the online offering since 1993 of *The Atlantic Monthly*, has offered readers an electronic window into politics, society, the arts and culture. In addition to content from its print sister, Atlantic Unbound offers a variety of interactive features, including "Post & Riposte," where readers discuss political and cultural issues raised in the magazine, as well as online-only articles.

Among those innovative Web publications unconnected to a paper parent is The Netly News, a Pathfinder creation of leading cyber-journalist Josh Quittner. Besides writing provocatively and critically about the evolution of the Internet, Quittner offers a Digital Sandbox, where visitors are invited to play with new technologies and gain first-hand experience.

Salon offers all the traditional intellectual fare of an opinion magazine, plus a meeting place for compelling online discussion as well. Called Table Talk, the discussion zone was inspired by a model developed at "The Well," where the first significant online community was born in the spring of 1985. Salon, as much as any online publication, tries to give its readers that elusive sense of belonging.

One of the most discussed sites is Slate, the Microsoft start-up edited by Michael Kinsley. Heavily promoted, Slate offers a rich set of articles and commentary on culture and politics, such as David Plotz's assessment of "Ralph Reed's Creed," or "Selling Seals of Approval," John Merline's investigation of how companies get charities to endorse their products. But Slate doesn't offer many digital bells and whistles, and critics say it does not fully exploit its online capabilities. It is also one of the most parodied online literary offerings. One send-up, called Stale (www.stale.com), recently traced the "surprising parallels" between changes in wind patterns and Clinton's electoral popularity.

Sports

These sites on the Web may not necessarily raise the journalistic yardstick, but they are compelling because they so effectively exploit the Web's capabilities.

The best overall sports reporting online is at ESPN SportsZone and CBS SportsLine. Both provide immediate coverage of games, after-games-analysis, and much more, from live-game statistics to interactive reader polls to video and audio highlights. Most of this content is free, although more specialized coverage is available for small monthly fees.

The Sports Network runs a distant second to these premier general interest sports services, and adheres to a more traditional approach to sports reporting with fewer interactive online features. *Sports Illustrated*'s SI Online provides mostly repackaged content from the magazine, though it had plans to increase its original content as part of a partnership with CNN starting July 1.

The Online Future

News content on the Internet has been evolving through three stages. In stage one, which still dominates most news sites, online journalists mostly repurpose content from their mother ship. In stage two, which gained momentum last year and characterizes most of the better news sites, the journalists create original content and augment it with such additives as hyperlinks (with which a reader can instantly access another web site); interactive features such as search engines, which seek out material on specific topics; and a degree of customization—the ability to choose what categories of news and information you receive.

Stage three is just beginning to emerge at only a handful of sites. It is characterized by original news content designed specifically for the Web as a new medium of communication. Stage three will be characterized by a willingness to rethink the nature of a "community" online and, most important, a willingness to experiment with new forms of storytelling. Often this is "immersive" storytelling, which allows you to enter and navigate through a news report in ways different from just reading it.

Sometimes this might be done through new technology. Just one example: Rob Fixmer, editor of CyberTimes, says that *The New York Times* is experimenting with omnidirectional imaging, which would permit you to explore a 360-degree field of vision. Such technology will allow viewers the experience of "entering" a live or recorded news event, or to see a still or moving photo in three dimensions.

But the promise of new media is not merely about dazzling technology. Most serious news organizations know that young people are turning to online media.

News organizations know too that audiences for online news in the future will be drawn by a site's unique content and perspective, and by its quality. New media represent the future. For editors and for publishers, a commitment to quality online news today is the best way to ensure that your news organization will be there when the online business matures a decade or more from now.

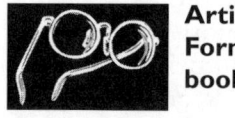 **Article Review Form at end of book.**

Why Web Warriors Might Worry

Andie Tucher
Andie Tucher is CJR's associate editor.

Part of the pleasure and excitement of online journalism is smashing antique rules, overturning taboos, and rethinking the very idea of news. Part of the danger is that some of those antique rules still make sense and some of those taboos can still keep us from eating our mothers—or our standards. In the brave but chaotic new world of online journalism, rethinking the news doesn't always mean improving it.

Even some optimistic observers have several areas of concern:

INTERACTIVITY. This is supposed to be the most distinctive contribution of online journalism. Webheads see interactivity as a way to draw millions of mouse potatoes together in a virtual community, to engage and involve them in the news, and to stimulate public debate. Well, sometimes.

Take, for example, the CNN-*Time* web site AllPolitics, which runs the gamut of interactive devices and gimmicks: free-form bulletin boards, instant "Take a Stand" polls ("Is FDR the greatest president of the 20th century?"),

Reprinted from *Columbia Journalism Review,* July/August 1997. Copyright © 1997 by Columbia Journalism Review. Andie Tucher, a longtime print and broadcast journalist is the author of *Forth, Scum: Truth, Beauth, Goodness and the Ax-Murder in America's First Mass Medium* (UNC Press, 1994).

an e-mail forum called "Voter's Voice" on the issue of the day (late-term abortion, the budget), and a daily trivia quiz that can earn you a totebag and your name in lights, or at least in HTML. Throughout 1996 the site offered a riot of campaign-theme games, including a post-election single-elimination tournament called "Pitfalls" designed to predict Bill Clinton's biggest second-term problem. (Campaign fund-raising beat out Hillary and Bosnia, among others.)

Bulletin boards and e-mail may make for discussions as feisty as anything that iconic old town square ever saw—but much of this famous "interactivity" is closer in spirit to *Jeopardy* than to a C-SPAN call-in. Why should a web site's instant poll on FDR's status be hailed as constructive engagement when the networks' overnight tracking polls on Bob Dole's status were routinely denounced as shallow or undemocratic? Why is sitting alone pondering a trivia question about Millie, the former First Dog, more communitarian than sitting alone heaving your shoe at the television set?

Some new-media mavens also boast how much more accessible—and thus accountable—online journalists are than traditional newspeople. But while reader feedback can help keep reporters honest, some new-media journalists are toying with another use of reader opinion that skates close to an abdication of their editorial judgment. MSNBC, for instance, invites you to rate the stories you read on a scale of one to seven according to how highly you would recommend each one to other "viewers," as MSNBC calls them. After you submit your rating, you're whisked to a page that lists the Top Ten stories of the minute with their scores.

According to Merrill Brown, editor-in-chief of MSNBC Interactive, the goal of the ranking is "principally and almost solely" to help people "share good ideas about interesting stuff they found in a deep, rich news environment that can be difficult to navigate, and also to give us some clues about what people are interested in." He insists that the rankings play no role in editorial decision-making. "In the hands of Rupert Murdoch it would turn out that way," he says, "but we're pretty serious about this enterprise." Serious or not, it's hard not to notice how many health stories land in the Top Ten—and how many new health stories crowd the MSNBC site every day.

CREDIBILITY AND AUTHORITY. On the Web, journalism, parajournalism, and pseudojournalism don't just coexist; they invade each other, through the handy online device of the hypertext link. While a newspaper editor can—theoretically, anyway—maintain iron control over the content of her four sections' worth of newsprint, no online journalist, no matter how scrupulous his own standards, can predict where his readers might daisy-chain their way. Even the most respectable news site has the potential to launch the unwary surfer straight through the looking glass.

The Web browser interested in the JonBenet Ramsey case, for instance—the Christmas-night murder of the children's-beauty-pageant queen in Colorado—might logically choose to start with the perfectly credible *Denver Post*, a local paper that has devoted extensive coverage to the crime. But the *Post* web site includes a link to the home page of the Boulder sheriff's office. The sheriff's page links to a resource called "Law Enforcement Sites." And that site can take you to something blandly entitled "JonBenet Ramsey Homicide Web Sites," a page, maintained by one Ken Polzin, Jr., of links to some four dozen other web sites pertaining to the case.

Polzin's standard for inclusion is clearly "relevance," not accuracy or even sanity. His page can take you to MSNBC's search engine, transcripts of press conferences, or a redacted version of the official autopsy report. Or you can just as easily surf right into the "Reverse Speech" site and listen for yourself to the "smoking gun" in the case: snippets from the audiotape of the Ramsey parents' CNN interview played backwards, supplemented with helpful transcripts in case you can't quite make out on your own that John Ramsey's tergiversated voice is in fact saying "I done it. It's a show you're running."

You can almost make a Six-Degrees-of-Kevin-Bacon game of it: how many links does it take to get from the home page of *The New York Times* to, say, a news release announcing authoritatively that "Pressure is growing on Capitol Hill for immediate impeachment hearings on President Clinton and Vice President Gore"? (Or so says the Committee to Impeach the President, which has just doubled its roster of supporters in Congress—to two.) How about a guide to the "hanky code" used by gay men to signal their preferences? (I made each connection in eight links.) But the question remains: how many rushed or inattentive surfers will end up wondering whether *The Denver Post* also has new evidence that Paul McCartney is dead?

CHURCH AND STATE. The rules seem to be different for online advertising, too. A survey by the Newspaper Association of America points to a disturbing trend: while no decent newspaper would dream of assigning its metro reporter to write headlines for its advertisers, most of the newspapers with separate new-media staffs routinely ask editorial employees to design or produce banner ads for their web sites.

Chris McKenna, a producer for Time Online, says that while her own organization has never asked her to do any business-side work, there does seem to be a sense among many news organizations that all standards are a bit looser online. "Some print media don't seem to take their online sites quite as seriously," she says. "They don't give them enough resources; they might expect a producer, say, to be a researcher and fact-checker and editor, too. It's as if they're saying 'Hey, we can compromise a bit, it's not our flagship product.'"

 **Article Review Form at end of book.**

Show Me the Money!

How the FUD factor has online news in its thrall

Denise Caruso

Denise Caruso (dc@technomedia.com) is a technology analyst, on leave from The New York Times, *where she writes the "Digital Commerce" column. She is a visiting lecturer on interactive media at Stanford and a visiting scholar at Interval Research, a technology think-tank in Palo Alto, California.*

I didn't see the movie *Jerry Maguire*, but God knows I've heard "Show me the money!" enough to drive me nuts.

As is Hollywood's wont, that catchy little phrase was thrust with so much velocity into the mass media that it instantly became a cultural spore, propagating itself into countless headlines and stand-up routines. Its ubiquity almost lulled us into believing we actually knew the story without ever having seen the movie. In fact, "Show me the money!"—in a dual role as rallying cry and cultural spore—is an appropriate starting point for as-

Reprinted from *Columbia Journalism Review,* July/August 1997. Copyright © 1997 by Columbia Journalism Review.

16 Perspectives: Online Journalism

sessing the wretched state of financial affairs for news organizations online.

First, and at long last, it appears that many people with financial responsibility for online news operations on the World Wide Web are weary of hemorrhaging cash. After far too many years of talk about revenue and nary a peep about profit, they would very much like for someone, anyone, to show them the money.

Second, the questions that one would assume are most critical to news organizations online—i.e., "Where is the money?" and "How long will we have to wait to see it?"—should have been answered long before now. If anyone had ever bothered to really demand some old-fashioned financial accountability, today's state of affairs would likely be less dismal.

And third, the idea that news organizations had no choice but to make a transition to the Web in the first place was very much the result of a virulent spore that infected the entire media industry, causing everyone therein to believe they could survive only if they invested mightily in an online presence. Like those of us who only heard about *Jerry Maguire*, they knew a lot less about the story than they thought.

The progenitor of this particular spore was the awesome hype machine of the technology industry, which back in the early 1990s started issuing press releases about how newspapers and television were on the brink of being replaced by new, interactive services delivered over the global Internet. These new services, not incidentally, were based on products that it just so happened technology vendors were selling. News folks, some of whom continue to brag to this day about their computer illiteracy, didn't have enough knowledge or courage to challenge the industry's assertions. They believed what they were told.

In Silicon Valley, the conscious creation of this environment of Fear, Uncertainty, and Doubt is a marketing tatic that actually has a name. It's called the FUD Factor, and in its thrall news organizations began racing to get online before it was "too late."

In the seven-plus years that I've been writing about technology and media, I never once met an editor or a publisher who asked, "Too late for what?" Instead, because no one would admit he or she was being driven by FUD, media companies scrambled to come up with some kind of business rationale for their online efforts.

Some said that their "investments" would yield fruit when the market catches up to their vision (a subset of this group have now decided that that market will never happen). Others—companies like Time Warner, for example—started out thinking online was a business, but in light of no profits have since shifted perspective. In fact, Time Inc. c.e.o. Don Logan may have been the first media executive to publicly note that the emperor had no clothes when, in November of 1995, he called Time's online efforts a "black hole" for money.

Time, and others with enough cash to stay the course, now choose to see their online efforts as an opportunity to experiment, testing new media concepts on real customers (which is what everybody should have done in the first place).

But none of these rationales, then or now, was based on a realistic economic model. That's because there isn't one. And there won't be until at least these three nasty and very tightly coupled problems are attended to:

One: News has become a commodity, like laundry soap or videocassettes. It is ubiquitous and cheap, if not free, to millions of people every day. But unlike soap or tapes it is incredibly expensive to produce and the cost of producing it does not go down as a function of volume. This was an impossible situation even before the Web.

Enter online and the situation gets worse. The easy money many organizations thought they could make by simply digitizing and slapping up onto the Web the stories already filed for today's newspapers or news broadcasts never even came close to materializing.

Two: Advertising support, which provides much or all of the funding for news organizations' traditional offerings, is unreliable at best as a revenue source for online news.

Because online news is a commodity and customers don't pay real money for it, once an organization takes its product and its revenue model online, it becomes vulnerable to a phalanx of new competitors. Geography no longer matters. News providers are no longer competing only with each other, but also with content aggregators like America Online and the Microsoft Network and Netscape and Yahoo!, all of which court advertisers as aggressively as any publication or television network in history.

What's even more worrisome is what has already started happening to classified and local advertising dollars because of online technology. Smaller and independent papers, which now survive on local news and advertising because global and national news is a commodity, are seeing companies like the omnivorous Microsoft Corporation fire up its Sidewalk local listings service.

The problems with online advertising are not limited to revenues. The Web was not designed as a commercial medium, but as a way to distribute and connect information to communities of interest; thus any line drawn between advertising and editorial is unnatural by definition.

For example, most news stories online link to other web sites; you can jump from site to site with the click of a mouse. Linking is integral to the medium, and readers should and do expect it. But readers do not expect news sites to include links that were inserted because they were paid for. Today there's no way of knowing if that happens. In fact, there has already been a furor or two over paid links, unidentified as such, on popular non-news sites. If and when online news publishers are tempted to sell commercial links inside news stories, we will already be way down the slippery slope of credibility.

At some point, a sentient being may be inspired to ask, "If the online news business is so ridiculous, why are we doing it?" Given the absence of reason outlined so far, the only apparent response is: "Because everyone else is." Which leads to the final point, one which my mother used on me, to great effect, in grade school.

Three: "If everone else jumped off the bridge, would you do it, too?" So far, no one has demonstrated there is any great customer benefit—besides immediacy—to online news. Unless you're a sports nut or a stock investor or an information junkie in some area or another, immediacy doesn't have much real value except as a marketing tactic.

And the much-vaunted "community" aspect of having an online news organization—chat and bulletin boards about stories—is hardly worth the effort. Online communities are extremely valuable where people share specialized interests; that's why sites such as Parent Soup, a place where parents can find resources and electronic discussion about parenting, are so popular.

But for a news organization? I don't think so. Sure, every once in a while something interesting comes out of electronic discussions on them. For the most part, however, people who participate seem to have a bit of trouble socializing. Often enough, if the messages aren't banal, they're offensive.

Still, everybody's trying to do whatever's possible, from chat to photos and audio and video and Java and games and contests—dangling any carrot they can to get visitors. They're all being very stoic about hanging in there because they don't want to be seen as past their prime.

This is a bad reason to spend millions of dollars. Instead, online news organizations ought to be taking a giant step back and asking themselves, "How can we be of service? What is the value proposition for our customers? What can we give them online that they can't get any other way—that they will thank us, and pay us, for?"

Maybe the answer is, "Nothing." Seriously, it's possible. But it is also possible for news organizations to set aside everything they think they know and look at the landscape with fresh eyes.

So, news is a commodity? Then maybe it's time to think about how to create and sell high-value information to a subset of one's existing customers. Everything on the Web has to be free? Then detour the Web. Use other paths through the Internet. Think about how to use the cost advantages of digital distribution without the Web and its freebie culture.

After all, it's not like there are any rules. It is entirely acceptable to make something up and if it doesn't work, try something else. As says Nick Donatiello, president of the consumer research firm Odyssey L.P., "It is much less important to be first than to be right."

Creative problem-solving, not business as usual, is the only thing that will allow the news business to wrest control of its destiny from the forces of FUD, which got it into this mess in the first place. It won't be as easy as digitizing a newspaper page or video footage and pretending that's the future, but I suspect it will be a bit more fruitful.

 **Article Review Form at end of book.**

READING 4

Customized news services enable consumers to create personal news sources, set boundaries on information access and expand their options without the limitations or filters imposed by editors. But are these services in the best interest of consumers? Are they too limiting? If consumers rely only on such services, are they being exposed to an adequate view of the world? Or should such services be viewed as supplements to traditional media? Christopher Harper explores these issues in the following article, with a look at free and subscription services.

The Daily Me

Christopher Harper

Christopher Harper teaches journalism at New York University. His book on digital journalism will be published next fall by NYU Press.

Brad Bartley is not the only student from Oklahoma at the Massachusetts Institute of Technology, but he is the only one from Quapaw. His tiny hometown, population 985, lies in the northeastern corner of the state. When Bartley arrived in Cambridge, he wanted some news from back home but couldn't find much in the Boston-oriented media. Maybe you get an occasional score of a game involving the local football or basketball teams. Maybe you get a glimpse of the weather in Oklahoma when a local television station shows the national radar map. But Boston is Boston, and Oklahoma is not exactly on the radar screen of the media in Beantown.

Bartley is a clean-shaven, jut-jawed, no-nonsense kind of guy who might have been cast in the play or movie "Oklahoma," in which Gordon MacRae sang about the winds sweeping across the Plains. But Bartley was able to do something about his info-gap. He and seven other freshmen set out to solve the problem as part of a class at the MIT Media Lab. That's where Nicholas Negroponte, the author of "Being Digital," holds court in a futuristic building constructed from an odd array of ornamental cement, white tile and glass. The building is named for Jerome Wiesner, the eccentric late MIT president and science adviser to John F. Kennedy who helped Negroponte start the lab 11 years ago.

If Mohammed were to go to a mountain in the age of new media, it would be the MIT Media Lab in Cambridge. The lab is Mecca for those who want to know what the new millennium will bring, be it the newspaper of the future, virtual reality or any other current buzzword.

Fortunately, the Media Lab's ayatollahs also listen to good ideas, and Bartley and his fellow freshmen had a good one. Together with researcher Pascal Chesnais, the freshmen devised a customized, personal news service, named FishWrap, which is updated continuously via computer.

Today—three years after the creation of FishWrap—the mainstream media from the Wall Street Journal to Time Warner offer dozens of variations of what the MIT freshmen conceived. The San Francisco Examiner and Chronicle's Internet edition, The Gate, actually uses the personalized computer structure developed at MIT, as do newspapers in Italy and Brazil.

But there are questions about customized news services, sometimes called the "Daily Me." The services are egocentric; a user chooses what he or she wants to read and can filter out other information. The roles of the newspaper reporter and editor—the traditional gatekeepers of information—are limited, if not eliminated altogether, in deciding what news the user receives. The user may become isolated from his or her neighborhood, city, state and nation because he or she has filtered out any information about the global village. "It's more isolation and less real life," says media critic Edwin Diamond, a former MIT professor who writes about online issues.

Customized online news services allow readers to receive news content tailored to their interests. But do readers risk missing important developments that don't fit their profiles?

From Christopher Harper, "The Daily Me" in *American Journalism Review,* April 1997. Reprinted by permission of American Journalism Review.

20   Perspectives: Online Journalism

But this problem is addressed, in part, by FishWrap's unusual front page. Readers decide what news they'd like to see at the top and what news they think is important for others to read.

"It's really about control, decision making," says Chesnais, a bearded ex-New Yorker who has been working on projects about news in the future since 1986. "We have no editors making decisions involving what people should read. The readers do that."

While there are a number of variations of personal news services, here's how the original, FishWrap, works. More than 700 people subscribe. A computer program asks three questions. First, the computer needs to know the zip code of the user's hometown. Second, the computer asks about the subscriber's academic interests and then his or her personal interests. From that profile, computer programs seek out key words, such as "computers" or "Oklahoma," to construct a daily news and information site from news stories filed into the computer's database by the Associated Press, the Boston newspapers, Knight-Ridder, Zagat's Restaurant Guide and a host of other news providers.

The main page shows what news sources have provided the information. The reader can then focus on a news category and view summaries of stories. If a summary seems interesting, the reader can call up the full text with graphics or audio. As a navigation aid, FishWrap displays a bar at the top of each computer screen that indicates the reader's current location in the document.

The roles of newspaper reporter and editor—the traditional gatekeepers of information—are limited, if not eliminated altogether, in deciding what news the user receives.

Like its printed cousins, FishWrap has a front page called Page One. But unlike other personalized services, in the spirit of democracy—perhaps news editors would call it anarchy—each of the 700 FishWrap users can determine what goes on the front page. If someone thinks that the group should read a particular story, that individual can put it on the front page. There is no limit to the number of front page stories that FishWrap can handle. These selections allow the reader to enjoy the breadth of community interests and force the user to be exposed to ideas outside of his or her personal choices.

Today, the lead story is about a Turkish politician who was physically attacked in Hungary. "I'd read that," says Bartley, an electrical engineering student. "It's weird enough." But if there are not enough people who read the story, it falls down to the bottom of Page One and then off the front page after 36 hours. The addition of the Page One stories came after a survey found that students were indeed concerned about becoming isolated from events outside their own interests.

But democracy can create some distinctive news decisions. When the Oklahoma City bombing occurred, for example, the disaster story placed second on page one behind a story about the mugging of Big Bird on the same day. "The icon of your childhood getting pummeled was more important to the students," Chesnais says. "It struck a chord among (them)."

After the front page, the MIT subscriber can access a constant stream of up-to-the-minute stories from the Associated Press. When the bombing in Oklahoma City happened, for example, Bartley turned to his computer to monitor what was happening in his home state and watched television on CNN from the corner of his eye. "Generally, I like to read more than watch television because it's more complete," he says. "It's better here on the computer because it was more restrained. I get this when I want it on the computer, and it's up to date."

The next section provides local, national and international news from a variety of sources. Bartley's local news comes from Oklahoma. Most of the time, Bartley does not find much that interests him, but he's glad to know that the weather in his hometown this day is better than in frigid Cambridge.

For his personal page, "Stuff That I Like," the MIT student has chosen computer technology, book reviews, architecture and photo essays. Today he gets nothing that interests him in the book review section, which includes books about Fergie and Oprah Winfrey and a reading by singer Johnny Cash. Under the photo essays, he retrieves photographs of George Gershwin and from South Africa.

When Bartley finishes reading his FishWrap, the computer retrieves all the articles he has scanned and offers him an opportunity to save any stories. After he logs off, the computer will reorganize the personalized edition if Bartley has changed his reading choices or has added new topics to his personal choices.

The computer program also responds to changes in reading habits. For example, Chesnais' sister was in Rwanda when the genocide began in 1994. As he started reading more about Rwanda, stories about the country moved up in importance as the computer determined he wanted more news about what was happening there. When his sister left Rwanda, the computer program pushed the stories down in importance as he selected fewer of them.

The customized news service at MIT, which is available only to students and faculty, also offers travel information. If a user is going to Finland, for example, news about that country appears on his or her FishWrap 48 hours before he or she travels and ends after the user returns.

FishWrap also tries to provide more detail and context for readers about specific stories. PLUM, which stands for Peace Love and Understanding Machine, is a software program that augments news on natural disasters reported in FishWrap. By placing news events in the context of a reader's home community, PLUM helps the reader better understand distant disaster news.

Here, for example, is the Reuters dispatch from June 30, 1995, about floods in China:

"China fears its worst flooding disaster this century with rising waters already killing hundreds of people and devastating farms and fisheries in its eastern region. Spring rains which annually bring calamity to tens of millions have been compounded by the effects of global warming and some meteorologists predict the worst inundation in a hundred years."

After reading the lead, most users would say: "What a pity!" Then the reader would move on. Bust FishWrap makes the story more relevant to people in Cambridge by incorporating a variety of data easily accessible on the Internet, such as material from the CIA Fact Book. The MIT news service pulls out the details on the worst floods in the United States. FishWrap points out that more than 14,000 people in Boston speak Chinese. The service creates a graphic of the area in China affected by the floods and places it on a map of Boston, showing that nearly all of the Boston suburbs would be under water if a similar flood occurred in Massachusetts. The damage of $500 million would cost every person in Boston $2,200, or about 7.5 percent of the average yearly income in the city. The number of households affected by the Chinese flood—220,000—would mean roughly all the houses in Boston.

None of the customized news services provides as many options as FishWrap. Some cost money. Others are free. You have to drop by a World Wide Web site to view some—known as "pull" technology, like pulling you to a local newsstand to buy the newspaper. Others send electronic mail messages to your computer—known as "push" technology, like pushing your newspaper onto your doorstep once you subscribe.

The Wall Street Journal's interactive edition costs $49 a year for those who don't subscribe to the printed version of the newspaper, or $29 for subscribers. Interactive Journal lets a user select stories from a number of categories of news and also flags stories that mention companies in the user's stock portfolio, providing a daily accounting of how investments performed. The Interactive Journal also offers briefing books about companies and a variety of stories related to business throughout the world. Articles that appeared during the past two weeks can be easily searched and retrieved.

Mercury Mail offers NEWspot, a daily e-mail of headlines and brief customized story summaries on a wide variety of topics. Because the personal edition comes as e-mail, it's like getting your newspaper delivered at home rather than buying it around the corner or going each day to a World Wide Web site.

Personal News Page is the newest offering from Individual, Inc., a company that was one of the first to offer customized news. PNP offers news from more than 700 publications, emphasizing science and technology, with secondary focuses on medicine, media and general business.

Pathfinder, Time Warner's online service, is arguably the deepest and most intimidating site on the Web. For free, a reader can search Time, Fortune and People, or learn about problems with old houses and progressive farming. For a fee of $4.95 a month or $29.95 a year, Pathfinder sorts through the material and provides the user with information on specifically requested subjects.

PointCast offers news and information from CNN, Time, People and Money magazines, Reuters, AccuWeather and a host of local newspapers. The service allows the user to select topics of interest, delivering matching stories by displaying them as a screen saver.

> **While some customized services like FishWrap force users to read headlines about international, national and local events, other services offer only those subjects the reader selects.**

While some customized services like FishWrap force users to read headlines about international, national and local events, other services offer only those subjects the reader selects. That troubles some editors, particularly because of their reduced role as gatekeeper and the isolation it creates for readers.

"Say you have a user who has set up a customization agent so that he or she gets favorite sports teams' news and selected stocks," says Leah Gentry, managing editor of Excite, a search engine and information service. "OK, the president is assassinated. That's a gimme. You override and give them that headline regardless of stated news preferences." But even Gentry is not certain if she would immediately flash a bulletin on a plane crash or a hijacking. "At what point do you stop respecting the wishes of the user and start feeding them what you think is important?" she asks.

If a company provides the option for an exclusive, personal news service, then the provider should stick to its commitment, maintains Melinda McAdams, a former content developer for the Washington Post's Digital Ink. "I am a user who absolutely does not want that allegedly important news flash. I will *never* have only one source of news on my desktop or in my life," she says, "and these news flashes would surely, certainly, undoubtedly be redundant and thus unwelcome for me."

Several editors suggest that the user should be asked to specify if he or she is absolutely certain that the news editors should not override the desire to be left alone when big news breaks. Steve Yelvington, editor/manager of the online edition of Minneapolis' Star Tribune, thinks the other customized services will eventually gravitate toward a shared community experience much like FishWrap. "There's a belief that computers are changing the ground rules, but those ground rules aren't what we thought they were, and when we look closely at the World Wide Web experience, we find that computers aren't very good at handing power over to individuals anyway," he says. "They're incredibly clumsy devices for navigating through information space. They're slow and unreliable. I think the market will demand that broad-but-shallow 'Daily We' element in any customizable environment."

What impact will these customized news products have on the future of the printed page? No one really knows. The Wall Street Journal says its online edition attracts a younger audience than the print edition. And many of the online edition's readers do not subscribe to the print version. Perhaps it's useful to go back to Bartley the MIT student who helped create the "Daily Me," who will be one of the news users in the future. "I think it would probably be fine if personalized news replaced newspapers," he says. "You get it in a lot more convenient form. You get it where and when you want it. It's easier to keep it around rather than clipping it and watching it get yellow."

Bartley sees an upside for newspapers. "Costs can go down for a newspaper, like maintaining a warehouse full of paper and a fleet of truck drivers. You can get the quick response time of television with the completeness of text. It will get easy to compare things by reading news from different sources side by side. It just seems like a big win situation."

But with only nine percent of America's homes wired to the Internet, it's likely that many people will still find their daily newspaper at the drugstore, on the doorstep or in the rose bushes.

Article Review Form at end of book.

Customized News Services

Do you want good news? Sports news? Trekkie news?

Tired of the same old headlines about murder and mayhem?

Welcome to the "Daily Me," and you're the publisher. If you don't like what you read, the only one to blame is you.

Here are some of the customized news services:

Newspapers

NEWS.COM
www.news.com
Cost: Free

The Los Angeles Times Hunter
www.latimes.com
Cost: Free except for archival material

The Philadelphia Inquirer and Daily News Clipper
www.phillynews.com
Cost: Free

The San Jose Mercury News NewsHound
www.sjhound.com
Cost: $7.95 a month

The San Francisco Chronicle and Examiner The Gate
www.sfgate.com
Cost: Free

The Times of London
www.the-times.co.uk
Cost: Free

The Wall Street Journal
www.wsj.com
Cost: $29 to $49 a year

Magazines

Time Warner's Pathfinder
www.pathfinder.com
Cost: $4.95 a month or $29.95 a year

Ziff-Davis ZDNet
www.zdnet.com
Cost: Free

E-mail

Farcast
www.farcast.com
Cost: $9.95 a month

Individual, Inc. Personal News Page
(Also available on the World Wide Web)
pnp.individual.com
Cost: Free to $6.95 a month, depending on service requested

Mercury Mail
www.merc.com
Cost: Free

Netscape In-Box Direct
www.netscape.com
Cost: Free

MSNBC
www.msnbc.com
Cost: Free

Screen Savers

After Dark Online
www.afterdark.com
Cost: Free

PointCast
www.pointcast.com
Cost: Free

WorldFlash News Ticker
www.scroller.com
Cost: Free

Search Engines

Excite
live.excite.com
Cost: Free

Infoseek
www.infoseek.com
Cost: Free

Yahoo!
www.yahoo.com
Cost: Free

Online journalism isn't limited to print publications. Broadcast news is also hopping on the bandwagon. Television stations are offering World Wide Web sites with the latest news. Although the sites are not as common as their print counterparts, the experimentation represents another direction in the online world. In the following article, Marc Gunther explores the elements that are attracting broadcasters to the Web. How are broadcasters using the Web's strengths to bolster their traditional offerings? What is the role of the consumer? What is the downside of instant access?

News You Can Choose

Marc Gunther

Marc Gunther has covered television since 1983.

On a typical weekday afternoon, Allison Davis, a former producer for NBC's "Today," is leading a tiny band of cyberjournalists who are bringing NBC News into the online world.

In cramped quarters strewn with computer cables and phone lines, they are preparing stories on Bosnia and Medicare, coaxing an NBC correspondent to write an analysis of Time Warner's merger with Turner Broadcasting, and selecting audio clips and still pictures from a Katie Couric interview with House Speaker Newt Gingrich.

Within hours, the stories, pictures and clips will be uploaded into the vast storehouse of information that is already available from NBC News on Supernet, a part of the new Microsoft Network (MSN) online service.

Television networks are staking out their turf in cyberspace. It's a brave new world where viewers, not producers, decide what goes into their customized "newscasts."

What can you find there? A detailed history of the conflict in the Balkans, a list of the most damaging hurricanes of the 20th century, a sound clip of O. J. Simpson's explanation of why he didn't testify in his own defense, a guide to the 1996 presidential campaign, excerpts from the latest NBC News/Wall Street Journal poll, transcripts of last week's "Meet the Press" and last night's "Dateline NBC," local weather forecasts, maps of the world, and bios and photos of, among others, Bill Clinton, Bob Dole, Maria Shriver and Willard Scott.

What can't you find? This afternoon Davis is struggling to check the latest headlines from NBC and the Associated Press. They're buried in her hard drive somewhere, but she can't manage to retrieve them. "Something's wrong with my computer, not the system," she explains. Still, she's the executive in charge—if her computer can't get along with Microsoft, what hope is there for the rest of us?

That, in a nutshell, is what network news online looks like these days. There's lots of excitement, enormous potential, plenty of promises and, to put it kindly, erratic delivery.

To take another example, CNN recently opened a site on the World Wide Web that provides an overview of the day's news, again with pictures, sound clips and video as well as text. What's more, unlike NBC's joint venture with Microsoft, CNN's Web site is open at no cost to any computer user with a link to the Internet. But frustration awaits subscribers to America Online, the nation's most popular commercial online service, who want to get their online news from CNN. Some AOL members say their screens freeze because CNN's software isn't compatible with AOL's Web browser. Says one AOLer: "You can't get there from here."

If that sounds confusing, well, it is. The online world is the new frontier of journalism, and

From Marc Gunther, "News You Can Choose" in *American Journalism Review*, November 1995. Reprinted by permission of American Journalism Review and NewsLink Associates.

veteran television news producers like NBC's Davis, Scott Woelfel of CNN and Les Blatt of ABC News are charting unmarked, ever-changing territory.

Adam Schoenfeld, an online analyst with Jupiter Communications, a New York consulting and publishing firm, says, "All the major news organizations know there's something there online, but they don't know what it is yet. They're feeling their way along."

But Schoenfeld believes there is a growing market for online news that is bound to be filled by the networks or newspapers or wire services. "People don't have a TV set at work, but they have a computer," he says. "If they want real-time news, it's a natural. You can get stories from the AP and Reuters midday today that won't hit your driveway until tomorrow morning."

The network news business should mesh neatly with the online world—the networks, after all, have as much access as anyone to the raw materials of news, the words, pictures, sound and video that can all be delivered online. They also have valuable brand names and the power to promote their online projects.

But to deftly manage the transition from television to online, the networks will have to radically rethink their ideas about how news is packaged and delivered. For starters, online news is viewer-driven, not producer-driven. It's part of a broad social trend that is offering people more choices than ever about how, when and where to get information.

"Essentially, when TV was created, the only power the viewers had was to turn on the set, change the channel and turn the volume up or down," says Dan Werner, vice president of MacNeil/Lehrer Productions, which is about to take PBS' "MacNeil/Lehrer NewsHour" online. "Now the people at home are gaining almost as much power as the creators. Now they can see a story on the air or on their computer screen and say, 'Hey, that was interesting, I'd like to learn more about that.' Online gives people the opportunity to go deeper, to make connections."

Or, as ABC's Blatt puts it: "We're quickly coming up on a time when people are going to be able to turn on their computers and basically punch up their own newscasts."

If nothing else, what the networks are doing online provides a peek into the future of television news, when viewers will turn on their sets and face a menu of choices: world news, national stories, local happenings, weather, sports, business or entertainment. With a flick of the remote they'll scan the headlines, skip stories that bore them, seek out more depth or watch highlights of only the sports events they want to see. News you can choose it's been called, and it's a business all the networks would like to be in, someday.

"There's no doubt that, at some point, you're going to go home at night and face a menu of items," says Michael Wheeler, president of NBC Desktop Video, a new venture that delivers business news to computers. "One choice might be the nightly news. Or you could say, 'I want to see news about O. J., an update on the Detroit Tigers and an update on the stock market.'"

Tomorrow's glitzy future is, however, a long way from today's glitchy online world. For now, getting the news online can be maddening, even for a patient and fairly knowledgeable computer user with good equipment. (To research this story, I used an IBM-compatible PC with a Pentium chip and a 14.4 modem, connecting to the Internet through America Online and Prodigy. Even so, surfing the 'Net was rarely smooth sailing.) What's more, once users get plugged into ABC, NBC or CNN online—CBS News has only a minimal presence in cyberspace—it's no simple task to find what you are seeking.

More important, at least from the industry standpoint, no one knows yet whether the networks can make money by delivering news online. Jon Petrovich, a CNN executive who oversees interactive ventures, says, "There will be a business there. How big it will be, I don't know." It's too early even to predict whether news online will be supported by advertising sales, subscription fees or both.

Keeping all those caveats in mind, it's still easy to see why television executives are excited by the online world. Here's where each network now stands:

▶ CNN launched an ambitious service at the end of August on the World Wide Web, a part of the Internet that can be accessed through any of the commercial online services. CNN also retains a smaller presence on CompuServe.

The advantage of being on the Web is its reach. In the long run, CNN should be able to attract more traffic and generate

> "All the major news organizations know there's something there online," says online analyst Adam Schoenfeld, "but they don't know what it is yet. They're feeling their way along."

more advertising revenues than rivals who are tied to one of the online services.

The downside is that CNN must bear all the costs of creating and maintaining its site. The network has sold ads to several sponsors, but revenues are negligible. And the costs are substantial, because most of the technical work is done in-house and a staff of 45 full time employees has been assigned to CNN Online. They update the Web site round the clock, seven days a week.

"If you look at the other broadcast networks, I don't think there's any doubt that we're ahead of what they're doing," says Woelfel, editor in chief of CNN Interactive, a division of CNN Online. CNN's online effort stands out for its breadth of coverage, with areas devoted to world and national news, sports, entertainment, business, food, health and weather.

For the all-news cable network, the stakes are high: An obvious appeal of news online is that it can be accessed at any time. Already, computer users who want information about a fast-breaking story have two choices—they can go online or turn on CNN.

Woelfel says that if he does his job right, many news junkies may prefer CNN Interactive to cable. "Online, you can get the news at any instant, when you choose to browse it," he says. "On television, you may watch an hour of news and never see the story you want."

CNN makes finding a story online even easier by providing a search function. Users can plug in keywords, and the system will search its library for whatever stories have been produced about, say, Bosnia or the Unabomber. Neither ABC nor NBC offers a search function yet.

➤ NBC News made its online debut with the launch of Windows 95 and the Microsoft Network in August. The Microsoft connection is both the strength and weakness of NBC's venture.

On the plus side, NBC's exclusive deal with Microsoft made the network a lot of money up front, better than $4 million, executives say. Essentially, the software company underwrote all of NBC's costs of going online.

Microsoft also enjoys some technical advantages over the other online services that enabled NBC to immediately provide a graphically appealing site with lots of multimedia content. More than the other networks, NBC exploits the richness of the online medium by including hypertext links—highlighted words and images that, with a mouse click, lead to additional information or related topics. "People have likened this to a mini CD-ROM," says Davis. "You can do so much to add perspective and depth to the news."

But NBC has dramatically limited its reach by dealing solely with Microsoft, which projects only one million subscribers by next summer. Most experts think MSN will grow rapidly, but the World Wide Web can already be reached by an estimated 9.7 million computer users.

What's more, despite Microsoft's largesse, NBC News is going online with fewer than a dozen staffers. Davis and her staff are covering four stories a day—fewer than the "Nightly News"—and their coverage is mostly repackaging of material created elsewhere, in addition to providing background materials, transcripts and other more indepth information. There's nothing wrong with that, but Davis would like to do more original reporting.

"We're ambitious, but tired," she says.

➤ ABC News became the first network news division to enter cyberspace in a major way when it launched ABC News on Demand with America Online in October 1994. A year later, ABC finds itself slipping behind its competitors, a sign of the breakneck pace of change.

As a result, ABC is planning to relaunch its online project this fall. "This medium changes so fast that you have to reinvent it every six to 12 months," says Bill Abrams, a former Wall Street Journal reporter who is vice president for business development at the news division. "It's just an endless game of hopscotch."

None of the networks will discuss their budgets for online news, but ABC News appears to be spending less than CNN or NBC, with just four full time editorial employees. ABC's deal with America Online gives the network a share of the hourly fees paid to AOL by users when they are in ABC's areas.

As an information provider, ABC News online isn't very impressive. Its breaking news coverage, which is limited to very brief wire reports from Reuters, can't compare to CNN's or, for that matter, to the AP wire, which is also available online. Nor has ABC organized its background material as well as NBC, which offers greater depth on news topics.

But ABC's online area on AOL has something neither NBC

nor CNN can claim—an active community of users who keep coming back, not to read the latest headlines, but to interact with each other, on bulletin boards and during live "chat" sessions.

This is a key to success online, say ABC executives. "I want the user to react," says Abrams. "We have to focus on stories that people talk about, a story that leads you to do something else, whether that's to download video or go to a chat room or a message board."

The popular bulletin boards offered on ABC News online draw daily comments from users. Many are trite or inane—"I think it is time for Sam [Donaldson] to get a toupee with a little grey in it"—but some offer thoughtful or heartfelt observations about issues in the news and ABC's coverage. "Nightline" town meetings about right-wing militias and about teen sex, for example, set off lively online debates that continued long after Ted Koppel left the air.

Live online chats with ABC anchors and correspondents have also drawn crowds, and occasional controversy as well. One night last spring, ABC's "Day One" correspondent John Hockenberry described capitalism as "amoral" and President Clinton as "a crowd-pleasing fanatic trying to look like a Republican." When asked if he thought the Contract with America would work, Hockenberry replied tartly: "Yes. . . . I'm moving to Switzerland."

Said Abrams: "He went a little too far in terms of what we like ABC News correspondents to say or not say." Conservative media critics circulated Hockenberry's comments.

All the networks say they would like to take fuller advantage of the interactive capability of the online world. NBC's Davis and CNN's Woelfel say they plan to send "cyberjournalists" equipped with laptop computers to major events, such as the 1996 political conventions. There they will seek to hook up newsmakers with computer users for live question-and-answer sessions.

Had CNN Interactive covered the Oklahoma City bombing, Woelfel says, he would have brought rescue workers or police online. "You run over to them with a laptop, and say, 'Would you mind answering some questions from our online users?' That gives a real connection between users and the people on the scene."

Perhaps so, but the networks may find they're neither needed, nor welcomed, as intermediaries. Typically, when major news stories break, online users create their own connections. During the Los Angeles earthquake and riots, for example, city residents provided firsthand accounts of events on all the online services. And a perennial online topic is how the mass media get stories wrong.

In a new study called "Tabloids, Talk Radio and the Future of News," Ellen Hume, a senior fellow at the Annenberg Washington Program, argues that online news challenges traditional journalists to get their house in order, or be bypassed. "Citizens can program their computers to retrieve their own 'news,' assembled easily from original sources far more diverse than the journalist's official Rolodex," she writes. "Newly empowered, they also can second-

> "Citizens can program their computers to retrieve their own 'news,' assembled easily from original sources far more diverse than the journalist's official Rolodex," Ellen Hume writes. "Newly empowered, they also can second-guess what professional journalists produce."

guess what professional journalists produce."

Indeed, the influence that the networks ordinarily wield may not be assets in cyberspace. "The early [users] seem to like to thumb their noses at the mass-market news providers," says Peter Krasilovsky, an analyst with Arlen Communications in Bethesda, Maryland.

Moreover, the differences between television news and print blur online. The networks must compete with magazines, newspapers and specialty publications, many of which have big cyberspace plans. Time Warner, for example, has created a site on the World Wide Web called Pathfinder that draws upon all of Time's publications to deliver more varied content than any of the networks are offering. Hours after the Unabomber's 35,000-word tract was printed in the Washington Post, for example, it was available online at Pathfinder.

While network executives focus on how to develop online news as a business, social critics and traditional journalists worry about the social implications of delivering news on demand. Interactive news, for all its dazzling promise, could widen the gap between the information-rich and the information-poor and erode the sense of community and shared knowledge now provided by over-the-air television.

"The consequence of all this fragmentation is that mainstream news organizations are being perceived as less and less relevant," says Andrew Kohut, a pollster and media critic. "The downside of all this, from a civic point of view, is disengagement. In the 1960s, when the American public watched Walter Cronkite . . . a lot of information got force fed. The public knows less about what's going on in the larger world than it did in those days."

In a speech last year, ABC News anchor Ted Koppel worried out loud about the dangers of news you can choose, whether delivered online or through pay television. "The wealthiest, the best off, will have more: more choice, more access, more control," he said. "Those that have the least will continue to have the least."

Evidence suggests he's right. Today's early experiments with interactive news target affluent viewers. NBC Desktop Video, for example, provides live television coverage of business news, delivered to the computers of Wall Street traders, mutual fund managers and corporate executives. It's a kind of C-SPAN for business, covering corporate news conferences, congressional testimony that affects the markets, presentations to securities analysts and interviews with CEOs.

When AT&T split up, NBC Desktop Video covered the entire news conference by the company's CEO, Robert Allen. "The wire story moved, but our customers want to hear Allen explain his vision," says Michael Wheeler, the president of Desktop Video. "If I'm MCI or Sprint, I don't want to depend on a third party to interpret the nuances that matter to me."

Wheeler believes that niche programming like Desktop Video will eventually migrate from offices to the home. "Every technological innovation has moved from business to the home, from the lightbulb to the fax machine," he says. "Some people will always get their news in a linear fashion. But others are going to pull up what they want to see, when they want to see it."

ABC's Blatt agrees. "It's no longer a case of people sitting there and watching the evening newscast and saying, 'That's the way it is.'"

How to Find the Networks Online

CNN INTERACTIVE

World Wide Web at http://www.cnn.com

ABC NEWS ONLINE

Available through America Online

NBC NEWS ON SUPERNET

Available through the Microsoft Network using Windows 95

CBS NEWS

World Wide Web at http://www.cbs.com

Article Review Form at end of book.

The newspaper industry is reinventing itself. Facing an onslaught from new media technologies that shift news access from media corporations to the consumer, the industry has to improve its content. Chris Lapham explores what steps are being taken to attract readers. What do the new newspaper models look like? How will news consumers adapt to these changing models? These are the questions posed by the following article.

The Evolution of the Newspaper of the Future

Chris Lapham

(laphac@rpi.edu)
Chris Lapham, Chief Correspondent for CMC Magazine, is an online content consultant and freelance writer and reporter who lives in the Capital Region of New York. She recently received a Master's degree from Rensselaer Polytechnic Institute in Troy, New York.

As we approach the end of the twentieth century, two powerful forces have emerged to change the mass communication model. The first is the use of computers as a means of processing, analyzing, and disseminating information. The second is the constantly accelerating capacity of that technology to enhance communication so it is almost unbounded by time and space. Because older communication technology required a huge investment of capital, a one-to-many model dominated, with those owning the broadcasting equipment or newspaper presses disseminating information to the masses. Current technology, specifically the digital transmission of text, audio, and video, has altered the traditional one-to-many communication model; instead, audiences are becoming producers as well as consumers of information, and a new many-to-many communication model has emerged. Today anyone with a modem, personal computer, and a telephone line can become a publisher, as we now know the term. But it is a mistake to eliminate totally the old model in favor of the new. By juxtaposing the best of the new model—computerized access, delivery, and packaging of information—with the best of the old model—insightful reporting in a well written story—a better hybrid model that combines the best of both is created.

CMC Is the Natural Next Step

Because this change in the mass communication model is occurring so rapidly, some are calling it a "technological" or "information" revolution. However, we are actually experiencing a natural step in the evolutionary progression of communication from orality and literacy to computers. If we can accept that writing is a form of technology (Ong 80), then it follows that computer-mediated communication (CMC) is simply another way of technologizing the word. While many squawk in alarm and anxiety, the millions of people using the Internet illustrate that society is now ready for this next stage in the evolution of communication. In fact, computer-mediated communication may return to human exchanges what the process of writing removed. In his text, *Orality and Literacy: The Technologizing of the Word*, Walter Ong describes the limitations of writing as a form of communication:

"Writing is in a way the most drastic of the three technologies (speech, writing, computers). It initiated what print and computers only continue, the reduction of dynamic sound to quiescent space, the separation of the word from the living present, where alone spoken words can exist."

From Chris Lapham, "The Evolution of the Newspaper of the Future" in *CMC Magazine,* July 1, 1995. Copyright © December Communications, Inc.

As the appropriate next step on an evolutionary continuum, CMC can return to language (the word) the immediacy lost in writing and give it a real-time presence. In fact, this is the very reason that the most popular form of CMC is electronic mail, fondly referred to as e-mail. People around the world have embraced CMC and instinctively formed "virtual communities" of like-minded individuals. Communication theorist Marshall McLuhan anticipated this warm response to the technological changes in communication more than 30 years ago. He predicted the formation of a "global village," which in many ways is coming true in the form of the Internet. The network has experienced astronomical growth—475 percent over the last year and 31,155 percent over the last three years (Rutkowski 7).

Emergence of the Many-To-Many Model

As people all over the world begin to produce and then share information within McLuhan's prophetic "global village," they naturally depend less and less on the information that flows from more traditional sources. Howard Rheingold, who describes himself as a high-tech social historian, explained this phenomenon at a Canadian writers conference:

"A tremendous power shift is underway, and despite the obscure or phony terminology used to describe it, this power shift is about people, and our ability to connect with each other in new ways much more than it is about fiber optic cable and multimedia appliances. The revolution triggered by the printing press was about literacy, and what literate populations are capable of doing (eg: governing themselves), long after it had anything to do with the mechanics of moveable type. The technology enable the power shift, but the power shift was created by the people who used the tool to educate themselves."

As Rheingold aptly states, this new communication revolution is shifting power to the people. This power shift seriously threatens the dominance of traditional mass media forms, specifically television, radio stations, magazines, and newspapers, which were built from the one-to-many communication model. Newspapers, which currently print and then deliver information on paper, are particularly vulnerable. Astute editors and publishers have recognized the threat digital delivery poses to the nation's estimable "Fourth Estate," and in an effort to reach today's "wired" audiences, they are creating new, electronic publications. But so far, creating a successful, futuristic model has eluded most publishers. Many outlets have opted simply to put the content of the "paper" product online, only to discover that the online world has its own, often mysterious ethos. Writing in Wired Magazine, Jon Katz, a media critic and former executive producer of the *CBS Evening News*, succinctly summarizes the dilemma facing newspaper publishers:

"So far, at least, online papers don't work commercially or conceptually. With few exceptions, they seem to be just what they are, expensive hedges against on rushing technology with little rationale of their own. They take away what's best about reading a paper and don't offer what's best about being online. That's the point of a newspaper . . . to filter the worthwhile information, then print it . . . . The newspaper needs to reinvent itself . . . . The object is not to replace, or put into a different format, but to gain a toehold in cyberspace and even absorb some of its values."

Newspapers Must Redefine Their Mission

Reinventing itself is a tall order for an industry that works under constant deadlines to produce a new product each day. How can the industry begin to construct a new model that takes advantage of state-of-the-art technology? Paradoxically, the answer comes from reflecting on the past. By analyzing and paring down the essentials of journalism as a craft and a profession, the real essence of the industry will emerge and a predictive model will begin to take shape. To its credit, the newspaper industry has conducted research and written and thought a great deal about what to do in the future. *In Come The Millennium, Interviews on the Shape of our Future*, a project of the American Society of Newspaper Editors, Michael Hooker, former president of the University of Massachusetts, says this is a pivotal moment in the history of newspaper publishing.

"The challenge for you will be perhaps your greatest ever. As a producer of newspapers, what you must do first is determine how you conceive yourself. Are you an organization that supplies newspapers or are you an organization that supplies information? Remington and Underwood saw themselves as being in the typewriter business. IBM saw itself as being in the word-processing business. The rest is history."

This self-analysis is being conducted in turbulent times when conflicting forces threaten to pull the industry apart. Reading a daily newspaper is a habit of millions of middle-age and older Americans. However, today's young people often prefer more sophisticated media to the daily ritual of the morning newspaper. We are also experiencing what some call an information explosion that threatens to bury even the most avid reader and intellectual. Ironically, it is the glut of information that holds the key to the survival of the newspaper industry. The digitizing of information has created a vast expansion in the amount of information that is readily available to audiences. Books and manuscripts, that previously consumed libraries and other physical spaces are now contained in digital bytes that can move with great speed over vast distances. Quite simply, more information is available to more people more quickly then ever before.

Mass media evolved because people from all walks of life needed help to understand the world around them. Throughout history, newspapers have excelled at collecting, recording, and distributing information at many different levels and geographic locales. As they evolve in light of technological change, newspapers need to embrace that mission anew. In fact, defining what is news is now more critical than ever. And it is their ability to do this within the context of new technology that is the key to newspapers' survival. Writing in a recent *New York Times Magazine* column, veteran journalist Max Frankel prognosticates:

"The newspapers that prosper in the next century will be the ones that offer the best journalism, that master the subjects about which they write and acquire the talent and expertise to appraise and explain an infinite variety of events ... Newspapers can trust the fermenting computer industry to perfect the technologies that will gradually replace their presses and delivery trucks. It's talent that they will need to survive in the digital age—gifted editors, reporters, and image artists who can find meaning in the approaching information glut."

Using Technology to Improve Content

In addition to improving the delivery of news, computer and telecommunications technology can improve the research and news gathering processes of newspapers. Unlike the one-to-many model where information came from the top, news on the Internet bubble up from the bottom and meanders its way upward. The daily reality of the many-to-many model means that the journalist now has a chance to really know and interact with his or her audience that goes way beyond traditional letters to the editor. This closer interaction should ideally lead to a better knowledge of the audience, and writing and reporting that more closely reflects readers' values and interests.

In today's more competitive information delivery environment, better research, better reporting, and better analysis are critical. Of the three, research is the priority. Speaking at a Neiman Foundation conference, J.T. Johnson explained the importance of the pre-reporting process:

"The quality of the information out can only be as good as the data flowing in. . . . Hence because of this shift in the data environment, educators and journalists must immediately turn more attention to the left side of the equation, the research, reporting, and analysis aspects if we are to improve the quality of the data in analysis components."

The value of research and analysis in creating the newspaper of the future may best be illustrated by one of the industry's leaders, the *News and Observer* (N & O) in Raleigh, North Carolina. While the paper has attracted attention for its World Wide Web site, Nando Land electronic service for children, and multimedia forays, the newspaper's real muscle comes from its research prowess. Nora Paul of the Poynter Institute, a journalism think-tank, claims that Raleigh's research operations are unparalleled. Writing in the *American Journalism Review*, Philip Moeller identified the N & O's real strengths:

"... what sets Raleigh apart is the fact that digitized information skills—for using computers, databases, online services—are becoming standard for nearly everyone in the newsroom."

He outlines what sets Raleigh's operation apart from the norm in the industry: a 21-person research department with a network of databases; staffers who write software to create research pathways to access databases; the creation of a database to track state legislation that was turned into an online service; and three generations of hypertext software that enables writers to search their own notes. These developments were the precursors of other innovative ventures, such as a multimedia series in collaboration with a local television station, and an electronic version of the newspaper.

Journalism Returns to Its Roots

In building a successful digital enterprise, Raleigh's N & O is a good model because it uses the new technology to improve its primary product at a grassroots level. This is a good lesson for the industry as a whole, which is now being called upon to turn information into knowledge—the ultimate goal. In her essay, "Writing For The Third Millennium," Beth Agnew talks about a return to the historical and literary roots of journalism:

"Writers have always been society's visionaries. We now have too much information to rationally deal with on a daily basis, and we need skilled professional help to turn that information into the currency of the next millennium—knowledge."

Along with its muckraking and investigative roots, there is a long history of the newspaper reporter as a writer of literature. In fact, the first newspapers in this country were partisan reports of events. It was the organization of the Associated Press in 1848 that introduced the requirement of objectivity in reporting, and reporters have been walking a tightrope ever since trying to be both observer and participant.

The insightful reporter interpreting reality ultimately has the same goals as McLuhan's highly intuitive "artist," who is capable of understanding the present as well as the future.

"The artist is the man in any field, scientific or humanistic, who grasps the implications of his actions and of new knowledge in his own time. He is the man of integral awareness . . . The artist picks up the message of cultural and technological challenge decades before its transforming impact occurs."

The Creation of a New Hybrid Model

The real beauty of the new technology is its ability to enable newspapers to not only enhance their researching and reporting capabilities, but also to deliver a better, more audience-aware product in an immediate and inexpensive way. Digital delivery is greatly improved by publication on the World Wide Web, the fastest growing part of the Internet. One of the main attractions of the Web is hypertext, a system that seamlessly links computers and files continents apart. For example, a story about a poll on the performance of a government official could include color-highlighted links that readers simply click on to get more in depth information about his or her voting record, recent speeches, or a news story about campaign promises. Using the hypertext capabilities of the Web totally eliminates the proverbial "news hole" and opens up an unlimited amount of "space" for presenting the news product. George Gilder neatly summarizes the marriage of the computer and the newspaper:

"The computer is a perfect complement to the newspaper . . . . [It] enables the existing news industry to deliver its product in real time. It hugely increases the quantity of information that can be made available, including archives, maps, charts and other supporting material. It opens the way to upgrading the news with full screen photography and videos, while hugely enhancing the richness and timeliness of the news. The computer empowers readers to use the "paper" in the same way they do today—to browse and select stories and advertisements at their own time and place."

By using computer technology to produce and deliver a new product, newspapers have welded both the old (literacy-print) with the new (computers-digital delivery) and created a better model. McLuhan explains this process as the creation of a hybrid which blends the old and the new to create a superior medium.

"The hybrid or the meeting of two media is a moment of truth and revelation from which new form is born. For the parallel between two media holds us on the frontiers between forms that snaps us out of the Narcissus-narcosis. The moment of the meeting of media is a moment of freedom and release from the ordinary trance and numbness imposed by them on our senses."

Innovative Solutions

The priority of this new model will be listening to the audience and creating innovative opportunities for ongoing communication. The WELL, which stands for Whole Earth 'Lectronic Link, recently became the first online service to offer self-publishing on the Web. The WELL, which is based in Sausalito, California, helped nurture author Howard Rheingold and the Electronic Frontier Foundation. The organization celebrated its 10th anniversary in April of 1995 by creating a Community Page that provides an index to the individual home page publishing efforts of its members.

One of the many newspapers embarking on an electronic future is the *Arizona Daily Star*. The *Star* is working on a new service called StarNet that offers a comprehensive mix of features and services. Some of those features include Internet access, news from the paper edition, local discussion groups, and access to the paper's archives. The *Star* is attempting to become an electronic home base for its readers and will give nonprofit organizations (with a budget of less than $1 million dollars) space on their service to publish local newsletters. While this service may be too ambitious for some publishers just beginning to venture into cyberspace, the concept of the newspaper as the community's electronic publishing hub is a critical component of the newspaper of the future.

While many are searching for the yet elusive answer, the only certainty now is that there is no one right way to do things: each newspaper must discover its niche and provide insightful and innovative content in a format its readers want. And that format may range from a hand-held tablet to a personalized newspaper created by an intelligent agent searching the Internet for customized news. Living the many-to-many model means that the flow of information is fluid with readers responding to and creating information and ideas. In addition to providing access to information, the newspaper publisher is now a facilitator of public discussion. By building community discussion, what is reported in the news takes on new meaning, and people come to better understand not only the world around them, but themselves as well.

References

Agnew, B. (1994, June). Writing for the third millennium. *Writers' Retreat on Interactive Technology & Equipment Conference.* University of Vancouver, Vancouver, British Columbia.

Frankel, M. (1995). The Daily Digital. *The New York Times Magazine.* 9 April 1995:38.

Gilder, G. F. (1994). Fidler's Electronic News Panel is a better bet for the future than home shopping." ASNE Bulletin.

Hooker, M. (1994). Interview. *Come the millennium: Interviews on the shape of our future.* Kansas City: Andrews and McMeel.

Johnson, J. T. and Markoff, J. (1994). What skills does the journalist require to take advantage of new technology? *Neiman Report.*

Katz, J. (1994, September). Online or not, newspapers suck. *Wired.*

McLuhan, M. (1994). *Understanding media: The extensions of man.* Cambridge: MIT Press.

Moeller, P. (1994). The age of convergence. *American Journalism Review*, 22–28.

Ong, W. (1982). *Orality and literacy: The technologizing of the word.* London: Methuen.

Reingold, H. (1994, June). The electronic landscape: A writer's perspective. *Writers' Retreat on Interactive Technology & Equipment Conference.* University of Vancouver, Vancouver, British Columbia.

Rutkowski, A. (1995, May). Statistics on the growth of the Internet. *Web Week.*

Article Review Form at end of book.

READING 7

Unless newspapers combine the strengths of print and cyberspace, traditional media may have trouble surviving. But what are those strengths and how can they be combined for a newer, stronger product? How can newspapers retain their audience when faced with additional competition? Does journalism have a new definition in an online age? Will advertising dollars drive the product, or will the product drive the advertising? David Shaw, a reporter for *The Los Angeles Times*, looks at these issues in the following article.

Can Newspapers Find Their Niche in the Internet Age?

David Shaw
Times Staff Writer
David Shaw's e-mail address is david.shaw@latimes.com
Jacci Cenacveira and Rebecca Andrade of The Times editorial library assisted with the research for this series.

Unless they combine the strengths of print and cyberspace, traditional media may have trouble surviving.

With public opinion polls consistently showing reduced respect for the traditional news media, the Internet now looms as potentially the gravest threat to survival that these media—and newspapers in particular—have ever faced.

Newspapers long ago lost out to television as the place most people get most of their news. Nowadays, many people do not even have to wait for the TV news to come on. They can get headline stories, sports scores and stock reports instantly on their computer terminals.

As Internet access becomes increasingly common, many people who are attracted by its unique features—and who are fed up with what they see as the bias, inaccuracy, sensationalism and arrogance of the traditional media—may migrate to the Internet in such large numbers that today's primary providers of news and information will become tomorrow's journalistic ghost towns.

Or—and this is the hope of establishment media moguls from coast to digitally monitored coast—the Internet could prove to be the greatest opportunity for salvation their business has ever had.

"We see the Internet as the best opportunity to create real economic value in the media over the next 75 years," says Peter Winter, president of Cox Interactive Media, a division of Cox Newspapers, based in Atlanta.

If newspapers can improve their print publications to take advantage of what the Internet can't do and, at the same time, create their own Web sites to capitalize on what the Internet can do, they could thrive both journalistically and financially—and reclaim the media dominance they once enjoyed.

"Paper is very valuable for certain kinds of uses, and electrons are very valuable for other kinds of uses," says Paul Steiger, managing editor of the Wall Street Journal. "They're going to coexist and mix and match, but over time, electronic transmission is going to be more important."

Marshall McLuhan argued 30 years ago that "The medium is the message," but Steiger and

From David Shaw, "Can Newspapers Find Their Niche in the Internet Age?" in *Los Angeles Times*, June 16, 1997. Copyright© 1997 Los Angeles Times.

other print editors who see the Internet as more opportunity than threat insist that newspapers will continue to be newspapers—news, information, insight and entertainment—no matter what the format or transmission mechanism is.

The Internet, after all, is just a delivery system—electrons and wires rather than ink and paper.

"It doesn't change the nature of what we do. It just changes the tools we use," says Owen Youngman, director of interactive media for Tribune Co. in Chicago.

But print journalists must avoid the shortsighted approach that fatally afflicted the railroad and typewriter businesses. Railroad executives saw themselves as being in the railroad business rather than the transportation business, and failed to meet the challenge of airplanes and automobiles.

Companies such as Remington and Underwood saw themselves as being in the typewriter business rather than the word processing business, and were buried by IBM, Apple and Microsoft.

Newspaper executives and the people who work for them must see themselves as being in the information and communications business, not the newspaper business.

The heart and soul of any serious news organization is its newsroom—the men and women who report and edit the news. Newspapers not only have the experienced staffs necessary to gather the news, but they also have the editorial standards, the connection to their communities and the record of public service that would seem to give them a head start in any race to establish a journalistic beachhead in cyberspace.

Moreover, a newspaper on the Internet can publish the sort of "extra" (as in "Extra! Extra! Read all about it!") that big-city newspapers routinely published when news broke in the days before television; on the Internet, a newspaper can update itself constantly, reclaiming from television the role of being most people's first source of news.

If a newspaper can provide good, traditional journalism—updated during the day and augmented by the graphic, personalized and interactive features of online publishing—will it really make any difference if the consumer downloads the material to his home or office computer and prints it there rather than having the newspaper print it and deliver it?

"As long as we can get the news to people . . . I don't think the trade-off from print to electronic is intrinsically bad," says Neil Budde, a former reporter and editor at the Louisville Courier-Journal and USA Today and now editor of the Wall Street Journal Interactive Edition.

But there is a significant difference between the two media: The Internet effectively shifts the decision-making process from the publisher/broadcaster to the consumer/user.

No Guarantees on Reliability

Historically, a relative handful of news media elites have served as gatekeepers and agenda-setters for a large and increasingly diverse society. Guided by their own standards of newsworthiness, relevance, taste and public interest—and severely limited by the available space and time (a certain number of columns or pages per issue, a certain number of minutes per newscast)—major newspaper and magazine editors and top radio and television news directors have long decided what (and how much) their audience will be exposed to every day.

There are no time or space limits—and ultimately no gatekeepers—on the Internet. Cyberspace is infinite. Anyone can disseminate information instantly, throughout the world.

This tidal wave of unfiltered information imposes "more responsibility on the . . . news consumer," says Brock Meeks, editor and publisher of Cyberwire Dispatch, an online news service, and chief Washington correspondent for MSNBC, the cyberspace alliance of Microsoft and NBC News.

"When you pick up the New York Times or the Los Angeles Times, there is an unspoken guarantee that what you pick up will be factual—it's been vetted by lawyers and editors," Meeks says. "There isn't that kind of unspoken guarantee [on the Web]. The news consumer has to be smarter, do his own filtering . . . ferret out the people who are good and responsible as opposed to those who are sloppy or wacko."

But most people have neither the time nor the skill to find, sort and evaluate all the information they find on the Net. Thus, for all the talk in some quarters of a process that has come to be called "disintermediation"—the elimination of intermediaries an middlemen—the Internet is unlikely to render obsolete the reporters and editors who serve as journalistic middlemen.

"The more material there is, the more need there is for filters," says Howard Rheingold, an Internet pioneer who was the first editor of hotwired.com, the Web site for Wired magazine, and has since created the provocative Web site Electronic Minds. "You don't need a printing press anymore, but you do need people who know how to cultivate sources, double-check information and put the brand of legitimacy on it."

Because the Web is so informal and errors are so easily and quickly corrected, many people writing for the Web are "less concerned" with accuracy than are most traditional journalists, say David Weir, vice president for content management at HotWired.

A reporter who makes a mistake in an online story can correct it almost instantly, rather than having to live with it until the next news cycle, as traditional journalists must do. That has made some online reporters lazy about verifying original source material, Weir says. As a result, he says, early online reporting has often been "sloppy and careless."

When that problem is combined with the tendency of some conspiracy-minded Net buffs to turn the Web into a hotbed of rumor and speculation, it becomes clear why proven reliability and brand-name credibility may be even more important to wanderers in cyberspace than to readers and viewers of more conventional media.

To illustrate this point, many critics cite the reports that circulated on the Internet that a U.S. Navy missile downed TWA Flight 800, which plunged into the Atlantic Ocean last year, killing all 230 aboard. The rumor—resoundingly denied by federal investigators—originated in a speculative e-mail scenario sent by a retired airline pilot, and it was widely picked up on the Net.

But it was the mainstream media that brought the story to the attention of most people, after Pierre Salinger reported what he had seen on the Internet.

Because Salinger is a "brand name"—former presidential press secretary, former U.S. senator and former ABC news correspondent—the story received more attention in the traditional media than it otherwise would have. Indeed, many people on the Internet had debunked it before it surfaced in the mainstream media.

The story won't go away, though, and the Internet continues to be disconcertingly fertile ground for crackpots and conspiracy theorists, as well as for responsible purveyors of legitimate information.

Many Web sites have "competently written . . . frequently updated pages [that] look as professional as those of brand-name news media sites," as Kurt Anderson wrote in the New Yorker this year. "Thanks to the Web, amateurism and spuriousness no longer need look amateurish or spurious."

Will New Media Replace Old Media?

Even though the ethos of cyberspace is freedom, sophisticated Internet users recognize the need for "a filter that can help the public separate the bunk . . . from mostly accurate news sources," as Brooke Shelby Biggs wrote in Slate, the online magazine published by Microsoft.

Responsible news organizations, online and in print, can provide that filter, and that is why many people in the forefront of Web journalism hope (and believe) that traditional media will survive in the Digital Age.

"I love my daily newspaper, and I don't think it will die. I don't think TV news will die," says Meeks.

Not only is a newspaper cheap, but it is much easier than a computer to take into the bathroom or to bed or on the bus. It's also possible to throw away when you're finished. Computers will certainly become smaller and cheaper in the years ahead—after all, 30 years ago, a computer cost $18,000 and weighed 250 pounds—but not even the most optimistic soul in cyberspace suggests that computers will ever sell for a quarter and be completely disposable.

"With every new medium, the question arises, 'Will it replace the old media?'" says Mark Pincus, chief executive officer of Freeloader, an Internet delivery system that ceased operating May 31. "The correct answer is always 'No!'"

In 1927, an editorial in Editor & Publisher magazine warned: "If news is known by the public through radio broadcasts, there is no logical incentive to buy a newspaper to get the news." Twenty-five years later, many "experts" also predicted that television would kill newspapers.

Television has certainly hurt newspapers in many ways—cutting into the circulation and advertising and helping to kill many afternoon papers. But the better newspapers have adapted and improved in response to the challenge from television—no longer simply reporting what happened yesterday but explaining how and why it happened and what might happen tomorrow and next week and next year.

That is why, when a major news event is heavily covered on television—whether it's the

Oklahoma City bombing or the Super Bowl—newspaper circulation goes up as people look for more detail, for analysis and for a confirmation of their own observations.

Many newspapers have also become much more like television in recent years, though, "dumbing down . . . aping TV rather than challenging it," in the words of Lincoln Millstein, vice president of new media for the Boston Globe.

In an effort to retain their dwindling and increasingly distracted audience, newspapers are emphasizing celebrity, sensationalism and "sound bite journalism" more than ever before.

Some critics worry that newspapers will misread the true appeal of the Internet and focus only on its bells and whistles—flashy graphics, constant updates, interactivity and instant links to other sites—and dumb down even further to try to compete with this medium as well. That, Millstein says, would be "the death knell" for many papers.

Competing to Deliver the News

The Internet is a bigger threat than television. It is growing faster than television did and it offers far more services than television does—and it has come along at a time when newspapers are in a weaker competitive position than they were when television began making its inroads. In fact, when a big news story breaks, many people already turn first not to newspapers or television but to the Internet.

On the day the jury returned its verdict in the wrongful death suit against O. J. Simpson, "we set a new record . . . 550,000 people visited our [Web] site," says Boots Rykiel, editor of the online edition of USA Today.

Many of the daily newspaper's longtime staples—sports scores, stock market tables, entertainment listings, the daily TV schedule, the weather report—can all be provided more efficiently (and updated more frequently) on the Internet.

"Newspapers are the medium most threatened by [the] personalization" of local news and information, says Norman Lehoullier, managing director of the interactive arm of Grey Advertising in New York. A newspaper is "the most local, most relevant piece of content you put your hands on," he says, and Internet companies are "going after that newspaper franchise."

The Internet, with its infinite "news hole," can—at least in theory—provide more detailed local news and information than even the best local newspapers. Online services could list every home sale, every school lunch and standardized test ranking, every police blotter entry, every high school and youth league sports score, every service club speaker and PTA meeting agenda, the minutes of every school board and city council and planning commission meeting—anything and everything that could conceivably be of interest to the residents of a given community.

There is no reason newspaper sites can't do this themselves—if they are willing to embrace what Terry Schwadron, deputy managing editor of the Los Angeles Times and supervisor of the paper's Web site, calls "a new definition of 'journalism.'"

"Much of the useful, practical information we'll be able to give on the Web is more straight facts than what we think of as traditional news coverage," Schwadron says, "but that kind of information has a higher profile in the electronic world, where people tend to look at everything from a standpoint of personal utility. Can we help you get a building permit online . . . and do other things that aren't classic journalism but will make your life more convenient?"

Some online sites have started tentatively down that path, offering a variety of services built around guides to local entertainment and recreation.

The Internet is competing with newspapers for more than news, though. It is also competing for advertising, which provides about 80% of the income for a typical newspaper.

Online ad expenditures skyrocketed from $12 million in 1994 to $55 million in 1995 to $300 million last year, according to Jupiter Communications in New York, a research and consulting firm that specializes in interactive technologies.

That is still a tiny fraction (less than 1%) of the $38 billion spent on newspaper advertising in 1996, but the figure is continuing to grow. Jupiter forecasts $5 billion in annual online advertising by 2000.

Meanwhile, many of the primary newspaper advertisers—retailers, grocery stores and financial institutions—have been merging, liquidating and turning to direct mail and other advertising venues at an alarming rate in recent years. If advertisers start spending significant portions of their budget on the Internet, they will probably reduce further what they spend in newspapers.

That is what they did when television began to make inroads

against newspapers. Although newspapers still draw a larger share of the total advertising dollar than television, the margin grows smaller almost every year.

Newspaper advertising increased 8.9% in the first quarter of this year, the best quarterly performance in 10 years, but it has increased only 17.6% over the last seven years—compared with a 40% increase in the gross domestic product in that time—and much of the advertising increase was attributable to increased advertising rates, not increased linage.

Aggressive cost-cutting and the declining cost of newsprint have spurred newspaper stocks to strong performances on Wall Street in the last year after several years in the doldrums, but a revitalized financial performance, even it if continues, may not be sufficient to respond to the challenge of the Internet, especially if the Internet continues to aggressively seek local advertising.

Competition for Ad Dollars

Except for a few major national newspapers—the Wall Street Journal, New York Times and USA Today—most newspapers get the vast majority of that revenue locally.

The most local advertising of all—and the one most vulnerable to the Internt—is classified advertising, a $15-billion-a-year business that accounts for about 35% to 40% of a typical newspaper's advertising revenue.

Cox Interactive Media and two Internet search engines, Yahoo! and Excite, are among several services that offer classified ads on their local Web sites, and many others are sure to follow. Even the most dedicated newspaper executive will admit that people looking for jobs or homes or virtually anything else sold through classified ads can search far more efficiently online than they can by flipping through newspaper pages filled with tiny print.

An Internet user just types in a precise preference—"a four-bedroom house with three baths, a large backyard and a swimming pool in the Pasadena area," and—click!—the computer screen instantly fills with information and pictures on all the houses that fit the description within the price range requested.

Because many people resent the face-to-face haggling and high-pressure tactics so often encountered at automobile dealerships, Irvine-based Auto-by-Tel is one of the most popular of the online services that are challenging traditional newspaper classified ads.

Through Auto-by-Tel, customers can go online and specify the make, model and features they want in a new or used car, get a price quote from the nearest participating dealer, "link" to other sites that will provide the dealer's invoice price, arrange financing and buy insurance, all without leaving home.

There are several similar online automotive services, including a joint venture announced in May by USA Today Online and AutoWeb Interactive.

In addition to the obvious savings in time and effort that online shopping affords the customer, it also enables the seller to save a great deal of money by eliminating various middlemen, from wholesalers to sales personnel. At least some of this savings is passed on to the consumer, providing yet another incentive for online shopping.

Fear over the potential loss of classified advertising revenue is the single most important force driving most newspapers to create not only their own Web sites but other online classified services as well.

"Classified will go [to the Internet]," says Richard T. Schlosberg III, publisher of the Los Angeles Times," and we have to be there to catch it on the other end" or someone else will.

Thus, until The Times Web site was redesigned in April, the largest type on the first screen a user saw was not a reference to the day's biggest news story but Classified Sources, under which appeared links to the HomeSource, AutoSource and JobSource classified ad listings. Those headings and links are still there, albeit less prominently, and The Times Web site also provides other real estate information—including mortgage calculators, sales records and neighborhood profiles.

The interactive edition of the Houston Chronicle has created Directory Center, which combines classified ads with community information and residential and business telephone directories.

Although he declines to provide specific figures, Gene Wiley, director of Houston Chronicle Interactive, says Directory Center has been "extraordinarily profitable" and may turn out to be "the magic bullet for making a buck" on the Web.

Some newspapers charge a relatively small extra fee to people who want their classified ads in both the printed paper and online. Others have instituted slightly larger than usual rate increases for the printed paper and then include all printed ads in the online edition at no additional charge. At present, virtually all papers refuse to sell classified ads exclusively for their online editions; a customer has to buy an ad in the printed edition as well.

Some Internet experts believe newspapers are doomed to lose most of their classified ads no matter what they do.

Most big-city newspapers have become local monopolies—and have been charging the high advertising rates that monopolies make possible, says Bill Bass, senior analyst in media and technology strategies for Forrester Research in Cambridge, Mass. There will be too many online competitors for most newspapers to sustain either their monopolies or their high rates on classified ads, Bass says.

Typically, an online classified ad will cost about 30% of what the same ad would cost in print, and Bass predicts that large alliances such as National Job Bank, CareerMosaic, Auto-by Tel, Monster Board and the Realtor Information Network of the National Assn. of Realtors will ultimately take about 70% of the total classified market with their online services.

That is a frightening forecast for the nation's newspapers. Miles E. Groves, chief economist for the Newspaper Assn. of America, estimates that if newspapers lose "only" 50% of their classified revenue, the profit margin for the average paper would plummet from 14% to 3%. If they lost 70% of their classified ad revenue, "they'd basically be losing money."

In an effort to prevent that scenario from becoming a reality, many newspapers are creating their own classified advertising networks. Times Mirror, parent company of The Times, has invested in Listing Link, one of the largest online real estate sites, with more than 200,000 listings nationwide, including most properties in California.

The Times has also joined the New York Times, Washington Post and more than 25 other newspapers in creating CareerPath, an online site that links employers and job seekers. More than 400 small- to medium-size newspapers have similarly joined forces in the AdOne Classified Network.

Further alliances—and more experimentation—will be necessary for newspapers to survive, and "the ones who will do well are those who innovate, who look at the Internet in a positive way, not purely defensively," says Pete Higgins, vice president in charge of interactive media at Microsoft.

That won't be easy.

"As an industry," says Robert Brisco, vice president for marketing and new business development at the Los Angeles Times, "newspapers are not used to the competition out there for niches, large and small, which require a much greater speed to market and tolerance for risk and need for innovation than the core business historically required."

So far, most newspapers have been unwilling to invest huge amounts of money in their online ventures. Even the biggest papers—most of which have annual revenues of several hundred million dollars apiece—are spending less than 1% of that on their online papers this year; almost all are investing far less. They are reluctant to be left behind, but equally reluctant to commit too much money to so new and unproven a medium.

That reluctance could be dangerous.

"We want an ROI [return on investment] on everything," Bob Cauthorn, director of new technology at the Arizona Daily Star, said at an interactive newspaper conference in Houston in February. "We are bound to these incredibly fat profit margins. . . . We are investing almost nothing in risk capital. We need to change that."

Because a newspaper's online start-up costs are so low—no trucks, no newsprint, no presses and relatively small staffs—most online newspaper executives say profitability for them is ultimately inevitable. Many predict a profit as soon as 1998 or 1999.

The real profit question, however, is neither if nor when but how much; a small profit on a small investment may look nice on the balance sheet, but if newspapers lose significant amounts of their classified advertising revenue, that small online stream may represent a pyrrhic victory in a war that could be nasty and brutal and not necessarily short.

Internet Advertising

Advertising Expenditures (in millions of dollars)

1994: $12

1995: $55

1996: $330

2000: $5 billion

Source: Jupiter Communications

Web Sites

These are the names and Internet addresses for Web sites mentioned in today's stories:

The Arizona Daily Star
http://www.azstarnet.com

Auto-by-Tel
http://www.autobytel.com

Boston Globe
http://www.boston.com

CareerMosaic
http://www.careermosaic.com

Career Path
http://www.careerpath.com

Chicago Tribune
http://www.chicago.tribune.com

Cox Interactive Media
http://www.cimedia.com

CyberWireDispatch
http://www.cyberwerks.com/cyberwire

Electronic Minds
http:/www.electronicminds.com

ESPN SportsZone
http://www.espn.sportszone.com

Forrester Research
http://www.forrester.com

Houston Chronicle Interactive
http://www.chron.com

Instant Sports
http://www.instantsports.com

Jupiter Communications
http://www.jupiter.com

Los Angeles Times
http://www.latimes.com

Monster Board
http://www.monsterboard.com

MSNBC
http://www.msnbc.com

National Job Bank
http://www.nationaljobbank.com

New York Times on the Web
http://www.nytimes.com

Real Audio
http://www.realaudio.com

Realtor Information Network
http://www.reinfonet.com

Slate magazine
http://www.slate.com

USA Today
http://www.usatoday.com

Wall Street Journal Interactive Edition
http://www.wsj.com

Washington Post
http://www.washingtonpost.com

Wired magazine
http://www.hotwired.com

Article Review Form at end of book.

READING 8

As Microsoft expands, is it quietly turning itself into a media powerhouse? The "Sidewalk" project calls for the creation of city guides chock full of entertainment news in a number of major U.S cities. In the process of building Sidewalk, is Microsoft going to take market share from traditional publishers? If you were a publisher of a daily newspaper in one of these targeted cities, how would you react? Would you believe Bill Gates or think more like the author of this article?

Stealth Sidewalk

Brooke Shelby Biggs

Microsoft's Sidewalk project spearheads a plan that will see Redmond own the news.

The traditional media may be a lost cause, what with the Disney-Turner-Westinghouse-Murdoch orgy in full swing. Big money owns and influences the media, and they aren't even trying to deny it any more. And for those of us who'd hoped that the inherently populist Internet would provide a purer, more spin-free media environment, it's time to stop dreaming.

We need not worry about Ted Turner buying CNET, or Michael Eisner swooping down on Tweak. Just think back to that Econ 103 class you slept through way back when, and remember what that slope-shouldered guy with the taped glasses at the chalkboard said about the means of distribution. He who owns them owns the ends.

And guess who owns the means of distribution in the world of new media. Forget the antitrust blather about Microsoft's naked ambition to rule the desktop. That's over and done, and Microsoft won. The powerful payoff—which I doubt Bill Gates even foresaw—is that with the promise of instant information delivered to your desktop, Microsoft also happens to control the main thoroughfare between you and your news.

Within the next five years, Microsoft will be the most powerful news media company in the world. Not only will everything you read have been created with assorted Microsoft software, but it will also be filtered and aggregated within sundry Microsoft media ventures, and delivered over Microsoft-controlled networks to your Microsoft-saturated machine.

If you happen to live in a major city, you'll see the existing media fortresses begin to crumble at the end of this year. Microsoft's biggest endeavor yet to insinuate itself into the general culture is its stealthy Sidewalk project. Sidewalk is the Yellow Pages with a glandular disorder. With it, Microsoft aims to create localized directories for select urban areas, such as Sydney, London, New York, Boston, San Diego, San Francisco, Chicago, and of course, Seattle.

Dailies and weeklies should be afraid. There are already strong indicators that the Internet will siphon classified advertising revenues away from newspapers. Localized sites like Sidewalk hope to cash in not only on classified revenues, but also on the mountains of arts and entertainment listings, and ads. With real-time weather and traffic updates, local news reports, restaurant reviews, area maps, and more, Sidewalk is positioned to trounce local print-media outlets.

What's going to make it even easier for Microsoft is the fact that some poor sots are plunging into the online city-guide pool blithely, not seeing the two-ton elephant poised on the high dive. Outfits like CitySearch and the regional Yahoos are compiling some outstanding content and infrastruc-

Some poor sots are plunging into the online city guide pool blithely, not seeing the two-ton elephant posed on the high dive.

From Brooke Shelby, "Stealth Sidewalk" in *HotWired*, 1997. Copyright © 1997 HotWired, Inc. Copyright © 1994-97 Wired Digital Inc.

ture. If I were Microsoft, I'd just as soon let the little fish mature or drown on their own, then swallow up the survivors' intellectual capital in a takeover down the road. I'd let the competition do the work (and make the mistakes) for me.

For the time being, those newspapers with robust online efforts won't feel much of a pinch, since Microsoft Sidewalk and its ilk are still in their larval forms. Those online papers that have invested in easy-to-navigate site designs—including powerful search technologies—can also rest easy . . . for now.

Local newspapers have a clear advantage here because they have long-standing business relationships and high profiles within their communities. They already have the listings and a system for managing them. The city-guide business is really just a fancy repurposing of the entertainment pages.

The newspaper sites that will hold their own are ones that both embrace the new technology and shovel, shovel, shovel their back-of-the-book content onto the Web. The winners will be the ones that add an intuitive interface—simple, elegant image maps—and most importantly, solid, reliable entertainment and restaurant listing and classifieds. Good examples in one of Sidewalk's targeted cities, San Francisco, include the *San Francisco Chronicle's* The Gate, and the weekly *San Francisco Bay Guardian* site.

But consider: Seattle Times users are not accessing their content with a Seattle Times Explorer Web browser. Web-savvy Australians aren't logging onto the Fairfax@Martket site via a Fairfax@Market online service. And online patrons of the weekly Boston *Phoenix* aren't running a Boston Phoenix operating system.

But Microsoft's Sidewalk will buddy up with The Microsoft Network (featuring Slate), which comes bundled with Microsoft's Windows 95 operating system and Microsoft's Internet Explorer Web browser.

Imagine Gutenberg with as many advantages back in the 15th century as Microsoft has in this one. He'd have had to own not only the printing press, but 90 percent of the ink and tree pulp in the world.

Article Review Form at the of book

Going online is not the sole province of white, middle-class males. African-Americans, Asian-Americans and Hispanics are also flocking to the Web. But how do the percentages compare to national demographics? How are minority groups using the Internet? What impact does economics have on Web utilization? What is the impact on groups who do not have significant access?

The Haves and Have Nots

Some surprising cyber demographics

Christopher Harper

New York City—It's been a long day for McLean Greaves. Rapper Biggie Small has been killed, and Greaves, a former reporter for the Canadian Broadcasting Company, has been going nonstop for three days on the Smalls' story. "We're trying to provide a Generation X black point of view," he said, including videotape of Small's performances here in New York's Bedford-Stuyvesant neighborhood before he became famous.

But you won't find the extensive coverage in any newspaper. You'll find it in Root Stand," an on-line publication that's part of Cafe Los Negroes, a cyberspace meeting place for news, entertainment and chat at (www.vmelanin.com).

Blacks & Latinos

The 31-year-old Greaves and 20 producers are attracting a great deal of attention in the publishing world by aiming at a market of young blacks and Latinos. But the cafe is not an exclusive club; whites are welcome, too.

Greaves and his partner, Arzie Hardin, a former commodities trader, are not convinced that there is such a significant divide between blacks and whites in the digital age. "With the price decline in computers, WebTV and more computers being brought into schools, the Internet is becoming much more accessible," said Hardin, chief financial officer of Virtual Melanin. "There may be a gap between blacks and whites, but it's narrowing really fast."

Who exactly are the haves and have nots in a digital age? Is it based on race, income, gender, age or something else?

The Latest Surveys

Gleaned from a variety of surveys, including Nielsen, the Wirthlin Group, and the Pew Research Center, a rough sketch of those using the Internet is beginning to emerge. Those on line tend to follow the demographics of the nation as a whole. Whites represent 86 percent of the total users, one percent higher than their percentage of the American population. Blacks represent nine percent of all digerati, one percent less than the number in the general population. Non-whites comprise 14 per cent of the Internet users, the same percentage in the general population. Asians tend to use the Internet at a higher rate while Hispanics use on-line services at a lower rate.

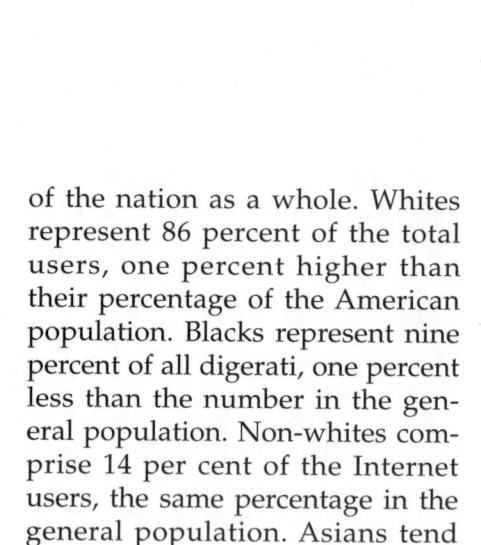

Those who use the Internet earn slightly higher incomes than the general population but those with incomes between $30,000 and $50,000 still use the Internet in higher percentages than their numbers in the general population. Those who earn under $30,000 are less likely to use the Internet. More than four out of 10 people on the Internet are female, a significant increase in the past two years.

Simply put, there are relatively few differences between those who use the Internet and the nation as a whole.

From Christopher Harper, "The Have and the Have Nots" in *Editor & Publisher*, May 16, 1997. Reprinted by permission of Christopher Harper.

"A Genuine Mass Media"

Adam Clayton Powell III, a longtime media analyst who is now vice president for technology at the Freedom Forum, sees a good deal of promise in the years ahead for Internet use and minorities. "The Internet is coming to resemble television, especially among the young, who are abandoning broadcast television in droves. And just as we do not talk about the television-rich and the television-poor, the inequalities of Internet access are rapidly becoming moot as it has evolved into a genuine mass medium," he said. Just after the turn of the century, Powell believes that Internet users will be a microcosm of the U.S. population as a whole.

Age, more than income, could actually divide the nation in the digital age. Jupiter Communications, a New York research company, projected that the number of children who go on line will jump from more than four million to more than seven million this year, increasing exponentially through the year 2002.

Older Americans

On the other hand, significant numbers of older Americans may become the "have-nots" because they have little desire to use computers or feel intimidated by their complexity. While a Merrill Lynch study found recently that one in 10 senior citizens have used the Internet, many older Americans remain infrequent participants in the on-line world.

Despite the fact that a large number of Web sites are aimed at older Americans, only five per cent of those between the ages of 55 and 64 use an on-line service, and less than three per cent of those over 65 have access to the Internet.

Simplicity is the key, observed Edwin Diamond, a longtime media critic and writer joined the Internet generation in his seventies. He maintained the computer and the Internet must be easy to use for "a three-year-old and an 80-year-old." He mused that the same should be true for video-cassette recorders, which about 10 percent of the American public can program properly, microwaves and consumer video cameras. "As for me, I'm a journalist. I use whatever medium available for my messages. If I have to learn how to beam stuff directly into the audience's cortex, I'll do it."

But Diamond remains relatively rare among the senior citizen. As a result most of those over 50 depend on newspaper and television for news—a trend that already provides much older audience for most traditional media and may be exacerbated as more of those now under 50 turn toward the Internet for news and information.

Online News

What are the implications for newspapers and television news? Those who want on-line news are from 18 to 50, including a large number of college graduates. Slightly more than half of Internet users watch television news. That's down significantly in only one year. Slightly less than half of Internet users read a daily newspaper. Some may interpret those figures to mean computer users are simply ill-informed. That would be a mistake. Surveys have shown that on-line users spend as much time seeking information as those who do not own a computer. Simply put, many people are getting information from the Internet rather than local newspapers and the evening news. That is particularly true for those under 50 years old.

"The habit of picking up the daily newspaper religiously is found only among those over 50," a recent newspaper industry survey found. "Network television news is joining newspapers as a medium for older citizens. . . . TV network news may be in danger of becoming an anachronism in the next century."

What Do People Want to Know?

What do people want to know about? Here's where the dichotomy between what those under 50 and those over 50 exists.

Crime stories interested all age groups in recent surveys, and they received the highest rating among all age groups. Four out of ten people ranked crime as what most interested them. The same interest existed among those in three age groups—those 18 to 29 years old, those 30 to 49, and those over 50. All groups have roughly the same interest in sports and science, but after that the taste in news varies widely between those under 50 and those over 50. Those over 50 ranked health, local government, religion, politics and international news as important news categories far more often than those under 50.

Crime does make the front pages and often is a major story on many local television newscasts. Simply put, if it bleeds, it leads. Newspapers tend to stress political news on the front page, leaving many younger readers scurrying for other sections. But what comes next? The metropolitan section. Again, older readers find interesting stories here but many younger readers generally do not. The next section usually is sports, which does interest younger readers. The business section often comes next—a section again that interests older readers. Almost all age groups are equally interested in science and technology, but it's rare that these stories make the top of the news, or for that matter receive extensive coverage in the print and television media.

Take a look at the structure of most television news broadcasts. Government stories be they local, state, national or international—often dominate the first segment of the news. The survey clearly showed that people have limited interest in these stories. If there is interest, those over 50 tend to have greater interest than those who are younger. Newspapers and television stations should ignore at their own risk the nearly 40 million Americans aged 16 to 24. When it comes to news and information, what exactly do they want? During a typical week, many young adults read the Sunday per and at least one newspaper during the week, according to a recent American Society of Newspaper Editors study. Newspapers do remain the primary source for local news and in-depth information. Regular readers in this age group describe newspapers as easy to use. That's the good news. The bad news? Nearly half of these young adults reported they could get along just fine without reading a newspaper.

What do young adults want? Like the rest of the nation and the world, it is impossible to provide a simple answer. More and more are turning to the computer to access the Internet and the World Wide Web rather than using conventional media.

"Does everybody care about what's going on? Yeah. Actually, they do care," observed one young computer designer from New York City. "Why doesn't everybody watch the news? Because they don't care about THAT news. I see several problems with news context, relevance and sensationalism. When I watch the evening news, I am appalled at what I see—It's almost a marketing decision rather than a news decision for newspaper and television broadcasts. Do editors want an increasingly older audience or is there a desire to reach out to a younger audience either in a traditional medium or online? It somehow seems appropriate to use one of the worst clichés in the news business: Only time will tell. Unfortunately, the clock is ticking faster than what most editors would like to admit. That's just fine as far as McLean Greaves is concerned. Virtual Melanin and others like it will offer people what they need to know and what they want to know. And that seems to be what a lot of people, particularly those under 50, want these days.

Article Review Form at end of book.

Cultural diversity is part of the Web. Pamela Mendels explores cultural diversity dynamics in the following article. What are the issues facing Hispanics, Asian-Americans and African-Americans on the Web? Is the Web being used to cross bridges between cultures? What are the problems faced by minority groups underrepresented on the Web?

Minorities Seek Online Identities

Pamela Mendels

We all know the stereotypical Internet user: A he. A teen-ager. A white person.

Well, the gals are swiftly catching up to the guys in Web savvy, if you believe the people who keep track of those things. Meanwhile, even mold-covered fortysomethings are beginning to be able to distinguish a URL from an e-mail address.

And according to a panel of experts at a forum in New York City last week, America's non-white ethnic groups are also eagerly turning to the World Wide Web.

McLean B. Greaves, chief executive and executive producer at Virtual Melanin Inc., a Brooklyn-based new media company aimed at what he describes as "the Generation-Xfro crowd," said that his Cafe Los Negroes site has attracted a loyal following in the year and a half it has existed.

Meanwhile, another panelist, Luis R. Cancel, president of a Manhattan-based Esperanto Internet Services LLC, said his 3-month-old InfoLatino site, providing bilingual information on Hispanic nonprofit and trade associations, is drawing about 1,000 visitors a week—and it hasn't officially been launched yet.

For Jeffrey C. Yang, publisher and founding editor of A. Magazine, these are welcome developments. Yang's company provides much of the content found on Channel A, a site about Asian news and culture. The Internet, he says, is a great tool to help ethnic communities delve into questions of their own identity while forging bonds with the rest of the world. Channel A, he noted, is targeted not just at Asians but at what he describes as Asia watchers.

> "The challenge for entities like ourselves—the Asian sites, the Latino sites—is to find a means to make sure those who don't have access to this language are not left behind."
> **Jeffrey C. Yang, Publisher of A. Magazine**

"It's an attempt to create a bridge, effectively, between East and West," Yang said.

Yang and company were addressing a crowd of New York Web industry types—lots of goatees and T-shirts and short skirts—at a meeting of the World Wide Web Artists Consortium.

The Web may be young, the panel's moderator suggested, but the emergence of ethnic voices on it is younger still.

Omar T. Wasow, whose business card describes him as "el presidente" of New York Online, a Brooklyn-based Web design company that began life as an online service aimed at a racially diverse audience, described the reaction of the naysayers when he launched his company in 1993.

"They said: 'Who's going to hang out there? You and the three other black nerds in America?'" he recalled.

Such misconceptions were not confined to one ethnic group. Yang said that despite the image of Asian-Americans as a techno-proficient "model minority," many Asians living in the United States are locked out of the Internet. The reason? The predominance of English online.

Significant numbers of Asian immigrants, he said, lack sufficient grasp of English to use the Internet. It's a problem affecting the Spanish-speaking community, too, Cancel said.

"The challenge for entities like ourselves—the Asian sites, the Latino sites—is to find a means to make sure those who don't have access to this language are not left behind." Yang said in a follow-up telephone interview. "It's not an easy thing."

From Pamela Mendels, "Minorities Seek Online Identities" in *The New York Times*, June 16, 1997. © 1997 The New York Times Electronic Media Company. Reprinted by permission.

Wacow challenged the panel to justify the need for ethnic sites at all. Wasn't the beauty of the Internet its very ability to allow communication without revealing a person's age or race or other characteristics, he asked? He provoked a laugh from the audience when he recalled a cartoon in which a pooch declares, "On the Internet, nobody knows you're a dog."

But Cancel argued that another treasured feature of the Internet is its ability to build what he termed "communities of common interest."

> "I think people like to know that they can go to a place and find people like them."
> **McLean B. Greaves,**
> **Chief executive and executive producer at Virtual Melanin**

Greaves agreed. "I think people like to know that they can go to a place and find people like them," he said after the forum ended. "Our site is definitely not a 'Cosby' crowd. We appeal to black and Latino Generation Xers."

In Asian newsgroups, Yang said later, Asian-Americans feel free to discuss pressing topics that matter to them, everything from the pros and cons of interracial dating to the question of whether the term "Asian-American" is appropriate for people who come from a huge continent with a myriad of cultures.

"On the Internet," he said, "you can be a woman, a man; gay or straight; black, white or other and no one knows, because no one sees your face. The question is: What does identity mean online?"

Article Review Form at end of book.

Creating news online costs a newspaper more money. Newspaper industry analysts predict that not all publications in existence today will be here tomorrow. David Shaw examines these issues in the following article, with a look at the losses incurred by several major online providers. How have some online publications handled the cash-flow problem? Will free access continue to be the norm, or the exception? With advertising expected to increase, what techniques are being explored to capture customers' attention? How will security issues be handled?

Internet Gold Rush Hasn't Panned Out Yet for Most

David Shaw
Times Staff Writer
David Shaw's e-mail address is david,shaw@latimes.com
Jacci Cenacveira and Rebecca Andrade of The Times editorial library assisted with the research for this series.

Amid unrealistic expectations, many ventures have failed. A shakeout period is expected soon for online media.

Even as Internet use continues its dramatic surge, many if not most Internet ventures are losing money, and many others—including some run by the titans of the industry—are shutting down, consolidating or cutting back.

The standing joke on the Web is that the letters "ISP" don't really stand for "Internet service provider" but for "I'm still profitless."

Already this year:

- Microsoft closed half the Web sites it created last year, fired several hundred part-time employees, announced the termination of 10 programs on its Microsoft Network and was reported to be considering getting out of the Internet service provider business altogether.

- CompuServe, an online pioneer, announced financial losses, the resignation of its chief executive officer and a shift from the mass consumer market to business and professional users.

- Time Warner was said to be losing as much as $10 million a year on Pathfinder.com, the Internet site that features Time, People, Money and other Time Inc. magazines. (Dan Logan, chief executive officer of Time Inc., has described Pathfinder as giving a "new definition to the term 'black hole.'")

- Politics Now, a popular World Wide Web site run by ABC News, the Washington Post and the National Journal, closed down. So did such Internet magazines as Out and Spiv and an online Web directory called Netguide Live. American Cybercast, producer of "The Spot," widely hailed as a prototype for Internet entertainment, filed for bankruptcy (although "The Spot" itself remains up and running).

Industry analysts believe these problems are a forerunner of the massive shakeout coming the rest of this year as companies are forced to come to terms with what Bill Bass, senior analyst in media and technology strategies for Forrester Research in Cambridge, Mass., calls the "amazingly unrealistic expectations" engendered by the potential of the Internet.

Many saw the Internet as the cyberspace equivalent of the California gold rush, and having invested hundreds of millions of dollars, they have been stunned to see the glitter of early growth turn into fool's gold. Although a number of online newspapers and other services insist that they will be profitable by next year, Bass says that in many cases, "that's because they made

From David Shaw, "Internet Gold Rush Hasn't Panned Out Yet for Most" in *Los Angeles Times,* June 19, 1997. Copyright © 1997 Los Angeles Times.

three-year plans in '95, and if they didn't show that revenue would equal expenses [by the end of three years], they wouldn't have gotten funded in the first place."

Some sites could be profitable already, though, if they weren't reinvesting their revenue in their ongoing operations.

"The question 'Are you profitable?' is exactly the wrong question," says Dick Glover, vice president of ESPN, whose Web site is one of the most popular on the Net. "The real question is, 'Should you be profitable now?' and the answer is no. You should be reinvesting . . . building a business for the future."

There are exceptions, of course—most of them commercial transaction sites rather than news and information sites—but by and large, as Neil Budde, editor of the online edition of the Wall Street Journal, says, with just a hint of hyperbole: "The only people making money on the Internet right now are the ones hosting conferences on how to make money on the Internet."

Proud Tradition of Free Access

For now, most sites on the Web are free to the individual user. Sex sites on the Web do charge for access, as do a relatively few other sites (the Wall Street Journal among them); some other sites (ESPN and Pathfinder among them) permit free access to the basic site but charge for what they call "premium" or "personalized" services. Many more sites say they ultimately expect to charge at least a nominal fee for some services.

But several online publications that said they would begin charging—like Slate, the online magazine published by software giant Microsoft—have abandoned those plans, at least for now.

"To be honest, we chickened out," Michael Kinsley, the editor of Slate, wrote in an online announcement in January.

A few weeks later, in an interview, he said he still believed that charging for access to Slate was "the most realistic way for it to become self-supporting," but he said he had decided "it would be better to establish a brand name with wide readership first, and you would short-circuit that process if you started charging too soon."

Nathan Myhrvold, group vice president and chief technology guru at Microsoft, pointed out in Slate itself four months earlier that Internet users would not pay for access to one site when "a million free sites are just a click away. . . . There's no incentive until people are too addicted to the Net to turn off their computers, yet are bored with what's available.

"In the very long run," Myhrvold wrote, "addiction and boredom seem as inevitable as death and taxes, and user fees will then be viable, at least in some cases"—much as some people who are "addicted" to TV but bored with its regular programming now pay extra for HBO and other premium channels.

But the basic culture of the Web is free access, and there will probably always be many free sites. At present, even those who charge for access keep the cost low. That means most of the revenue to support the Internet must come from advertising and commercial transactions.

In the earliest days of the Web, it was widely assumed that the free spirits who used it would not tolerate the intrusion of advertising. But most Web sites have ads now—America Online even sells ads on about a third of its chat rooms, a heretofore sacrosanct precinct—and users often have to click their way past two or three ads, rejecting various commercial come-ons just to get to the site they want.

In time, commercialism on the Net will grow. Black Sun Interactive of San Francisco has developed what it calls ad "robots," avatars that, in effect, will be able to eavesdrop on chat rooms, and when they "hear" a phrase that matches one in their memory bank, they could make an advertising pitch. (If a user mentioned that he was having car problems, for example, the avatar might recommend a particular kind of car or car dealer.)

Because many online sites require users to register and provide demographic data on themselves, software is being developed that will ultimately allow Web advertisers to achieve the merchandiser's dream—targeting an audience far more precisely than it can with either newspapers or television by advertising a product only on sites that draw people likely to be interested in that product.

Moreover, they will be able to get nearly instantaneous electronic feedback on whether their ads are effective: How many people saw the ad? How many "clicked" on it and went on to a more detailed presentation? How many bought the product right then, online? Relatively crude versions of some of these technologies are available now.

Web Makes Ideal Marketing Tool

The Internet has the potential to be the best sales tool—the best advertising and direct marketing vehicle—ever devised. The Internet can turn any advertiser—any product manufacturer or service provider—into the equivalent of a direct marketer. On the Internet, consumers looking for a particular product or service can shop over the entire country—the entire world—looking at photographs and comparing prices, features and terms, and then buy what they want with a credit card and arrange to have the purchase delivered to their door.

During the last Christmas season, 14% of all retailers were online, up from 4% the previous year, according to a survey by the accounting firm of Deloitte & Touche. That's why retailers ranging from FAO Schwartz to Macy's to Eddie Bauer have created Web sites.

Meanwhile, one online shopping mall—America's Choice Mall—already has more than 1,200 "storefronts," Dell Computer Corp. has sales of more than $1 million a day, and Amazon.com has been so successful selling books online—more than $16 million worth since July 1995—that Crown Books has expanded its online site, and both Borders and Barnes & Noble recently launched their own sites.

As a story in Slate pointed out this year, Amazon.com isn't necessarily as convenient, as quick, as cheap or possessed of as encyclopedic an inventory as it claims. But it is a comprehensive, user-friendly service, and it does provide links to many reviews and comments by typical buyers, thus creating a unique, online book community.

Many other sites also take advantage of the special features of the Internet. Omaha Steaks can't let you taste a porterhouse online—not yet anyway—but CD-Now, the most popular compact disk site on the Web, does allow customers to hear 30 seconds of various songs before making a purchase. In time, people may be able to log on to a Web site, type in a credit card number and download a full CD onto a blank disk.

Online shoppers spent more than $500 million in 1996, and Forrester Research predicts that that number will increase more than tenfold, to $7 billion, by 2000.

Newspapers would like a share of that money—both advertising money and fees for serving as a middleman in various commercial transactions—to offset the losses they are likely to incur if advertisers shift dollars from the print media to the Web. USA Today has already created an Online Marketplace that links breaking news to both commercial product information and opportunities for electronic shopping.

Security Concerns Over Purchases

But for all the online shopping that's available, the Web still accounted for less than 2% of all retail sales last year—and 10% of those sales involved sex-related merchandise.

Many people do like shopping for cheap air fares and other travel-related services on the Internet, so for the moment, online shopping is more of a threat to travel agents and mail order businesses than to retailers. Many problems remain before shopping by computer replaces a visit to the department store, toy store or any store for most Americans.

Some shoppers enjoy the personal contact with sales personnel and the serendipity of walking into a store looking for one item and then finding something altogether different that proves suddenly irresistible.

Of far greater importance, many people remain uneasy about sending their credit card numbers into cyberspace, despite the insistence of various online entrepreneurs that online credit card transactions are at least as safe as faxing a credit card number or leaving a receipt with a credit card number on a restaurant table. To counter this uneasiness, most online merchants offer customers the option of not providing credit card information by computer but of listing a telephone number at which they can later be called.

InfoDial, a Malibu company that develops software for online merchants, announced in April that it had developed the online equivalent of "checks"—software that makes it possible for shoppers to pay for goods purchased online by giving merchants, in encrypted form, all the information that appears on a check.

But as with credit cards and various Internet tracking devices, this raises further concerns about security and privacy. A survey this year showed that one-third of Internet users say they give false demographic information on the Web because they are concerned about how such personal information will be used.

A Better Hybrid: Trends from Changing Technologies

Web-savvy snoopers can go online and find such once-private information as driver's license registrations, probate records, Social Security numbers, previous telephone numbers and addresses, individual financial information and encounters with the law. The Social Security Administration suspended access to one of its online programs amid concerns that the privacy of individual wage, tax and benefit information was at risk.

Yet another hurdle for online merchants: Women account for 70% of all retail sales in the United States, but so far, men outnumber them in the online world. Although a Business Week/Harris Poll in May said the percentage of women on the Net has jumped from 21% a year and a half ago to 41% today, women tend to spend less time online then men do. The WorldWide Internet/Online Tracking Service of IntelliQuest in Austin, Texas, said this year that among heavy users, men still outnumber women by a 3–1 margin.

The Question of Regulation

Prospective advertisers—and the Web sites who need their support—face many other problems as well.

One involves government regulation. Last year, Congress passed the Communications Decency Act, a bill that outlawed "indecent" material on the Net and was designed in large part to protect children from such material. Last week, the Federal Trade Commission conducted a public workshop that included complaints by children's advocacy groups that many online marketers take advantage of kids' susceptibility by using interactive games, contests, quizzes and video clips to ignite their interest in various products. Online marketers use some of these same devices to do market research on kids without their parents' approval.

The Communications Decency Act is now before the United States Supreme Court, and with an estimated 4 million children under 18 using the Internet regularly, a similar legal battle may be necessary to deal with advertising material on the Web.

But online advertisers have enough issues to worry about even without the threat of government regulation.

No one has ever been sure just how effective any particular advertising is, which is why John Wannamaker, the department store magnate, once said, "Half the money I spend on advertising is wasted, and the trouble is, I don't know which half."

On the Internet, Wannamaker would be even more uncertain.

Advertisers base their spending on the size of the audience they are likely to reach, and while five separate companies—including Nielsen I/PRO, a subsidiary of the company that provides ratings for television shows—now measure the Web audience, none has yet attained the industrywide credibility that Nielsen's parent company has in television or that the Audit Bureau of Circulation has in the newspaper industry.

"Advertisers will not be totally comfortable advertising on the Web until confidence builds that Web advertising measurement is accurate and auditable by a reliable third party in a 'Nielsen-like' way," says Mary Meeker, managing director of the Morgan Stanley investment banking firm, in a 142-page report on Internet advertising.

In the beginning, Web sites measured their audience in terms of "hits," but everything downloaded by an individual user counted as a separate "hit," so amid the hyperbolic millions of daily hits reported by many sites, there was no way of knowing how many individual people were visiting any site. Many sites now measure in terms of "page views"—the number of pages that are downloaded. But that figure, too, is meaningless because one user might download just one page while another downloads 20.

The best audience measure would be what is known as "unique users"—i.e., individual users. But the only way to get that number is to require everyone to register, and most sites don't do that. Even those that do require registration can't be terribly precise because, for example, everyone who comes to a site via AOL is counted as being the same, single "unique user."

Most estimates of "unique users" are little more than educated guesses, based on widely varying methods—some of them seemingly about as scientific as throwing a fistful of pennies into the air and trying to count them as they come down. Bernard Gwertzman, editor of the New York Times on the Web, says his site receives 80,000 unique users "on a good day." But Boots Rykiel, editor of the online edition of USA Today, says his site receives almost 500,000 unique users a day.

Is that possible? USA Today has 50% more circulation for its print edition than does the New York Times; could it actually receive 500% more online visitors? Rykiel refers the question to Allegra Young, who is in charge of such matters for USA Today.

Yes, she says. In fact, she pegs the exact number of unique users each day, on average, at 447,222.

She may well be right. But how did she arrive at that number?

"We have 264,000 distinct hosts—like Harvard University or America Online—that people come to our site from. We multiple that figure by 1.7."

Why 1.7?

"We figure that there is probably more than one person and, on average, not more than two for every distinct host."

How does she know that? Aren't there likely to be tens, hundreds, thousands of users from some sites? How does she know the average is between 1 and 2 . . . and why decide on 1.7 rather than 1.5 or 1.3 or 1.8?

Young has no explanation.

Many other sites don't even try to arrive at these numbers. Nor can advertisers agree among themselves how the audience should be measured and how advertising rates should be calculated. Should it all be based on the number of people who see the Web page with their ad on it? Or on the number of times people "click through," moving from that first small ad to a more detailed sales presentation on another linked site? Or, given all the hoopla about the Web as a boon to direct marketing, should ad rates be based on actual sales? Or on some combination of these?

When Forrester Research polled more than 50 advertisers on these questions recently, they were so divided that not one of these four mechanisms was supported by more than a third of the respondents.

While some advertisers insist on paying only on a click-through basis, many people who run online are resistant.

"It makes me responsible for something I have no control over," says Bob Ingle, president of new media for Knight Ridder Newspapers. "I can get people to see your ad, but if you did a poor job" [designing it, and no one clicks through], why should I lose money?"

Indeed, click-through rates generally hover in the single digits—3% or 4% or so—and many in the Internet community say that's because most Web ads are just not very creative or imaginative. Although some advertisers use animation and interactivity, most ads are static "banners"—generally small, horizontal, rectangular graphics at the top of a Web page.

"I don't know what ads on the Net will look like in the future," says Nick Donatiello, president of the Odyssey research firm in San Francisco. "But I know what it's not going to be. It's not going to be . . . banner ads—which are just billboards on the Web. Someone is going to come along and say, 'This is not like anything we've had before,' and he'll define advertising in a new way for a new medium."

One of the problems with banner ads is that if a user does what the advertiser wants him to do and clicks on the ad to go to fuller presentation of the advertising message, he leaves the original site—which creates a Catch-22 situation for news organizations and other creators of online content: They want effective advertising so they can make money, but they don't want advertising so effective that it lures users away from the non-advertising information they're providing. Unlike printed newspapers (in which most ads are right next to the stories) or television (in which commercial breaks lead right back into programming), Internet ads are only successful if they pull the user-cum-customer away from the site.

Net Traffic Lags Far Behind Papers, TV

Most important of all—both in terms of shopping and advertising—no Web site has yet attracted the huge volume of traffic that warrants the massive advertising expenditures made in traditional media.

The Los Angeles Times Web site, for example, estimates that it has 50,000 "unique users" on an average day. But the printed edition of The Times sells a million copies every weekday, and most studies suggest that each copy is seen by at least two other people—a total audience of about 3 million.

The gap is even greater—astronomically so—between online sites and television.

ESPN's SportsZone is the most popular destination site on the Web—i.e., it has more users than does any other Web site except the browsers and search engines. That translates to 480,000 "unique users" a day—one-sixth the size of the audience of the largest daily newspapers in the country and one-sixtieth of the most popular television programs in the country. Even the 15th-rated cable TV show in a typical week draws more than six times

A Better Hybrid: Trends from Changing Technologies   53

as many viewers as does the ESPN Web site.

A Nielsen I/PRO independent audit last fall said that Netscape, the leading Web browser and, as a result, the single most frequently visited site on the entire Web, was receiving more than 2.9 million visitors a day. Netscape now claims 4.5 million to 6 million visitors a day. Even assuming that the latter figure is correct, that's still fewer people than watch about 90 of the 114 prime-time network television shows.

No wonder each of the three major television networks received several billion dollars in advertising last year, while Netscape—which earned more advertising revenue than any other online company—received only $27 million.

Apart from Netscape, the Internet search engines are the most heavily trafficked sites, so it's no surprise that they received about 40% of the total online ad revenue last year, almost quadruple what the news or general interest sites received.

Much advertising on the Internet today consists of a small group of companies taking money from their left-hand pockets and putting it in their (or each others') right-hand pockets. The companies spending the most money on Internet advertising are, almost without exception, companies that have a major stake, directly or indirectly, in the Internet—Microsoft, AT&T, IBM, Netscape and four Internet search engines, Excite, InfoSeek, Lycos and Yahoo! The biggest recipients of online ad revenue also tend to include Netscape and the search engines.

On television, the networks also spend a lot of money to advertise and promote themselves and their programs—$500 million per network this season, according to the Wall Street Journal—but they at least are not alone. Both Procter & Gamble and General Motors are expected to spend about the same amount—or more—in network advertising in 1997, and half a dozen other companies also spent more than $300 million apiece in network advertising last year; that sum represents more than all advertisers combined spent on all the sites on the World Wide Web.

Online advertising increased more than fivefold last year, from $55 million to $300 million, but that's still less than one-fifth of 1% of the $173 billion spent on advertising in all media in 1996. Even cable television—the smallest of the existing media—outdistanced the Internet by a 20–1 margin, with $6 billion in advertising revenue.

The Internet is still in its infancy, though, and its potential is enormous. As technology continues to improve and its audience continues to grow—as users and advertisers alike become more comfortable with it and knowledgeable about it—the Internet could ultimately attract the kind of audience and generate the kind of advertising revenue that would enable it to revolutionize human communication even more dramatically than Johann Gutenberg's first printing press did more than 500 years ago.

Web Sites

These are the names and Internet addresses for the primary Web sites mentioned in today's stories:
Alta Vista
http://www.altavista.com
Amazon Books
http://www.amazon.com
America Online
http://www.aol.com
America's Choice Mall
http://www.choicemall.com
Barnes & Noble
http://www.barnesandnoble.com
Borders Books and Records
http://www.borders.com
CD Now
http://www.cdnow.com
C/Net: The Computer Network
http://www.cnet.com
CompuServe
http://www.compuserve.com
Crown Books
http://www.crownbooks.com
CyberWireDispatch
http://www.cyberwerks.com/cyberwire
Dell Computers
http://www.dell.com
Electronic Newsstand
http://www.electronicnewsstand.com
ESPN SportsZone
http://www.sportszone.com
Excite
http://www.excite.com
Forrester Research Inc.
http://www.forrester.com
Herring Communications
http://www.redherring.com
InfoSeek
http://www.infoseek.com
Knight Ridder Inc.
http://www.knightridder.com
Los Angeles Times
http://www.latimes.com
Lycos
http://www.lycos.com

MSNBC
http://www.msnbc.com
Netscape.
http://www.netscape.com
New York Times on the Web
http://www.nytimes.com
Nielsen I/Pro
http://www.ipro.com
Pathfinder (Time Inc.)
http://www.pathfinder.com

San Jose Mercury News
http://www.mercurycenter.com
Slate magazine
http://www.slate.com
The Spot
http://www.thespot.com
USA Today
http://www.usatoday.com
Wall Street Journal Interactive Edition
http://www.wsj.com
Washington Post
http://www.washingtonpost.com
Wired magazine
http://www.hotwired.com
Yahoo!
http://www.yahoo.com

Article Review Form at end of book.

WiseGuide Wrap-Up

Forecasting trends is always a tricky business. We all know how often the weather forecast is wrong. But there are some trends in online journalism that can be used to make predictions.

We've seen from the readings in this section that demand for online access to news and information can be expected to increase. We've also read about strong trends toward more customization of news. And, while reader demographics could change dramatically, the myth that white males dominate the Web has been shattered. We know also that news stories will contain accessories not found in their print counterpart and that, like print, online publishing will be supported to some degree by advertising.

What is not clear is what economic model will sustain online publishing. Most online publications are still figuring out how to turn a profit in a marketplace not limited by time or space. Economic pressures will contribute to shifts and turns as the field develops.

Despite the economic uncertainty, most experts believe the future of online journalism is promising. Increasing readership and significant savings in production costs are two certainties. While the economic model develops, smart online publishers are integrating basic journalism skills with new ways of publishing. Competencies in writing, researching, interviewing, reporting and analysis are being integrated with skills in advanced media technologies and a keen awareness of new consumer needs.

What form the online future will take is unclear. But, by honing a portfolio of technical, analytical and creative abilities, journalists will be prepared to take on the task of online journalism in the new media age.

R.E.A.L. Sites

The adjacent list provides a print preview of typical CourseWise R.E.A.L. Sites. (There are over 100 such sites at the CourseLink™ Site.) The danger in printing URLs is that Web sites can change overnight. As we went to press, these sites were functional using the URL provided. If you come across one that isn't, please let us know via email at webmaster@coursewise.com. Use your Passport to access the most current list of R.E.A.L. sites at the CourseLinks™ Site.

Site name: Net Gain by J. D. Lasica
URL: http://www.newslink.org/ajrjdguide.html
Why is it R.E.A.L.? A look into online journalism. More interesting than a textbook. The series is filled with quotes and anecdotes. It is broken down into short chapters and written with a light touch. The future of online journalism looks good. The series offers a window into the field.
Key topics: careers, current issues, desktop journalism, future trends, economic models, history, journalism administration, mass communication, Net usage, skills, online journalism, online newspapers, webcasting

Site name: The Media in Cyberspace III by Steven S. Ross and Don Middleberg
URL: http://www.mediasource.com/study/cont.htm
Why is it R.E.A.L.? Here is the data needed to support the field. Written in short sections with lots of charts and diagrams. Online usage, viewpoints and trends about online journalism are profiled in a scientific format.
Key topics: careers, computer-assisted reporting, current issues, economic models, history, research, online journalism, future trends, mass communication, Net usage, reporting, webcasting

Site name: Driving a newspaper on the data highway by Melinda McAdams
URL: http://www. well.com/user/mmcadams/online.newspapers.html
Why is it R.E.A.L.? A classic article on creating an online newspaper from the woman who did it at The Washington Post. McAdams traces the issues and answers that led the Post to create a separate paper located far from the traditional newsroom.

Key topics: advertising, careers, current issues, desktop journalism, economic models, future trends, history, marketing, mass communication, online journalism, online newspapers, skills, webcasting

Site name: A seat at the table: the role of journalism in the digital era from the Radio and Television News Directors Foundation
URL: http://www.rtndf.org/rtndf/new/foreword.htm
Why is it R.E.A.L.? This article is of interest to broadcast journalists and those considering online careers. It tracks how television is responding to new media and offers suggestions for the future direction of the industry.
Key topics: access, advertising, broadcast, careers, current issues, desktop journalism, economic models, future trends, history, legal issues, marketing, mass communication, regulation, skills

section 2

On the E-Beat: Moving to the Center of the Newsroom

Key Points

- Become familiar with computer-assisted reporting and how it is being used in today's newsroom.
- Understand what online skills are in demand and how these skills are being integrated with the traditional "street-beat" skills.
- Develop a sense of how these combined skills will need to evolve with the changing technologies.

"[Computer-assisted reporting has now moved] from the computer nerd in the corner to the center of the newsroom."
—Rose Ciotta

WiseGuide Intro

The Internet is already the fastest growing medium in history. It took 38 years for radio to reach 50 million homes and 13 years for television to reach that mark. Some experts predict the Internet will reach 50 million in five years. This number has not been lost on traditional publishers. A survey conducted by Newslink.Org in July 1997 reported that there are 3,622 newspapers publishing online. To effectively produce these, and other kinds of related online publications, a whole new way of working the beat is required.

In this section, we'll explore different perspectives on working the beat in the emerging field of online journalism. The term "online journalism" is used to cover a wide array of activities and processes. These include harnessing the Internet for research and investigation, using e-mail for interviewing and soliciting comments and creating databases for the analysis of stories and, of course, the development and distribution of online content, which includes text and multimedia.

As we'll see in this section's readings, new technologies are changing the beat in many ways. One change is within the job market. Online journalistic skills are highly sought after by employers. Publishers are seeking computer-literate journalists, because their strong analytical skills are adaptable to developing new media technologies. A recent Freedom Forum report found that 86 percent of new journalists say it is "very important" for journalism students to know how to harness computers for research and writing.

Another change comes from computer-assisted research. Reporters can now access a rich array of news resources that previously were out of reach due to time or access constraints. Reporters can now zero in on highly specific information and sort through tons of records within seconds—leaving more time for developing, verifying and rewriting the story.

Yet another change is in the reader's expectations. The e-beat is not the exclusive purview of the journalist. As readers increasingly go online to find firsthand information, they will expect more from the media. If the public can locate supplemental information on a Web page, consumers will have a hard time accepting news stories that lack additional information, analysis and appropriate depth. The skills that separate a professional journalist from a consumer surfing online are many. Placing information within a context, filtering the real from the unsubstantiated and turning chunks of data into stories are ways the professional journalist adds value.

And so, while the use of computers for reporting and delivering the news represents a significant change in journalism, traditional journalistic skills that make a reporter effective on the street beat will play a large role on the e-beat. These skills include interviewing, researching, organizing material and writing the story. In this section we'll see that being effective on the e-beat requires an integration of specific online skills with the traditional street-beat skills.

Questions

1. How would you define online journalism? How does it differ from its print and broadcast counterparts?

2. In what ways is online journalism changing the role of the reporter? What specific online skills are needed to be effective on the e-beat? How should these skills be integrated into the traditional street-beat skills of interviewing, researching, writing the story and so on?

3. What skills do you currently possess that will make you effective on the e-beat? What skills do you need to develop? What types of jobs in online journalism appeal to you?

Katherine Fulton offers a reassuring look at new media technologies for students just beginning to explore the field. By taking a long look at the field, she also opens the door to additional exploration, raises questions for further discussion and takes note of trends. Along the way, she raises these interesting questions: Will the newspaper of the future be a handheld electronic tablet? Will interactive media communications be as common as the telephone? And who will use electronic media in the future?

Future Tense

The anxious journey of a technophobe

Katherine Fulton

Katherine Fulton helped found The Independent, *an alternative weekly based in North Carolina's Raleigh-Durham-Chapel Hill area. She worked as its editor for nearly a decade before leaving last year for a Nieman fellowship at Harvard. She now teaches a course on media technology at Duke University.*

"Once a new technology rolls over you, if you're not part of the steamroller, you're part of the road."— Stewart Brand, author of The Media Lab: Inventing the Future at MIT

I can't pinpoint the moment my attitude about technology changed, because there wasn't a single one. I never wore the label technophobe as a badge of pride, the way some writers do. I just felt mystified by machines, and sheepish about my ignorance.

I think it was the passion of the people creating the electronic future that eventually seduced me into learning more. A few years ago I had gone to a workshop on group dynamics and organizational change; it had been filled with corporate technology types from places like Microsoft. I learned a lot and found myself telling one of the organizers, a computer scientist who had worked in the space program, that I wished he would give the workshop for people in nonprofits, "people who are trying to change the world." He looked at me with a puzzled expression on his face and said, "But, Katherine, that's exactly what these computer people are doing."

You don't forget a moment like that, when you feel the sting of a blind spot revealed. But I was too busy to do anything about it. Not to mention depressed. My feelings about technology and the future of newspaper journalism in those days ranged from denial to gloom and doom. And that had been on a good day. Finally last year, after fourteen years as a reporter and editor, I left my job, and was considering leaving journalism. But first I wanted to step back and take a long look around.

As I began a fellowship year at Harvard, it came suddenly to me that it was time to stop being so stupid about machines. Naturally, I found my way down the river to MIT, to the gleaming I.M. Pei-designed Media Lab. I wandered through its corridors as though in a foreign land, forcing myself to remember the reporter's most basic lesson: there's no such thing as a dumb question. But it didn't really help. I still felt dumb and lost in a place that seemed to represent everything I found impenetrable about computers.

Some months later, I went to hear one of the Media Lab's scientists, Walter Bender, who's working on electronic newspapers. I hoped he'd be able to translate for me, but I only understood about half of what he said. He'd brush off a question or a challenge with a simple dismissal. "That's a no-brainer," he'd say, usually just at the moment my

It came to me suddenly that it was time to stop being stupid about machines.

Reprinted from *Columbia Journalism Review,* November/December 1993. Copyright © 1993 by Columbia Journalism Review.

60 Perspectives: Online Journalism

brain was most taxed. Still, he captured my imagination.

To Bender, the key new technology is electronic mail, because it is interactive. The word "interactive" hadn't become a buzzword yet, and it took me a while to grasp what he was talking about—that the one-to-one, two-way personal communication of the telephone will merge with the one-to-many, one-way mass communication of the newspaper or the television network. Bender wants news knit into the fabric of people's lives. The newspaper he envisions is a computerized assistant that can, for example, read your calendar, then provide you with articles and ads about the place you're going this weekend. And much, much more.

It's a disturbing vision, because it conjures up a nation of people so "personalized" that we don't even have today's headlines in common. I pushed myself beyond an easy, high-minded dismissal to take a closer look.

Bender throws off little phrases that have years of thought behind them. He says, for instance, that he wants the television to have "content knobs, not channel knobs." Again, it took me a while to understand what this means. Think of it like this: reading today's newspaper or watching today's news broadcast is like riding a passenger train. The news of the future will be like driving a car. It will be a service designed to appeal to the tastes and judgments of the user.

What if you could control the content, Bender asks, by talking back to a documentary film that engages you? Suppose, having watched for an hour, you could instruct the great computer in the sky to scan the ninety-nine hours of interviews that didn't make it into the film, and show the profile subject answering the questions the documentary left unanswered for you?

That's exactly what you'll be able to do in the world to come, Bender says.

I still had some doubts. But I was engaged, excited even, by aspects of this vision.

I found myself thinking back to the gulf war, to the massive amounts of daily coverage that illuminated very little. I had wanted to read the most revealing and insightful stories each day, and I couldn't have cared less what newspaper or country they came from. I had wanted a major U.S. newspaper to do the unthinkable: to provide me with an edited news summary from all sorts of sources, not just its own. I had wanted the kind of service Bender described, not a traditional news product.

A New Medium

My encounters with Bender, as it turned out, were the first tentative steps on what slowly became a lively intellectual and emotional journey. I had caught a glimpse of what might be ahead. But I was still searching for other views of the horizon.

I found one in the Miami airport, of all places, when I spotted a *Rolling Stone* article by media writer Jon Katz touting computer bulletin boards as "the purest journalistic medium since smoke signals."

I knew a little about bulletin boards, though I hadn't signed on to one yet. Here was just what I needed—a guide who didn't make me feel stupid, who was instead inviting me to take a look at a media world "up for grabs."

Modems, telephones, and computers have created a new two-way communications medium already used by millions of people worldwide, Katz explained. The many talk to the many, rather than the few to the many, and everybody talks back, creating more accountability for anyone who provides information.

It's a radically democratic vision—one I now wanted to explore, because it explained a lot about the motivation of the computer industry's visionaries, the ones driven to change the world.

I imagined that, ideally, the video equivalent of the existing bulletin boards would be neighborhood C-Spans, controlled by the block council, announcing the arrival of new neighbors, providing political alerts, organizing day care co-ops, generating conversation. Everybody would be a reporter, and episodes like the chance filming of the Rodney King beating would become commonplace. Facts and opinions would flow without intervention, and most definitely, without the blessing of journalistic gatekeepers, who in this new world must surrender control and share power, "things that journalists are trained not to do."

So when do people need a "journalistic filter" and when does it get in the way? I was just starting to chew on such questions when another view of the new landscape opened up. My friend and fellow journalist Francis Pisani had organized an outing to the MIT laboratory that develops technological tools to teach the humanities. Francis was way ahead of me in exploring the new technology; he'd been taking a course on how writing can evolve once the writer sees that the computer is much more than a fancy typewriter.

Come down to MIT, Francis said. If you want a look at the media future, you should have a look at education, because the applications, as they call them, are more advanced than they are in journalism. So I went, and soon found myself sitting in a darkened classroom as an English professor began demonstrating his interactive, multimedia program.

The text of *Hamlet* flashes on the screen. Run across a word or an allusion you don't understand? *Point. Click.* The definition is before you. Want to know more? *Point. Click.* And off you go for a journey into Elizabethan England. You like that scene, and want to see it performed? *Point, click, choose Zeffirelli's* Hamlet, *or Olivier's* Hamlet. Presto. You're watching the scene you just read.

Honestly, I think my mouth fell open. This was serious, fun, and something quite new. I was experiencing the user-controlled future for the first time. But I was also glimpsing another new medium—the multimedia future that destroys the old boundaries between print and video.

I had read about multimedia, of course, but I had to encounter it before I could fully grasp its significance. In the developing digital world, the messages, distilled to a common mathematical language, can include words, pictures, sound—any medium, because they'll all be the same medium. We won't be just print journalists, or radio journalists, or television journalists. We may all be digital, multimedia journalists. And things will be possible that no one has yet imagined.

I could see the potential for the new medium to become an alloy that merged the best of print with the best of television. I could see how viewing television could be more active, and how reading could be more sensuous. I could see the fascinating challenge involved in combining the talents of writers, photographers, filmmakers, information designers, graphic artists, animators, and computer specialists. And I could see that this new medium, like television before it, could begin to have an impact before it was in widespread use.

The excitement of this vision, together with its frightening underside, was driven home to me a little later when I was gaping my way through a beautiful book called *Understanding Hypermedia*. I got to the chapter called Applications, which comes as close as a book can come to illustrating how the technology can be used in schools, corporations, stores, museums, in entertainment and infotainment.

I flipped to the book's index. The word "journalism" was not to be found.

"The Next Wave"

Journalism . . . I remembered that. Has something to do with trained reporters, determined to find facts someone doesn't want them to have. Has a lot to do with hard work and good judgment. Doesn't have much to do with graphic interfaces, high-definition television, or my sexy new PowerBook.

What if you could control the content by talking back to a documentary? asks Walter Bender of MIT's Media Lab.

What *would* happen to journalism, and to journalists who refuse to become infotainers? Just about the time I was starting to wonder, I listened to a tape of Roger Fidler speaking to the American Society of Newspaper Editors last spring. Fidler is directing the new Knight-Ridder Information Design Lab in Boulder, Colorado, and has just finished a book called *Mediamorphosis*.

For the time being, Fidler said, that future is not an either/or proposition—either paper or electronic delivery. The electronic world will develop in parallel for some time to come. Look for the process to quicken beginning in 1995, as the hardware becomes available. Like television, it will be an "elite medium" at first. Then the prices will drop.

You have to get the current complex electronic world out of your mind, he said, and imagine the computer as an affordable, portable, notebook-sized consumer appliance, as easy to use as a toaster. Other industries, such as entertainment, will drive the development of this technology, and journalism will just ride along.

When you load this computer of the future with Fidler's newspaper of the future, you'll see something like today's front page, only it will actually be a three-dimensional map for exploring layers of information. Liberated from the space constraints of paper, the newspaper in tablet form will offer the reader features not now available, and provide various levels of detail and depth about every story. No longer will a key background sidebar run only once; it can run every day. All you'll have to do is touch the story, or ask out loud, and the tablet will deliver a few paragraphs, or a few thousand words, complete with maps and comments from the writer.

This ability to navigate in the electronic world—for each writer to break a narrative down into connected pieces, and each reader to devise a different path through the pieces—is called hypertext: It's what my friend Francis Pisani had been studying at MIT, and it truly is a major development in the his-

A Journalist's Guide to Survival in The Digital Age

What to do with the feeling that it's all too overwhelming? My strategy is to plod along patiently, playing tortoise to the technological hare. It's just like building a ball of string on a big story you plan to do someday. You don't have time to focus on it, but you can work on it a few hours here and there, until before long you actually know a fair amount.

Here's a doable technological training program for tortoises and other breeds of journalistic animal.

Put your feet up

For a quick and enjoyable introductory read, complete with gorgeous graphic design and a glossary of technical terms, pick up *Understanding Hypermedia: From Multimedia to Virtual Reality.* (Phaidon Press, 1993). The authors, London designers Bob Cotton and Richard Oliver, are thrilled "to be present at the birth of a new medium," they believe "will dominate mass culture in the twenty-first century."

Demystifying Media Technology: Readings from the Freedom Forum Center, (Mayfield Publishing, 1993) is less fun but much more thorough, and it includes a glossary. Order from the publisher at 800-433-1279, and be sure to ask for the computer disk being offered with the book, so the most up-to-date articles will be included.

By all means, though, also contact the Freedom Forum Media Studies Center (212-678-6600) at Columbia University, which produces publications and seminars and has a state-of-the-art technology lab. The fall 1991 issue of *Media Studies Journal,* still in print, has a number of interesting articles on "Media at the Millenium." Roger Fidler's *Mediamorphosis, or the Transformation of Newspapers into a New Medium,* is among them.

If you want to know the immediate outlook for everything from digital audio broadcasting to videophones, turn to *Communication Technology Update: 1993–1994.* It's edited by August E. Grant and Kenton T. Wilkinson; published by Technology Futures (800-TEK-FUTR), and updated annually at the University of Texas at Austin.

For a deeper overview of the complex interplay between the forces of technology, economics, and audience psychology, dig into *The Future of the Mass Audience,* an impressive scholarly work by W. Russell Neuman (Cambridge University Press, 1991).

The best way to keep up with the rapid changes is to read *The New York Times* every day and *Wired* magazine every month. I read the *Times* because it is easy to find and because it's doing an excellent job covering the digital age—in major features, in the business section, in the computer columns, and in the Monday special media page. *Wired* is the most accessible and affordable of the new magazines on digital technology. *Newsweek* dubbed it, "a techie *Rolling Stone.*" Order it at 800-SO-WIRED with a credit card.

Get paid to learn

If you're a working reporter, write about the new technology, no matter what your beat happens to be. You'll find schools, government agencies, businesses, libraries, and museums to write about—and you'll get to see what interactive multimedia is all about. There will also be plenty of political and moral issues to explore as the fiber-optic information highway gets built.

If you haven't done so already, badger your boss to train and equip you and everyone else in your newsroom to do computer-assisted reporting.

Investigative Reporters & Editors (314-882-2042) offers training at its periodic conferences around the country, and has just received a major grant from the Freedom Forum to expand its services in technology training.

Of course, you can also teach yourself. Order "Computer-Assisted Research, A Guide to Tapping Online Information," from the Poynter Institute for Media Studies. The thirty-two-page manual will be updated in early 1994 to include information about the growing global network, the Internet. The guide, which costs $3, can be obtained by writing to Research Guide, Poynter Institute for Media Studies, 801 Third Street South, St. Petersburg, Florida 33701.

One of the online commercial services, CompuServe (800-848-8990), has a lively journalism forum that includes a little library of conversations on the future of the media. Once online, you can ask both journalists and computer junkies for help with your stories and technical problems. It isn't free, so insist that your newsroom have access.

Explore

Find the computer junkies in your area—join a users group, take a tour of the local online bulletin boards, find a new friend who will translate the technical gobbledy gook and be your guide. This stuff isn't easy. Have someplace to turn when you get discouraged.

Whatever your specialty, get your head out of it and learn what the new technology will mean to someone else. Writers need to talk more to artists and photographers, and vice versa. Print people need to understand more about video. Start seeing the big picture, not just your own lens on it.

Pick one of the new technological experiments and follow it closely. The *San Jose Mercury News* and *Time* magazine are both on America Online. Times Mirror and Cox have chosen Prodigy. Time Warner and U.S. West are planning an interactive cable television system in Orlando, Florida. Magazines like *Newsweek* are offering editions on compact disks. You won't have any trouble finding some action

Finally, if you can afford it, or can find someone to pay your way, by all means go to one of the big conferences, where lots of people gather to gape at what's new and gab about what's not. The annual Digital World conference, presented by Seybold (800-433-5200), focuses on issues and trends as well as exhibitions. The 1994 conference, to be held in late spring, will bring together people from entertainment, consumer electronics, publishing, and computing.

In short, make time to see the world through different eyes.   —K.F.

tory of writing. Reporters, it seems, will face as many new creative choices as their readers in the nonlinear world in the making.

Remember, too, Fidler said, all the things a multimedia and interactive world will offer. His newspaper will enable you to touch a photograph or ad, opening a window to a slice of video. And you can send as well as receive. Having read your paper, you can instruct your notebook computer to clip and file what you need, to send a copy of an article off to a friend or to dial up that idiotic columnist.

Some things probably *won't* change, he predicted. You'll still want edited packages of the top stories, so you won't have to search for them yourself. You may continue to turn first to the sports scores or the stock listings, just as you do now—and some days that may be all you read. The difference will be that you can also have the new personal news packages, with as much information as you might want about your most passionate interests.

And don't forget, Fidler said, that all this will come with benefits the defenders of print often overlook. Delivering news electronically will save enormous quantities of money, trees, and landfill space.

At last, the landscape ahead began to come into focus for me. Here were all the pieces of the puzzle, assembled in a coherent fashion: the newspaper as a service delivering content, not a product forever wedded to paper. Control in the hands of the user. The power of multimedia to tell a story in different ways.

Far from debasing newspapers, the electronic world, as Fidler described it, was poised to improve them immeasurably, especially for a generation that will grow up on interactive multimedia. Fidler told the newspaper editors to take heart: "I believe that we have an opportunity to catch the next wave and be the predominant medium for communications."

But then Roger Fidler, representing one of the nation's most powerful media companies, *would* say that. He's being paid to figure out how Knight-Ridder can protect its interests. What will happen to the journalists? Will reporters have to carry new point-and-shoot videocams everywhere? Will editors do nothing but create hypertext links from the ballooning online libraries? How much will a personal newspaper cost to produce, and who will be able to afford to buy it?

My questions kept coming, and keep coming nearly every day now. I remain concerned about what will be lost in the digital future. But I'm even more worried that journalists will lose this opportunity to question assumptions and be more creative—to recapture lost audiences and capture new ones for the stories the shopping channels won't sell.

It will take guts to face the uncertainties. It won't be easy to live with unk unks—the unknown unknowns I heard a Harvard professor describe as the inevitable products of any technological revolution. But we have no choice but to face them, because computers are driving a change far larger than computer-assisted reporting, or paint programs, or digital photography. The economic infrastructure of whole industries is going to change, and journalism along with it.

At this point, all I know for sure is how I've changed: the "next wave" doesn't scare me so much anymore. I'm actually looking forward to riding it.

> **I'm worried that journalists will lose this chance to question assumptions and be more creative.**

Article Review Form at end of book.

Training reporters in computer-assisted reporting techniques can sometimes be a hard sell. Some reporters have phobias about technology; others are content with the status quo. But, as Rose Ciotta, computer-assisted reporting editor at *The Buffalo News*, points out in this article, CAR is for every reporter. What impact has CAR had on print and broadcast newsrooms? What are the arguments for CAR programs? How are reporters getting training they didn't receive as undergraduates? And what makes a CAR story like a traditional news story, but better?

Baby You Should Drive This CAR

Rose Ciotta

Rose Ciotta is the Buffalo News' computer-assisted reporting editor and an IRE director.

Computer-assisted reporting (CAR) has produced excellent journalism and won fans among high-level newspaper executives and investigative reporters. But some technophobic journalists have been slow to embrace it.

Rena Singer, a suburban correspondent for the Philadelphia Inquirer, took a "loaded gun" to her interview with the budget official. Before firing off a question, she knew that the borough of Norristown had been running in the red in recent years by as much as 25 percent.

A spreadsheet analysis told her that the borough had overspent and then used a cash fund to close the gap. To taxpayers, the books looked better than they should have. Thanks to Singer's story, Norristown last fall issued its first true budget in three years.

Singer's piece was a mere blip on the Inquirer's journalism screen. It was a daily story on one borough, not a massive series destined for a Pulitzer. It didn't have the impact of the paper's more ambitious computer projects like "America: What Went Wrong?" or a voter fraud investigation that ultimately overturned the results of a state Senate race.

But Singer's story underscores the fact that computer-assisted reporting is no longer solely the domain of computer wizards working on long, time-consuming packages. It's an important ingredient in daily beat reporting as well.

"I couldn't have done that story without the computer," Singer says. Adds Neill A. Borowski, the Inquirer's director of computer-assisted reporting, who worked with her on the analysis, "This story opened a whole new world for her."

Now being practiced by a third generation of journalists, computer-assisted reporting, or CAR, faces a new frontier as it moves from the computer nerd in the corner to the center of the newsroom.

Thanks to the computer's power, reporters are tapping into data and producing high-impact stories on topics ranging from criminals among nursing home workers and school teachers to unsafe elevators and the influence of political contributions.

Pulitzer winners in each of the last six years used computer techniques to uncover racism in mortgage loans, arson fraud, medical malpractice, government waste and lax building codes.

While cutting back in other areas, editors and television news directors are buying equipment and creating new CAR jobs because they see the value in the stories computers make possible.

CAR specialists are delighted, but they also realize they have a long way to go before computer skills become routine in the nation's newsrooms. Teaching journalists to see computers as essential tools for obtaining information requires a shift in newsroom culture in an industry that is notoriously slow to change. As a result, they are struggling to find the winning formulas for selling the

From Rose Ciotta, "Baby You Should Drive This Car" in *American Journalism Review*, March 1996. Reprinted by permission of American Journalism Review.

Spreading the Gospel of CAR

Here are some tips on how managers and computer-assisted reporting specialists can make CAR an integral part of the newsroom:

Make local data that reporters use frequently—political contribution lists, motor vehicle and voter registration records and the like—available online.

Use software tools that make searching for data as easy as typing in a name or address.

Offer Internet e-mail and encourage staffers to use it.

Start small, with stories based on data that are easy to handle.

Train senior editors so they can see that CAR is neither magic nor brain surgery.

Select an unlikely candidate to do a CAR story.

Focus on those who want to do CAR stories. Fear of being left behind will motivate the others.

Publicize CAR stories on bulletin boards, newsletters, in-house publications.

Look at stories in progress and suggest where CAR could make them better.

Include CAR skills in job evaluations.

Have patience. Building a program takes time.

Set up a buddy system so reporters can learn in pairs.

Offer all types of training: classes, one-on-one instruction while doing a story, tapes, CD-ROMs, regular sessions, month-long sabbaticals.

Do slide shows of CAR stories so everyone can see the possibilities.

Include news research professionals to help spread the skills.

Build alliances with data processing and other departments outside editorial.

Set up brown bag lunches with outside speakers on CAR topics.

Identify newsroom helpers.

Survey the newsroom on computer skills and training needs.

Offer interest-free loans so reporters can buy computers for home use.

Set up a CAR reading corner for reprints, tip sheets.

Host a Net-surfing party to introduce staffers to the Internet.

Recognize that not everyone will learn everything.

Send reporters and editors to conferences so they can see what's happening elsewhere.

Put PCs in the middle of the newsroom; don't keep them locked in an office or hidden in the corner.

Don't force CAR on those who want no part of it (just as you wouldn't—couldn't—force someone to fall in love).

---

tools and for teaching wary journalists how to use them in a time of dramatic technological change.

"What everyone is having a difficult time accepting is we're in a revolution in terms of news gathering," says Brant Houston, managing director of the National Institute for Computer-Assisted Reporting (NICAR), a joint program of Investigative Reporters & Editors and the University of Missouri School of Journalism.

From the mid-1980s to the early '90s, CAR journalists spent much of their energy trying to persuade top editors to invest in CAR. In recent years, their focus has shifted to winning over the rest of the newsroom.

"We're beyond, 'There's no money for hardware or software,'" says Nora Paul, director of news research programs at the Poynter Institute in St. Petersburg, which hosts an annual seminar on CAR. Paul says journalists applying to attend the program have a new lament: "Universally, the biggest hurdle is, 'The guy sitting next to me doesn't get it and doesn't want any part of it.'"

There's also the challenge of fitting CAR—and the new jobs it is creating—into the newsroom organization. CAR editors (a.k.a. project or database editors) rarely have a reporting staff of their own, so they often must convince other editors or reporters to use computer data for a daily story or as the starting point for a larger project.

"CAR still needs an interpreter, a leader, someone who can show where it applies," Paul says.

The inexorable march of technology could cure the problem, experts say. As newsrooms shift to PC-based production systems, more and more reporters will be able to gather and analyze information via computers at their desks.

"Every newsroom must move toward the PC-based system. That's the tool for modern day reporting," says Jonathan Krim, a San Jose Mercury News assistant managing editor who is overseeing his paper's conversion from the so-called "dumb terminal," which allows reporters only to write and edit stories, to the personal computer, which can use other software. With PCs, he adds, comes the critical need to make reporters "technologically literate," regardless of how many CAR stories they produce.

At Newark's Star-Ledger, the recent switch to a PC-based operating system to produce the paper means reporters are getting basic training in Windows, handling a mouse and word processing. That significantly shortens the journey to using a spreadsheet, software used for calculations, or a database manager, software that organizes large volumes of information.

"The advantage," says Tom Curran, the Star-Ledger's projects editor and computer expert, "is people will lose their fear of computers."

There's little doubt that CAR is catching on. Recent surveys show increases in the newsroom in online use, computer training and staff devoted to CAR. When news organizations evaluate candidates for reporting and editing positions, computer skills are a plus. And the voices promoting CAR are increasingly at the highest levels of the newsroom.

"CAR is really exploding. It's growing exponentially," says Houston. "We're over the hump of whether it belongs or it doesn't."

At TV stations, competition is creating an appetite for CAR. "I've been astounded at how open my shop has been to these stories," says Mike Wendland, who heads the I-Team at WDIV-TV in Detroit. Wendland has used the computer to do stories on dirty restaurants, unsafe highways and nursing homes.

At KSTP-TV in Minneapolis, Joel Grover routinely uses computers for investigative stories while daily reporters also tap into computer data for quick-hit pieces. "Every single story we do now we find some way that computers help make the story a lot better," Grover said at last fall's CAR conference in Cleveland.

As newspapers struggle to stem declining circulation, CAR is one way to produce stories that readers are demanding, says Philadelphia Inquirer Editor Maxwell E. P. King. Despite Knight-Ridder's orders to cut spending, King has made money available for CAR. He not only formed an in-house unit headed by Borowski to spread the gospel, he also promotes computer-assisted reporting within the chain as the chair of its CAR task force.

At U.S. News & World Report, with Senior Editor Penny Loeb leading the way, CAR has not only produced award-winning projects on special education and tainted blood supplies, but has become an integral part of the magazine's competitive strategy to produce investigative reporting based on "almost courtroom-quality evidence," says Brian Duffy, the magazine's assistant managing editor for investigations. And while CAR costs money, he adds, it's a wise investment that will help restore confidence in American journalism.

New York Times Managing Editor Gene Roberts, whose reign at the Philadelphia Inquirer produced a record number of Pulitzer Prizes for investigative stories, calls the CAR tool "critical to journalists." Roberts says he has been a "fan of computer skills for more than 20 years," since Inquirer reporters Donald L. Barlett and James B. Steele used a mainframe computer to analyze the Philadelphia court system.

Roberts recently told journalists at an IRE/University of Maryland conference that while he has no plans to venture into the online world—he prides himself on being the "last boss in the newspaper business who never uses a computer"—he has seen its value, particularly in covering major breaking news stories like the Oklahoma City bombing.

Forces outside the newsroom help ensure CAR's place in daily journalism. Governments are increasingly storing data on computers. Online data sources are mushrooming. The World Wide Web is rapidly growing as a prime venue for obtaining and publishing data. Hardware and software keep getting easier to use.

There's also growing interest in public journalism, which uses computer tools to research community issues.

All of which means that CAR should not be regarded as an exotic toy; it's an essential element in the craft of journalism. "Computer-assisted reporting is not for the getting ahead," says Jim Mosley, the St. Louis Post-Dispatch's CAR specialist. "It's for the getting by."

As the practice proliferates, more and more reporters must learn how to carry it out. IRE has made training in computer-assisted reporting a key part of its mission. Some 5,000 journalists have attended training seminars hosted by IRE/NICAR in the past 18 months, and CAR training will be available at IRE's national conference in Providence in June.

"Demand has jumped and the skill level has gone up," says Rosemary Armao, IRE's executive director. "The demand isn't just for beginning training. People also want to know about mapping software and other higher-level skills."

Newspaper chains and major news organizations are teaching their employees computer-assisted reporting. The Associated Press last year sponsored 15 training seminars and plans 27 with NICAR for 1996. Gannett hosted three regional programs involving 22 newspapers and 52 people in 1995, and will sponsor three in 1996 involving 60 people from as many as 20 papers.

"We're making progress," says Anne Saul, Gannett's news systems editor. "We require at least two people to come from every newspaper, one of them an editor, so there is someone there to spearhead the CAR program and not leave the reporters swimming upstream by themselves." Still, Saul concedes that Gannett papers, like many others, "have a long way to go" before CAR becomes a tool as commonly used as the telephone.

At AP, the emphasis is on equipping reporters with the CAR tools to do daily stories. All 236 bureaus worldwide can access a library of CD-ROMs offering reference works ranging from telephone numbers to association names to the full text of the New York Times and Wall Street Journal. The wire service's 143 domestic bureaus are receiving new, powerful computers loaded with spreadsheet and database software.

AP sees a payoff. When Orange County went bankrupt, reporter Rob Wells used a spreadsheet to examine each investment to show how the county collapsed. In Wisconsin, Robert Imrie typed details about hunting accidents into a database manager, and learned that young hunters were shooting older hunters.

"This sort of stuff works," says Bill Dedman, AP's director of CAR. Dedman, who won a Pulitzer Prize in 1989 at the Atlanta Journal and Constitution for an exposé of mortgage lending practices, has spent his first year at AP building the infrastructure to assist daily reporting. He's also shaped a nine-member team headed by Bob Port, a computer specialist who came from the St. Petersburg Times, and data wizard Drew Sullivan, formerly with NICAR, to supply data to the bureaus and do national stories.

At Cox Newspapers, the driving force behind computer-assisted reporting is Elliot Jaspin, the godfather of the genre known for his pioneering work at the Providence Journal-Bulletin.

Jaspin, who recalls the early days when skeptics doubted he could analyze 30,000 records, is breaking his own records. Last August, nine Cox newspapers published stories on doctors who were making millions on Medicare. Jaspin tackled the initial data—100 million records that took up 290 reels of magnetic tape—and gave each paper its state's data so it could report on local doctors.

The project, which involved 25 staffers, revealed that 72 doctors nationwide grossed at least $1 million each in a single year from treating the elderly.

Jaspin, systems editor in Cox's Washington bureau, says the effort to embed CAR in newsroom culture "is still in its infancy." At Cox, he's focusing on linking the newspapers with high-speed data lines so they can share information.

The idea of chains sharing data isn't new. Gannett Special Projects Editor David A. Milliron routinely supplies all 92 newspapers with ready-to-use national data on CD-ROM. The papers can also tap into Gannett's private forum on CompuServe for data and assistance and Gannett News Service's electronic bulletin board. "Every single one of our papers has used at least one of the databases for a story or package over the last year," says Milliron.

He's especially proud of reporters and editors at small newspapers, like Buster Wolfe at the Monroe News-Star in Louisiana (circulation 38,949) and Cheryl Phillips at the Great Falls Tribune in Montana (circulation 34,471), who produce CAR stories using antiquated equipment. Phillips was recently rewarded with a high-speed Pentium PC after writing a series on gangs in Montana using a database she created herself.

"It's our smaller papers that are pulling off the 'well dones,'" says Milliron. "The biggest misconception is that you have to be a large paper with the latest equipment to do CAR."

"I fiddle with my databases on planes, at home over the weekend, whenever the mood strikes me," says Stephanie Reitz of Connecticut's Waterbury Republican-American. "It's like fiddling with my hair in the morning. I just want to see what's possible."

At Knight-Ridder, two developments are aimed at encouraging more CAR throughout the chain: a data library for all of its newspapers and a mentor program so that the experts can help the beginners.

While interest in CAR is growing dramatically, so is anxiety about its arrival. Journalists who consider themselves writers above all else are especially apprehensive.

At the Poynter Institute, journalists attending a writing seminar were brought together with computer types interested in new media. "You could feel the anxiety level in the room go up 300 percent," Poynter's Paul says. "Writers were defensive, asking, 'What's wrong with just being a good writer?'"

Not everyone in the newsroom needs to be a computer wizard, experts agree. But, they add, even good writers can't afford to be left behind by the technological revolution. Some practitioners, like Steven S. Ross, who teaches CAR at Columbia University in a graduate program that emphasizes the marriage of computer data and narrative writing, say the ultimate CAR challenge is to produce stories about people with data in the background.

CAR enthusiasts recognize that they must do some proselytizing to bring computer atheists and agnostics into the fold. They want everyone to learn online searching, including on the Internet. Most should know how to use a spreadsheet and when to use a database manager. "Everyone should know the possibilities," says U.S. News' Loeb.

CAR specialists advocate a variety of strategies: assigning a powerful PC to those who show initiative to produce CAR stories, celebrating successes with in-house publicity and designing software to make computer work easier.

"CAR doesn't emphasize enough the using of the network in the newsroom to share information," says George Landau, manager of information services for the St. Louis Post-Dispatch. "I'd like to build a newsroom where any public record of any likely use to a journalist is updated and made available to journalists who are taught how to use it."

In Philadelphia, CAR specialist Tom Torok designed a way to search a database so Inquirer reporters could use voter registration records to identify New Jersey parolees who were encouraged to illegally register to vote in Philadelphia in order to collect welfare. The reporters needed only to type in a name or an address to get the information. Other newsrooms set up similar systems for motor vehicles information. Norfolk's Virginian-Pilot put police and school data on the World Wide Web for use by both its staff and the public.

It's also critical to smooth the transition into the world of computer-assisted reporting. Carol Napolitano, a public affairs team reporter at the Omaha World-Herald, urges papers to shy away from major projects when starting CAR. Rather, she says, easy-to-do stories "bring more people into it so a larger percentage of the newsroom can have that first experience." There's nothing like success with front page stories made possible by the computer to trigger excitement and break down resistance.

The best sales vehicle for CAR in the newsroom is word of mouth, says Jennifer LaFleur, former NICAR training director and now database editor of the San Jose Mercury News. "The best way to promote CAR is to get a few key people interested and using it and others will see it and see them getting stories in the paper."

Despite all of the cheerleading, CAR faces a variety of challenges on the newsroom floor, where there may be too little time and equipment for much computer-assisted reporting—or too little interest. Some journalists are satisfied to limit their CAR experience to Internet surfing. Others want no part of a skill that emphasizes mathematics and detail work.

Even the experts agree that not every journalist needs to master higher-level skills like mapping (transferring data onto traditional maps) and statistical analysis.

But equipment shortages can pose problems. Most newsrooms don't have enough PCs for every reporter, although most have a few for common use. Increasingly, they are linked on a network where data are available for general use. Few offer e-mail or Internet access to anyone who wants them. Time is also a problem, as cutbacks mean the doubling up of jobs.

"It's still a struggle for most people to find the time, both for training and reporting," says reporter Bob Warner of the Philadelphia Daily News.

Ray Robinson of the Atlantic City Press sees "tremendous interest" fueled by major awards won by computer-assisted projects and the work of organizations like NICAR that give reporters a forum for sharing techniques and stories. While CAR ideas are easy to sell, says Robinson, "the hard part is executing the idea after it's been sold. That's because our reporters are busy people, often producing three or four stories a day." Others describe a reluctance to embrace CAR because it's new, different and not user-friendly.

"A lot of newspaper reporters are not willing to try something new or to make the effort," observes LaFleur, who spent 20 months training journalists for NICAR. LaFleur says she often found more interest in learning CAR skills among bureau reporters on major dailies, who see them as a way of getting ahead, than among senior staffers downtown. She also found success stories at small dailies where management provides training and equipment for everyone.

Some say journalists should take it upon themselves to buy a computer and learn how to use a PC even before their companies make them available. Others say there's a lot to learn and that success has to be measured in small steps. And management support is crucial.

Stephanie Reitz, who has tasted CAR success at Connecticut's Waterbury Republican-American with page one stories on delinquent taxes and city workers' overtime, warns that some journalists shy away from CAR because they are intimidated by the jargon.

"I fiddle with my databases on planes, at home over the weekend, whenever the mood strikes me," she says. "It's like fiddling with my hair in the morning. I just want to see what's possible. If you make training fun, you've won half the battle."

While everyone agrees training is critical, there's no unanimity on exactly what a training program should look like. Newspapers increasingly are setting up their own newsroom "universities" to teach everything from Windows to spreadsheet and database software to basic mathematics.

The Raleigh News & Observer, which has won praise for its commitment to newsroom training, recently gave its program a second look and decided to start giving reporters month-long internships during which their primary task is learning how to analyze data.

"Our goal is to teach reporters how to analyze data so there isn't any question they can't answer," says Pat Stith, the paper's CAR editor, who will train three reporters this year. While Raleigh has more than 60 reporters who have written stories based on computer data, many can't do the analysis themselves. The N & O's goal is to produce reporters who are self-sufficient. "You can't get there if you're relying on nerds like me," says Stith.

Stith's training idea—immersing oneself in the new software language in the same way a student might go to Paris to perfect his or her French—has already been borrowed by Norfolk's Virginian-Pilot, where Toni Whitt, a city hall reporter, recently spend a month learning such skills as creating and analyzing a campaign finance database. "When you do it every single day, it sticks with you," says Whitt. Lise Olsen, the paper's CAR mentor, says she plans to offer month-long training to five others this year. Her goal is to have a CAR specialist on each of the paper's 12 news reporting teams.

Even a month—a luxury in today's newsrooms—won't turn reporters into computer wizards. "It's a real step forward but probably not enough," says Dwight L. Morris, a CAR high priest. Morris, a former Los Angeles Times staffer who is now a computer analysis consultant, says most editors don't appreciate the time it takes to teach computer skills, especially to professionals who generally shun math. "Most senior editors, when they decide they want to get active in CAR, they might send someone to one week of training and that's sort of it," he says. "There's no follow through and not enough training."

Teaching reporters to be self-sufficient also stems from the survival instinct of CAR specialists, who often find themselves with a bottleneck of reporters who want to do stories but can't do the requisite analysis. Add teaching and daily coaching duties and CAR editors find they have trouble getting enough stories in the newspaper.

Another source of angst for some CAR specialists is the issue of bylines. Sometimes the data person is denied a byline when others have done the traditional reporting and interviewing. The computer specialist may receive credit in a tagline, graphic or "nerd box." Some say this stems from a lack of respect for computer work and will fade as more reporters do their own analysis.

Others, like Stephen K. Doig, the Miami Herald's associate editor for research, are in management positions and choose not to receive bylines even when stories are based on their work.

At the Tennessean in Nashville, Database Editor Lisa Green is struggling with reporters who want data for their stories but don't want to learn how to get it. Her approach is to work with reporters until they are confident enough to do their own analysis. She looks for relatively simple stories, like a study of school field trips, to show reporters the power of the tools.

When the paper canvased staffers to see what type of training they wanted, she says, "computer skills came out number one." At San Jose, LaFleur's survey also showed high interest and low skills. The same gap exists in newsrooms across the country.

CAR pioneer Philip Meyer says the next wave of CAR stories will demand high-level statistical analysis, a skill lacking among most journalists. "That's the next hurdle," he says.

Gene Roberts agrees that computer training is important. But he warns against viewing CAR as a panacea. In some cases, he says, CAR "becomes a crutch. . . . We rely so heavily on reporting statistical data that you can overlook empirical evidence and journalistic footwork."

And, of course, data can't do the job by themselves. It's critical to flesh out the numbers with people, with the sights and sounds of the street, and strong narrative. Roberts says the Times is working on two projects that began with computer data. Once the numbers have been crunched and studied, he adds, reporters will hit the streets with the job of "breathing life into this data."

Article Review Form at end of book.

Computer-assisted reporting (CAR) techniques help reporters write deeper, more insightful stories. As an investigative reporter in New Jersey and Miami, Neil Reisner has seen CAR techniques applied to major investigations as well as to routine coverage. In the following article, Reisner examines how his colleagues use CAR techniques to enhance stories. Which reporters were writing routine stories, and which ones were involved in major investigations? Did they use the same CAR techniques? Which software programs were the most useful (and why)?

On the Beat

Neil H. Reisner

Neil H. Reisner is database editor at the Bergen Record in Hackensack, New Jersey, and teaches at Columbia University's Graduate School of Journalism. He is assistant system operator on CompuServe's Journalism Forum, where he leads a section sponsored by IRE and NICAR.

Computer-assisted reporting isn't just for projects anymore.

When a corruption scandal hit the South Hackensack, New Jersey, police department, Bergen Record reporter Deborah Privitera set out to get local reaction.

But before Privitera hit the streets, she stopped at her desk and typed "DO CENSUS" into her computer terminal. With a few keystrokes, she called up a U.S. Census Bureau profile of the blue-collar, ethnic town just 12 miles from Manhattan on Interstate 80.

"I punched in DO CENSUS and learned it was a township of 2,100, half of whom were Italian, and the rest a mixture of other nationalities," Privitera recalls. "From that I could tell that it was a very small neighborhood and

Bergen Record reporter Deborah Privitera accessed computerized census data for background on a small New Jersey town.

ethnically diverse; the education and employment data gave me even more of a sense of what the township was like."

Alan Cox, a reporter at WCCO-TV in Minneapolis remembers a day last spring when the Centers for Disease Control and Prevention questioned the wisdom of giving 16- and 17-year-olds driving permits.

"I sorted nine years' worth of Minnesota death records to look for teen traffic fatalities. Using Census Bureau CD-ROMs, I calculated accident rates, and mapped them by county," he says. "Within a few hours, I could show that teens in rural Minnesota were most at risk . . . and that we were entering the time of year with the greatest risk. It was the night that most Twin Cities high schools held graduation ceremonies, so the story led the broadcast."

Computer-assisted reporting—it's not just for projects anymore.

The same techniques that fueled Pulitzer Prize-winning investigations for the last six years can also help beat reporters—the ones churning out three stories a day, along with features and enterprise—add color and depth to their efforts. Journalists around the country are learning that a few keystrokes can often make the difference between routine efforts and real insight. It doesn't take much time and it often doesn't take lots of extra effort. All it takes is the willingness to learn a few new tricks and—perhaps more important—the flexibility to adopt new ways of thinking about old problems.

With tools like the Record's DO CENSUS, with free or inexpensive computer programs that let journalists quickly do the calculations or analyses that give context to stories, and with more powerful (but easy to use) spreadsheets or databases that calculate or sort data instantaneously, reporters can dig into stories in ways they never have before. And though computer-assisted reporting (CAR) on the beat may not be a fixture in every newsroom yet, the best and most ambitious reporters are adding it to their repertoires and using it to advance their careers in much the same way that reporters with VDT experience had an advantage during the transition from typewriters to computers.

From Neil Reisner, "On The Beat" in *American Journalism Review,* March 1995. Reprinted by permission of American Journalism Review.

"What CAR allows people to do on deadline and on their beat reporting is to relatively quickly collate information and analyze it," says Brant Houston, a former database editor at the Hartford Courant who last year became managing director of the National Institute for Computer-Assisted Reporting (NICAR), based at the University of Missouri's School of Journalism. "That adds a lot more depth to their reporting and allows them to ask much better questions of people who are involved in the story. That rests at the heart of good reporting—just knowing the right questions to ask."

Ralph Frammolino learned just how much knowing the right question to ask could help a day after completing a week-long NICAR-sponsored seminar at the Los Angeles Times last fall. Before the workshop, the Times reporter says he had only "tinkered" with computers. But literally minutes after returning to the newsroom, he was confronted by a deadline story that would not have been possible without CAR.

It was about, of all things, jury selection on the O.J. Simpson trial.

"It was truly instant gratification," says Frammolino. "We had a week-long boot camp where 10 of us, reporters and editors, were put through pretty rigorous training. And of course we were fascinated and kind of titillated by the kind of high-powered stories that had been done."

With visions of databases dancing in his head, Frammolino returned to the newsroom Monday morning.

"Before you can say 'Pentium,' my editor is chasing me down, saying, 'I need your help, I need your help. They've winnowed out the first members of the jury. We've got to find out who are these lucky people left.' ... I looked her in the eye and said, 'I've got exactly what you need. I'll use the computer.'"

What followed was a few hours of keyboarding as a Times researcher dictated to Frammolino portions of the lengthy questionnaire potential jurors had filled out, public information in California. Frammolino frantically typed the material into Microsoft Access, the database package he had learned only the week before. By deadline that day, the pair had entered 30 separate facts about each remaining member of the jury pool, including demographic items such as race, gender, address, education and employment. Potential jurors also were asked if they had heard recordings of Nicole Simpson's frantic call to 911; if they had seen video of the police chasing O.J. Simpson on L.A. freeways; and how they viewed the reliability of DNA testing. Once the information was entered, it took just a few minutes to come up with some quick analyses.

"We were able that first day not to come out with a stand-alone story, but really to add a lot of depth and texture to that first story. It was very helpful for the graphics and the chart," says Frammolino. "Most striking to me was that something like 92 percent of the pool had seen O.J. in the slow Bronco chase, but something like less than 50 percent had ever seen him play football, when he was in his glory."

Los Angeles Times reporter Ralph Frammolino was able to find details about the O.J. Simpson jury pool that eluded his competition.

Proponent Brant Houston says computer-assisted reporting allows journalists to quickly collate data and analyze it on deadline.

The next day other Los Angeles area newspapers, working from paper records, were able to present only the most rudimentary analyses, observing simply that the remaining jury pool contained mostly African Americans who might be more suspicious of police and favor Simpson.

Frammolino began to wonder who was being dropped from the pool and, more important, why. Many, of course, had been removed because they'd violated Judge Lance A. Ito's order to avoid media coverage of trial preliminaries. But Frammolino got an insight into the Simpson defense team's strategy.

"It was very clear that the people being excluded were the ones more likely to believe in DNA evidence, and also that they were more educated people," he says. "Why is that important? Because the entire prosecution case relies on the test results."

Thus the Times was able to run a comprehensive story on the fine art of jury selection, including comment from experts on the thinking that might lie behind the lawyers' tactics.

"If we had to do this by hand, with 30 different fields [categories of information], I don't think we would have gotten to it," Frammolino says.

Quickly finding elusive data is what CAR on the beat is all about. And to make it possible, newsroom tools such as DO CENSUS and computers mounted with database programs like Access or Paradox and spreadsheets like Excel or Quattro are increasingly common—or should be.

DO CENSUS is just one program that encourages beat reporters to access computerized information. Built by a Bergen Record editor who noticed that the CD-ROMs sold by the Census Bureau contain canned "profiles" of states, counties or municipalities, it took only a couple of days to compile basic information on the demographics, economy, housing stock and labor force for the 100 or so towns the Record covers. Then it was simply a matter of convincing the Record's mainframe computer mavens to mount the profiles on the ATEX system the newsroom uses to write and edit stories, though the data could as easily have been put on a desktop PC. Very quickly, reporters and editors began to use DO CENSUS every day.

Any newsroom with a desktop computer that can handle Microsoft Windows or a Macintosh can acquire a slew of other free or low-cost programs to make reporters' lives easier. They include:

➤ A program to calculate the impact of inflation: Developed at the Raleigh News & Observer (see "The Digitized Newsroom," January/February) and improved at the St. Louis Post-Dispatch, this tool lets a reporter enter the amount spent in one year and see what it is worth in another year. It's a quick, easy way to check an official's claim that a seemingly enormous increase in the amount of a city budget, for example, is really "just keeping up with inflation."

➤ A weights-and-measures conversion program developed by a staffer at the Spartanburg Herald-Journal in South Carolina that translates anything from cubits to light years into more common measurements: It can help reporters explain to readers (or to themselves) what it really means when a scientist says something is 100 light years away.

➤ Another program, also developed at the Spartanburg Herald-Journal, that quickly calculates that bane of journalists, the percentage change between two numbers: It's very handy for reporters who need to state the percentage by which taxes will increase this year over last.

➤ A program developed mostly for pilots and frequent fliers that calculates the distance and flying time between some 900 airports around the globe: This might be used to add detail to stories about faraway events.

➤ A simple tool that could be built in any newsroom to help reporters analyze local budgets: By using a spreadsheet to enter budget amounts for this year and next, it becomes a simple matter to see what internal items might have increased or decreased dramatically, perhaps much more or less than the budget as a whole. Reporters can then use the inflation calculator to see whether the percentage change seems reasonable.

Alan Cox at WCCO-TV is one of only a handful of television reporters doing CAR on deadline stories. He says this is because of television's need for visuals, a problem he encountered when preparing his report on teen traffic fatalities.

"Using 9-track tape, a database program, a spreadsheet program, a CD-ROM extract program and mapping software kept me glued to my chair," he says. "A field producer and a photographer visited a driving school for video and interviews to flesh out the story. I couldn't have done it without them."

CAR on television brings other challenges, because it requires another level of technology to bring the results of reporters' work to the TV screen. That technology can be difficult to master.

"When I did my story live on the air for our early broadcast, I used a [graphics] program, and I indulged in adding a computery sound effect to play when the graphics came on screen," he recalls. "In my haste, I embedded it improperly. When I called it up on the air, error boxes repeatedly popped up. I'd always planned to make a joke about technology if something went wrong during a live report, but given the subject matter, it seemed like the wrong time. I don't use that sound effect much anymore."

Still, Cox does not hesitate to use computer resources, even when they don't lend themselves precisely to traditional television. The night of the USAir crash in Pittsburgh he used a CD-ROM containing Federal Aviation Administration records of the downed plane's service history and accessed online services to get information on the aircraft's model.

"Television newsrooms tend to have limited printed reference materials, and the online sources are helpful in a crush," he says. "There was no time to compare the number of maintenance problems we found for that specific plane with similar makes and models. But in a way that tight deadline struck a chord with viewers. Because there was no time to put the information into a standard television graphic, I showed and read the records on the air directly from a database program. I later got calls from reporters at other news organizations, from a couple of airline employees and from a few home computer buffs wanting to know how to do the same thing."

Heather Newman, a city hall and urban affairs reporter for the Tucson Citizen in Arizona, uses CAR techniques to help her with her routine coverage.

Tucson Citizen reporter Heather Newman used computer-assisted reporting to produce a quick profile of a city councilman accused of wrongdoing.

Newman uses a database program as her Rolodex, keeping a continually updated list of names, addresses and phone numbers for everyone who sits on a city committee and a list of neighborhood association activists that lets her select a source by name, area of the city and other criteria. She uses her word processor to keep the minutes and reports from City Council meetings, enabling her to quickly call up the history of a council action.

"We needed to do a snap profile on a councilman who has been involved in an alleged kickback scandal," says Newman. "He had run on a strong campaign of neighborhood support. Having the neighborhood associations typed in enabled us to immediately pull the names of people representing all associations in his ward, allowing us to call them to see how he had kept up on his promises."

Neill Borowski, director of computer-assisted reporting for the Philadelphia Inquirer, rattles off a list of other ways beat reporters use CAR, noting that his newspaper encourages the quick-hit daily and the in-depth Sunday CAR story.

In one case, a correspondent phoned 44 public high schools, asking them to fax a list of colleges to which graduating seniors were accepted and how many went to each one.

"We in turn built a spreadsheet—it could have been a database, too—reflecting several thousand college-bound seniors . . . and found the hot colleges," Borowski says. "The story interviewed admissions counselors from those colleges and the graphics listed both the hottest colleges overall as well as the hot colleges at individual high schools."

For another story, the same correspondent made her job even easier. Rather than call each school with her request, she entered the principals' names and fax numbers into a program on her PC that sends a computer file as a fax.

"She wrote the letter asking her questions, set the fax on automatic and it sent out 44 faxes without a care. The reporter went on vacation for a week and came back to a pile of faxes with answers from the high schools," says Borowski. "Is this CAR? Sure it is. It is using the computer as a tool to facilitate reporting."

To encourage its staff to use computer-assisted reporting, the Inquirer established what it calls "Bit-by-Bit University." In the last year, more than 200 reporters and editors have studied everything from basic PC training to spreadsheets to databases to the Internet.

"The success stories are the people who can't wait to leave the classes and try to apply what they have learned," says Borowski. "In some ways, we're seeing the same reluctance to change that we saw in the mid-'70s when most newsrooms moved from typewriters to VDTs. The younger people quickly adapted. Some older editors never could change over, while others embraced the new technology and began to work on ways they could squeeze the most productivity out of it. We're seeing that now with CAR."

Glossary

Column: In a spreadsheet, one category of information, such as municipal spending on police protection in 1994. A column extends vertically. The equivalent of a database field.

Computer-assisted reporting: Using personal computer technology as an adjunct to traditional reporting methods. CAR permits reporters to go deeper into information by mining and analyzing larger volumes of information than they otherwise could. The technique, in a way, turns traditional reporting on its head: Normally, reporters collect anecdotes and from them deduce trends. CAR lets reporters find trends, then collect the anecdotes to illustrate them.

Database: A kind of computerized file card box or Rolodex, but very well organized. Database software lets reporters enter information into the computer in a standard format—name, address, phone number, zip code, for example. Then, much like pulling the aces out of a deck of cards, the computer can extract, for example, all the information on people living in a particular zip code or all the people named Smith. Databases and spreadsheets are somewhat interchangeable. A database is better for sorting and extracting information.

Field: One category of information in a database, such

as zip code. The equivalent of a spreadsheet column.

Mapping Software: Computer software that transfers data onto traditional maps, enabling a reporter to graphically show, for example, where crimes or accidents occur or where particular segments of the population live.

9-Track Tape: Magnetic tape on which many government agencies keep their computerized records. These records can be transferred from tape into a personal computer, and then examined using off-the-shelf software.

Record: All the information in a spreadsheet or database concerning a single person or event. A single database record might include name, address, city, state, zip and telephone number.

Row: In a spreadsheet, all the information on a particular person or event, such as municipal police spending for 1991, 1992, 1993 and 1994. A row extends horizontally. The equivalent of a database record.

Spreadsheet: A kind of computerized accountant's pad, organized into rows and columns. The advantage of a spreadsheet is its mathematical power. Once data are in a spreadsheet, it's a simple matter to add, subtract, multiply or divide, or run other mathematical operations on huge quantities of numbers. A spreadsheet is better for crunching numbers than a database.

Article Review Form at end of book.

Computer-assisted reporting (CAR) involves the independent analysis of databases—either acquired through other sources or created in-house. In the following article, Drew Sullivan explores the variety of records at a reporter's disposal. What type of records does the author consider as vital? How are newsrooms acquiring the data? To what extent are the databases being used in newsrooms?

Building Your Own Local Hall of Records

Drew Sullivan

In a newsroom in the not-so-distant future....

Do they have the story? The question locked up ace reporter Shelly Friday's thoughts like a bear trap as she nervously opened the late edition of the Daily Sun, her competitor. Nothing above the fold. Nothing below. If they had it she would have seen it on page one.

She quickly turned back to her own story. Her fingers blazed across the keyboard.

"An aide to Mayor Madeline Gambit admitted yesterday to hiding the mayor's ownership of two 10-acre parcels of land in her aide's name. The property was given to Ross Michaels by the Oklahoma Charlie Casino Corporation of Laughlin, Nev., in exchange for the mayor's help in getting approval for a license by the state gaming control board. The property was to be turned over to the mayor after she left office."

Friday swiveled her chair, simultaneously grabbing the phone and hitting the speed dial for the assessor's office.

"Thank you for calling the Green County courthouse. All offices are closed due to Arbor Day."

Dammit, Friday cursed. No wonder the Sun didn't go with the story. My competitor Rooker couldn't get the documents, and Michaels wasn't talking after he realized his blunder. No problem, thought Friday. She highlighted the names Ross Michaels and Oklahoma Charlie and right-clicked her mouse. Up popped a menu. She selected "search all databases" and hit return. Within seconds, the screen filled with dozens of citations. Her heart leaped again. Two records from the assessor's office. She clicked on the link and up popped the deeds listing the grantor as Oklahoma Charlie's and the grantee as Elisabeth Reynolds.

She clicked on a map and up popped a graphic of the town with the parcels shaded. Interesting, thought Friday. The parcels bordered the highway at the precise spot where the mayor had recommended an off ramp. That meant the parcels would be worth a fortune.

She checked out some other hits. Ahaa. Ross Michaels shows up on a marriage certificate with Elisabeth Reynolds.

"So they're using his wife's maiden name," Friday muttered to herself.

Within minutes, by simply highlighting a name and clicking, Friday was able to find background information on the casino from her paper's archives, articles of incorporation from the state listing Elisabeth Michaels as an officer of the corporation, and dozens of other properties and financial dealings.

While the story is fictional, the technologies aren't. A number of newspapers have found that a few byproducts of their computer-assisted reporting projects, electronic databases of local public records and reporters who know how to use relational database managers, have enabled them to build the electronic version of their local hall of records in an easy-to-use form.

"One of my jobs is now to make as many of the data sources people use available to them on

---

The article was published in *The IRE Journal*," in bi-monthly magazine of Investigative Reporters and Editors (IRE). IRE is a nonprofit educational organization that promotes investigative journalism through conferences, training seminars, publications, research and other services. For more information, write to IRE at 138 Neff Annex, Missouri School of Journalism, Columbia, MO 65211, call 573-882-2042, or use IRE's web site-www.ire.org.

their desktops," says Jennifer LaFleur, database editor for the *San Jose Mercury News.*

At the *St. Louis Post-Dispatch,* reporters can access drivers' licenses, vehicle registrations, state death and city payroll records from their computer using an easy-to-use search screen. The pages are accessible through the *Post-Dispatch's* Web server, meaning even if their reporters are on the road, all they need is access to the Internet to search the databases.

The system was designed and built by George Landau, who left the paper in November to start his own consulting firm, NewsEngin, Inc., that specializes in designing and building database libraries.

"We're planning on adding a database to the system every couple of weeks," says Landau, who still consults with his former paper.

Future plans call for adding databases of people who have been in the state's correctional system, city and county assessors' records, campaign finance records, voter registration records and real estate information.

"What we do is try to anticipate demand and put up records that a reporter on deadline is going to need," Landau said.

Many other papers are setting up or have set up electronic database libraries. At the Buffalo News, reporters can access voter registration records, city payroll and campaign contributor data. At the *Baltimore Sun,* computer kiosks in the library access—among other databases—Small Business Administration loans, building permits and school test scores. *The Star Tribune* (Minneapolis) offers its reporters criminal history and business licenses. *Fresno Bee* reporters have access to searchable 911 calls and local crime data.

Unlike commercial public record database vendors such as Lexis/Nexis, Autotrack and CDB Infotek, these electronic database libraries can be fully relational, meaning reporters can compare many databases together rather than enter a search one name at a time. For example, a reporter with access to a city payroll database can compare it to a database of parolees to find all the city employees who served time in jail.

Those papers that have electronic database libraries say it is making a difference.

"We've had pretty strong use," Landau says. "Drivers' license and vehicle registration get hit many times a day, and it's resulted in a number of front-page stories in the last couple months."

A number of other reporters agree.

"There is a huge demand for this," says Alan Levin of the *Hartford Courant.* "It is real handy in day-to-day reporting."

Levin helped build and maintains a library of nearly 20 databases that are accessible through the paper's network. He is currently working with reporter John Moran to migrate the library over to an Intranet where reporters in remote bureaus will have access.

"I'd say we have about 200 people use the system each month," Levin says. "That will double once we get the bureaus online."

While it is never easy to get the equipment needed to do computer-assisted reporting, building an electronic library is sometimes an easy sell.

Journalists have found that by using electronic databases of local public records they can build the electronic version of their local hall of records in an easy-to-use form.

"It definitely saves a lot of time," LaFleur says. "Anything that saves time has a lot of support."

Instead, LaFleur and others have found the more difficult task to be getting reporters comfortable with the use of databases.

"We still don't have everybody using it," LaFleur says. "Once they do, they're hooked. People who are more savvy with computers use it on a regular basis." LaFleur advertises the system and updates users through a monthly inhouse newsletter called Mouse Droppings.

Building an electronic library can be easy or difficult depending on how much support in time and money a reporter gets from his or her news organization. A simple system can be built with nothing more than a fast, powerful PC with lots of storage space. Also needed are a relational database management system (DBMS) software and some data. Using commercially available DBMS software like Microsoft Access or Microsoft Visual FoxPro, a system can be hooked to a network and front-ends built in a matter of days. The downside of these simple systems is that only a few reporters can use the system, and it's likely to be slow.

More sophisticated systems usually include one or more powerful server machines and massive amounts of storage and RAM. These systems can cost anywhere from $10,000 to $100,000 depending on the speed and power desired. Rather than Access or FoxPro, these systems might use larger and more powerful server software like Microsoft SQL Server, Sybase or Oracle.

Rather than reporters directly using SQL Server to search the data, designers like Landau typically build a user-friendly front-end. This can be done with Web pages and a Web browser, Visual Basic applications, other easier-to-use DBMS programs like Access or a combination of the above.

"I'm convinced that teaching the average reporter to become an Access maven is about as likely as teaching him the Koran," says the *Baltimore Sun's* Mike Himowitz. "On the other hand, if you can write a friendly, easy-to-use front end with little 'type here' fields and 'click here' buttons, you can make the information accessible to everyone."

When connected to a Web server, an electronic library has the advantage of allowing reporters to access the information from anywhere in the world.

Levin, like Landau, chose Web pages for the future of databases at the *Courant*.

"What we're finding is that with the advent of Intranets and Web browsers, it's making life a lot easier," Levin says. "Reporters only need to learn Netscape in order to use these systems."

Article Review Form at end of book.

Using a computer to research a news story has its hazards. Just because the information is available online does not guarantee its accuracy. Part of a reporter's job is to become familiar with accurate sources of information while creating a checks and balances system for determining accuracy. What are the five pitfalls Penny Williams offers in this article? How can they be avoided?

Database Dangers

More and *faster* do not always mean *better*

Penny Williams

Penny Williams, a television anchor/reporter for 10 years, currently is assistant professor of broadcast journalism at Buffalo State College in New York.

When reporters rely only on databases for their facts, they can get a story that is incomplete, inaccurate, or lacking in historical perspective. And sometimes they end up with no story.

Databases can be a handy resource for journalists: they allow reporters to obtain background information from published articles. They also can find potential sources and generate quotes from those sources. And they can do it all quickly.

But when using these electronic libraries, there are some pitfalls to bear in mind, according to several journalists and researchers experienced in database use.

Pitfall 1: You Can't Get the Whole Story

WMAQ anchor/reporter Allison Rosati calls the database "a springboard onto other things."

"My experience has always been that once you start getting your interviews and start getting your video together, the stories take shape. And no matter what you've read beforehand, the story gains a life of its own."

ABC News Correspondent James Walker recently did an investigative piece about law enforcement officials in several states, including Arizona, who were faking fingerprints to gain convictions.

For the story in Arizona, Walker went to the little community of Nogales, where he says he knew he couldn't get background information, sources, or quotes from a database. "The newspaper in Nogales was just not online because the town's so small," Walker says. So, Walker and his crew went to Nogales to do their own digging.

But the story didn't start in Nogales. "A source tipped me off that it was happening in Ithaca, New York," Walker says. He figured if people's fingerprints were being faked in one state, the same thing might be happening in other states. He found other cases in California, Alabama, Oklahoma, Tennessee, and Georgia. Walker did a database search, but the peculiar nature of the fingerprint story limited the use of databases.

"We did extensive searches to see if in fact there had been incidents of fingerprint faking around the country. We found out that the nature of the subject is such that it is seldom publicized. It's covered up, which made it even more difficult. Several instances had been handled quietly. So databases are a nice foot in the door, but that's all they are."

Pitfall 2: It's Not the Gospel

John Hanchette, a Pulitzer Prize-winning national correspondent for Gannett News Service, has used databases to great advantage, but he warns of their dangers.

"Reporters are too likely to consider it gospel because they see it on the screen," says Hanchette, who doesn't trust statistics found in databases, particularly when they originate from a press release. "People are realizing now that you can attract a

Reprinted by permission of Penny Williams, Ph.D., Assistant Professor, School of Journalism and Mass Communication, St. Bonaventure University.

print or electronic reporter's attention with imposing numbers."

Lynn Davis, a professional researcher with ABC News' Research Library in Washington, D.C., says she always checks numbers. "No one who is a good researcher will go only with a number out of another article. For me, it's never that final—I usually want to see it backed up some other way."

Davis says the technology has reached the point where even the most experienced investigative reporter should rely on a professional researcher to determine whether information gleaned from a database is safe to air or print. The field of facts available on databases has so many layers that it's a rare reporter who can master it without taking too much time from other reporting duties.

"There are plenty of reporters who are good researchers," she says, "but I also think there are times when people don't rely on the professional who has the knowledge to use the things correctly." An experienced reporter might not have used the database enough, Davis says, "to research well—to research efficiently, to get a good answer in good time and not cost a lot of money. They also probably might not have an awareness of disadvantages of certain sources."

Over time, she says, a researcher who repeatedly makes similar types of searches comes to know the strongest sources.

What can journalists do when their organization doesn't have a professional researcher? Davis suggests using the database frequently to become familiar with it, but "if they're totally on their own, I think they have to be aware of the fact that databases are not information that's perfect."

If you have connections with other bureaus, or even other radio or television stations, you might contact their librarians or researchers to check a fact, she suggests.

"The other thing, if they're in a small market and they have [just] one database, is to insist that the vendor" be available to answer questions, she says.

Pitfall 3: Knowing the Boundaries

Mastering all of the database services—and the boundaries, strengths, and weaknesses that separate them—can be a challenge.

Walker of ABC News is among those electronic journalists learning that one service does not do it all. "I though you'd do a search on NEXIS, and you'd get every newspaper in the country. Not so. If you want to get the *San Jose Mercury News,* I have to get it off of America Online. . . ."

Among the major online commercial database services are LEXIS/NEXIS, owned by Mead Data; Dialog, owned by Knight-Ridder; and Dow Jones News/Retrieval, owned by Dow Jones & Co.

Which is best? Depends on what you're looking for.

Dialog, for example, has the full text articles from thousands of journals and newspapers, including all Knight-Ridder papers; databases of article citations from thousands of magazines; the texts of books such as "Who's Who in America" and the "Encyclopedia of Associations"; and information from government agencies.

LEXIS/NEXIS also has full text articles from thousands of magazines, journals, and newspapers. The NEXIS service's main strength is that it has exclusive access to full text articles from *The New York Times.* The LEXIS service's part of LEXIS/NEXIS has the full texts of legal resources, court decisions, and legislative records.

Dow Jones News/Retrieval has the full text of many newspapers, including *The Wall Street Journal* and information from the Dow Jones News Wire.

In addition to online commercial databases, there are also electronic bulletin boards. The main difference between a commercial database and an electronic bulletin board is that users can interact with electronic bulletin boards; they can ask questions and get answers, leave messages, have conversations with other users. Commercial electronic bulletin boards such as CompuServe and America Online also can provide users access to full texts of newspaper articles not found in major databases.

The plus side of using an electronic bulletin board is the cost. It's cheaper than using a commercial database. The minus side, says Davis, is that it might be harder to find what you want, unless you're specific in your search. The electronic bulletin boards don't have what Davis calls "proximity searching."

With NEXIS or Dialog, says Davis, "you can ask for one key [search] word within a certain number of words from another key word. And that is just perfection in searching, because if you're good at it, you can guess where [the word] should be, and instead of pulling up 900 articles on a subject, you'll pull up 23. That's a good search, usually."

Pitfall 4: Finding the Right Words

If you put the wrong words into the database, you might not find what you're looking for. This takes a practiced instinct.

"It's the same problem you have in doing any original search," Davis says. "If you're using a database that has abstracts in it, they may not have used the words that you are told are in the full article."

For example, in searching for stories on guns, "it can be guns, it can be firearms, it can be handguns, it can be pistols, it can be assault weapons," Davis says. "If you don't cover your bases, you might miss something."

The same applies to corrections. "Corrections get entered in after the fact," Davis notes. While corrections are usually attached to the original article, a journalist might not find the correction if he does not return to that source, Davis says.

Pitfall 5: A Limited History

Most databases have information going back to 1980, Davis says, and a few have gone into the 1970s. This poses real problems if you're trying to research something that happened or was written earlier.

Marsha Bartel, senior producer for the investigative unit of WMAQ-TV in Chicago, recalls a recent story that sent her back to the books for data from World War II. "We just did a story on mustard gas testing, and all of that [information] was in the library's archive system. It was just like going back to college and digging through the library."

When ABC's Walker was with *Nightline,* he did a piece on what it would have cost in material and casualties if the United States had invaded Japan with troops instead of dropping the atomic bomb on Hiroshima and Nagasaki in 1945. "That required us to go back into the Library of Congress and to get whatever documents, magazines, newspaper articles, periodicals, military journals from those times that [used] intelligence reports that had been declassified," he says.

"I rely on databases as a launching point," Walker says. "That's where they give you an extraordinary leg up. Because as a launching base, you get all sorts of potential sources that you can call. I think that's the most important tool that they provide."

Article Review Form at end of book.

Gaining access to government documents, data and files is part of a journalist's job, yet how often do journalists consider the views and job responsibilities of the gatekeepers in government offices? The following article, written by a staff member of a county government manager's office, offers a look into those views. Sherry L. Horton explores these critical questions: When does access violate the privacy of the individual? How should access fees be determined? And who really owns the data kept on file by government officials?

"The Widest Possible Access":

Wake county's approach to computerized records, open government, and privacy

Sherry L. Horton

The author has been on the staff of the Wake County Manager's Office since December, 1991.

Wake County is caught in a dilemma. To provide its wide array of services—many of them required by law—the county collects huge volumes of information about its residents. The law says most of that information is public. Many citizens, however, believe information about themselves and others should be private. To make the issue even more complex, technology is making it ever easier to get to and disseminate stored information.

Wake is not alone. All local governments collect and maintain data about their residents simply for the purpose of providing services. Yet, once governments have the data, they may be called upon to make it available for commercial purposes, to analyze it in painstaking ways, or otherwise to invest time and effort in preparing it for somebody else's purposes. Who is to have access to the information storehouses of local governments, how easily, how cheaply, and for what purposes?

Though Wake is not alone in the dilemma, it is in the lead in the solution. This article looks first at North Carolina's Public Records Act, then at the issues it poses, and finally at Wake County's new policy on public access to computerized information.

The Law

The North Carolina Public Records Act[1] is broad and sweeping.

Its whole thrust is to make government information available to the public, except for particular kinds of information that the law specifically makes private, such as elements of county employees' personnel files. A 1992 decision of the state supreme court[2] emphasized the scope of the Public Records Act by expressly holding that all records in the hands of the state or local government are public unless a specific provision of law provides otherwise.

Further, the act includes information of just about every kind, regardless of the form in which it is recorded. The law covers "all documents, papers, letters, maps, books, photographs, films, sound recordings, magnetic or other tapes, electronic data processing records, artifacts or other documentary material, regardless of physical form or characteristics, made or received pursuant to law or ordinance in connection with the transaction of

From Sherry Horton, "The Wildest Possible Access: Wake County's Approach to Computerized Records, Open Government, and Privacy" in *Popular Government*, Vol. 58, No. 3, Winter 1993. Reprinted by permission of the Institute of Government, The University of North Carolina at Chapel Hill.

public business by any agency of North Carolina or its subdivisions."[3] A 1981 North Carolina Court of Appeals decision makes clear that records that are to be public include not only those that the government is required by law to keep, but also those "kept in carrying out lawful duties," even if not strictly required.[4]

The law's direction is unmistakable. Information that the government collects belongs to the public and is available for the public to see, copy, and use.[5]

The Huge Volume of Information: An Example

Wake, like all local governments, collects information for many different purposes. The tax assessor alone, for example, collects and maintains a mass of information in carrying out his duties. Each piece of property in the county is identified by its address, legal description, owner's name, and owner's address. All this data is maintained simply for the purpose of identifying who is responsible for the taxes on the property. In addition, information regarding property acreage and buildings is maintained in order to assess their worth. Information about a building includes details regarding design and style, exterior walls, roof type, floor and wall finishes, heating and air-conditioning systems, plumbing fixtures, and even the types of kitchen appliances inside. All of these details aid the assessor's office in determining the proper tax value to place on the property. And, because this information is all obtained and maintained in carrying out the tax assessor's lawful duties and is not specifically exempted by statute, it is, by law, public information.

More information is added to the public record as the revenue collector maintains files on the amount of taxes paid, due, or past due on each piece of property; on foreclosure proceedings; and on liens. These are all records "kept in carrying out lawful duties," and are public information.

The Geographic Information Services Department adds another layer to the record by maintaining maps of the entire county. This department maintains maps of property lines, administrative districts, voting precincts, townships, and topography, among others.

Then the register of deeds' information can be added to the total. Clearly, Wake County maintains a mammoth amount of tax and property information—just as do other local governments throughout North Carolina and the United States.

Concerning such information, the North Carolina Public Records Act requires the following: "Every person having custody of public records shall permit them to be inspected and examined at reasonable times and under his supervision by any person and he shall furnish certified copies thereof on payment of fees as prescribed by law."[6]

The Issues

Does easy public access threaten privacy? Not so long ago, prior to the information age, the tasks of collecting and maintaining these volumes of data were laborious and time consuming. However, the advent and wide use of computers within government agencies have made the job of collection and maintenance much more manageable. Also not so long ago, retrieving any particular piece of information could be equally laborious and time consuming. But now computers have made such retrieval easier than before and have made possible the analysis of information at a level impossible in earlier times. In short, computers have created an easy and efficient way to provide data to the public.

In its early stages, however, the computerization of public records could have been seen as a legitimate barrier to access. From the late 1960s, when such computerization was begun, through the late 1970s, when public-access terminals were first made available in Wake County, most people had little or no experience with the new technology and were hesitant to use it.

Now, however, computerized records can be made easier for the public to reach. Increasing numbers of people have had some degree of exposure to computers through their work or leisure activities and are more adept at using them. Many counties—including Mecklenburg, Catawba, and New Hanover—now allow the public to view computerized records in terminals in the county offices. Some new software packages allow users of these public terminals to quickly sort and analyze data on their own. Additionally, some counties-Mecklenburg and New Hanover among them—now have dial-in services which allow citizens in their homes or businesses to get access to the public information stored in government computers.

In fact so many people have personal computers, or access to them, that some groups worry that the mere existence of government databases poses a threat to citizens' privacy. The North Carolina Technological Information Study[7] commissioned by Governor Martin, which was released in June of 1992, concluded that computer access to government databases is quickly becoming a threat to privacy in North Carolina.[8] The study suggested enacting a Right to Privacy Law to expand and more clearly define the kinds of government records that are to be exempted from the Public Records Act and to establish a state commission to settle disputes over what is public and what is not.

Wake County Information Services Director Russ Goff says that codifying the laws relating to public records and individual privacy would be helpful. Citing statutory provisions which preserve the confidentiality of medical records, mental health records, and other records such as those relating to government employees, Goff says, "The law is generally clear regarding which government-collected and-maintained information is and is not available to the public. The problem is that the exemptions are currently spread throughout the statutes."

Does easy interagency sharing of information threaten privacy? Privacy concerns also come into play when various agencies share information. Often the information that agencies share may be necessary to their work, but it may not qualify as a public record. For example, revenue collectors often try to obtain access to any databases available to locate the assets of delinquent taxpayers, such as Employment Security Commission (ESC) records where they may find a trail to wages that can be garnished. Much of the information that the revenue collectors find in these ways, such as a citizen's place of employment and daytime phone number, is not in a strict sense relevant to records maintained regarding the amount of taxes paid or owed on a piece of property. But the revenue collectors obtain this information from the ESC and use it for the purpose of collecting taxes. So is it public or private?

How much should the government charge for access? Once it is determined whether information is public or private, there is the issue of cost. Should governments provide information to the general public free of charge, or should they charge a fee? What about businesses that use the information to make a profit? If there are fees, should they be based on the cost of disseminating the information or on the cost of collecting and maintaining the database?

Many governments have discouraged public access to computerized information either through limited facilities that prevent access or through prohibitive user fees. For example, Guilford County is currently being sued for attempting to charge the *Greensboro News and Record* five cents per record for property tax listings. This amounts to $8,200 for the entire database.

Other counties, however, have been proactive in structuring themselves to handle information requests as part of their daily routines. No matter which approach a government uses, the issue of public access to computerized public information can no longer be ignored.

Wake County's Statement of Direction Regarding Public Access to Computerized Information

The following statement of direction is adopted by the Wake County Board of Commissioners to provide planning guidelines for future automation development and to assure full public access to public information retained or processed by computer within the County.

Wake County is desirous of providing the widest possible access to public records and information stored in computers and on magnetic media to a wide spectrum of the general public, regardless of the purpose or end use. Consistent with the principle of first providing resource support to those agencies and interests for whom electronic data is captured and maintained, and for whom annual operating budgets have been appropriated; and consistent with the provisions of the public record laws of North Carolina as well as personal privacy issues; it is the intention of Wake County to:

- Facilitate public access to public records contained on, or processed by, computers to the maximum extent possible, within the limits of annual operating budgets.

- Make available magnetic copies of public information contained in County computers at cost of copy, not to include recovery of development or acquisition costs.

- Proliferate, share, coordinate and support computerized data files, resources and interests among and between the municipal, local and state government agencies and functions within Wake County.

- Provide special information research, consultation, and programming on a cost recovery basis, without impact to normal service delivery to authorized County functions.

- Assure equal access and use of computerized information to both special interests, capable of paying for the additional costs associated with "customized" handling of informational requests, and the general citizenry of the County.

- Assure the confidentiality of client records, personnel records and other records mandated by state or federal law to be so protected.

Adopted by the Wake County Board of Commissioners December 16, 1991.

One County's Response

Public Access

Wake County began providing free public-use computer terminals with access through the mainframe to databases in the tax assessor's office and the revenue collector's office in the 1970s, and to databases in the register of deeds' office in the early 1980s. However, even with these provisions, requests for public records increased at a rate that strained existing staff and resources.

As a result the director of Information Services, the director of Geographic Information Services, the tax assessor, and an assistant county manager began looking for ways to improve service delivery. In addition to relieving the stress on staff and resources, the group wanted to move beyond a basic level of service and actively promote access to county records. In the process, it wanted to create a decisive policy so that all departments would be clear on how to handle requests for information.

In December of 1991, prompted by this staff work, the Wake County Board of Commissioners approved a Statement of Direction Regarding Public Access to Computerized Information (see page 13*). This policy includes provisions for facilitating access, assuring equal access, sharing information within the county and with other governmental agencies, and providing copies of information at the cost of printing it. The policy also includes provisions for ensuring the confidentiality of clients, personnel, and other records as mandated by state or federal law.

Most notably, the Wake policy encourages providing access to information "regardless of the purpose or end use" intended by the user.

Since the approval of the policy, several programs have been implemented to facilitate access to and sharing of information. The most expansive aspect moves the county beyond providing public-access terminals in county offices to providing dial-in access to the county's mainframe, available to any caller from any location. Currently, Wake has four dial-in lines so that anyone with a computer, a modem, and compatible software can access the mainframe twenty-four hours a day. Two additional general-access dial-in lines can be easily added should they be needed, and the county is looking at ways to provide access to the mainframe to more than six users at once.

Using these phone lines, people are able to get access to either the county's public databases or the county's electronic mail and bulletin-board system. The databases so far include the records of the tax assessor, the tax collector, and the register of deeds. They do not include information about the clients of the county's social services or public health departments, or about personnel.

To date the dial-in service has been provided on request but not actively promoted. The county currently is upgrading its computer hardware and software to ensure that demands for public information will not disrupt the daily work of county employees. In late 1993, once the county is prepared to handle an even larger load of requests, a campaign will publicize the kinds of information available and the various ways and costs of getting access to it.

Usage of the county's dial-in lines increased significantly between late 1991 and late 1992 (see Figure 1*). Goff expects the usage to increase significantly again in mid-1993, when the register of deeds' records from 1974 to 1990 are added to the database. A new Geographic Information Services property-identification system should also increase the number of citizens interested in using the public-access terminals and dial-in services.

Dial-in lines allow people to get access to public information when it is convenient for them to do so. It eliminates the need for them to come to downtown Raleigh, pay to park, and wait to be served. It also relieves some of the demand on county employees who would have to wait on these citizens or provide the information to them over the telephone.

To illustrate: the Wake County Tax Assessor's office fields about 3,000 informational requests by phone each month. That number has held steady for the last several months, though dial-in mainframe usage has increased over the period. Had those dial-in users been calling the assessor's staff rather than the mainframe, there may have been a need for more phones and additional staff.

In an effort to provide the media with more timely knowl-

*Not included in this publication.

edge of meetings and other important county news, the county invited representatives of all area media outlets to obtain passwords and take a class in order to get access to the county's electronic mail system. The service and the class are offered at no cost to the user, other than the cost of his or her own computer equipment and any phone charges.

Dial-in lines also facilitate data-sharing among Wake County departments, as well as among the county departments and agencies of other government units. Sharing data allows governments to reduce duplication of data collection, thereby reducing costs. It also facilitates joint planning and better relations among local governments.

Special Requests

As progressive as Wake's policy is, the county is still wrestling with the issue of special-service requests. A citizen (or a business) may ask the county staff to manipulate county records in order to generate information that the county itself has no need for, but that the citizen or business wants to use, perhaps for commercial purposes. It is clear that the Public Records Act does not require the county to create documents or compile information in this way—the law merely requires access to documents and compilations of information that already exist. The county, in keeping with the spirit of the Statement of Direction Regarding Public Access to Computerized Information, wants the information in its computer storage to be as useful to the public as possible, "regardless of the purpose or end use."

Still, with budgets getting tighter and the proviso in the Statement of Direction that these services fall "within the limits of annual operating budgets," it is difficult for the county to provide a high level of service in this area without compromising day-to-day operations.

The solution has been for county employees to conduct special searches on a time-available, first-come, first-served basis. But if the special request requires extensive time, or if the staff is fully engaged in pressing county business that cannot be laid aside, the person making the request is offered two choices. He or she may purchase a copy of the entire database at just the cost of the magnetic tapes—$20.00 each for the five-tape set. Or he may be given the names of several commercial enterprises that have themselves purchased the entire database and will manipulate it, for a fee, as the customer wants.

For the searches the county staff itself handles, the customer pays only for the materials—the paper, the computer ribbon, diskettes, etc.[9] The Wake County Board of Commissioners and County Manager Richard Stevens have chosen not to try to recover the costs of data collection, hardware, or software necessary to create or maintain the databases. In the words of Stevens, "That data is public information. It belongs to the public, and they have a right to use it."

Data Sharing

An interconnected computer system for county municipalities is currently being implemented to facilitate the sharing of information advocated in the county policy. Raleigh and Cary already have direct leased-line connections to the county's mainframe through which they share much information with Geographic Information Services. The towns of Zebulon, Knightdale, and Fuquay-Varina have recently gained switched-dial access to the mainframe. They will use this to obtain up-to-date information on the status of building inspections in their jurisdictions. Additionally, the county recently gained access to the State Information Processing System (SIPS). The main benefit of this sharing is timelier, more efficient access to information by all parties. However, sharing this information is also saving untold amounts of money by preventing governments from collecting and maintaining databases for information that other entities already possess.

Comparison with Other North Carolina Local Governments

Although open records are mandated by North Carolina law, few governing bodies actually have been willing to facilitate the flow of information from the government to the citizens. In fact, Wake County may be the only North Carolina local government with a formal policy of providing as much information as possible to its citizens.

"I think it is an excellent policy, very well thought out," says Hugh Stevens, an attorney who often represents the North Carolina Press Association in public access cases. "I have commended it as a model to others studying the issue and trying to formulate their own policies. I have also had occasion to send copies of it to publishers in other states who are fighting to gain access to records which should be open to the public."

Debra Henzey, Director of Communication for the North Carolina Association of County Commissioners, also sees Wake's policy as progressive: "Wake County is the only county in North Carolina that has provided open access to this extent," she says. "I am not aware of any other policies that go this far."

Summary

Wake County's policy is bold in that it meets the issue of access head on. While taking into consideration issues both of the law and of ethics, the policy takes a proactive stance on making public information available to all citizens, regardless of their motives or ability to pay. It also attempts to promote efficiency within government. Wake County's leaders believe that this is the best approach, because providing citizens with proper access to information is the most important step toward having an informed, effective democracy.

Notes

1. N.C. Gen. Stat. (G.S.) Chapter 132.
2. News & Observer Publishing Co. v. Poole, 330 N.C. 465, 412 S.E.2d 7 (1992).
3. G.S. 132-1. A bill introduced in the General Assembly February 10, 1992 (H 121, sponsored by Rep. George Miller, D-Durham), would add provisions to G.S. Chapter 132 specifying, among other things, that public records stored on computers must be made accessible through development of a register clearly explaining what information is in the computer storage and how it may be accessed; that it is the responsibility of the governmental custodian of the record to provide it in any form that the custodian is capable of producing, even if the custodian would prefer another form; and that no public agency may purchase or lease computer equipment that impairs its ability to permit access to public records. The bill would also limit the fees that could be charged for access to computerized information.
4. News & Observer Publishing Co. v. Wake County Hosp. Sys., 55 N.C. App. 1, 284 S.E.2d 542 (1981), cert. denied, 305 N.C. 302, 291 S.E.2d 151, cert. denied, 459 U.S. 803 (1982).
5. "Every person having custody of public records shall permit them to be inspected and examined at reasonable times and under his supervision by any person, and he shall furnish certified copies thereof on payment of fees as prescribed by law." G.S. 132-6.
6. G.S. 132-6.
7. Earl R. Mac Cormac and M. Jane Bolin, *North Carolina Technological Information Study* (State of North Carolina, June 1992). Prepared at the request of Governor James G. Martin.
8. "Most of us are only vaguely aware of the implications arising by our names appearing on mailing lists and dossiers being maintained by private companies and our government. The social cost of the loss of our individual privacy strikes at the very base of the freedom envisioned by our founding fathers." Mac Cormac and Bolin, *N. C. Information Study*, 1.
9. The fee schedule now used covers paper ($0.01 per page), 3.5-inch (1.44 MB) diskettes ($1.00 each), 5.25-inch (1.2 MB) diskettes ($1.00 each), labels ($0.01 per label), nine-track tapes ($20.00 each), and microfiche ($1.60 per fiche and $0.20 per duplicate).

Article Review Form at end of book.

Online newspapers are as individual as their print counterparts. As with print publications, editors and publishers strive to meet their specfic market needs. Some online publications are mirror images of their print versions. Others strive to be quite different. Should original reporting occur for online publications? Or does it make more sense to repurpose content developed for print? The following article examines these and other questions about the identity and role of online papers in relation to their print counterparts.

Newspapers Take Different Paths to Online Publishing

David Shaw
*Times Staff Writer
David Shaw's e-mail address is
david.shaw@latimes.com
Jacci Cenacveira and Rebecca Andrade of
The Times editorial library assisted with the
research for this series.*

Most just repackage their paper without taking full advantage of Web's unique ways to deliver information.

The Internet is the new frontier in American life, the electronic equivalent of the Wild West. In these early years of the World Wide Web, about the only point on which even the pioneers in this still primitive digital culture seem to agree is that virtually everything being done now is so derivative of existing media that in the long run it will either have to change radically or fail.

This is especially true for daily newspapers, most of which are rushing to create online editions, often without a clear vision of how best to use the new medium.

"Newspapers are essentially repackaging what they do in print, and that's a waste of time," says Brock Meeks, editor and publisher of Cyberwire Dispatch, an online news service, and chief Washington correspondent for MSNBC. "If a paper goes online, it should have a different product than its print product."

But how different? If it's too different, does it sacrifice the brand-name identity that it spent decades developing—and that could give it a competitive edge in the battle on the Web?

There is no clear agreement among editors on how best to capitalize on—but not be cannibalized by—this powerful new medium. This is a problem both on such legal and ethical issues as copyright and plagiarism, and on the even larger question of how to maintain the core function, values and identity of a newspaper while taking advantage of the interactivity, synergy, graphic display and unlimited space the Internet offers.

Big-name newspapers are taking widely varying approaches to online publication. Even common ownership doesn't ensure a common approach; the New York Times and the Boston Globe are owned by the New York Times Co., but they have strikingly different Web sites.

"Our site is very much the New York Times," says Kevin McKenna, editorial director of the New York Times Electronic Media Co. "Theirs is very much Boston"—not the Boston Globe newspaper, but Boston, the city.

The Globe's Web site, unlike the New York Times and the vast majority of other online newspa-

---

From David Shaw, "Newspapers Take Different Paths to Online Publishing" in *Los Angeles Times,* June 17, 1997. Copyright © 1997 Los Angeles Times.

pers, doesn't look like its parent paper and is not named after it. It is called boston.com, and it includes content not only from the Globe—which originated, organized and anchors the site—but from more than 30 other Boston affiliates, ranging from other newspapers, magazines, radio and TV stations to museums, libraries, the local ballet and symphony orchestra, the Better Business Bureau and regional weather and traffic services.

"We decided we wanted to be the gateway to our region for news and information about our region," says Lincoln Millstein, vice president for new media at the Globe.

When a hurricane began moving up the East Coast last winter, boston.com was able to supplement Globe and wire service reporting with audio feeds from radio station WBZ and video clips from television station WHDH so that online users could "see and hear what was happening in Georgia before the storm got near here," says Gina Maniscalco, executive director of boston.com.

As with most newspaper Web sites, there is little or no Globe reporting done specifically for boston.com. But the staff of boston.com does supplement what's in the paper. When the Globe published a series of articles in March on "Hidden Massachusetts"—the "poverty, abuse, violence and desperation" in rural Massachusetts—boston.com put up databases that enabled residents in each of the state's 351 communities to find local statistics on everything from income and unemployment statistics to welfare caseloads, sex offender registration and child abuse complaint rates.

Online publication of such ambitious projects can give much wider exposure and recognition to a local or regional newspaper like the Globe. The printed edition of the Globe circulates almost exclusively in New England—mostly in Massachusetts—but 27% of the people who use boston.com live outside New England.

"Suddenly," Millstein says, "the Boston Globe has an entirely new audience, far beyond where trucks can take the paper."

Similarity Between Print, Online Image

The New York Times already has the kind of national audience that the Internet makes possible for the Globe and other papers. The Times sells about 40% of its newspapers outside its primary market area, so with the New York Times on the Web (the official name of the paper's site), the Times is not seeking to extend its reach so much as it is seeking to extend its brand name into a new medium for the new millennium.

Toward that end—and in direct contrast to boston.com—the Web site for the New York Times probably resembles its print counterpart more than does any other major newspaper site.

"We want it to feel and look like the New York Times," McKenna says.

The New York Times is generally recognized as the best and most authoritative paper in the country, and people who run the paper want to take advantage of that reputation in their online edition.

The New York Times on the Web provides little original reporting—apart from the coverage of cyberspace in its daily CyberTimes section—but virtually the entire news and editorial content of the printed paper is available online without charge (except for international readers, who pay $35 a month). The Sunday magazine is not yet online, the bridge and chess columns and the crossword puzzle are available in a package for $9.95 a year, and the restaurant reviews are available through a separate Times site on America Online.

In April, the Sunday Book Review was added to the New York Times on the Web—and expanded upon. The site has 50,000 reviews dating back to 1980, and readers of a particular book review can find online reviews of other books by the same author, as well as articles on and interviews with that author—some of them gathered together in the original, multimedia biography "Life & Times" that the site puts up every week. Through RealAudio—and in cooperation with various organizations—the New York Times on the Web also makes available online readings by many authors, ranging from Vladimir Nabokov to Stephen King.

Ironically, in a newspaper known primarily for its text rather than its graphics, many of the online forums the Times conducts are organized around original, online photo essays on such subjects as the war in Bosnia to the landless workers in Brazil.

Earlier this year, Editor & Publisher, the trade magazine of the newspaper industry, named the New York Times on the Web the best overall online newspaper service among papers with more than 100,000 circulation. Editor & Publisher also said the New York Times on the Web had the best editorial content of any online paper in that size category.

The Times has not yet made its archives available online, largely because previous contracts under which the Times sells access to its archives to other online services have been very lucrative, says Bernard Gwertzman, editor of the New York Times on the Web. But negotiations now underway should bring at least a year's worth of the paper's archives to its Web site by late summer.

While the New York Times is relying on its reputation as the country's newspaper of record and on its long tradition of general excellence and comprehensiveness to sustain it in the new medium, many other newspapers are trying to carve out specialized niches for their online editions.

Thorough Integration of 2 News Media

The Wall Street Journal, online as in print, is the preeminent specialized daily newspaper. But the Journal is "special" in more than its focus on the subject of business. Among other things, the Journal has integrated its print and online editions more thoroughly than most other papers. Editors even reconfigured the newsroom to include the staffs of both editions.

"Being that close, people [from the print staff] will come over and say, 'Did you see this?' and 'We're working on that,'" says Neil Budde, editor of the paper's online edition (officially known as the Wall Street Journal Interactive Edition). "Shortly after we launched, the print side said they were doing a story with a lot of documents on the tobacco industry, and we put the entire text of the documents online."

The Journal Interactive Edition has also published the full text of many government economic reports that a print newspaper would have to ignore or, at best, excerpt.

Paul Steiger, managing editor of the Journal, says it is still "relatively rare" for a reporter on the print Journal to write a story exclusively for the online edition, but there have been "notable exceptions." As at many other papers, online editors do attend the paper's daily news conference, and several Journal columnists appear online regularly to answer questions and participate in chat sessions with readers.

"We've had amazing cooperation for the print edition, more than I expected," says Tom Baker, business director of the Wall Street Journal Interactive Edition, and he attributes that in large measure to the attitude of Peter Kann, the publisher of the Journal, who made it clear from the beginning that "the online edition is the Journal, not some strange project."

There isn't much original reporting in the Journal's online edition yet, Budde says, but he expects that to change as the edition matures. Even now, because the printed Journal only publishes Monday through Friday, there have been times when editors put a story online Saturday to avoid being beaten by the competition and having to wait until Monday to catch up.

The Dallas Morning News created quite a stir this year when it did something even more unusual. The paper got an exclusive story reporting that Timothy J. McVeigh has allegedly claimed responsibility for the Oklahoma City bombing, and it published the story on its Web site on a Friday afternoon rather than waiting to put it in the Saturday paper and risk being scooped by other media.

Newspapers are reluctant to, in effect, scoop themselves this way, but some East Coast papers now routinely take that chance, putting the next morning's paper online late the previous night, early enough for editors on the West Coast to see those stories, have their reporters scurry for new information and match the stories in their morning editions.

But Dow Jones, the Journal's parent company, has long had its own worldwide news service, as well as overseas editions of the Journal, "so we've been struggling with this problem for years," Steiger says.

The Journal is different from most other newspapers in several other areas that have enormous implications for online publishing. Because it doesn't publish much classified advertising, Baker says, the fear of losing that revenue was not the "driving force" behind the Journal's online venture as it has been for most other newspapers.

"We wanted to see if we could reach a crowd of readers that we hadn't reached before," he says, "primarily young readers with our [upscale] demographics who didn't read our paper every day."

So far, he says, that's what's happening: "Two-thirds of our subscribers on the Web are not print subscribers. . . . The median age of our Web subscribers is 40. In print, it's 52."

Of course, it's early yet, and those numbers are based on a relatively small sample. The online edition has about 100,000 subscribers; the circulation of the printed Journal is 1.8 million.

But those 100,000 are paid subscribers, providing about 40% of the revenue for the online edition. (The fee is $49 a year—$29 for subscribers to the printed edition—compared with $175 for a printed subscription.)

One of the few online papers to charge for subscriptions, the Journal has substantially more paid subscribers than other major papers have free subscribers. The New York Times estimates that it has 80,000 users "on a good day," the Boston Globe figures it averages about 73,000 users, the Los Angeles Times about 50,000.

Because so many online sites are free, in keeping with the basic culture of the Web, there is considerable doubt that most people will pay to read a newspaper online. But Dow Jones has long charged customers for some online material—information from its Dow Jones News Retrieval Service, for example—so "our prejudice was to charge readers," Baker says.

Looking at Sites as Revenue Sources

Although no one has quite figured out yet how to advertise effectively on the Web, most newspaper and magazine executives—and most Internet professionals—think advertising will provide most of the revenue for online publications, much as it now does for traditional media.

Most newspaper executives are also looking at other online sources of revenue, including the development of electronic Yellow Pages and the possibility of serving as intermediaries in various consumer transactions. Most also believe they can charge for stories from their archives (as many papers already do), as well as for various other special services, features and/or personalized editions.

"We know those will be significant revenue streams down the pike," says Peter Winter, president of Cox Interactive Media, a subsidiary of Cox Newspapers of Atlanta, publisher of the Atlanta Journal and Constitution, "but we expect to make most of our money from advertising."

Although most online papers operate within the structural framework of their parent newspapers, Cox Interactive Media is an independent subsidiary of Cox Newspapers, "the only way," Winter says, "to have a self-supporting business and avoid having a product that reflects a traditional media sensibility."

Its first site, Access Atlanta, combines a city guide, profiles of local businesses, chat rooms, a travel guide and news from the Cox newspaper and radio and television stations in town. Cox has a similar service in Austin, Texas, and expects to be operational in 10 or more areas—including Orange County, San Diego and San Francisco—by the end of summer.

With its stable of 19 newspapers, half a dozen TV stations, 38 radio stations and one of the nation's largest cable systems, Cox hopes to be operating online city guides in 30 communities by year's end, all of them featuring heavy user participation.

Although the online editions of the major daily newspapers generally draw the most attention, several smaller and medium-size papers are also among the leaders in Internet development.

Nando Times, a pioneering Web site, began as a largely local service with early content provided by the Raleigh News & Observer. But when the paper was purchased by the McClatchy group, Nando shifted its focus. Nando now provides links to all McClatchy papers—including the Sacramento, Fresno and Modesto Bees—and by the end of the summer, says Christian Hendricks, president and publisher of the Nando Times, the site will have several areas of joint coverage with those papers.

But the Nando Times is now primarily a global rather than local or regional site. Its news coverage has a heavy emphasis on national and international events and will soon be continually updated. Thirty percent of the visitors to nandotimes.com live outside the United States.

Like the Cox newspaper sites, the Arizona Daily Star site has made interactivity an integral part of its operation. Visitors to the site can click on stories that interest them to create their own "community front page," and they can participate in online quizzes and polls embedded in the stories they are reading.

"Part of our mission is to provide a publishing platform for the entire community," says Bob Cauthorn, director of new technology for the paper.

Cauthorn says his Web site is already profitable—"meaningfully profitable"—in part because it has created its own Internet service provider, the necessary link between the home computer and the Web, a service generally provided by technology companies or, in some cases, by telephone companies. Users can access the paper's Web site without charge but if they want to contribute to it, either by selecting or commenting on stories for the community front page, they have to do so through the paper's ISP, which costs $20 a month.

Other medium-size dailies with well-regarded Web sites include the San Jose Mercury News, Arizona Republic and Phoenix Gazette, Indianapolis Star/News, Minneapolis Star Tribune and New Jersey Online (which combines the efforts of several

Advance Publications news organizations, the largest being the Newark Star Ledger).

But one of the most interesting experiments in online journalism is being conducted at the Houston Chronicle, which often sends reporters out with digital cameras and high-quality tape recorders to provide original, multimedia stories for its Web site.

One of the online paper's most popular—and most innovative—multimedia features is "Virtual Voyager." Chronicle reporters go out on a wide range of adventures and file multimedia, interactive reports to the paper's Web site along the way. One reporter went to Australia with her daughter. Another went to China. Two other Chronicle reporters traveled Route 66 from Chicago to the West Coast with cameras mounted in the back seat. From the Grand Canyon, they provided 360-degree photos that gave users back home a real feel for the grandeur of the setting.

Web Sites

These are the names and Internet addresses for the primary Web sites mentioned in today's stories:
Arizona Daily Star
http://www.azstarnet.com
Boston Globe
http://www.boston.com
Chicago Tribune
http://www.chicago.tribune.com
Cox Interactive Media
http://www.cimedia.com
CyberWireDispatch
http://www.cyberwerks.com/cyberwire
Dallas Morning News
http://www.dallasnews.com
Houston Chronicle Interactive
http://www.chron.com
Indianapolis Star and News
http://www.starnews.com
Los Angeles Times
http://www.latimes.com
Minneapolis Star Tribune
http://www.startribune.com
Nando Times
http://www.nando.net
New Jersey Online
http://www.nj.com
New York Times
http://www.nytimes.com
Phoenix Newspapers
http://www.azcentral.com
San Jose Mercury News
http://www.mercurycenter.com
Wall Street Journal Interactive Edition
http://www.wsj.com

Article Review Form at end of book.

WiseGuide Wrap-Up

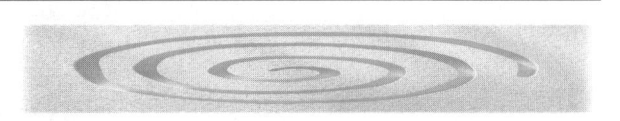

Increasingly the e-beat is journalism's beat. From the feature writer looking at movie trends to the investigative reporter uncovering government corruption, the e-beat is part of journalism's daily life. Like the street beat, it takes time, talent and skills to be effective with online journalism. Editors and reporters who view a mouse as a rodent and a monitor as someone who issues a hall pass still populate many newsrooms. Bypassing the laggards and hooking up with the explorers will create new opportunities for journalists interested in mastering the e-beat.

For beginners, the first step is to become skillful in the tools of the trade. That includes learning to develop good stories by mastering the street-beat skills of researching, interviewing and solid writing. But it now also means harnessing the computer to go beyond word processing and into the rich resources of the online world. Journalism students need to develop skills in Internet searching, database analysis and multimedia applications.

As the preceding articles indicate, the online consumer is looking for a different kind of story. We've seen that the successful e-beat journalist looks to add more depth and exploits opportunities to add other kinds of media into the online story. For example, picking up photos of the *Jupiter* landing off the wire for print publication is pretty tame compared with the online story that integrates actual audio and video. Given these kinds of publishing opportunities, it's no wonder that (borrowing again from Rose Ciotta) the e-beat has moved from the corner of the newsroom to center stage.

R.E.A.L. Sites

The adjacent list provides a print preview of typical CourseWise R.E.A.L. Sites. (There are over 100 such sites at the CourseLink™ Site.) The danger in printing URLs is that Web sites can change overnight. As we went to press, these sites were functional using the URL provided. If you come across one that isn't, please let us know via email at webmaster@coursewise.com. Use your Passport to access the most current list of R.E.A.L. sites at the CourseLinks™ Site.

Site name: Computer-Assisted Research, 3rd ed, by Nora Paul
URL: http://www.poynter.org/car/cg_chome.htm
Why is it R.E.A.L.? As head of the news library at The Poynter Institute, Nora Paul wrote one of the first handbooks for computer-assisted reporting. This is the third edition. Offered is a wealth of information for engaging in the most sophisticated form of reporting around.
Key topics: access issues, computer-assisted reporting, current issues, database searching, desktop journalism, future trends, information access, information retrieval, mass communication, Net usage, online access, online journalism, online newspapers, online searching, reporting skills

Site name: Investigative Reporters and Editors Inc.
URL: http:www.ire.org
Why is it R.E.A.L.? IRE is the premier organization for investigative reporting. This site offers journalism resources, training resources and handouts from conferences. A must look-see for anyone thinking about investigative reporting, good writing and topical issues.
Key topics: careers, computer-assisted reporting, current issues, database searching, desktop journalism, ethics, features, future trends, information access, information retrieval, legal issues, media writing, online newspapers, reporting skills, story strategies

Site name: National Institute for Computer-Assisted Reporting
URL: http://www.nicar.org
Why is it R.E.A.L.? The focus is on computer-assisted reporting in its varied forms. NICAR posts its training activities, its newsletter and information about its database library. Special interest journalism nonprofit organizations maintain home pages on the site.

Key topics: careers, computer-assisted reporting, current issues, database searching, desktop journalism, ethics, features, future trends, information access, information retrieval, legal issues, media writing, online newspapers reporting skills, story strategies

Site name: Student Press Center
URL: http://studentpress.journ.umn.edu/
Why is it R.E.A.L.? Working on your college paper? The Associated Collegiate Press offers links to academic and professional news organizations, story resources, a cartoon collection, style book and expert contacts. A must for the student journalist.
Key topics: carreer, computer-assisted reporting, current issues, desktop journalism, future trends, mass communication, media writing, online journalism, online newspapers, reporting skills

Site name: Federal government information
URL: http://www.fedworld.gov
Why is it R.E.A.L.? This site offers links to almost every government database online. Good information for campus stories and term papers. Invaluable reference material and databases for stories.
Key topics: current issues, legal issues, online access, research

section 3

Online Careers: A Specialty or Recasting the Mold?

WiseGuide Intro

In the online world, publications are reinventing themselves—editors are managers, reporters are producers and artists are graphic designers. Journalists from print backgrounds are planning multimedia products, broadcasters are focusing on how text looks on the screen and the public is demanding interactivity. The boundaries between media forms have blurred.

In this section, we'll meet journalists who have left traditional careers for jobs in new media publications. We'll look at day-to-day online journalism at specific newspapers. And we'll explore the new kinds of job skills needed in an online world. As you read, ask yourself if online journalism is a specialty or a mold being recast.

While exploring the e-beat in Section 2, it was obvious that certain technical skills are needed to be an effective online journalist. According to Steven C. Miller, assistant technology editor for *The New York Times*, the online journalist should know how to work in these environments: word processing, spreadsheets, relational databases, listservs, e-mail, newsgroups and the World Wide Web. Such basic skills enable a reporter to travel the online world in search of sources, to locate rich databases and to identify and reach experts who, in an offline world, may not be within reach. The information can then be sifted, analyzed, reviewed and merged with other information to bring immediate context to developing stories.

Jane Singer, a Colorado State University professor, told her peers at a journalism educators conference: "It is dangerous for journalists, whose job is deemed so crucial to society that it is protected by our nation's highest law, to stand on the sidelines as new technologies emerge, take shape and spread.... [Journalists] must be equipped— both in terms of their mind set and their technological skills—to maintain, practice and strengthen those values in the interactive media environment."

The number of journalists with these kinds of skills increases each year. Higher salaries and the opportunity to be at the forefront of online journalism are attracting people to the field. Job opportunities are expanding at a rapid rate even as newspaper circulation falters. Presently the field appears to be wide open for journalists with the interest, talent and skills.

In the early days of newspapers, magazines, radio and television, it was the pioneers who set the standards, developed the expectations and rewrote the rules to meet the needs of the medium. The online journalists you'll meet in these readings are risk takers cut from the

Key Points

- Develop a clear sense of the job market and what will be expected of entry-level journalists.

- Understand how different publishers are deploying online journalistic talent. Within this context, reexamine your career objectives.

- Examine your definition of a reporter and put it to the test as you read these articles.

"No one can forecast whether multimedia journalism will become just one more specialty, or fundamentally remake the mold. But for newspaper people restless about the future, taking a taste of new media seems wise."
—Charles Stepp

same kind of cloth. They welcome the challenges inherent in breaking new ground and see things that other people can't even imagine. These individuals certainly see their new careers as much more than a quirky specialty.

> **Questions**
>
> 1. Do you agree with Steven Miller's list of the skills needed to be an effective online journalist? What skills do you think you'll need to be a pro?
>
> 2. Why are some publications assigning journalists exclusively to online reporting?
>
> 3. Will you need different skills for an online magazine as opposed to an online newspaper? Would other skills be needed for reporting at MSNBC?

READING 19

Developing a successful career in journalism today takes more than just writing and editing skills. Charles Sessions Stepp's article illustrates why editors are interested in hiring reporters with multimedia skills and related analytical talents. What are you doing to prepare yourself for the online world that's described in the following article? Which publications interest you as a place of employment? Why? Do you think What balance should you strike between developing technical skills and conventional journalism skills? What changes might you make in your career goals after reading this article?

The New Journalist

Carl Sessions Stepp

Carl Sessions Stepp, AJR's senior editor, teaches at the University of Maryland College of Journalism and coaches writing and editing at newspapers. He wrote about the newspaper industry's angst in our October 1995 issue.

When author and college professor Jon Franklin hosted his former editor George Rodgers recently, the two old pals relaxed by the fireplace at Franklin's 50-acre Oregon spread and reminisced about their adventures at Baltimore's late Evening Sun. Then they cruised on to cyberspace, where they're masterminding a new pay-per-read site for literary journalism.

Perhaps they seem unlikely new-age pioneers—Rodgers didn't even own a personal computer when he retired last fall. But they have a Web-load of company. As new forms of journalism expand at a Pentium pace, more and more traditionally trained news hands are converting to jobs that were unimaginable when their careers began.

Not long ago, the typical beginning reporter faced a simple choice: print vs. broadcast. Those options remain. But today's growth area is in multimedia jobs that blur and often obliterate the old boundaries. It's a proving ground forging not just new kinds of journalism but a new species of journalist as well.

Expertise and versatility define the members of this new species more than attachment to one specific medium. They can think and work across the widening spectrum from print to television to new information technologies.

Some are wholehearted outriders on the information superhighway, fleeing mainstream newsrooms they consider constipated and obsolete. But many faithfully keep their old-world ties, just branching out a bit for growth and fun.

The online era demands added skills and innovative ways of looking at the profession.

Above all, whether by accident or calculation, they're positioning themselves to adapt and thrive wherever fickle technology flies next.

The changes already have influenced recruiting for both online and traditional media jobs.

When Associated Press editor Ruth Gersh considers a job prospect these days, for example, she often skims past the cover letter, resumé and references, and zeroes in on another telltale indicator: the applicant's home page.

Gersh, who is developing a new multimedia service for AP clients, demands solid news credentials. But she also looks for signs that candidates can roam comfortably on the cyberbahn.

In the new "technitorial" age, she says, she needs people with a blend of traditional and futuristic skills, who can work imaginatively with the rich swirl of text, photos, graphics, audio and video that multimedia embodies.

"The people who have expressed interest so far," Gersh

From Carl Sessions Stepp, "The New Journalists" in *American Journalism Review,* April 1996. Reprinted by permission of American Journalism Review.

Comic Strips Online

Wherever you find newspapers, you'll also find comic strips—even in cyberspace.

That's the philosophy that drove cartoonist Bill Holbrook, 37, to begin marketing his newest strip, "Kevin and Kell," online last fall.

"I was just looking at the business and where the business was going," says Holbrook. "Newspapers are launching online versions of themselves, and I figured I'd better follow where my clients are going."

Holbrook began publishing comic strips while majoring in illustration and visual design at Auburn. He later served as an artist at the Atlanta Journal-Constitution before launching his first syndicated strip, "On the Fastrack," in 1984; it now runs in about 100 papers. His second strip, "Safe Havens," runs in around 40.

But "Kevin and Kell" runs in no papers. It is produced exclusively for online distribution. About 40 online forums carry it, paying a flat $20 per month for the five-day-a-week strip. (It can be read at www.compuserve.com/kkhome.html, among other places.)

Holbrook says online artistry isn't much different from drawing cartoons for newspapers. He produces "Kevin and Kell" in hard copy and provides it to a partner who scans it onto the Internet.

About the only major difference is that he feels free to use more computerese. "If you're seeing 'Kevin and Kell,'" he figures, "it means you're already online, and you know the language."

In fact, the strip builds in an electronic theme. Kevin is a 37-year-old rabbit who works as systems operator for an online network. Kell, a 29-year-old wolf and Kevin's wife, works as a hunter for Herd Thinners Inc. She's a direct descendant of the Big Bad Wolf.

---

says, "range from very traditional print backgrounds to people who've come up on the broadcast side, the technical side, the photo side . . . people who've done design, even people who've done marketing.

"Of course," she adds, "what I'm looking for is all of this."

Editors across the country tell similar stories. At the Chicago Tribune, online editor John Lux agrees that applicants with a Web page have "a leg up." It shows their curiosity and commitment, much like previous generations of journalists got noticed by writing for any publication that would have them. One of Lux's recent hires worked for an online union paper. Another volunteered to produce a CD-ROM featuring prize-winning photographs.

> **The AP's Ruth Gersh, who is developing a multimedia service, says she needs people with a blend of traditional and futuristic skills, who can work imaginatively with the rich swirl of text, photos, graphics, audio and video that multimedia embodies.**

And while electronic media—online providers, Web sites, CD-ROMs, e-zines, desktop publishing—have fueled the trend, it spills over into the hunt for journalists of all kinds.

Recruiters for Gannett newspapers, for instance, examine online college papers for evidence their alums have the right flair.

"We're hiring more on potential and brainpower and far less on functional skills," says Mary Kay Blake, Gannett's director of recruiting and placement. The idea isn't to identify computer skills per se, but to recognize that computer-literate people often "show clear thinking, strong analytical skills and connective abilities."

No one can yet forecast whether multimedia journalism will become just one more specialty, or fundamentally remake the mold. But for newspeople restless about the future, taking a taste of new media seems wise.

Youth does help, it appears. But a striking number of veterans are enlisting, from celebrities like Michael Kinsley and Linda Ellerbee (both recently lured to online projects) to long-timers from the news trenches.

What kind of world are they encountering? What kind of skills and attributes do they need? And what early lessons have emerged from this potentially momentous migration?

Journalists infiltrating the new media encounter a world that's frantic, exciting and begging for creativity.

Online coverage is everywhere, from a real-time Super Bowl site visited by millions to CNN's multimedia daily news files to prodigious plans for covering the Summer Olympics and the presidential campaign online (see "The Boys on the 'Net," page 40*). The Newspaper Association of America's Web page lists over 150 newspapers with online services.

When you expand the definition to online magazines, the numbers skyrocket—one list counts 811 available e-zines. These online specialty publications range from crude tracts to sophisticated electronic magazines, and the topics and titles have mushroomed, from Bible study to dream interpretation, from Bad Haircut to Dead Pig Digest.

Online coverage of routine news is becoming, well, routine.

When a Groundhog Day snowstorm white-coated the Washington, D.C. area, for instance, the Washington Post's Digital Ink online service signed

*Not included in this publication.

A Farewell to Print

Susan Older didn't leave newspapers mad. Just tired.

"I was beginning to get tired of traditional journalism," says Older, now the managing editor/new content for the Raleigh-based online service Nando.net (http://www.nando.net). "Not because I was such a visionary that I saw the Internet exploding. But because I had been doing it for 20 years. I was just tired of the sometimes tedious process of training new people and getting the news out in the traditional way."

Older's path looked typical for a lifelong print journalist. She had worked for a small magazine and a weekly newspaper and had served as an assistant national editor, health and behavior editor and page one editor for the Life section at USA Today.

Then in 1992 she jumped, transferring into one of parent Gannett's new media divisions to work on a CD-ROM project. Later she became a founding editor of Inter@ctive Week magazine before joining Nando.net early this year.

Her varied background—plus the fact that she's "been through a lot of battles over journalism"—gives her the confidence to step into the unknown.

What was hardest about adjusting to cyberjournalism?

"It would be easy to say the most difficult thing is learning the technology, but that's not true," Older says. "The hardest part is giving up the gratification of daily reinforcement of what you do."

Online, she adds, "you may not have the gratification of seeing it on paper every morning. But you are updating the news all day long. It's even more gratifying—except it's not on paper."

---

on before dawn. Its news team tallied snow totals, updated forecasts, selected photos—and rummaged up a recording of Robert Frost reading his snow poetry to include as a "hot link."

Such is breaking news, Internet style: crossmedia, sometimes traditional, often cyber-clever . . . and unfailingly interactive. Digital Ink, for instance, coordinated minute-by-minute snow reports (under the whimsical headline, "Has anyone seen a snow plow yet?") from neighborhood "correspondents," subscribers who messaged in to the central database.

Charles Shepard, 41, is a decorated reporter who joined Digital Ink last year after 18 years with newspapers. Shepard led the Charlotte Observer to a Pulitzer Prize covering the financial troubles of televangelist Rev. Jim Bakker. Later at the Washington Post he helped break the story about sexual misconduct by former Sen. Bob Packwood.

> "You have to be able to admit that the old way of journalism—hundreds and hundreds of years—is changing," says Susan Older, managing editor/new content for Nando.net, a Raleigh-based online service.

Now Shepard is online manager for projects at Digital Ink, where he senses the need for both proven news judgment and imaginative thinking.

"If you think of the people who are most successful," Shepard says, "it's people with strong news instincts, but they also have a feel for the medium and how it's different. They aren't just print journalists wearing slightly different clothes. They can use new media in different ways."

A parallel view comes from Susan Older, 47, managing editor/new content for Nando.net, the widely praised online service begun by Raleigh's News & Observer. She looks for good journalists to begin with, but she also likes people who are "risk takers and renegades."

"What makes some journalists just sit in the newsroom, and what makes some break out?" asks Older, who first drifted from newspapers to a CD-ROM project in 1992. "You have to be able to admit that the old way of journalism—hundreds and hundreds of years—is changing."

Such a renegade and risk taker is Jon Franklin, 54, who won two Pulitzers for Baltimore's Evening Sun and now teaches writing at the University of Oregon.

Franklin moderates an online literary journalism discussion group, WriterL, and, with George Rodgers, 55, is creating Bylines, an online service to market in-depth articles and stories. A long-time science fiction buff, Franklin began pushing for computers from the moment he showed up in the typewriter-driven newsroom. He's considered himself a pioneer ever since.

People like himself "want novelty," Franklin says. "Sometimes they get into trouble, sometimes they don't. Pioneering is one of the constructive things you can do with that impulse. . . . It's intellectual swashbuckling."

Beyond this open-minded, go-for-it attitude, the new species of journalist needs other qualities as well. Editors and managers see some common traits in the new breed:

➤ They have a multimedia outlook. If anything characterizes the new age of journalism, it will be the need to integrate text, images, sounds and video into understandable packages.

Repeatedly, editors interviewed for this article stressed

An Online Entrepreneur

It was the 1994 San Francisco newspaper strike that led David Talbot to leap "out of the burning building" and into the Internet.

The burning building was the newspaper business, where he had been arts and features editor of the San Francisco Examiner. For Talbot, the strike "was the culmination of a downward spiral—declining morale in the newsroom, fewer resources. While things were looking grimmer and grimmer in the newspaper world, there was more and more excitement online."

Today, Talbot, 44, is editor of Salon (http://www.salon1999.com), an online magazine with a full time staff of 15 and ambitions to become an electronic showcase of sophisticated journalism. Launched last November, it's a biweekly but is updated often between issues.

One issue included Alexander Cockburn writing about Pat Buchanan, an interview with humorist/author Al Franken and a look at how teenage girls are "recharging kids' TV."

Talbot is anything but a high-tech junkie. He didn't own a decent computer when he left the Examiner. But he had an "entrepreneurial urge" to create a magazine. And the Internet offered the advantage of far lower start-up costs.

With seed money from investors, Talbot and his colleagues opened Salon last November. They are still "living off the investment," he says, but they hope, through some creative combination of ads, syndication and corporate sponsorship, to eventually prosper.

Talbot believes that many newspaper forms—columns, reviews, op-ed essays, even comics—carry over nicely to the Internet. Plus they get a boost from its interactivity.

"The greatest part," he says, "is that readers become part of your editorial process."

---

that they were not looking for hackers or techies (except for the jobs that are strictly technical). Mostly, they want journalists who can draw from writing, editing, design, imaging and broadcasting to meld seamless multimedia messages.

"Increasingly, we're looking at people with multimedia backgrounds, people who think visually as well as in the traditional sense," says Laurie Petersen, editor in chief of Media Central, a Cowles online service covering the electronic media.

At the Chicago Tribune's online service, John Lux uses the term "producer" to describe his electronic news editors. "Writing and editing on the Internet is different," he says. "It's no fun to read on the Internet, so what takes the place of colorful writing is images. What editing is on the Web is not word editing but finding ways to use graphics, images and sounds to tell the story."

A key, according to Older, is leaving behind the old world of linear thinking.

"After years of writing stories that go from the beginning to the end, you find yourself creating something that has tendrils in every direction. If you can't break open your brain and think that way—well, what if someone clicks this way or explores that way—it's going to be hard."

➤ They appreciate new technology and how people use it. Shepard of Digital Ink agrees that technical skills aren't paramount, but he does believe new journalists need to appreciate how computers work in order to master their potential. For Shepard, "the single biggest difficulty has been understanding how a database is constructed and how to build or rebuild one."

If you don't "understand the technical dynamics of the product—what's under the hood," says Shepard, it would be like "running a race car team without knowing what the carburetor is capable of."

Mastering the medium also requires knowing how your audience thinks.

Petersen points out that success depends on understanding how to search the vast Internet, how people actually use online machinery and how they think about processing information. All that requires a bit of technical competence and, she says, "a solid grounding in common sense, having a feel for how people go at things."

➤ They have an agreeable online voice and writing style. "Writing is what's important," says Jon Franklin. "Writing, and the ability to see what's going on around you."

Franklin believes that online readers will welcome long stories if they're compelling enough. Bylines, the service he and Rodgers are forming, is based on the assumption that online readers will pay to read extraordinary longer pieces.

Not everyone is sure that they will. Chicago's Lux argues the opposite point firmly. "People who are good writers and know it have to change their mindset that long, elegant stories are good," Lux maintains. "They are no good online, unfortunately. You may only get people for a screenful."

> **"People who are good writers and know it have to change their mindset that long, elegant stories are good," says John Lux of the Chicago Tribune's online service. "They are no good online, unfortunately: You may only get people for a screenful."**

A Double Threat

Laura Williamson got into cyberspace without leaving ink-and-paper space.

As health and welfare reporter for the Atlanta Journal-Constitution, Williamson writes for both the daily paper and its Web site for legislative coverage (http://web.ajc.com/insider).

Electronic journalism wasn't in her plans when she majored in English at Georgetown, mastered in journalism at Maryland, or took reporting jobs in Lynchburg, Virginia, and Annapolis, Maryland. But by her third paper, in Roanoke, Virginia, she had bought a personal computer and was exploring the Internet.

So she wasn't caught off guard when her next paper, the Journal-Constitution, wanted her to go online.

From a reporter's perspective, Williamson says, working for the Web doesn't change her routines much. She keeps separate files for online stories and often takes additional notes, knowing that the Web's more specialized audience can use the extra detail.

And writing for the 'Net, she says, is different from hard news for the paper. It's more conversational, like an essay or a column.

Williamson, 31, enjoys the traditional and online worlds. Like most journalists, she admits she can't predict where fast-changing media will end up, but she's convinced the changes will affect all journalists. While newcomers take naturally to cyberspace and other nontraditional media, Williamson warns that veterans shouldn't ignore them.

"You're missing something if you are not out there," she says, including vital sources, topics and audiences. "If you're a middle-aged reporter and you don't do this, you'll have a tough time."

Others point out that the very notion of length is a print concept. Online text is far less linear. Users have many choices. They can stick with a posting for many pages, or "tunnel" to different levels for more details or completely new topics. They can use hypertext links to leap from site to site, or from text to video to audio.

So, while the length question stands unresolved for now, many editors agree that new writing styles will undoubtedly emerge.

As Cowles' Petersen observes, "You have to be a good writer with a voice. Online writing in particular requires a very alive writing style. It's a more personal kind of thing."

Several writers have discovered that, at least in their infancy, online media encourage more humor and conversational writing than traditional media.

Laura Williamson covers health and welfare for the Atlanta Journal-Constitution. Her job may suggest one direction journalism will take; she writes stories for the daily newspaper and often files different versions for her paper's Web site.

For example, Williamson has been following several health and welfare issues before the Georgia legislature. For the daily paper she writes stories of general interest. But for the Web site she writes longer, more analytical, even more informal pieces, on the assumption, her online audience is already knowledgeable and wants the extra touches.

Williamson thinks the conversational style may keep people moving from screen to screen. "I don't mean flabby writing," she says. "But there's room for a little humor or inside baseball that they would never put in the paper because nobody cares. It's okay to be chatty and okay to be long, but it must be readable."

▶ They are willing to share control with the audience. "Allowing the user to control what they do is very annoying to some journalists, especially newspaper people," says Raleigh's Older. "But the user is taking over. People don't want to be controlled anymore."

Online users not only talk back to journalists (as audiences always have), but they often do so in real time. That two-way process actually shapes coverage, according to Petersen, and new journalists need to both accept, and anticipate, that interactivity. That means reporters, for instance, have to predict audience questions and gather and present information that accommodates them.

Ultimately— and perhaps ironically, given the high-tech drapings—this all may produce a powerful new kind of community journalism, not unlike old-fashioned weekly newspapering.

"This is a very democratic medium that encourages conversation between producers and users, that has room for all the material you can't fit into the newspaper," says Shepard of Digital Ink.

Like many other developments driving today's journalism, this raises questions about how much new material will be strictly

> **Online users not only talk back to journalists (as audiences always have), but they often do so in real time. That two-way process actually shapes coverage, according to Laurie Petersen, editor in chief of an online service covering the electronic media.**

market-driven and how much will reflect editors' concerns about social responsibility. Will new media just feed consumers what they want, or will they devote resources to investigations or serious topics that may have less popularity?

However the mix develops, the potential for reinvigorating community journalism seems high. In fact, Older thinks a stint in community news might be just the thing for the new species of journalist.

"If the Internet is not a community, then tell me what is," says Older, who got her start running a small publication in Bozeman, Montana. "I think community journalism is the best training for doing anything on the Internet, because you find out what community is all about."

So we return to Jon Franklin and George Rodgers, a couple of vets who, as Rodgers puts it, "had our journalistic adolescence at the tail end of the Front Page era."

Now they want to use a new format—the Web—to tell the kinds of meaningful stories they've loved for decades. And they're going at it with true trailblazer spirit.

"A fundamental new journalism?" ponders Franklin. "Oh yes, yes. Probably many of them."

Article Review Form at end of book.

READING 20

Despite a recent change in ownership, *The Raleigh News & Observer's* tradition of excellence in online journalism continues. The *N & O* won a Pulitzer Prize in 1996 for a computer-assisted reporting story on pig farming. What the following article shows is that online journalism isn't just about computer-assisted reporting. Why did the *N & O* become a leader in online journalism? What makes the *N & O* an attractive place to work? How have the *N & O* reporters adapted to new media technologies? How does the paper's Web site interact with its print version?

The Digitized Newsroom

Philip Moeller

Philip Moeller, a former business editor and electronic news editor at the Sun in Baltimore, is a consultant and writer based in West Hartford, Connecticut.

The Raleigh News & Observer shows how powerful databases, online research, and the new approaches to reporting and writing they encourage, are reshaping journalism.

It sounds so simple. Begin with a typical metropolitan newspaper newsroom—perhaps the staff is a little younger than at peer papers, but not noticeably different in most respects. Now, give serious thought to the computer and communication equipment that promises to revolutionize the news, information and entertainment industries. What if staffers could master these machines, making their use routine inside the newsroom rather than merely a topic they write about?

Welcome to the Raleigh News & Observer, one of America's few remaining family-owned newspapers. The N&O, as it's known, has been introducing its reporters to these new tools over the past few years. While its venture is clearly a work in progress, Raleigh offers a comprehensive look at how digitized information and new approaches to reporting and writing stories could reshape the nation's newsrooms.

At the N&O and other technology-friendly papers, the reporter's craft is changing, as are the roles of news librarians and other staff members. Team journalism, although not driven by technology alone, is becoming especially prevalent in newsrooms that make heavy use of computers. And such collective efforts in a digital era are regularly producing definitive stories that can pass muster as social science as well as journalism. The computer, once reserved for big investigative projects, is becoming a commonplace ally of beat reporters doing routine stories.

Readers are using computers and modems, too, and they have become active participants in Raleigh's Internet forays as well as in virtually every online forum involving news organizations. The interactive nature of online communication is changing how stories are reported. Perhaps more important, interactivity may fundamentally change the relationship between journalists and the people they cover.

The editors and reporters at the N&O have thousands of counterparts at papers across the country. Nearly every newsroom is blessed with a cadre of technologically savvy, highly motivated journalists who are trying to pull their institutions into new arenas. But what sets Raleigh apart is the fact that digitized information skills—for using computers, databases, online services—are becoming standard for nearly everyone in the newsroom. There are about 100 computer work stations now available to the roughly 150 professional newsroom staffers at the N&O, and Executive Editor Frank Daniels III says every staff member will have a personal computer by this summer.

From Philip Moeller, "The Digitized Newsroom" in *American Journalism Review,* January/February 1995. Reprinted by permission of American Journalism Review.

Several related developments underscore differences between the N&O newsroom and industry norms:

- The paper's 21-person News Research Department has created a network of databases, many built by N&O staffers, that can be accessed from computer work stations.

- Staffers in news research and in the N&O's 17-person New Media Department write software programs, which are often needed to create research pathways into valuable but inaccessible databases.

- The paper has turned a database that tracks bills in the state legislature into a successful online subscription service, which N&O executives see as a prototype for other profitable ventures.

- The paper is in its third generation of hypertext software, which allows writers on special projects to search their own notes much as they would an outside database.

- The N&O is getting involved with multimedia. The first effort included a series of feature stories in the paper, audiotext offerings on the paper's telephone information service and online stories that included text, audio and video elements. The series was done in collaboration with local TV stations, which aired their own versions of the stories.

- Finally, like a growing number of papers, the N&O has created an electronic version. But instead of affiliating with America Online, Prodigy or another commercial service, it started its own online service and has linked it to the Internet, providing a broad array of information for electronic readers.

The N&O's transformation into the premier digital daily dates to the naming of Frank Daniels III as executive editor in late 1990. The N&O, with roots back to 1865, has been owned by the Daniels family for a century. Josephus Daniels bought the paper in 1894 for $10,000 and ran it for more than 50 years. His grandson, Frank Daniels Jr., is now the publisher.

When Frank Daniels III was appointed to his position, Republican Sen. Jesse Helms was waging a brutal reelection campaign against former Charlotte Mayor Harvey Gantt, the Democratic challenger. The younger Daniels was struck by the Helms camp's sophistication in using computer and communications technology.

"That was the galvanizing factor" in getting the N&O into computers, Daniels says. "The Helms team beat the hell out of the news media. . . . In political campaigns, our competition is not the other media but the campaigns. And since the 1970s, they've been beating us. . . . It made me realize how stupid we were, and I don't like feeling stupid."

Neither did longtime N&O reporter Pat Stith, who took an 18-month sabbatical to, in Daniels' words, "explore what could be done with these tools from a reporting standpoint." Stith worked closely with Lany McDonald, then head of the N&O library. The library became the News Research Department, and has been expanded under McDonald's successor, Teresa Leonard.

Much of the progress at the N&O was sparked in late 1992, when the paper hired two database experts. This was the beginning of a restructuring that doubled the number of employees in the N&O News Research Department and tripled its budget. One of those experts was Dan Woods, a computer science major who, after several years in the computer industry, got a master's degree in journalism. Woods says he had perhaps five counterparts at other papers when he joined the N&O. He estimates there are now about 20 newspaper database editors.

Woods provides N&O reporters with information culled from databases, but he spends most of his time helping to create the large pool of networked databases from which the entire staff can draw. Much of this work, he says, involves the arduous task of writing computer codes and laboriously "cleaning" data so it can be used in the newsroom.

Reporters don't just rely on Woods and his staff, though. Everyone in the newsroom is encouraged to learn computer skills. Further, Stith says, the N&O "decided that computer analysis of databases would not be limited to 'investigative' stories, or even major projects. We intend to benefit from economy of scale. We are going to use databases to create or improve everyday front page stories and second fronts."

Computer literacy is voluntary, but management has made it clear it will grant resources and opportunities to those who learn such skills. To prod its staff, the N&O provides interest-free loans for members who want to buy their own PCs; more than $500,000 has been loaned so far.

> **When he saw the sophisticated way the Helms campaign used computer technology "it made me realize how stupid we were, and I don't like feeling stupid," says Executive Editor Frank Daniels III.**

The paper also keeps track of computer literacy rates: Computer skills are included on formal job performance evaluations.

Most newspapers have introduced computers into the newsroom through small reporting teams, usually composed of investigative project reporters. What sets the N&O apart is the extent to which computer skills are used in daily coverage.

"I haven't seen an effort on the level of Raleigh's anywhere," says Philip Meyer, a professor at the University of North Carolina at Chapel Hill and a pioneer in computer-assisted journalism. Meyer says he prefers the Raleigh model for other newspapers, "but there may not be enough talent available at the price that newspapers have historically been willing to pay."

Still, it's a new era. Many younger journalists are computer literate. Coincidentally, many newsrooms are replacing their aged text-editing systems, which generally can't be used for even simple computing tasks. And a high percentage of these papers will be installing PC-based systems, providing a stimulus to develop new communication tools.

At the N&O, the routine use of computer tools owes much to the paper's efforts to develop and update databases that can provide quick information and context even for spot news. For example, the N&O's Computer-Assisted Reporting Network, called CARnet, contains electronic versions of several phone and public sector personnel directories; economic and demographic information; and extensive data on state and county government property, tax and business records, and motor vehicle information. Another useful database, other than the aforementioned legislative tracking system, is the N&O list of contributors to major state political races. Called the Money Machine, it is updated regularly and can be searched by contributors' names.

Beyond these powerful tools, there's another major distinction between the N&O and other newsrooms, namely the central role played by its news library, now called the News Research Department.

Unlike the newsroom, says Daniels, the news library can serve several masters without ethical or pragmatic conflicts. It can help create and maintain a database on state legislation that reporters find invaluable, for example, and then also help turn that database into a for-profit product sold outside the newspaper. And with revenues from such ventures becoming increasingly necessary to pay for the digital newsroom, Daniels sees the importance of creating an efficient way to do this.

The N&O's Teresa Leonard says that having the resources to assemble and maintain databases has been a major benefit of expanding the News Research Department. "Because of the way we're organizing and keeping track of what's coming in, we're able to keep track of things that otherwise would be too much trouble to keep track of," she says. "It has allowed us to create stories that otherwise wouldn't have been there."

Nora Paul, former library director at the Miami Herald and now director of the news research program at the Poynter Institute, has noted that a number of newsrooms are developing cooperative relationships among reporters, editors and library researchers. "For the possibilities of online research and computer-assisted reporting to be fully and successfully explored," she said in a 1993 speech, "I believe that librarians need to define and enhance their role and that librarians and reporters need to forge a whole new relationship."

Those enhancements include working with reporters and editors to evaluate data sources even before stories have been assigned or defined, doing actual reporting on secondary research sources, training newsroom personnel in database and online searching skills, acquiring and developing databases, and coordinating newsroom information systems. Raleigh is doing all of these things and Paul says its research operations are unparalleled.

One of the major changes made possible by computer-assisted journalism is that newsrooms no longer have to depend on outside sources for information. The day of the story based on two sources and a press release is over.

For example, when the N&O did a story on repeat offenders who clog state and local jails, it "analyzed how many misdemeanants have cycled through the system more than 10 times," explains Metro staff writer Steve Riley. "We found 185 of them. There was no way else to find those people. The old way to do that story is to ask someone at the prison. This way you find them yourself. You don't have to rely on someone else to tell you what news is."

Executive Editor Daniels feels strongly that newsrooms need to be able to define the news, not just reflect self-interested statements from skilled spin doctors. This ability, he adds, will help newspapers maintain their attractiveness as information providers in an era when raw hard news is available from a growing number of electronic news services.

Daniels' comments echo the work of the University of North Carolina's Philip Meyer, who has written extensively about journalists' need to develop statistical and related social science skills. The traditional passive approach of the reporter to covering the news must give way, Meyer believes, with newspapers becoming more comfortable setting the news agenda.

"The old ethic of media passivity encourages most journalists to sit back and let government or special interest groups take over the role of information processor," he says. "For media to rely on interest groups, even public-spirited ones, for information processing is dangerous."

Tom Koch, a writer and consultant, also sees technology changing the traditional relationship between the journalist and his source and, ultimately, the nature of journalism itself.

"Online data technologies empower writers and reporters by providing them with information equal to or greater than that possessed by the public or private official they are assigned to interview," he wrote in his 1991 book, "Journalism for the 21st Century: Online Information, Electronic Databases and the News."

"The effects of this empowerment," he says, "will eventually redefine the form of the news . . . and of public information in general."

If digitized technologies are contributing to changes in the type of journalism practiced in newsrooms, they also seem to be playing a role in how those newsrooms are staffed. That's because journalism is becoming a team sport.

Historically, Meyer notes, reporters were bred to be independent and often isolated observers who were detached from the consequences of their work. They didn't interact much with the communities they covered. They were given a lot of freedom, but not much money. "The economics of the newspaper business therefore pushed the journalist toward the characteristic moral profile: a lone hero wandering from market to market like the archetypal cowboy of the movies, settling scores on behalf of the common man against the rich and the powerful," Meyer said in a 1990 speech.

This profile, however, is at odds with new information technologies, says Meyer. Computer-assisted reporting requires a team approach.

"The new media are team products," he says. "Increasingly, there is less room for the lone-hero, reporter-as-cowboy figure."

Multimedia projects especially demand team efforts. The N&O made its first foray into this uncharted territory last summer with a 16-week series called "North Carolina Discoveries." The series, which focused on state topics, ran in the paper, aired on local radio and television, and was uploaded onto the Internet via NandO, the paper's online service.

This joint effort entailed multiple interviews for the different formats. The participating TV stations did their own interviews while the N&O shot still photographs and gathered its own audio material. These were used for the N&O's own multimedia effort on NandO. The paper also used the audio material on its audiotex information service.

N&O reporter Julie Ann Powers points out that the project required broadcast skills that are unfamiliar to traditional print reporters. "From the very beginning of the process it [the reporting] is different," she says. "I had to think in terms of sound and motion as well as whether it would support a full length story in the paper." Sound, which is not a factor for print stories, proved a major new concern, she says, as did the need to compensate for the lack of visual elements in radio stories and, to some extent, print stories. She needed to pose questions that would elicit answers in a form suitable for recording, she explains, whereas her traditional interview style was much more conversational.

N&O State Editor Ben Estes stresses that the series, which was a "valuable experience," was still a test run. "I view this in a lot of ways as an experiment getting us ready for things to come," Estes says. "Eventually, I want to be able to do this on all stories."

Estes also notes that coordinating all the series' elements was difficult and extremely time-consuming. "The tradeoff," he says, "is that Julie is doing one story a week instead of five, and I'm editing one story a week."

Although multimedia efforts may require new skills and approaches to reporting, the most far-reaching impact of digitized information will likely stem from its interactivity. Readers talk in cyberspace. They become instant critics, sounding boards and easily reachable sources.

> "The new media are team products," says Philip Meyer, a professor at the University of North Carolina. "Increasingly, there is less room for the lone-hero, reporter-as-cowboy figure."

Raleigh's NandO is developing new services to interact with the public. For example, NandO staffers have created NandO Land for children and have made it available for free at local schools. The service will both acclimate teachers and students to the world of online and give the N&O a better idea of how to appeal to a generation that has become increasingly disinterested in traditional newspaper content.

Bruce Siceloff is the newsroom online editor who works with N&O staffers to provide, among other things, a digitized edition of each day's paper. Online journalism and interactivity are new to the paper, Siceloff says. And while he wants newsroom staffers to "start dreaming in different media," he acknowledges that this evolution will require more staff familiarity with online tools, particularly the Internet and its increasingly powerful software aids.

Another way that newsroom types will be "engaged" in the online world, Siceloff hopes, will occur as they find themselves participating in two-way communication with readers. Such interaction is a staple of online life but print journalists generally aren't used to the kind of probing, constant online chatter that fills cyberspace. Siceloff and his counterparts at other newspapers believe this interactivity will have a major impact on the profession.

If the 1990 elections were a major factor prompting the N&O's interest in using technology to bolster its reporting, it might be fair to say that the 1994 elections created an equally strong mandate for using new information tools to communicate better with an alienated electorate.

The elections revealed how unhappy and disconnected voters feel, and the paper, in the spirit of "public journalism" wants to foster community participation in the electoral process. Siceloff says in future campaigns the N&O will use its online tools to stimulate communication among voters, government and the press. Beyond interactive discussions, the paper will provide voters online data on candidates and issues, and help them do their own online digging for additional information.

Such efforts will include material on Internet's World Wide Web, which permits the use of sound, still photos and graphics, and full-motion video, as well as text and E-mail services. This is a major improvement over NandO's early Internet offerings, which were limited to a text-only electronic version of the N&O daily paper and a range of bulletin board services.

On the Web, as it's called, the N&O now is posting an impressive display of multimedia content (the N&O's Web address is "http://www.nando.net"). Online content includes several newspaper projects, such as the 16-part "North Carolina Discoveries" series; the NandO Times, a daily electronic edition of the paper; NandO's Entertainment Server, with listings of area movies, concerts and other community events; and a User's Guide to the Triangle, which features databases of information on the region.

Other N&O Web products aren't directly related to the newspaper. Sports information services are available. There's a service called Music Kitchen, which features text, images and sound cuts from a number of rock bands. And NandO is working with a travel agency to offer airline reservations and no-fee ticket services over the Internet. With the Internet's global audience, these products give the N&O access to consumers—and revenue opportunities—far beyond its circulation area.

Although the Internet is a different entity than a newspaper, NandO's new online products are an extension of the dramatic changes taking place in the N&O newsroom and its research library.

"Once you create digital information you can do anything with it," says Executive Editor Daniels. "And once you build the infrastructure for that, assuming you don't skimp, you can support much more than your news department with it."

It's Daniels' systemic approach that differentiates the N&O from other newspapers. "You've got good stuff going on in most every other newsroom in the country, but there's no synergy to it," Daniels says. "They're not helping their newspapers evolve, and that's what this is all about: How do you help the company evolve?"

Article Review Form at end of book.

Elliot Jaspin and Brant Houston were pioneers in the developing field of computer-assisted reporting. In the following article George Landau looks at the men, their work and some of their peers who also had success applying the power of the computer to the newsroom. What lead newspapers to begin adapting C.A.R. (computer-assisted reporting) techniques? What impact did computer technology have on the stories cited? What resources are needed to set up a C.A.R. program?

Quantum Leaps
Computer journalism takes off

George Landau

George Landau, a reporter for the St. Louis Post-Dispatch, is a specialist in computer-assisted journalism.

Two and a half years have passed since reporter Elliot Jaspin left the Providence *Journal-Bulletin*, moved to the Midwest, and began preaching the gospel of computer-assisted reporting. Jaspin is not alone in the field, but as founder of the Missouri Institute for Computer-Assisted Reporting (part of the University of Missouri's School of Journalism) he is generally credited with having been the first to promote the use of personal computers to analyze mainframe-size databases.

His methods have caught on. While the precise number is hard to pin down, at least two dozen newspapers in the U.S. have a reporter who specializes in working with computer data, according to Jim Brown, executive director of the National Institute for Advanced Reporting, at the Indiana University School of Journalism in Indianapolis. And judging by attendance last April at the Indiana institute's conference on computer-assisted journalism, hundreds more reporters and editors from print and broadcast want to learn how to use a computer for a lot more than just word processing.

PC journalism has caught on quickly in newsrooms because PCs have evolved at a dizzying pace in recent years, while their price has dropped. These days, $6,000 can buy you a PC with more than enough storage capacity to handle files from most mainframes. Another $3,000 buys a nine-track tape drive to read the data from those mainframes. Finally, state-of-the-art software costs only about $800.

Here's what some of us ordinary reporters and editors have been able to accomplish in the last year or two using PCs to analyze data from mainframes:

Ghost Voters

In an account of possible vote fraud in East St. Louis, Illinois, the *St. Louis Post-Dispatch* proved the existence of an afterlife. My colleague Tim Novak and I had been comparing a listing of voter addresses with a database of vacant lots, trying to gauge the extent of illegal registration. (With the city's registered voters outnumbering the voting-age population, this was no fishing expedition.)

In the middle of that project, another database we had long been seeking arrived: eleven years of Missouri's computerized death certificates, 1979–1989. We had haggled with the state health department for months to get those tapes. The bureaucrat in charge didn't understand the words "public record," and feared we would print a list of every AIDS victim since 1983.

What did Missouri death certificates have to do with East St. Louis? More than we expected. St Louis, it turns out, is a popular place to die; the best and biggest hospitals are on the Missouri side of the Mississippi River. By having the computer scan those eleven years of death certificates—550,000 records altogether

Reprinted from *Columbia Journalism Review*, May/June 1992. Copyright © 1992 Columbia Journalism Review.

—we derived a list of more than 1,000 East St. Louis residents who had died in Missouri.

Of those, 270—most of them dead for several years—were still registered to vote. Two dozen had kept on voting from the grave. We started our story this way:

A man named Admiral Wherry, an army veteran who owned a barbecue pit and tire repair shop in East St. Louis, died more than two years ago.

But that didn't stop him from voting in the Illinois Democratic primary on March 20.

Since then we've used the Missouri death certificates to identify coroners who repeatedly failed to investigate suspicious deaths, listing the cause as "unknown" when an autopsy might have revealed child abuse, elderly abuse, or other evidence of homicide.

Justice Jailed

In Connecticut, reporter Brant Houston of *The Hartford Courant* had been working with a relatively small set of computerized court records when he learned of an intriguing, and much larger, database: a computer file kept by the state bail commission that listed defendants' bail, the highest crime of which the defendants were accused, any other charges pending, prior convictions, race, age, and sex.

Two months after Houston began working with a nine-track tape of bail commission data, the *Courant* published a three-part series describing the racial inequities in the state's bond system, the tendency of some judges to impose excessive bonds as pretrial punishment, and the failure of the bond system to assess its own fairness despite a 1981 legislative mandate that it do so.

Houston and reporter Jack Ewing's series started on June 16, 1991. Six days later they reported the response of Connecticut's chief justice: he ordered a comprehensive study of racial bias throughout the state courts.

Recently, in order to make databases available to as many reporters as possible, the *Courant* purchased several PCs and printed a directory of what's available in-house or online. Among the offerings are databases of state and federal campaign finances, industrial toxic emissions, death certificates, federal contracts, census data, and real estate records.

Deadline Demographics

Early last year, when the U.S. Census Bureau released the first detailed population counts from the 1990 census, the information wasn't available on paper. Months before printed reports would be ready, journalists with the right tools got the counts from nine-track magnetic tape, the format in which the bureau initially releases all its information.

San Francisco Chronicle special projects editor Judy Miller, who had attended one of Jaspin's seminars, was ready when the Census Bureau released the California counts in February. The *Chronicle*, of course, wasn't the only paper in line for a copy of the tape on the release date. Also present at the state data center in Sacramento were couriers from other California newspapers.

It was 9 P.M. when the tape reached Miller in San Francisco. "I knew exactly what the writers needed, what the graphics people needed," she says. "It took maybe five minutes." On the front page of the next day's *Chronicle*, sharing space with news of the allied thrust into Kuwait, was an account of California's "astonishing population changes."

Ramon G. McLeod and demographics editor Jim Schreiner wrote that "California is rapidly becoming a state in which minority groups will constitute a majority of the population." The story jumped to a page brimming with maps and charts listing ethnic populations in the city of San Francisco and every county in the state.

Miller says that while the state's other newspapers also had census stories that day. "We were one of the first California newspapers to print detailed census results." She says the experience taught her that "computer-assisted journalism doesn't have to mean it takes three months to do. It can also give you a competitive edge in a very tight, tight deadline situation."

Since those initial stories, Miller has bought a tape of more detailed census data, listing population by age, sex, household size, and family type (single mothers as opposed to married couples, for instance).

"I'd like to do some trend stories, where you use the numbers to get at news features," Miller says. "For example, the population of single dads increased. Now that men are having to deal with issues like child care, will we get better child care?

"We want to get behind the numbers and see how they reflect changes in society, how we live," she says.

Resources

There are two keys to the kingdom in this information age: access to data and the ability to

Online Careers: A Specialty or Recasting the Mold? **109**

analyze it. Neither requires mainframes; personal computers can deliver both.

With the addition of just a $70 modem, any PC can be used to explore the rapidly expanding universe of online databases. Services like Lexis/Nexis, Vu/Text, DataTimes, and Dialog offer more kinds of information than can be described here. Newspaper morgues, municipal real estate records, appellate court rulings, SEC filings, abstracts of obscure research journals—it's all out there, waiting to be found.

Online research can be expensive—many services charge about $100 an hour—but it's an unbeatable way to get background for a story. In an ideal newsroom, online research would be the responsibility of the reference library. But in newsrooms where libraries haven't risen to the challenge (or in newsrooms without librarians), reporters have to learn what there is and how to get it.

In addition to online services, data can come from such sources as government tapes or manually entered facts and figures gathered from paper sources or interviews. You might want to fetch census data by modem for analysis with mapping software, for example. Or you might only need to type a few hundred records into a database by hand.

Yet even then, having gathered data, you'll have solved only half the equation.

A well-equipped PC can swallow a database of almost any size. The trick is in getting the PC to digest the data. Here's a quick overview, with examples, of three different kinds of software that a reporter can use to analyze information:

Database Managers: This software allows you to take a database and do basic things like search, sort, and "group" data.

- Searching: with the right software, computers can find needles in haystacks without breaking a sweat. In a matter of seconds, for example, a PC could extract from a master database of death certificates a list of everyone who had died from brain cancer.
- Sorting: using the same database, you could have the computer list those brain cancer victims by zip code. You could also sort by name, age, weight, or whatever else is in the database.
- Grouping: if you wanted to identify the zip code with the most brain cancer deaths, you could tell the software to "group" on zip code, counting up the occurrences within each zip, then displaying the resulting list in descending order of frequency.

This isn't as hard as it may sound. Luckily, there's an elegantly simple but extremely powerful language we can use to get information from a computer database. Called Structured Query Language (SQL), it is being used increasingly in software for everything from mainframes down to PCs.

To master SQL you need learn only a few rules governing the use of a few key phrases, and once you've learned SQL you can instantly use any software that employs it.

Several brands of PC software with SQL are available; after testing a few, I'm happiest with FoxPro 2.0, from Fox Software in Perrysburg, Ohio. FoxPro is extremely fast, even with very large databases. It is also easy to learn and, once mastered, provides sophisticated and powerful programming tools that go beyond SQL.

Statistical Packages

These are database managers with built-in formulas that can be used to isolate cause-and-effect relationships in a sea of variables. Such software would allow you to analyze court records, for example, to show a link between sentencing and defendants' race—independent of defendants' age and sex, the kind of victim and crime, and the specific judges and attorneys involved.

Philip Meyer, a journalism professor at the University of North Carolina at Chapel Hill, has been urging reporters to use statistical tools since 1973, when he published *Precision Journalism*. (A 1991 updated version, *The New Precision Journalism*, is available from the Indiana University Press.) Back then, you needed to master a mainframe, a slide rule, and statistical theory. These days, Meyer says, journalists can teach themselves statistics using PC software called SPSS/PC+ studentware.

But he suggests that the journalist master a traditional database manager (like Paradox, or dBASE) first.

Geographic Information Systems (GIS)

This is a new breed of PC software that allows mapping of any data with a geographic component, from real estate records to census counts. Analyzing the 1990 census, for example, can be daunting if you don't have software to plot the hundreds of census tracts in a metropolitan area. With a GIS, the computer can instantly color each tract to reflect data values—for example, red for tracts that saw increases in median income from 1980, blue for tracts that saw a decline.

Reporters can use a GIS to monitor the political redistricting process. Just trace the latest boundary proposal onto the screen and tell the computer to total up the ethnic populations for all the census "blocks" inside it.

A good GIS can also plot anything that has a street address. In St. Louis, we used software called Atlas*GIS to "pin map" a database of 18,000 vacant lots. By merging the pin map with a map of the city's twenty-eight political wards, we were able to publish a ranking of vacant lots by ward.

Mastering the PC as a reporting tool requires four things: hardware, software, data, and diligence. There's still a learning curve to climb, but it's a lot less steep than it used to be. Computer skills are largely self-taught, but to get pointed in the right direction, reporters may want to take advantage of the following resources:

• The Missouri Institute for Computer-Assisted Reporting in Columbia, Missouri, offers week-long seminars that teach neophytes how to handle data in a variety of formats, including nine-track tape.

Elliot Jaspin, executive director of the institute, sells a software package called NineTrack Express that makes it easier for reporters to transfer data from mainframe tape to PC. The institute also publishes *Uplink,* a monthly newsletter on computer-assisted reporting. (For more information call 314-882-0684.)

• The National Institute for Advanced Reporting at Indiana University, Indianapolis, has an annual conference on computer-assisted reporting that draws hundreds of journalists from around the country for a weekend of inspiration and idea-swapping. It is usually held in March. (For more information call 317-274-2774.)

Article Review Form at end of book.

The *Chicago Tribune*'s online newspaper was unique at the outset, because its staff worked only for the online publication. The result is that its reporters were among the first dedicated digital journalists. What skills do they need to work in the online world? How are these skills different from those needed for print and broadcast? How are their stories different from stories in print?

Doing It All

Christopher Harper

Christopher Harper teaches journalism at New York University. His book, "And That's The Way It Will Be: News in the Digital Age," will be published by NYU Press next September.

Cornelia Grumman presses the sixth-floor button on the elevator at the Henry Horner public housing project. The City of Chicago has planted flowers outside the building in the West Side neighborhood often run by gangs and drug pushers. But the elevator does not work well and reeks of urine. After two tries at the button, Grumman finally reaches the fifth floor and walks up a flight of stairs strewn with garbage. Two young boys climb on a safety fence that's supposed to keep them from falling into the garden below, but the fence seems more like a cage to keep them in.

Grumman, a reporter for the Chicago Tribune, wants to know what people on welfare think about massive changes in the federal program. She visits 24-year-old Melineice Reed and her three children who live in a well-kept but tiny three-room apartment. Reed has lived in the projects all her life. The next day she has an interview for a job as a cleaning woman, and she's a bit nervous. "Do you have anything to wear that's nice?" Grumman asks. "Nice enough," the woman says.

Nearby, a group of worshippers gathers at a Baptist church for Sunday services. Grumman finds several people willing to talk about the federal plan that would limit benefits to the poor. One woman, Demitraius Dykes, has spent all of her 26 years on welfare. A recovering drug addict, she has five children. Dykes says she's trying to turn her life around, attending a course in office skills. "I don't want my kids to grow up and think they should sit around and wait each month for their check," she says. Grumman scribbles notes, runs a tape recorder and later takes a picture. Although she does not like using video cameras, Grumman wishes she had one along for this interview because Dykes is a good talker.

> **The Chicago Tribune is one of the few papers with reporters devoted exclusively to its online version. Staffers cover stories, take pictures, operate video cameras and create digital pages.**

> **"The traditional role of the editor stays the same . . . ,"** says Associate Internet Editor Thomas Cekay—the gatekeeper of what makes it online and what does not. But, he admits, "I have to edit a whole lot faster" because of the constant deadline pressure of the up-to-the-minute Internet edition.

The 33-year-old reporter is one of a new breed of journalist—the digital journalist. Although more than 200 American newspapers offer an online edition, most are simply an electronic version of the printed newspaper—a "shovelware" version, as it's known on the Internet. The Tribune, however, is one of the few newspapers in the country that has devoted reporters like Grumman to work exclusively for the Internet edition. The reporters write stories, take pictures, operate video cameras and even create digital pages. With more than 20 other staff members, the seven reporters produce one of the most innovative online editions available today.

Forty-three-year-old Owen Youngman, director of interactive media for the Chicago Tribune, seems like a high school science

From Christopher Harper, "Doing It All!" in *American Journalism Review*, December 1996. Reprinted by permission of American Journalism Review.

teacher behind his glasses, and his nasal-dominated cadence can put some people to sleep. But his zeal for the future makes this son of an evangelical minister come alive.

"My neighbor on one side buys the Tribune because he's a stockbroker," Youngman says. "My neighbor on the other side doesn't. Why? It's not really fulfilling for someone with two kids in school in suburban Chicago. She cares a lot more about what affects her kids. It's not her fault. It's my fault. Now I have a technology to provide information to her. We need to do a better job of understanding what is valuable to people and deliver on what we say we will deliver."

Online consultant Leah Gentry, who started the online version of the Tribune, wanted to deliver to users what she thinks they should have and what they want. She proudly called her team "the hardest working band in the business." Gentry was the band leader, and the 36-year-old former editor for the Orange County Register put into place a set of exacting standards, called "Leah's Rules," that would make any conductor envious:

1. All the regular rules of journalism apply. Reporting and editing must be solid. Facts must be checked and rechecked. 2. If you're going to use this week's gizmo, it has to help advance the telling of the story in a meaningful way. 3. No instant publishing. Everybody has his or her finger on the press, but nobody is allowed to post a page that hasn't gone through the editing process. 4. Reporters need to think of the medium while reporting. In addition to story information, they must gather or assign information for animated or still graphics, video and audio.

"The main rule: What we're doing is journalism, not stupid technology tricks," she says.

The Tribune Internet edition, which started in March, contains most of the information from the print version—news, sports, job listings, real estate and automobile advertisements, weather, stocks and television listings. For its readers, the Internet edition offers in-depth stories, special technology reports, games, discussion groups and everything someone would ever want to know about the Chicago Bears and the Chicago Bulls. The Internet edition also provides audio interviews and information from the company's radio station, as well as video from the Tribune's 24-hour news service. ChicagoLand Television News (see "The High-Tech Trib," April 1994).

The Internet band includes 44-year-old Thomas Cekay, a former financial editor of the Tribune. He is the associate Internet editor—the gatekeeper of what makes it online and what does not. "The traditional role of the editor stays the same. Do the readers need to see this? Is it intelligently done? Is it sophisticated reporting? Is it what the Chicago Tribune wants?" observes Cekay, a longtime Tribune editor who also has worked for newspapers in Ohio and Oregon.

"The differences are the demands on the editor are much higher because the editor has to know a lot more stuff than on the paper. The editor has to know about the audio that goes into these packages. The editor has to know about the video that goes into these packages." And, he admits, "I have to edit a whole lot faster" because of the constant deadline pressure of the up-to-the-minute Internet edition.

The rest of the band is young, energetic, serious and sometimes irreverent. The newspaper editors and reporters at the Tribune tend toward blue shirts, khaki pants and expensive shoes. With few exceptions, this group tends toward T-shirts, blue jeans and tennis shoes.

Grumman, by far the best-dressed in her business suits, studied public policy at Duke University and the Kennedy School of Government at Harvard. She worked as a freelance reporter in China and scouted rock 'n' roll bands there. Another reporter, Darnell Little, 30, studied computer programming and developed telephone software for Bell Labs before becoming a journalist. Stephen Henderson, 26, wrote editorials for newspapers in Lexington, Kentucky, and Detroit before joining the Tribune's Internet staff.

During the Democratic convention in Chicago, the Internet edition of the newspaper reached nearly 100,000 users a day by putting together a mixture of original reporting, audio reports from the Tribune's radio station, video clips from two Tribune television stations and articles from the printed edition.

Reporter Little had an idea for a historical tour of some of the 24 previous political conventions in the city, starting with the one that nominated Abraham Lincoln in 1860. Little, who received master's degrees in both engineering and journalism from Northwestern, went to the Chicago Historical Society to get a visual sense of how to conduct a tour on the World Wide Web.

"The idea was to take people on a tour that was a virtual museum. There were three parallel streams. There was the tour guide—a walk through six conventions. The second was a behind-the-scenes look at what was happening in Chicago at the time. The third part included archives and political cartoons," Little explains. "The reporting is the same as working for a standard newspaper—gathering the information and talking to people. But you put it together and write it differently."

Before writing the story, Little designs a story board for what each of the main pages will show—a practice used extensively in the film, television and advertising industries. The story board contains an outline of a page's content, graphics and computer links to other stories.

After Little reports a story, he then follows his original story board—with adaptations—to make certain that the reporting, photography, headlines and navigation make the story easy for the reader to enjoy.

Little likes to imitate the articles on the front page of the Wall Street Journal, a style that he says works well on the Web. The first page uses an anecdotal lead to draw the reader into the story. The second page broadens the story with the nut graph. The other pages flow from these first two pages to allow the reader to follow a variety of links that expand on each report.

The process is called "layering." Because a computer screen contains less space than the front page of a newspaper, the first layer or page of a digital story contains a headline, a digital photograph and text designed to make the user continue to the next layer. The pages are usually about 500 words, with the option for the reader, with a click of a mouse, to follow a highlighted path. But a user may want to follow another path. He or she could read about the 1860 convention and want to learn more about what was happening in Chicago during that period. After searching through the archives of that time, the user can proceed to the next convention or even skip ahead to another convention. The layers provide a logical way to proceed, but they also enable the user to read the digital pages in any order.

"I write the story in chapters," Little says. "What works the best is when you have a design on the Web that is the equivalent of the layout of a magazine and your eye and attention are focused on one part, which is easily digestible, and it flows and leads you into other parts."

Reporter Grumman found her first weeks at the Internet edition frustrating. She started on the newspaper's print side, where she covered suburban police departments. "My first instinct was to do quick hits," she recalls. "They went nowhere. They were up for a day and, boom, they're gone." The reporter's first attempt at using the Internet for a more complex story involved the murder of a 24-year-old woman in suburban Chicago and the police investigation into the crime. The main story of "Who Killed Stacey Frobel?" appeared in both the online and print editions without significant editorial differences. In the Internet edition, however, readers could click on a chronology of events, descriptions of people involved in the crime and its investigation and a variety of background stories—far more than would have been available in the daily newspaper. Simply put, there are no space limitations on the Internet, and an online story can be as long as the reporter and editor think it should be.

Reporter Henderson studied political science at the University of Michigan. Within days of his arrival in Chicago, he noticed a story about the 1995 murder rates in the city.

"It wasn't a big deal. It was a story that the paper does every year," he recalls. "I said to myself, 'I bet there's a lot more there.'" Henderson asked the print reporters for all the information about the murders—the time, the neighborhood, the cause of death and a variety of other statistics. He put together a map of the city and allowed readers to look for information about their neighborhoods—again with a click of the mouse rather than a visit to the records office at the police precinct. "We got thousands of people interested," he says. "If we use a big database in telling a story, you also have to give the readers a chance to use that database. That's giving people information that's important to them."

Now he intends to do the same with fires in Chicago to allow readers to find out when fires occurred, the causes and how well the authorities handled the alarm. "The medium really shapes the writing. It makes you write shorter and sharper. I try not to write long stories, but break the story up into digestible parts that people can read," Henderson says. "When I worked on the city desk, I would go do my story and I might assign a photographer. Then I'd just pass the thing on. Somebody else edits it. Somebody else copy edits it. Another person would read it and decide whether it would go on page one. Someone would decide where the photos would go. Here, it's so much more important for me to be there through the whole process, shaping the thing so that it makes sense in the medium."

A large portion of the Tribune online readership mirrors that of the Internet—men with middle-class incomes between the ages of 25 and 35. As a result, the most popular section of the Internet edition is sports, where fans can follow the Bears and the Bulls, as well as college and high school sports. Internet Sports Editor Mike Reilley says that "the section becomes your bar stool."

The Bulls' site is a good example of what can be done online when there aren't the space limitations that there are in a newspaper. The pages include a list with stories about every game of the Bulls' 1996 championship season. There's even a reprise of how fans tore up the city during previous victory celebrations. And there's a section on forward Dennis Rodman, whose bestselling book and dramatic appearances in drag at book signings have attracted readers from throughout the world. "The Bulls and Dennis Rodman have been great for us," says Reilley, a former Los Angeles Times reporter.

The next step is taking the stories and sections and putting them online. Unlike the front page of a printed newspaper, there often is only one story that's promoted with a photograph and a large headline in the Internet edition. For other parts of the online edition, there is immediate access by section or specific story. "We looked at the daily paper and said, 'What works?' Our brand name—the Chicago Tribune—works," explains Andrew DeVigal, the 27-year-old producer and designer of the online edition. The

At the Tribune and elsewhere, digital journalism remains in its infancy, and there are growing pains. Reporters sometimes resemble one-man bands, carrying a variety of technical instruments without the necessary skills to do the job properly.

major differences between the online edition and the printed version are immediacy, interactivity and multimedia, DeVigal says. During the Democratic convention in Chicago, for example, the online edition updated stories throughout the day, including the resignation of Clinton political adviser Dick Morris. In addition, "Buzz" and "For Junkies Only" provided offbeat tidbits and gossip of what was happening at the convention, the parties and on the streets.

Interactivity allowed the Internet edition to include a Tribune poll of 500 people about President Clinton and Robert Dole, and then asked readers of the Internet Tribune how they would respond to the same questions. The online Tribune's poll results tracked rather closely with the official poll.

Multimedia allowed users to listen to every speech at the Democratic convention through a program known as "RealAudio," which stores audio programs for use at any time. Video clips included interviews with ordinary people and delegates from the convention and a reunion of protesters from the 1968 convention. A new technology, PhotoBubble, presented a still picture of the convention site with an amazing 360-degree view of the United Center. The viewer could zoom in to take a look at the television network skyboxes, or widen the shot to see the entire convention floor.

Along the left side of every page is something called "the rail," which starts at the top of the page and runs all the way down to the bottom. The rail guides readers to featured stories in the Internet edition. By clicking the mouse, the user can travel to a particular section or story. Basically, the editors do not want users to get lost going from one section to another. If the user chooses a section, the title will turn from red to blue. That shows the user where he or she is.

The bottom line of any publication, however, is the bottom line. How will this operation make money? It's difficult to pry much specific financial information from anyone. The Tribune Co. has spent several million dollars on Internet publishing in 1996. Youngman says he has a business plan that he thinks will make the digital operation a profit center after a few years.

"The newspaper business is really good at charging a token amount of money for an expensive product. Fifty cents doesn't cover the paper and ink, let alone the transportation, the gasoline," Youngman says. "We can recover a token cost by saying if the Chicago Tribune thinks something is interesting, it's free. If there is something you think is interesting and you ask me for it, that's going to cost you something. It might cost you something like information—your e-mail address or your zip code—a nickel or a couple of bucks a year. But it's going to cost you something."

At the moment, the Internet edition costs subscribers nothing. That is expected to change. There are no comics, no crossword puzzles and no business section—all of which will be added soon—possibly for a charge. A reader can search the archives of the newspaper—another service that may be provided for a charge in the future. The special sections for the

Bears and the Bulls will almost certainly cost a fee.

At the Tribune and elsewhere, digital journalism remains in its infancy, and there are growing pains. The reporters at the Internet Tribune sometimes resemble one-man bands, carrying a variety of technical instruments without the necessary skills to do the job properly. At a printed newspaper the reporter generally takes a pen, a notebook and sometimes a tape recorder. At the electronic version, the reporter carries a pen, a notebook, a tape recorder for audio clips, a digital camera for single snapshots and sometimes a video camera for video clips. At the GOP convention in San Diego, Grumman sent back videotape after videotape.

"You have four things slung over your shoulder," she chuckles. "I had to run to Federal Express at 6:45 p.m. every day to ship the tapes. When they got them in Chicago, they said that there was too much movement and too many zooms. It was just a comedy of errors." The era of digital specialization, in which a reporter reports and a photographer photographs, is likely to come soon. But some glitches will continue to arise. Malia Zoghlin, who worked as a television reporter and producer in Hawaii, got separated from a reporter while shooting videotape of a reunion of protesters from the 1968 Democratic convention in Chicago. Zoghlin tried to conduct an interview while holding a microphone and a camera. She asked the interview subject, activist Bobby Seale, if he could hold the microphone. Unfortunately, Seale accidentally turned the microphone off, so there was no audio when Zoghlin returned to the office.

More important, there sometimes remains a gulf between those who work at the newspaper and those who work at its electronic edition. "When I first was going to the Internet edition, people would nod and say, 'It's the wave of the future,' and they would smile and that was it. They couldn't think of anything to say about it,"

The Tribune Empire

The Tribune Co. has been at the forefront of many journalistic innovations—some bad and some good. One publisher instituted a series of spelling changes because he thought the English language was too complicated. "Through" became "thru," for example, a practice that did not die until the 1970s.

While other newspapers worried about the encroachment of radio and television, the Tribune added the new media to its holdings. In Chicago, it owns and operates ChicagoLand TV, its own local television news venture. The company has also expanded its radio and television businesses in New York, Denver, New Orleans, Atlanta, Los Angeles, Philadelphia and Boston. The company has 10 television stations, seven in the top markets; five radio stations; Tribune Entertainment Co., which produces programming such as "Geraldo"; and joint ventures, such as a significant holding of Warner Bros. Television Network.

In 1991, the Tribune began to invest in online technology companies, buying a stake in America Online. In 1996, the company also invested $7 million in Excite, a firm that indexes and searches World Wide Web sites on the Internet.

The company has also teamed up with AOL on a variety of projects. The most ambitious is a $100 million plan called "Digital Cities," which will offer news, information and entertainment to more than 100 cities throughout the United States, from Peoria, Illinois, to Portland, Oregon. Only a few sites are up and running, but the venture is a clear signal to Microsoft that big-time daily newspapers are not about to surrender to Bill Gates' similar project, "Cityscape."

Is the next competition going to be Cityscape vs. Digital Cities? "I think that's one of the battlegrounds," says Owen Youngman, director of interactive media at the Tribune. "Because we believe their focus is on entertainment and leisure listings and materials newspapers have always presented, we think it's an important battleground. But we're not focusing on any one opponent. We're looking to the opportunities to perform all the traditional functions we provide. If we do provide that information, we think we will be competitive and then the marketplace can decide about the value and content and who's doing the best job."

Digital City Chicago is one of the biggest projects. The Tribune will offer 342 different sites for towns, villages and cities in the reading area, similar to what the Tribune did two decades ago in zoned editions. In the past, these editions offered specific news and advertising to local communities. Youngman plans to start the online sites with what he describes as "horizontal communities," political and geographical locations throughout the Chicago area. Then he hopes that "vertical communities" sprout up with readers interested in subject areas such as religion, parenting and politics. "Microsoft, CNN and the Chicago Tribune are all going to cover a bombing at the Olympics," Youngman says. "Not everybody else is going to worry about Fox River Valley Gardens."

A leading Internet research firm is not convinced that Digital Cities will make it into the next century. "We believe the next five years will see a bloody battle for control of the local online market," Forrester Research wrote in October. Ultimately, Forrester thinks that Microsoft will win that battle, but that it will be costly for Gates.

Another ambitious project is the online "New Century Network," to which newspapers nationwide, including the Tribune, contribute articles for readers in another part of the country. In its promotional material, the New Century Network says it "aims to marry the interactivity, breadth and cool conversation of the net with the credibility and dedicated insight of hometown newspapers across the country . . . and eventually, maybe, across the world."

Grumman says. "People think it's an interesting diversion. A toy. It's not meaty. But it's another way for people to get their news."

There also is resentment among some print reporters because of the huge infusion of capital into digital technology. "There isn't much money for raises," grumps one writer. And there is some fear that the electronic newspaper may someday replace the printed edition.

In one rift, the print newspaper published a series about medical emergencies on airplanes, "Code Blue: Survival in the Sky," which went online in June. The stories ran more than 20,000 words—a daunting task for anyone to read. It was decided that the series should be added to the Internet edition with graphics, audio clips, video clips and even a demonstration about how a defibrillator—a device to help heart attack victims—works. One well-known journalist criticized the approach of the Internet version, and copies of the complaint circulated all around the Tribune. Still, there are converts from the printed paper. One reporter whose story faced severe cuts at the newspaper offered the original version to the Internet edition, which ran it. Reporters who saw stories left out of the newspaper for space reasons brought them to the Internet edition, where they were published online.

Those closest to the electronic product realize the medium must win converts—both readers and fellow journalists. "This medium is in its infancy," Gentry explains. "There are thousands of ways to do things. We just have to figure them out and convince people we're right."

Article Review Form at end of book.

The following article contains profiles of seven Generation X journalists who have opted for the online journalism world instead of the traditional newsroom. Their views go a long way toward explaining why online journalism is growing so fast. The digital journalists and editors also pinpoint some challenges faced in the online world. After readinig the following article, which career path might you consider? Will the online and print career paths begin to merge? Do you think online journalism is more about producing the article or reporting the news?

It's a Job but Is It Journalism?

Answers from the first generation of content-providers

Christina Ianzito

Christina Ianzito is an assistant editor at CJR.

Before Robin Sparkman graduated from Columbia University's Graduate School of Journalism in May, she dutifully sent out her cover letters and résumés to New York-based magazines, and spent four months talking back and forth to one of them about a reporting position. "Finally they called me and asked me if I wanted to be a fact-checker," she says, with disdain. "Can you *believe* it?" Twenty-seven years old, she felt she'd already done her share of fact-checking, for *Newsweek,* and leaving New York was out of the question. So she did what dozens of other young journalists did this summer: landed a job at MSNBC.

There has never been an obvious or easy first step for young journalists on the road to a successful career. That is still true. But budding journalists do have new options these days, in new media, which offers a way to hit the ground running and, for better or for worse, to avoid unpaid internships and small-town newspaper jobs. Journalism-school grads, semi-seasoned reporters, and untested twenty-year-olds are all heading to online jobs for the money, the opportunities, and the excitement of seeing a new kind of journalism unfold. Their titles range from "associate editor" to "assistant producer" to "production associate." Some are thrilled, some are disillusioned; some are writing, some are coding HTML. Some are finding real journalism in this new world, and some are not.

Sparkman, for one, is an "online producer," which she says means: "I'm thinking about content design and product."

Um, *what?*

She takes CNBC-TV shows and puts them up on the Web, reworking sound and video into an online form, a process somewhat like turning TV back into print. "Right now I'm not doing traditional journalism—reporting and writing—and I definitely strongly miss the writing part."

Sparkman nonetheless believes that MSNBC was right to hire someone like herself with a journalism background, someone with news judgment and certain standards. "Because it's so new, there are no rules," she says. "So it all comes down to me and my not putting garbage on the Web."

This first generation of online journalists has no professional

Reprinted from *Columbia Journalism Review,* November/December 1996. Copyright © 1996 by Columbia Journalism Review.

model, so "there's a loose atmosphere," says Vladimir Edelman, twenty-two, an associate producer at MSNBC. He is also the cofounder, with Emily Field, also twenty-two, of the Interactive Media Writers Association (*http://www.imwa.com*), an online organization meant to encourage discussion about writing standards in this new electronic medium.

"Looseness," of course, is a friend of the young and ambitious. After working for *Inc. Online,* Edelman was recruited by MSNBC this summer. "It's sort of a window of opportunity that opens in history very rarely," Edelman says, "to establish yourself amid really professional journalists, in what would take a decade normally."

And the window seems to be widening. A recent "New York New Media Industry Survey" by Coopers & Lybrand estimates that the new media industry employs 71,500 in the New York area alone and expects that number to increase by between 40,000 and 120,000 new jobs through 1998. These jobs will include programmers, designers, and administrators, but there's plenty of room for eager, techno-savvy journalists.

Not all will stay so eager. Some online journalists have been frustrated, especially those working for the Web sites of established print publications. The sites, they say, often feel like afterthoughts, marked by too much repurposing-morphing print stories into Web format. It's not that repurposing is inherently a bad thing, it's just that doing it doesn't make for a very interesting journalism job.

Publications like *The New York Times* (*http://www.nytimes.com*), the *San Jose Mercury News* (*http://www.sjmercury.com*), and the Raleigh *News and Observer* (*http://www.nando.net*) have tried to approach their sites with some imagination by adding original content, hypertext sidebars, and other enhancements to repurposed pieces. Along with repurposed content, for example, *The New York Times* offers "CyberTimes," a section reserved for reporting on Internet-related issues, most of which is original. Editor Rob Fixmer says good journalists are the key to making this kind of project superior. But they have to learn that the inverted pyramid style doesn't work online, he says; you can't assume that the reader starts with the lead and ends with the kicker. "We have to conceive of the stories in the medium's own terms," says Fixmer. "That means thinking links rather than sidebars."

Seth Effron, forty-four, executive editor of the well-regarded *Nando Times,* affiliated with the Raleigh *News and Observer,* says that this shift in organization is why he hires less-experienced journalists along with practiced veterans: "they don't have preconceived notions."

Thirty-four-year-old Laura Italiano is one experienced journalist who's quite happy with the inverted pyramid, thank you very much. She spent eight months last year as a free-lance consultant for New Jersey Online (*http://www.nj.com*), where she did some reporting (see "Launching the Pope in Cyberspace," CJR, January/February). But "it was not journalistically satisfying,"

"You have to conceive stories in the medium's own terms"

she says. "You're sitting at a computer writing about people sitting at computers."

Now she's working for the *New York Post,* and loving it. "Last week they sent me out to cover Hurricane Fran," she said in September. "I was out at an elementary school in Hampstead, North Carolina, and the roof was blowing off, and I had a notebook and a pen. I was the most low-tech journalist. It's a blast."

The young people who seem happiest in new media are those whose jobs include reporting, writing, editing—journalism, in short, at least similar to what they might be doing had they chosen print. How much room for this journalism there will be in the online world of the future, however, is open to debate.

Mark Stahlman, co-founder of the New York New Media Association and a multimedia consultant, is one who insists that there'll be no pot of gold for journalists at the end of the infosuperhighway. "The essence of new media is that it's a two-way process. Talk radio is closer to new media than *Slate* is," he says of the Michael Kinsley/Microsoft e-zine. Stahlman thinks new media is about creating conversations and connections, and that's where the growth will be.

Today only 8 percent of people go online for news once a week or more, according to a Pew Research Center study, and nobody has yet figured out a viable way to make online journalism profitable.

Neither of these facts has slowed down many journalism schools' rush to teach new media. Dean Brent Baker at Boston University's school of communication says proudly, "We are wired!" A retired admiral, Baker speaks with military-style enthusiasm about how he was hired to "kick the college into the twenty-first century." Since 1992, he's built two major multimedia labs for the school, and "on the front of the catalog is a computer—not a quill pen or a typewriter or any of that crap."

He's convinced that his students won't make it in journalism if they stick with a single dimension, and points out that his print graduates are making $20,000, while those going into new media are bringing in between $45,000 and $65,000; the brave—and rich—new world, he suggests, is one of multimedia.

MSNBC's Vladimir Edelman, a graduate of Baker's journalism program, agrees, but believes that young journalists' open door to online jobs today will soon be quietly closing. "It's an incredible opportunity," he says, "but I think it'll shut down in about half a year. A lot of older people are starting to catch on."

They're starting to catch on to the bold facts that HTML coding isn't difficult; that the mumbo-jumbo lexicon of hyperlinks, repurposing, and URL's is pretty easy to grasp after a few hours of Web surfing, and that all you need to become a production associate, or even a "Webmaster," at an online publication is the ability to write and think. Places like MSNBC, meanwhile, already have templates of HTML codes, an innovation that shears countless hours and headaches from the repurposing process. It's all starting to look less and less like rocket science and more and more like . . . something else.

"I don't know if it's journalism," admits MSNBC's Robin Sparkman, "but it's interesting."

Mark Hull, 21

job title: Online editor, Mercury Center (*http://www.sjmercury.com*), May 1996 to present

job description: Updates site during evening shift, builds links, designs, edits, occasionally reports

location: San Jose, California

background: Majored in journalism at Pepperdine University, worked on campus newspaper and magazine, put magazine online, interned with four different print newspapers

ten years from now: Unsure, but "I'd love to pursue this and see how it unfolds."

Hull says he was visited recently by a strange and foreboding dream: "Geraldine Ferraro told me, 'You've got to get out there and report!'" Why Ferraro was the messenger is beyond Hull, who, despite the dream, insists that he's made the right choice in forgoing the traditional entry-level newspaper beat—covering cops, city hall, or 2 A.M. fires—for cyberjournalism.

Hull points to his recent efforts helping report and build the links that turned *San Jose Mercury News* staff writer Gary Webb's investigative piece "Dark Alliance" into an interactive mind-blower. Printed as a three-part series in the *Mercury News* beginning on August 18, the piece reports that a San Francisco-area drug ring sold cocaine to Los Angeles street gangs and used its profits to help fund a CIA-run guerrilla army in Nicaragua (see page 00*). The online documentation includes a small library of court depositions, letters between senators and the attorney general, photos of evidence, and even sound clips of taped conversations between the drug dealers. The report has become something of a journalistic controversy as other media follow up on its findings, but it has prompted three separate federal investigations.

Hull is obviously proud of his work, and believes that unlike many established newspapers that either half-heartedly or unskillfully attempt Web versions of their reporting, Mercury Center has taken online journalism to a higher level. "To be at the place that I am at my age," he says, "it's a real blessing."

Bill Frischling, 24

job title: Online producer, Digital Ink Company, a subsidiary of The Washington Post Company (*http://www.washingtonpost.com*), January 1995 to present

job description: Surfs the wires, updates business section, locates new content, builds links

location: Rosslyn, Virginia

background: Majored in journalism at Michigan State, worked for two years as an intern for *The Philadelphia Inquirer*

ten years from now: "I'll be with new media as long as it's fun."

Frischling likes building better than reporting. That's building links, building references, then linking what he's building to what's already been built. "I love what I'm doing right now," he says. He's surrounded by a sea of computers and low partitions in Digital Ink's sleek offices, where

*Not included in this publication.

the decor is all windows, indirect lighting, and open space. The look is t-shirts and jeans—and a pair of Birkenstocks for Frischling.

He may build, but he doesn't really write. "It bothered me a lot initially," he admits. "Your friends' first reaction is, 'Hold a funeral for the guy. He's stopped writing.'" But his job is very much about journalism, he insists, since it requires highly tuned news judgments: What's important? What information should be linked to what? He compares himself to a kind of high-tech librarian, creating information that lasts—at least longer than it does on newsprint.

washingtonpost.com averages seven million hits a week and updates six times an hour. In early September, Frischling helped update links about the Iraqi crisis, for example, which included a military briefing on security issues in Iraq, a detailed map of the country, and background on Kurdish history. Fast-talking and seemingly tireless, he often works a twelve-hour day, from 6 A.M. to 6 P.M.

Since new media is so, well, *new,* its rules and hierarchies are often more fluid than in established media. It's a world where the young and talented are viewed as serious players. "I'm a twenty-four-year-old punk kid going up to an editor with an idea," says Frischling, "and the usual response is, 'Try it!'"

Trisha Smith, 32

job title: Free-lance writer

job description: Writes for various e-zines, including *Charged* (http://www.charged.com)

location: New York

background: Managing editor of trade magazine *California Builder.* Graduated from Columbia University's Graduate School of Journalism in May 1995, took job at Newhouse's site, New Jersey Online (http://www.nj.com) until August 1996

ten years from now: Expects to continue working in new media, creating original content.

Smith isn't shy about sharing her feelings about her former job at New Jersey Online: "It's been one of the worst experiences of my life."

The site won "Best Online Newspaper" in the 1996 Digital Edge Awards from the Newspaper Association of America's New Media Federation, but Smith was not so impressed. She quickly became frustrated by what she sees as the site's lack of original content and a limited editorial vision. And she's not alone—at least five of her twenty-five former colleagues have given notice since she dropped out.

"There was never a real plan," Smith said disdainfully during her last week on the job. "It's total chaos. All we can use is the paper [*The Star-Ledger* of Newark, a Newhouse affiliate]. We can't do anything original anymore." Smith believes that worries about the bottom line steered the site away from the innovative and toward the mundane, and now "all the talent that they have there is being wasted." Like many young journalists, she shivers at the thought of spending days "repurposing," coding and reloading print pieces onto the Web.

So she's free-lancing for new media. She isn't bringing in as much cash, but she's discovering the ins and outs of tax write-offs, and is relishing her freedom from New Jersey Online: "I'd rather not have a job than have to repurpose the paper," she says.

Marcy Harbut, 26

job title: Staff writer, Earthlink Network (http://www.earthlink.net), an Internet service provider, April 1996 to present

job description: Writes an online humor column and customer newsletter about the Internet

location: Pasadena, California

background: English major from University of California, Riverside; news assistant/staff writer for *San Gabriel Valley Daily Tribune* and education reporter for *The Glendale News-Press* in California

ten years from now: "I don't think I want to go back into print. It's such a dying industry."

For a former print reporter like Harbut, there are journalistic trade-offs to this kind of work—like having to write about and within the narrow world of the Web day after day. "The biggest sacrifice is having a much more limited subject to talk about," she says. "And stories get cut down to 600 words. Even though we don't have to worry about ad linage, we have to worry about download time."

But Harbut had simply had it with the grueling competition, long hours, and low pay-off she found in print. Her salary jumped $8,000 when she moved from daily newspaper journalism to Web writing. And because she's a level above those doing the grunt work of HTML coding, her job can be fun. One of her tasks, for example, is writing a sarcastic Web surfer's guide to cool and outrageous sites on Earthlink's own Web site, which is designed to help users navigate around the Internet.

She admits she doesn't consider herself much of a journalist anymore. "My friends joke that I'm a sellout," she says. "But I'm a lot happier."

T. Trent Gegax, 30

job title: Online reporter, *Newsweek Interactive* on America Online (key word: Newsweek), June 1995 to October 1996

job description: Wrote headlines and hyperlink sidebars, and did some original reporting

location: New York

background: English major from University of Minnesota; wrote for the alternative press in Minneapolis and *The Peoria Journal Star*; summer internship at *Newsweek* that segued into a researching position. Moved to Interactive division, then back to the print edition as an assistant editor

ten years from now: Hopes to work as a print writer for a New York-based weekly print magazine.

For Gegax, working in new media was more a "detour" than a transforming trip down the infosuperhighway, although it did help him get one notch closer to his ideal job. He showed *Newsweek* he was cut out for print when he was in Atlanta reporting an online story about the women's field hockey team. When the bomb went off at the Olympic games, Gegax was the only *Newsweek* reporter in the area to fill in the blanks. A month later, he was promised a job in *Newsweek's* back of the book section—a ticket out of new media, or, as he calls it, Cyberia.

It's not that it's awful, he says. It's just *marginal*. "What was boring was that you know that 20,000 people at the most would see your stuff, but working for the magazine, 10 million might see it."

Gegax would dissuade young journalists from heading online for work, since he thinks so many new media jobs involve more production than reporting, and, more importantly, because he believes that even the best online journalism will have fizzled out by 2000. "There's no business model on the Web that's making any money. *Feed, Salon,* and *Slate* are all witty, well-edited publications that could sell on the newsstand, but they won't last two years."

Cyrus Krohn, 25

job title: Assistant editor, *Slate* (*http://www.slate.com*), February 1996 to present

job description: Writes occasionally, updates "The Fray," submits story ideas

location: Redmond, Washington

background: Majored in journalism and edited school paper at Lynchburg College in Lynchburg, Virginia; worked as a college intern for Vice President Dan Quayle; researched for CNN's *Larry King Live* and *Crossfire*

ten years from now: "To one degree or another, I'll be involved with this technology."

Krohn has seen *Slate* grow from a four-page memo on Michael Kinsley's desk into the over-hyped, hyper-criticized e-zine for critical thinkers that it is today. That critics bemoan its restrained use of electronic media—its format is more *New Republic* than new media—is no cause for concern. "When you flip through the cable channels," Krohn asks pointedly, "would you rather watch CNN or public access?"

A combination of print and broadcast experience made this young Republican ripe for Kinsley's picking; he snatched Krohn from *Crossfire* and placed him in an office adjacent to his own. Krohn's work day—typically ten hours-starts at 7 A.M., when he reads through the e-mail and begins working on story ideas and guest suggestions. Part of Krohn's job is to introduce "threads" to "The Fray," *Slate's* reader discussion forum, in the form of a summary paragraph and a follow-up question. The National Rifle Association, for example: "A respectable organization representing a legitimate cause or an exploitation show taking cover behind the Constitution?" He's also written one piece, "White House Confidential," comparing the questionable conduct he saw in the Bush White House with Gary Aldrich's allegations of debauchery under Clinton's reign. The piece is now stored in "The Compost," the online bin of *Slate* artifacts too old to be "HOT!" but too choice to be trashed.

"The opportunities are endless," says Krohn. "This is just a big adventure for me."

Michael Broadhurst, 26

job title: Interactive news reader, *The Wall Street Journal*, Interactive Edition, July 1996 to present

job description: Repurposes newspaper for Web, updates stories, copyedits, writes roundup of activity in Asian markets

location: New York

background: Graduated from The University of Western Ontario where he edited school paper for two years and wrote for various college publications; graduated from Columbia's Graduate School of Journalism in May

ten years from now: "Will be in print, definitely."

After a few weeks of late-night on-line repurposing, what once seemed old-fashioned and unplugged begins to look pretty cool.

When most of us are still hitting the snooze button on our alarm clocks before work, Broadhurst is heading home to sleep: he works the 11:30 P.M. to 7:30 A.M. shift at the *Journal's* Interactive Edition, which is staffed twenty-four hours a day so online news can be continuously updated. Broadhurst helps prepare wire-service pieces for the Web, copyediting and formatting them. "I certainly don't like the hours," he admits, "and I would rather be writing."

He "writes"—sort of—when he does his daily summary of the Asian markets, "but there's no by-line," says Broadhurst. "And it's not really substantive journalism."

New media seemed to offer the best job options when Broadhurst graduated from journalism school this spring: he wanted to stay in New York City, so small-town newspapers were out and, as he soon discovered, big-name magazine jobs are tough to come by. Since Broadhurst eventually wants to do original reporting, the jury's still out on whether he's made the right career move. "Unless the online medium evolves in the next few years," Broadhurst says, "it's not where I want to be."

Article Review Form at end of book.

MSNBC isn't a conventional newsroom. It's the creation of a software giant teamed with a broadcast news giant, yet the following article shows that journalists with significant reporting and editing backgrounds in traditional newsrooms are leaving to sign up with MSNBC. What differences are they finding between the two working environments? Which working environment would you prefer? Do you see any dangers in an organization with a nonnews background, such as Microsoft, entering the news business?

Webward Ho!

Alicia C. Shepard

AJR contributing writer Alicia C. Shepard wrote about the CIA/crack cocaine controversy in our January/February issue.

Tom Brew looked down the road and didn't like the view. He'd been a mid-level editor at the San Jose Mercury News for 12 years and didn't see much room for dramatic career advancement.

On a whim in the summer of 1995, he sent his resumé to Microsoft's new news enterprise in Redmond, Washington, which had already hired some of his Mercury News colleagues. Soon a Microsoft recruiter called. Was Brew interested in an editing job with the Microsoft Network, a job that offered not only a new challenge but also stock options in the company that made founder Bill Gates a billionaire?

"Unlike a lot of people, I still retain a lot of affection for newspapers," says Brew, now 45. "But the last 10 years, I wasn't getting job offers. It was flattering when Microsoft called."

Microsoft flew Brew and his wife, Dawn, up to Redmond and wowed them. That was when the soul-searching truly began. Was he really ready to give up the newspaper business? Was Microsoft really interested in journalism or was this just another way of promoting Windows 95? Was working for Microsoft "selling out"? Would his friends still consider him a journalist? Was he willing to move his wife and two small boys away from his parents and the San Francisco Bay Area to a region where thick, gray skies are as common as blue?

Eventually, the sky-high housing market in the Bay Area helped make the decision easier for the Brews, who moved to Redmond in September 1995. But there was a more compelling reason. "I knew it would be rough making the transition. But I also didn't want to spend the rest of my life as a mid-level editor," Brew says. "They put us in a newsroom and said, 'Don't worry about money.' Who knows how it will work out? But how many times do you have an opportunity to create a new medium?"

Brew made the move at just the right time. Shortly after he got there, Microsoft signed a joint venture agreement with NBC to create MSNBC. The newly formed 24-hour information and talk network married NBC's cable and television expertise with Microsoft's extensive Internet and personal computer software knowledge. Debuting in July 1996, MSNBC enjoys the deep pockets of Microsoft and the credibility and prestige of NBC.

Soon the migration to the Redmond outpost began. But not only high-tech geeks wearing their baseball caps backwards have moved to Redmond. Since the unconventional media marriage, traditional journalists have left secure jobs at such news organizations as the Wall Street Journal, U.S. News & World Report, ABC News, the Associated Press, CBS News and the Los Angeles Times to be part of a forward-looking experiment mixing network TV, cable and the Internet.

The chance to be a pioneer in an exciting new medium is luring traditional print and broadcast journalists to MSNBC on the Internet.

"I find it easier to talk to the technical people than to understand them," says MSNBC's Merrill Brown. "The journalists here are often forced to stop and say, 'Wait a minute. Let's switch to English.'"

Some simply came for the challenge of trying to make something new work. Some made the move because they feared that their industries were stagnating.

From Alicia Shepard, "Webward Ho!" in *American Journalism Review,* March 1997. Reprinted by permission of American Journalism Review.

Others had grown tired of the predictability of their jobs. And many came so they wouldn't miss the boat sailing into journalism's future. "This is like television in 1947," says Merrill Brown, editor in chief of MSNBC on the Internet. "It really is, 'Whoa!' "

Once there, the media pioneers have encountered the snafus that often accompany a start-up: equipment malfunctions, disorganization, biweekly reorganizations, brutally long hours.

Other challenges are not so commonplace. It's easier, for example, to get a hard drive than a reporter's notebook. And rather than providing a familiar newsroom setting, MSNBC is a virtual Tower of Babel with its refugees from the worlds of print, television, radio and computers speaking in their own strikingly different languages.

It's a land where writers are called "content providers" and most journalists find themselves working next to people who think with a different part of the brain, to whom "getting granular" means getting down to specific details.

"I find it easier to talk to the technical people than to understand them," says Brown, who has worked at the Washington Post and Court TV. "The journalists here are often forced to stop and say, 'Wait a minute. Let's switch to English.' "

The pluses, though, are formidable. A chance to find completely new and creative ways to tell stories. Endless space for copy and graphics (witness the 10-part series on the 11th anniversary of the Challenger explosion). The money. For some, stock options. An endless supply of free coffee, sodas and juice. A Starbucks coffee kiosk on site. An architecturally dramatic cafeteria with restaurant quality food (so you won't have to waste time going out for lunch). No suits and ties. And high-caliber people. The only dead wood is in the nearby forest.

The Microsoft compound sprawls across 296 acres with 62 low-slung red buildings and could easily be confused with a college campus. As on many campuses, there are few signs of gray hair or serious wrinkles. It's dominated by the young, peopled with the best and the brightest clad in jeans, T-shirts, cutoffs, sweaters and sandals. Casual is cool. So is long hair on guys. A tie or suit is a dead giveaway that you are either a job supplicant or a visitor with something to sell. Spiffy shuttle buses with baskets of Tootsie Rolls, bubble gum and hard candy whisk employees from one side of campus to the other.

In the midst of the main campus is glass-enclosed Building 25, home to the 200 or so journalists taking a gamble on MSNBC. Most sport yellow badges, pegging them as part of the joint venture, while the rest of the Microsoft employees wear blue tags. With a yellow badge, one can walk past doors with signs bearing such ominous sounding nameplate as the "cryogenic vat room" before entering MSNBC's secured newsroom.

"The notion of Microsoft people wandering through here is something we have to be a little sensitive to," says Brown, who joined the enterprise last May. "It's not Microsoft per se, it's that the Microsoft people and those in the computer software business shouldn't be looking over the reporters' shoulders. When people come in and say, 'How is Microsoft doing?' I say, 'This is not Microsoft. It's MSNBC.' "

What's happening inside the MSNBC newsroom is really not top secret. MSNBC is trying to become one brand with two operations—an NBC-dominated cable shop in Fort Lee, New Jersey, and a multimedia, interactive Internet arm in Redmond. Programs are developed simultaneously for cable and the Internet, with some original material created for the Web. The goal is cross-pollination. MSNBC journalists are constantly searching for ways to make television and the Internet compatible, to create material for the Internet that's complementary to what's on NBC, CNBC (NBC's cable station) and MSNBC, as well as to figure out ways for users to interact with the news.

"We are pushing software development in ways it's never been pushed before," says Michael Silberman, a CNS refugee who is MSNBC's executive editor. If a graphic or an interactive chart can't be created, journalists tap into the infinite brain power available from the legions of Microsoft employees. The attitude is always the same: "We've got the brain power to do it. So let's do it."

Last fall Sports Editor Ed Macedo, formerly of the San Jose Mercury News, decided he wanted to poll the site's visitors on how they ranked pro football teams, updating the results as soon as each respondent weighed in. So he turned to program manager Brenden West, asking West to come up with a plan in eight hours. "It was one of those things that looked simple, but it took me a couple of days. There's no way I could explain to them [the journalists] what was involved," says West. "Oh yeah, they were impatient because I didn't make the deadline. In this case, it was something that broke new ground. I wasn't even sure I could do it." But he did.

Says Merrill Brown, "We are constantly trying to figure out how to tell the story, how to integrate multimedia, how to use computer software to tell the story, and striving to operate at some level in sync with our cable counterpart."

It isn't easy. Having Jane Pauley at the end of her MSNBC cable show, "Time & Again," suggest viewers turn to the Internet for more information on that day's program is the easy part. Getting video from her show to stream across a computer screen for longer than 15 seconds is a technical hurdle of the first degree. But the potential is there.

Potential is what it's all about. Right now, when someone goes to http://www.msnbc.com, they encounter a graphically charged Web site not unlike other media venues. The cover page has the day's headlines, updated every three hours. Occasionally, there's a bulletin encouraging viewers to tune into CNBC or MSNBC cable or "Dateline NBC" or to watch "InterNight," a cable program designed to visually explore the Internet. "Readers" can scroll through the categories: World, Commerce, Sports, SciTech and Life, each with two stories, often staff-generated. One day in late January, the cover page offered stories on Charles Murray's latest book, a bomb blast at an abortion clinic, the lack of competition between cable and phone companies and an interactive quiz on one's financial health.

Interaction is what the new medium is seeking. Not only can you customize a front page to reflect your interests by filling out a questionnaire, it's possible to type in your opinion about a story or issue, or follow link after link on any topic that grabs your attention—until you are drowning in more information than you ever needed. During President Clinton's second inauguration, MSNBC had a live still camera trained on the swearing-in ceremony. Viewers on the Internet could operate the camera, zooming in on people or playing with the camera angles. Although designed to handle many requests, the feature was swamped and difficult to use. But it certainly was novel.

It was the potential that drew Michael Silberman and his wife, Emily Eldridge, to Redmond in October 1995. After almost 11 years at CBS in New York City, Silberman saw all too clearly what the next five years would be like. When "Eye to Eye with Connie Chung" was canceled, Silberman lost his job as a producer of that show. CBS talked to him about a variety of positions, but each was all too reminiscent of what he'd been doing.

Then a friend of his wife who works at Microsoft called the couple. Silberman perked up. He liked what he heard. "The appeal was to develop or create interactive television news," says Silberman, whose wife, a former associate producer for "Dateline NBC," now works for "Underwire" on MSN. (While MSNBC is a joint venture, Microsoft continues to maintain its own online service, MSN.)

"I can't think of another place in journalism where you can be doing something completely new that's never been done before," Silberman says. "I didn't leave traditional journalism because I felt disillusioned, as many have. It was much more the draw of doing something new. The easy thing is to stay with what you know."

What Silberman knows is how to produce a television news show, and that expertise, he says, lends itself nicely to the World Wide Web. "A lot of what I learned as a television producer translates to the Web because it really is a visual medium," he says. "We are now always trying to figure out how to best present layers and layers of information to folks."

During last summer's Democratic National Convention in Chicago, Silberman and his team produced a multimedia retrospective of the 1968 convention using still pictures, text, audio spots from the time and footage from the NBC archives.

Silberman says that things are settling down after the bumpy early days. "We're getting into a rhythm," he says. "We are sort of moving out of the start-up mode and focusing on who we are writing for and what we think is important."

And coordination between the two media has improved sharply, in his view. "The main way we used NBC correspondents before was to do a phoner and put that in a story as an audio link," he says. "Now we are starting to work with them to produce stories for the Internet that have an NBC correspondent's byline."

The irresistible challenge of a start-up drew Mark Pawlosky to MSN News, MSNBC's forerunner, from the Wall Street Journal's Dallas bureau in 1995. Pawlosky rejected the company's first overture. But as he thought more about the prospect of developing new and exciting ways of providing news and information to computer users, he became intrigued.

Now he's business editor and executive producer, supervising a staff of 16 and happy he made the move. "I really wanted to make an impact and have some influence on journalism," he says. "And it's more likely to happen here."

Newspaper people, disheartened by the cutbacks that have plagued their industry, are particularly drawn to Redmond. There they encounter a world where money appears to be no object, and new ideas are eagerly embraced.

Dan Fisher, who spent 27 years as a reporter and editor at the Los Angeles Times, decided to take the leap soon after new Times Mirror chief Mark H. Wiles arrived in 1995 with budget ax in hand ready to cut, cut, cut. Fisher's last job at the Times before he joined Microsoft in January 1996 was working on starting TimesLink, the company's online service, which debuted in October 1994. "We'd been looking at a three-year lease to see if we could make money," Fisher says. "Then at seven months they were trying to cut it back. That was disturbing."

When a headhunter called in August 1995, Fisher jumped at the chance to be managing editor of Microsoft's "Sidewalk," an online city entertainment guide set to debut in March. "This would be like getting an opportunity to do this new thing called television in 1931," says Fisher, who has since become managing editor of MSN's "Investor" Web site.

The advent of MSNBC had special resonance for Sheila Kaplan, a former investigative producer for ABC. When she was working on a master's in journalism at the University of California at Berkeley, she watched "as half the class" went off to join an offbeat experiment in Atlanta launched by someone named Ted Turner: an all-news cable network. After graduating, Kaplan took the safe route as a newspaper reporter.

"I thought at the time I wouldn't go there," she says. "It had just started. Who knew what it was going to be?" Now, she adds, "the people I went to journalism school with are all running CNN. I didn't want to make the same mistake twice."

Kaplan is an investigative producer for MSNBC on the Internet. "I wanted to do something more substantial than television, but I missed print," says Kaplan, who move to Redmond from Washington D.C., last June. "But once in TV, I liked what you could do with sound and video. To me MSNBC was the best of both worlds: taking the substance of print and adding in the creativity of TV, without having the constraints of length and space."

What inspired many to defect to the Microsoft campus were mid-career ruts. Some who have flocked there had been doing journalism for over a decade. Too many stories seemed formulaic. While some might have eventually left the field, MSNBC provided a new way of getting them jazzed about journalism again.

That was the case for Andrea Hamilton, now an MSNBC writer/editor (or content provider) who left a good job (metro desk reporter) in one of the biggest cities in the world (New York) with one of the world's best news organizations (the Associated Press). "I needed to do something else," Hamilton says. "I'm 39. I'd always wanted to be a writer, but I'd been slotted as an editor."

Hamilton was impressed by the people who interviewed her at MSNBC. "They asked really intelligent questions," she says. But she was also told: "Do we know where we are going to be in six months? No. Can you live with that?" How do you feel about working in a completely chaotic enviroment? Can you live with that? She could. Hamilton packed up her apartment in Greenwich Village and began work last July.

While it can be exciting, the transition from traditional news to the culture of this new world of journalism is not always seamless. When television producers talk in a meeting about b-roll, or print people refer to the nut graph, no translations are necessary. But here former television types are apt to throw around jargon that baffles their print partners, and vice versa. Add computer whizzes to the mix and the need for translators can arise.

Microsoft has its own language," says Kathleen Flinn, a "Sidewalk" producer who left a job as editor of the glossy magazine "Internet Underground" to try Microsoft. "They say things like, 'You own that link, I'll own getting data on coffee houses.' It's odd because they use three-letter acronyms like BTW (by the way) and TIA (thanks in advance). I'm used to seeing that in e-mail, but they speak it. That's why you sit in meetings and say, 'Huh?' "

"Microspeak," as it's come to be called, is a combination of technical terms, business school-ese and, now, journalistic shorthand. It's not unusual to hear that one must "disambiguate," which

> "To me," says producer Sheila Kaplan, "MSNBC was the best of both worlds: taking the substance of print and adding in the creativity of TV, without having the constraints of length and space."

Online Careers: A Specialty or Recasting the Mold? **127**

means to clarify. The expression "We've got the cycles" baffled ex-L.A. Timesman Fisher at first, but now he knows it means "We have the available brain power to work on the problem."

"This is the first place I've worked in where I sit in on conversations and I don't understand what someone is saying," says David Guilbault, who worked as a producer for ABC for 20 years.

But there are bright moments. Mike Gordon, who worked for newspapers for 22 years, most recently at the Atlanta Journal & Constitution, offers one. "We can baffle the software guys with newsroom slang at will," he says, "although they're catching on. One of the program managers was heard saying, 'Let's cut to the nut graph.'"

To combat the sense of alienation in a strange culture, last August Flinn formed the Society for Displaced Journalists' Microsoft Chapter. She came up with the idea after attending an opening party for Slate, Microsoft's online magazine edited by Michael Kinsley. "It was really nice to talk to people like me," she recalls. The group meets monthly at various watering holes and has a pool tournament coming up.

Flinn's opening salvo seeking disenfranchised journalist read: "If you've ever found yourself lost by technobble in meetings, then SDJ is for you. (e.g., 'We were working on the OLE init conflict with the ODBC drivers but we couldn't make any progress because the repro case wasn't happening in our domain.')"

The sense of participating in the birth of a new medium and finding a new place for original journalism, however, buoys spirits. No one seems to care much that MSNBC is available to just 30 million households. As to how many people read the daily report on the Internet, no one really knows. (PC-Meter, a kind of Nielsen ratings for the Web, reported that MSNBC ranked sixth in usage in the news, information and entertainment category in the last quarter of 1996.) Those toiling in Fort Lee and Redmond work as hard as they would for the networks or major newspapers, yet without a network-sized audience or the influence of a dominant local daily.

"It doesn't bother me yet," says Kaplan. "If three years from now it's still like that, I might be bothered. Right now, I'm not paying attention to who is looking at it. I'm just having fun."

Article Review Form at end of book.

While change is a constant, accepting and adapting to change can be a challenge. *The Dayton Daily News* changed its approach to the news and overhauled its newsroom as a result. This included incorporating computer-assisted reporting techniques across the newsroom, eliminating traditional departments, revamping writing guidelines and seeking community input for stories. What was the impact of these changes? What makes the *Daily News* an innovator in computer-assisted reporting? What impact has the additional writing emphasis had on the final product? What role does community-assited journalism have in the overall product?

Doing It in Dayton

Newsroom culture turned upside down; staff tries to avoid culture shock

Hugh Morgan

Hugh Morgan teaches journalism at Miami University in Oxford, Ohio, and is a former writer for the Associated Press.

Editor's note: The previous stories identify three newsroom trends for the '90s—computer-assisted journalism, community-assisted journalism, and a renewed interest in writing/storytelling. In this context, trend means change, and change is anathema to most newsrooms. While we report on change every day, we struggle mightily to accomplish change within our news organizations while continuing to meet our hourly and daily deadlines. Integrating any one of these trends into a newsroom is a major challenge; attempting all three at once may sound like foolishness. The Dayton Daily News *in Ohio is trying just that—and more. Hugh Morgan, a former AP correspondent, spent three months visiting, observing, and interviewing folks in Dayton to see what could come of intentional chaos.*

Technology such as the Linotype, rotary presses, photoengraving methods, and the telephone ushered in a new era of journalism a century ago.

This technology made it possible to create mass circulation newspapers, which in turn explored new ways to cover and report stories. Newspaper circulation mushroomed.

A century later, with newspaper readership in decline, a new wave of technology again promises to enable us to develop new ways of reporting and delivering the news.

Computers are enabling newspapers to experiment with writing techniques that depart from the government-focused, inverted pyramid writing style of decades past, and they are trying to explore what it means to write for the readers.

The technology and new ideas have converged at the *Dayton Daily News*, a Cox newspaper, where these widespread changes are causing editors and reporters alike to hold their breath—some in apprehension—others in expectation. They are seeing whether these approaches will fit together.

Compared with a century ago, the changes facing newsrooms are "cubed," says Steve Sidlo, the managing editor.

"It's rare to have an opportunity to be on the cutting edge of anything, and this is an opportunity for editors, for newspaper people, to bring about some really important changes," he says. "I find that very exciting. It is certainly threatening in some ways, and it's also—to my mind—a tremendously exciting opportunity."

Recognizing the challenges, Editor Max Jennings says, "I don't know too many newspapers that are doing more innovative things at the same time as we are. In fact, I don't know any."

From Hugh Morgan, "Doing It In Dayton" in *Quill*, May, 1994. Copyright © 1994 Society of Professional Journalists, Greencastle, IN. Reprinted by permission of Dr. Hugh J. Morgan.

Among the changes are computer-assisted reporting, community-assisted reporting, and experiments in writing that vary from the use of narrative style to development of high-density, fact-filled pages that have no traditional stories. At the same time, the *Daily News* is:

- Switching to pagination,
- Wrestling with a thorough newsroom restructuring that has jettisoned traditional departments, and
- Developing many new media projects such as audiotext and niche publishing. (See related story on page 000*.)

In studying the changes during the first three months of the year, it became obvious that the greater change was not the technology, but the new philosophical approaches to the gathering, writing, and dissemination of news that the technology makes possible.

One theme throughout all these projects is egalitarianism. In the corporate world it is known as total quality management. In newsrooms, reporters are told to write for the readers—rather than for politicians or experts—and editors are told that writers have rights. This decentralization of power—or breakdown of hierarchy—is facilitated by technological breakthroughs.

The changes started with major projects, and they have generally been successful. The challenge on all fronts is to make them a daily part of the lives of reporters and editors.

"The idea is to get people to embrace the changes and the new culture and to have them feel energized by it and stimulated by it and not threatened by it, and also to try to convince people that we can make these kind of dramatic changes . . . and still not sacrifice [our] principles," says Jennings, a former wire service journalist and university professor who became editor in 1988.

"I ain't giving up on defending the First Amendment. I ain't giving up on being the champion of open meetings and open records and the free flow of information from government, or giving the voice to the little guy, or propping up somebody who needs some help, or putting the bad guys in jail," he says. "But, nonetheless, you got to sense that we are going to have cultural change."

Databases Open New Doors

A key element is computer-assisted journalism, which has already earned the *Dayton Daily News* a national reputation as the first paper to be directly wired to the county's computers—making such items as police reports, court files, election results, and property records instantly available. In addition, the paper has learned to manipulate databases on major projects, such as an analysis of more than 1.8 million records from the Occupational Safety and Health Administration. The investigation, a finalist for a Pulitzer Prize, found the federal agency did not fine people very severely when they were at fault in workplace deaths.

To help the paper learn the database ropes in the late '80s, the *Daily News* brought in Elliot Jaspin to teach the basics to a handful of staffers.

Jaspin, a pioneer in using databases, has since joined Cox's Washington bureau and continues to help the *Daily News*. A recent collaboration analyzed a computer record of the National Bridge Inventory from the U.S. Department of Transportation to reveal that almost a third of the nation's bridges could not support standard loads, or were designed and built for a time when traffic conditions had practically no relevance to today.

"What we learned is that you can find things using a computer that you can't find anywhere else," says John Erickson, *Daily News* projects editor. But he has two warnings for any paper going into computer-assisted reporting.

"We are trying to be very selective in choosing computer-assisted reporting stories that have impact," he says. "Pick your targets. Think of your stories first and think of how a computer tape or a couple of computer tapes will make your stories better. You are going to build up those stories that don't read like computer stories. And we try very hard to do that."

Another problem is not just in training, he says, but "If you don't do it all the time, you are going to lose anything you learn, you are going to forget it."

Only about 10 staffers routinely use the computers for calling up government records. And fewer are comfortable playing with databases.

One reporter who maneuvers comfortably through the databases is Cheryl Reed, who has covered the police beat since October 1992. She learned from Erickson, former assistant metro editor Mizell Stewart, and from four days of classes at a local company where she studied Paradox software and DOS (PC operating system).

Now that she accesses police records rather easily, Reed says, "I don't know what I would do without it."

It has become routine, like in late January when she picked up a

---

*Not included in this publication.

report of a 20-year-old suburban man who was shot to death. The victim was not identified. A source in the coroner's office gave her the victim's name. Since he died in a known drug area, she thought he might have a criminal record. Her next stop: the computer.

Using the same e-mail system millions of users call up daily, she queried the Montgomery County jail. She soon found the victim's rap sheets and discovered such facts as arrests on charges varying from burglary to drug abuse, height (5-foot-11), various employers, physical characteristics (a moon tattooed on his back), and the name and telephone of his mother. Reed found the man had been in trouble elsewhere, so she called another suburban police department and it faxed a misdemeanor report to her. She then called the mother, who told Reed about her son, "Deep down he was a great kid. He got hooked up with drugs—that's what killed him."

Reed arranged an interview, but when she arrived at the house, the mother was overwrought. Her husband—the stepfather—gave the interview.

All the while, the police had not yet released the name.

Reed then wrote the hard news story in the narrative format. The first three paragraphs read:

> Michael Mosley's short life played out like a bad country song, his stepfather said.
>
> Mosley's father drowned when the boy was 3 years old, he was kicked out of school when the assistant principal caught him with a bag of marijuana, and his best friend died in his arms last year.
>
> On Wednesday night—Mosley's last night in town before moving south to a new job and a new world—a bullet ended his life.

One last caution, from Stewart, is that sometimes reporters can get so caught up in crunching computer data that "they can forget to go out and talk to real people."

Listening to the Community

Another key element to the *Daily News* transformation is what executive metro editor Martha Steffens calls "community-assisted reporting," which she defines as having "heavy input from the community." Jennings labels it "public service journalism." Jay Rosen, an associate professor of journalism at New York University and director of the Project on Public Life and the Press, terms it "public journalism."

Whatever the name, the idea is to go beyond the newsroom admonition to write for the readers, to first consult the readers—and the nonreaders—to learn how they view an issue before devising a strategy to cover the story.

Rosen's project is funded through a grant from the John S. and James L. Knight Foundation to the Kettering Foundation, a research foundation in Dayton that has explored public life in communities. The *Daily News* has been conferring with Rosen and with the Kettering Foundation staff—especially Dr. David Mathews, its president, who once served as President Gerald Ford's secretary of health, education, and welfare.

Consulting with the foundation on ways of proceeding, Steffens is spearheading a major reporting effort in which the journalists are first going to the community, including young people, in a project focused on youth violence. The stories, planned for the fall, will emanate from those discussions.

"Basically, the thrust of this is to go out and have focus groups with citizens and let them determine what the story is about and where it is going," says Mickey Davis, a feature writer on the five-member team preparing the series. Staffers plan to listen to separate focus groups of middle school pupils, high school students, and adults.

"Maybe what we are is listeners—the key here is listening. It is a different perspective of what we are used to doing. And we haven't sorted it out yet in terms of really letting the focus groups determine the direction of the stories. That's a new kick for us," Davis says.

This will be in conjunction with similar projects around the nation by the foundation. The idea is to learn what is valuable to citizens about various issues dealing with youth violence and then to frame stories from their standpoint. This differs from the standard practice of pursuing preconceived ideas developed in the newsroom or by consulting experts and politicians.

Mathews says the public has been unhappy with the way journalism has presented issues. "If the options for action that are presented in the paper were recalibrated around how various options affected what is valuable—both pro and con—there would always be more than two options—and each option would have both some attractive and unattractive things about it."

"The *Dayton Daily News* is attempting to speak to this most fundamental problem of the rift between the public and journalism by changing in fundamental ways journalistic practice—the way they cover stories, the way they report stories," Mathews says. "That gets to the very heart of what journalism is all about."

"We can't tell them how to do it. We don't write newspapers.

We don't know," Mathews says. "So they are truly on the frontier in this project. You have to admire their courage."

The *Daily News* has already published a few such projects, including a February report dealing with ninth-grade proficiency tests that must be passed before seniors in Ohio's public high schools can graduate. The package included sample questions with answers given on the paper's NewsLine audiotext service, an experiment that drew more than 9,200 calls in four days.

But the concept for the stories grew out of calls for assistance by the Alliance for Education, a nonprofit third party advocate for strong public schools that was concerned about the low turnout rate in Dayton for the test last October. Through contacts with Brad Tillson, publisher of the *Daily News* who was the immediate past president of the Alliance's board, and with editor Max Jennings, the Alliance created a task force composed of the Alliance's staff, community leaders, and school administrators to discuss the challenge. Steffens was brought over from the *Daily News* to listen to the deliberations, and then she assigned education writer Jim DeBrosse to prepare the story package, which was published two weeks before the next round of tests.

Steffens says she initially thought they just wanted a story focused on getting students to show up for the test, but after several meetings, the participants realized they needed to create an understanding within the community about how the tests came about, how the tests have changed the curriculum, and how they are important to not just the students but to the community.

In DeBrosse's package, he used as the major story an explanation of how educators are employing innovative techniques to teach students basic concepts needed to pass the test. It started with a lengthy anecdote on how a teacher uses origami cubes to teach students the definition of volume. A secondary theme dealt with the history and reasons for the test. Also on Page One were a box outlining the importance of the tests and a photograph showing a student holding one of the cubes. Inside were two full pages that included the jump of the main story, sample questions, photographs and illustrations, and stories that dealt with businesses teaming up with schools to given incentives for taking and passing the test, business people tutoring students (the story focused on one student and a bank employee), and a software designer's program for teaching basic skills in math and writing.

On the heels of the survey, other media, including Dayton's radio and television stations, began doing takeouts on the test.

John Swann, a testing consultant for the Dayton schools, says preliminary figures for eighth graders indicate that 88 percent took the tests. This is an 18 percent to 28 percent increase over what was expected based on past experience. In addition, suburban Dayton schools reported high enrollments for the tests.

Steffens also developed a 20th century package of the tornadoes that destroyed the nearby town of Xenia and killed 33. Steffens says that about a dozen members of the Xenia community were invited "to get together with us—people who have had some longevity in the community—and have pretty valid historical points of view—to talk with us on how they see the community changing during this time period, whether or not the disaster changed the course of Xenia forever, perhaps in a way that they didn't want the community to go."

"Perhaps they also have lessons for other areas that have been hard hit by disasters," she says.

According to Rosen, "The major benefit [of public journalism] is that the community comes closer to grappling with its problems and the newspaper is centrally involved in that."

"There's also a benefit, I think, for the staff which gets to see itself in a form of public service that can be quite inspiring and engaging to people in the newsroom," he says. "And also educational, by the way. People learn that there is a certain wisdom that resides within a community and that it may not ever come from experts or reporters or official sources or any of the other people journalists routinely talk to."

The risk, he noted, comes if a paper crosses the line and becomes "an advocate in the old-fashioned and dangerous sense." That is something the paper is not prepared to do in any project with the community, Steffens says, adding that the paper's watchdog role is as important as ever.

A Return to Good Writing

While developing computer-assisted and community-assisted journalism, the *Daily News* is also working to make people notice them and other types of stories by making them more readable. As at papers throughout the country, reporters are breaking out major stories into packages and they are accompanied by photographs and information graphics. There are experiments in narrative writing daily, but the workhorse—as elsewhere—is the inverted pyramid, although the style is more conversational and from more of a human perspective than in the past.

Editor Jennings says, "In one sense, we are breaking out of the traditional format . . . like putting in new kinds of pages in our paper, new kinds of information pages, and I am telling you we are embracing the oldest forms of journalism, which are good writing."

The paper has particularly recruited four news staffers for their writing abilities. "They are wonderful writers and they still have a great love and passion and affinity for the feel and the cadence and the rhythm and the sound and the texture of a good sentence," Jennings says. "And I don't want to—for a second—send out a signal to our readers or to our newsroom that we are not interested in good writing in this newspaper."

To ensure that reporters have ownership of their work, Jennings explained, the paper adopted a writers' Bill of Rights by Charlie Waters, assistant features editor of the Los Angeles Times. It guarantees reporters certain rights during an assignment, a pre-writing conference, a chance, if time allows, for the reporter to make a case for a version an editor might not want at first, and the chance to be involved in the final editing process so long as the writer acts professionally. A tie goes to the editor.

One of the paper's major experiments in 1993 came after an 11-day state prison riot at Lucasville in south central Ohio. The Daily News published a 12-page special section filled with illustrations, a two-page center-spread color information graphic, photographs, and 950 inches of copy written like a nonfiction novel.

Reporter Mary McCarty used New Journalism techniques as the lead writer for the chronological narrative.

"We wrote it as a narrative tale, a detective story," says assistant metro editor Ron Rollins, who edited the project and wrote part of it. "We eliminated attribution. We were heavy on moods. . . . But it was all based very solidly on reporting and on the printed record of what had happened."

The story was told chronologically from the riot to the surrender followed by a brief epilogue of what had occurred since. "It put people there when guys were getting killed, it put people there when officials were planning what to do. It was a history," Rollins says.

Five other writers—Tom Beyerlein, Adrianne Flynn, Tim Miller, Cheryl Reed, and Sandy Theis—and Rollins also wrote various days depending on who had the best sense of the events of those days. Other reporters contributed. McCarty gave the project a read and suggested changes. Then Rollins finished the editing.

"It was a team effort. It was an entirely unique project for our paper," Rollins says.

McCarty, who came to Dayton from a career as a writer for Cincinnati Magazine, used a similar approach to a major series that detailed what happened to several women who had been imprisoned for violence to their husbands, fathers, or boyfriends, but who had been paroled by an outgoing Ohio governor. In one part of the series, for instance, she started from the point of view of one of the women and put it in first person—based upon McCarty's saturation reporting and court records. She says the article, about a sexually abused woman who shot and killed her stepfather, sparked a healthy electronic debate among reporters on their terminals as to whether this approach was appropriate.

The first few paragraphs read:

I have to kill him now.

The small, still voice came to Antoinette Taylor as if from outside her body. The refrain tuned out all other thoughts, like a bad jingle on an E-Z listening radio program.

And for once, Taylor, the most timid, indecisive of women didn't hesitate.

As to daily writing by the staff, McCarty says it could probably be improved despite the demands and stresses they face.

"There's a lot of productivity on this staff and we are all working on trying to insert into our writing style liveliness and experimental techniques," says McCarty, who meets with various staffers in a writers group. "Some people don't agree with the nonfiction novel approach, but I think everybody is trying to make their writing more sprightly."

Rollins says narrative writing works well at times, but, "On a day-to-day basis the inverted pyramid is kind of our cornerstone because we know that it is a good readership tool. It tells the story the way that scanning readers want. So, the inverted pyramid is not a nasty, you know, it is not a four-letter word."

Rollins says, "On the other hand, we encourage writers to try different approaches. A couple of years ago we put anecdotal leads on everything and we got out of that. We go through phases like everybody, but we really try and think about what to do. . . . We also look for offbeat ways to tell a story that may surprise people a little bit."

Rollins says the paper tries to "mix it up. We try to use the inverted pyramid as a tool, not as the be all and end all."

Article Review Form at end of book.

The newsrooms of many online publications bear little resemblance to traditional newsrooms. They differ in physical appearance, attitude and mission. But the concerns of online editors and publishers are similar to those of their print counterparts. What are some of those concerns? What do writers and editors say is different about writing for online publications? How have these differences helped *HotWired* and *Salon* survive in a field where online magazines die quickly?

Cyberspace Journalism

Carol Pogash

There's no doubt that electronic newspapers and magazines are the flavor du jour. But are they more flash than substance? And will they ever make money?

They said HotWired looked like a newsroom. Not like any newsroom I've ever seen. Ringed with cloudy windows, the former sewing factory has been transformed into a cavernous space. As HotWired grew, seamstresses fled; walls were crushed and open space now is brimming with young, enthusiastic cyber-editors and producers pioneering their way onto the World Wide Web.

Hot pink and black wires snake across the ceiling. Evian and Crystal Geyser waters are the beverages of choice. Maria, a yellow lab belonging to the design director, moseys by, wearing a blue ribbon to protest censorship on the Net and a tasteful set of pearls. She's the most dressed up member of HotWired. Women don't wear makeup. With a few exceptions, men don't wear ties.

The chief operating officer, the marketing director and the legal counsel share space with the newsroom staff. Nobody has an office. A surreal six-foot flower-like lamp looks like vegetation from Neptune. On the sign-in sheet, one person gave us a reason for visiting: "spiritual enlightenment"; another wrote "kicks and giggles."

"I'm working more hours, making less money, but I'm happier," says HotWired's copy chief, Pete Danko, a recent emigré from the San Francisco Examiner. "I feel better about my future. I have a feeling it's going somewhere."

The switch meant a departure from tradition, a new way of thinking, of editing, including the incorporation of audio and video into stories. It meant tossing out the AP Stylebook in favor of rules established by Wired magazine, the ad rich, beautiful print cousin of HotWired, Wired's Ten Commandments, which sit by Danko's elbow, include "Don't Sanitize" and the "We're not in newspapers anymore" directive: "Invent New Words."

So much happens so fast on the Net that HotWired, which has been in existence since October 1994, is considered old and established. To Danko, Web years are like dog years. Flourishing for a few fortnights is a feat. Stagnate and you die.

HotWired is constantly evolving, not into a newspaper, not into an entertainment magazine, but into something interactive and different. But is journalism being committed here? Or are these people simply larding up cyberspace with splashy graphics, news of the Net and fun factoids? Is this the future of news? Or is it some fantastic but short-lived journey?

The stampede to put information on the Net may have begun with individual self-expression. Now it's clearly market driven. Stand-alone news and feature services have popped up online while the number of *daily newspapers in cyberspace* has tripled in a year, with some 175 now on the World Wide Web. Millions upon millions of dollars are being spent, even though no one yet knows how to turn a profit, or what effect newspapers online will have on circulation figures at their print parents.

Despite the costs, nearly all the news on the Net is being

From Carol Pogash, "Cyberspace Journalism" in *American Journalism Review,* June 1996. Reprinted by permission of American Journalism Review.

served up free to everyone (although that's beginning to change, so enjoy these halcyon days). Each site is trying to make itself so clever, colorful and appealing that it becomes a daily habit. Each is competing not only against other forms of media, but also against thousands of other sites. So much experimentation is going on so fast that you can observe the changes daily. In the two months since AJR's last Internet-related feature (*The New Journalist,* April), the *Wall Street Journal* (full text) and the *Los Angeles Times* have been launched online. And other sites have changed dramatically.

"This is not a land grab," says David Simons, president of Digital Video Corp., an online business development firm. "This is jockeying for position in sand dunes. Nobody is making money that I know of. Certainly not on the content side."

Observes Paul Sagan, president and editor of new media for Time, Inc., "It's the chicken or the egg. Which comes first, the content or the audience with the money?" *Pathfinder,* Time Warner's megasite, offers a Coney Island of publications, including People (updated daily), a daily Time, Asiaweek, Money Magazine, Fortune, Sports Illustrated, Sports Illustrated for Kids, Entertainment Weekly, dozens of others—enough detours to get lost for days.

Most of the newspapers on the Net are producing "shovelware," print stories reproduced on Web pages, with few changes other than key words painted hypertext blue that offer readers links to stories with greater depth.

For the most part, HotWired's features tend to be about the Web. Swathed in natural fibers, young people are scrunched over HotWired's computers, trolling for sites and stories on the Net that they can write about for their site. A basic difference between this setting and a traditional newsroom is that these people don't go out to cover stories. They largely cover what's on the Internet, which is what many sites do. It's as if most of those working on the Web are standing in a circle holding up mirrors to one another. HotWired just does it better than most.

"We make plenty of mistakes every day," says Chip Bayers, one of HotWired's executive producers, "and we're proud of it. We're still learning the form. It's like the early days of radio when people read newspapers on the radio." And HotWired has begun branching out, producing stories from around the world beyond the Net. Newspaper journalism with attitude.

Under the direction of David Weir, a onetime editor at Mother Jones and Rolling Stone, and cofounder of the Center for Investigative Reporting, HotWired runs some of the best political coverage anywhere. It's politics among consenting adults.

The Netizen, HotWired's political section, provides "Daily Braindumps from the Campaign Front," spicy, incisive accounts of the candidates' activities. A piece by staffer John Heilemann, formerly of the Economist and now HotWired's "boy on the bus," described Sen. Robert Dole, the presumptive Republican presidential nominee, as "muttering, mumbling, spitting out staccato bursts of simplistic assertions that have been the hallmark of his campaign this year."

Authored by such writers as iconoclastic media critic Jon Katz and Netraker Brock N. Meeks, HotWired's political pieces may be laced with the kind of street lingo that would cause mass cancellations if they ran in daily newspapers. Stories tend to be heavy on opinion and angle, zippier, looser in language yet tighter in length than in a newspaper or magazine.

After the Republican primaries wound down, the Netizen seemed to falter. But by late April, it was breaking ground again with Heilemann shadowing Clinton in Japan. One piece contrasted a Clinton speech praising Japan's receptiveness toward more American imports, specifically cell phones, with a visit to Japanese electronic stores, where Heilemann had a tough time finding a Motorola.

"We have to prove there is an audience," Weir says. If enough people visit the Netizen (you can track the number of "hits" or visits to a site per day) there could be more news-driven stories to follow.

"I think what you're looking at," Weir says, "is honestly the birth of a new mass media. It's happening right before our eyes . . . it's global . . . and it's headquartered in San Francisco."

Article Review Form at end of book.

Michael Bloomberg's Wall Street skills helped him build a media empire by focusing on financial information. This empire includes information-service terminals in public facilities, a business news service, a Wall Street magazine, a TV network and a radio station. Why has Bloomberg been successful? What niche market did Bloomberg discover? What makes his news service unique? What predictions does he make for the future? Why did we include a publisher like Bloomberg in this section on the e-beat?

Baron of Business News

Linton Weeks
Washington Post Staff Writer

Michael Bloomberg's relentless ambition to create a global business news empire has put his little electronic boxes just about everywhere. Now he's reveling in recognition and riches—and says he's just begun.

Bloomberg. The name is everywhere here in the capital of money. On the magazine in the Delta shuttle seat pockets. On a computer terminal in a LaGuardia Airport corridor. On a billboard above the Holland Tunnel. On the walls of Penn Station and the World Trade Center. The whole burg is abloom with Bloomberg.

And that's exactly the way Michael Bloomberg wants it—especially on days like Friday, when the stock market is in a tailspin and the world is hungry for information about the financial markets. He wants the Bloomberg name to be the source.

It's "a cute, ethnic name that's easy to remember," he says.

Like a cowboy with a branding iron, Bloomberg has burned that name on a whole herd of financial products. His news service. His magazine for Wall Street insiders. His magazine for Wall Street outsiders. His energy newsletters. His publishing house. His three-year-old radio network. His two-year-old TV network. His radio station in New York.

And, most important of all, his "boxes"—the information-service terminals that have become ubiquitous in the financial world. These versatile Bloomberg terminals provide about 67,000 users around the world with in-depth securities analysis, detailed financial histories of companies worldwide and up-to-the-second news, weather, sports and entertainment [See related article, Page 000*].

In just 15 years, Bloomberg has built his company into a worldwide purveyor of financial information. In the process, he has made a personal fortune estimated by Forbes magazine at $1 billion. He's giving lavishly to charity, including a $55 million gift last year to his alma mater, Johns Hopkins University in Baltimore. Yet to hear this intensely ambitious man talk, he's just getting started.

To understand what drives Michael Bloomberg, you need to start with the fact that he worked as a securities trader at Salomon Brothers Inc.—arguably the most macho job at what was then the most macho company in the world. During the 1970s, he ran Salomon's equity block trading desk. He also supervised the company's computerized information services. John Gutfreund, the former Salomon chairman, has said that Bloomberg's gift to the company was to reprogram a Quotron—an old-fashioned stock quote machine—so that it could perform some basic stock analyses and comparisons.

When Salomon Brothers went public in 1981, Bloomberg left the company with $20 million or so. Some say he was pushed, some say shoved. Regardless, it was the best thing that could have happened to him. His buddies at Salomon continued to wheel and deal—their antics were chronicled in Michael Lewis's 1988 "Liar's Poker"—until the bottom fell out in a 1991 bond trading scandal,

*Not included in this publication.

From Linton Weeks, "Baron of Business News" in *The Washington Post,* December 8, 1996. Copyright © 1996 The Washington Post. Reprinted with permission.

and several go-go executives, including Gutfreund, went-went.

Bloomberg, meanwhile, used his analytical and trading skills to set up a business—30 percent of which was, and still is, owned by Merrill Lynch & Co.—that could pump vital information to money managers. In the beginning, he offered nothing but comparisons of stocks and bonds. He leased to his customers specially designed Bloomberg machines; using dedicated phone lines, he was able to provide them with high-speed data that could contrast and compare stock prices, price-earnings ratios and other information.

Rusty Todd, a journalism professor at the University of Texas and a former middle-level executive at Dow Jones Telerate, one of Bloomberg's competitors, said that the analytical tools Bloomberg created to help bond traders are exceptional.

"Bonds react to economic changes in predictable ways," he explained. "You can use quantitative ways to predict all kinds of things about bonds, such as the movement of the price of the bond over its lifetime. As you build a portfolio, you want a variety—when they'll expire, how volatile they are."

The Bloomberg, he said, helps bond watchers follow a complicated market easily.

Eventually, Bloomberg learned that his clients hungered for the news behind the numbers, so in 1990 he launched Bloomberg Business News. Today, the news service employs reporters around the world and publishes a 24-hour electronic news wire that covers the financial scene like paint.

As part of his campaign to spread his name, Bloomberg offers his news service free to select newspapers, including The Washington Post. He asks only that his service be credited at the end of each story. Pick up a financial section from The Post or the New York Times on a given day, and you'll nearly always find a handful of business news stories credited by Bloomberg Business News. There's that name again.

His corporation, Bloomberg L.P., has grown 30 percent a year and will take in more than $850 million in 1996. Via the Bloomberg machine, the company provides financial and general interest information to 145 radio affiliates and 200 TV stations worldwide.

Yet for all his success, Bloomberg is still hungry. Many observers say he's still got the heart of a Wall Street equities trader. "He's got a gift for making quick judgments," says Lewis. "That's very much a part of a trader's mentality."

But Lewis believes Bloomberg has one other essential, distinguishing characteristic: patience. "Traders don't build businesses," Lewis says. "He's obviously got a knack for long-term planning. Traders don't."

A Day at the Office

Bloomberg seems anything but patient as he stands in the doorway of his newsroom.

Though he's not very tall, he cuts a striking figure. Today, he's wearing dark pants, white shirt, black tie with yellow stripes, half-glasses. He chatters with passers-by.

He's in fairly good shape—the body of a man who isn't an exercise nut and remains an undisciplined eater. He snacks all day long, maybe grabs a cup of sweet-and-sour soup for lunch. He wakes early every morning and runs when he feels like it. He goes to sleep at midnight or a little later. He's usually at the office from 8 to 8.

Bloomberg leases 12 floors in two buildings at the corner of Park Avenue and 59th Street. But the main action is on the 15th floor of 499 Park Ave.

This is where Bloomberg has his equivalent of the old trading desk. He doesn't have an office. No one at Bloomberg has an office, he's delighted to point out, though he does have a small glass conference room behind his desk.

Newsroom activity swirls about an abundantly stocked, absolutely free junk-food bar. Six islands, in the center of the 15th floor lobby, spill over with bins of drinks and goodies. Five kinds of cookies, three kinds of pretzels, three kinds of cereal, microwave snacks—soups, popcorn, pasta—tuna lunch kits, bowls of fresh fruit, plates of cheese, 56 boxes of chocolate candy.

Here and there are handsome aquariums.

Salesfolk are demonstrating Bloomberg machines in glass cubicles. In another see-through square, Annie Bergen is lobbing softball questions at writer Scott Turow in a taped TV interview that will be shown on Bloomberg TV and written up for Bloomberg News and excerpted on Bloomberg Radio. She tells Turow to keep his answers short.

Financial gurus, bestselling writers, Hollywood stars and other rich and famous newsmakers parade through Bloomberg.

It's 5 P.M. Bloomberg's people scurry past. "Have you gotten Sharon Stone yet?" he asks Clare Hickey, entertainment producer of the Bloomberg Forum.

Hickey says she's called, but Stone's people won't call back.

"Did you tell her she has the chance to be the next Mrs. Bloomberg?"

Hickey just smiles.

Bloomberg gets quasi-serious. He tells Hickey to put it this way to Stone, and he charts a graph in the air. "As I get older, I get more valuable," he says, moving his left hand up. "As she gets older, she gets less valuable," he says, moving his right hand down.

His hands meet. Now, he says, would be the perfect time for, um, an intersection.

"How many single, heterosexual billionaires are there out there?" Bloomberg is fond of asking.

When he's not talking about business or his charity work, Bloomberg—who was born on Valentine's Day, 1942—is talking about women. Women he knows, women he sees, women on the phone. "You look smashing," he says to an employee in a red dress. "You're all made up."

"Got a hot date," she says, scrunching up her nose.

Asked if he's sexist, Bloomberg insists not. He's proud of his record. He boasts about the high percentage of women in the top tiers of his organization.

At one point during his busy day, a charcoal-suited Charlie Rose, who tapes his PBS-TV show in Bloomberg's studio, stops by Bloomberg's desk and says something. "We're two bachelors in New York," Bloomberg explains later. "We've got a lot to talk about."

"I like him enormously," Rose says of Bloomberg. The two have known each other for several years. "It's fun, it's a locker room thing with us."

Beyond a long glass wall, the Bloomberg Business News service clanks and clamors through the late afternoon. At a cluttered, medium-size desk, surrounded by a Bloomberg terminal and other sophisticated computer equipment, Charlie Pellet works like a maniac. A boom mike hangs over his head. From his chair, he produces and files two-minute radio reports—based on dispatches by Bloomberg's 250 business reporters worldwide. Several times a day he slips over to a makeshift TV studio in the corner of the room to film business reports for Bloomberg Information Television.

The digitized newsroom is run by bow-tied bespectacled Matthew Winkler, a former Wall Street Journal reporter. At the Journal, Winkler coauthored a 1988 profile that pegged Bloomberg as "breezy" and "profane." A short time later, Bloomberg called Winkler up.

What would it take to break into the news business, Bloomberg wanted to know. "I thought Bloomberg was already in the news business," Winkler says now. "I thought he was able to show very important people what was going on—with historical and real time data—what we as reporters weren't able to show them in words in the paper."

Bloomberg invited Winkler to a Japanese restaurant and offered him a job. His goal was to marry financial data with financial news.

"What excited me at the time," Winkler says, "is that wire services were pretty crappy. Show-up and throw-up stuff." Winkler says he wanted the opportunity "to build something that would go beyond news services."

The grueling hours don't faze Winkler. "I love the newsroom, the scoops. I've always been a newspaper guy. I think it's a very romantic occupation. I love being around reporters."

Recognizing the Name

It's all in the name. The proliferation of the Bloomberg name, says Bloomberg, helps the newsroom run better. "The more people know us," he says, "the better our sources."

He loves the simplicity of the cycle: Because of his growing business he's getting more recognition. Because of his recognition, his business is growing.

Bloomberg is sitting now in the small glass conference room behind his desk. Surrounded by shelves of magazine stories about himself, he tears open a small bag of Cheez-It snacks, licks his finger and picks up every last crumb.

What, he is asked, is he scared of? Is he concerned that Dow Jones, or some other company, will beef up its analytics and block his growth? No, he says, other groups—including a consortium of six of the world's largest brokerage firms—have tried to compete directly with Bloomberg and he has whipped them every time.

Is he concerned that he's locked into antiquated hardware? No, he believes his keyboard and his machine, including the new flat-panel, remote-keyboard version, provide state-of-the-art delivery to his customers. And for the past year and a half, Bloomberg information has been available on personal computers and workstations. About 3,000 users receive their news this way.

Is he concerned that the Internet will overpower his company, offering essential information to money managers at a cheaper price? No, he believes the Bloomberg offers historical and real-time financial information that cannot—and never will—be found on the World Wide Web.

He maintains that the Internet is nothing but a distribution system.

Bloomberg doesn't fret about the future so much as try to dominate it. He believes, for example, that the Newspaper of Tomorrow will be made of cloth. "There [will be] transistors hidden in the fibers," he says. When you want to read about sports, he says, you will choose it on a menu and sports information will appear on the cloth page.

"You keep all the reasons that people read newspapers," he says. And you take advantage of up-to-the-second technology.

Bloomberg continues to fast-pitch his vision of the future. And it's hard not to get swept up in his energy. He's got good health, a good shtick, a booming business and a nonstop life.

In fact, he's got to go now. He's speaking to a new radio affiliate this afternoon, then he's launching a new magazine in the evening and he's going to the stylish 21 Club with an old girlfriend from Atlanta.

"I go to restaurants, people are pointing at me," he says, still some amazement in his voice. "They call out my name."

Financial Information in an Instant: High-Speed Network at Heart of Bloomberg's 'Real-Time' Service

The center of the Bloomberg universe is the classic "Bloomberg box"—75 pounds of machinery that includes two 15-inch monitors, one keyboard and more than 4,000 functions. The monitors display a small window for Bloomberg TV and a panel for the news service.

The key to Bloomberg's real-time capabilities—instantaneous quotes, functions and analytics communications—is a high-speed network, using a dedicated digital phone line that allows for interactive communications.

Other financial information companies, including Reuter and Dow Jones & Co., offer similar services. According to Robert Crooke of Reuter, more than 300,000 users worldwide regularly access Reuter's financial information. Reuter also sells its news to newspapers, radio and TV networks and broadcast outlets worldwide and has developed news applications for the new online and Internet media.

Dow Jones is another competitor. More than 100,000 people worldwide subscribe to Dow Jones Telerate, a financial news and information service that is available through special hardware of a desktop PC. Paul Ingrassia, executive editor of Dow Jones News Services, said that 3,000 Bloomberg subscribers pay as much as $730 extra each month to receive Dow Jones news on their Bloomberg terminals. "We're on 90 percent of the desks of people who buy real-time corporate news in the U.S. and Canada," Ingrassia said.

Those services, Michael Bloomberg is quick to point out, sell financial information a la carte. The Bloomberg is prix fixe. Subscribers pay a flat fee—$1,140 a month—for the hardware and everything Bloomberg offers.

Like Reuter and Telerate, Bloomberg also offers premium services, such as Moody's Investor Service Inc. information.

Trip Strauss, a stock broker at Stephens Inc. in Little Rock, uses his Bloomberg for keeping track of his clients' holdings. "You enter in the portfolio of stocks you are watching," Strauss said, "and the Bloomberg can arrange them in ascending or descending order. Hit another button and get their P/E ratios."

In the old days, Strauss explained, if Goldman Sachs & Co. downgraded a stock, the company called up its best customers and passed along the news. With Bloomberg and other financial news services, that information is available to anyone.

As the user delves deeper and deeper into the Bloomberg service, the analytical information—pulled together by more than 1,000 Bloomberg number crunchers in Princeton, N.J.—gets more arcane.

But the Bloomberg offers much more than financial analysis. Subscribers use Bloomberg for planning trips, reading horoscopes, following sports scores, sending flowers, everything but playing liar's poker. "Besides its product," said Sharon Lawrance, an analyst at Salomon Brothers Inc. in New York, "the Bloomberg has a fun side. If traders are not trading, they have other things to do."

Ask founder Michael Bloomberg about the health of his company and he shrugs. He says that 67,000 users are paying $1,140 a month. "You add it up."

Hmmm. You can even use the Bloomberg as a hand calculator.

Let's see. Twelve times $1,140 times 67,000.

In annual revenue, that's $916 million and change.

Article Review Form at end of book.

WiseGuide Wrap-Up

Change is constant. It is a part of our lives. When we embrace change, we open up ourselves and our careers to an infinite set of possibilities. These possibilities can only enhance us as individuals, as journalists and as representatives of the people we serve—the news consumers.

In academic institutions throughout North America, journalism departments are teaching online journalism skills. Educators recognize that, to compete in the marketplace, their graduates need the technical and analytical skills required by the online world. These Section 3 readings (and their CourseLinks counterparts) illustrate how these skills can be applied in the real world. Note that these skills are used in both traditional and nontraditional newsrooms from Raleigh, N.C., to Redmond, Wash., and every state in between. In these newsrooms, reporters are working on computer-assisted reporting projects, turning to the Internet to research background information and e-mailing sources for more information. They are writing for Web pages, developing multimedia projects and pushing the medium as far as it can go. The result is a new outlet for news, as well as new opportunities for creative journalists.

For the journalist in today's world, embracing change presents new career possibilities. The same is equally true for today's journalism student. Keep an open mind about this rapidly changing profession. Be flexible and prepare by honing a wide range of journalistic skills. No one can predict how the journalistic mold will be cast.

R.E.A.L. Sites

The adjacent list provides a print preview of typical CourseWise R.E.A.L. Sites. (There are over 100 such sites at the CourseLink™ Site.) The danger in printing URLs is that Web sites can change overnight. As we went to press, these sites were functional using the URL provided. If you come across one that isn't, please let us know via email at webmaster@coursewise.com. Use your Passport to access the most current list of R.E.A.L. sites at the CourseLinks™ Site.

Site name: Society of Professional Journalists
URL: http://spj.org
Why is it R.E.A.L.? SPJ offers this site as its electronic resource for journalists. You'll find media news, reports, FOIA information, award winners, a merchandise catalog and convention information at this site.
Key topics: careers, community journalism, computer-assisted reporting, current issues, database searching, desktop journalism, economic models, ethics, features, future trends, information access, information retrieval, legal issues, media writing, minority issues, online newspapers, online magazines, personalized news services, push technologies, reporting skills, story strategies, webcasting

Site name: American Journalism Review
URL: http://www.newslink.org
Why is it R.E.A.L.? Articles related to online careers and journalism, story archives and sites of interest can be found here.
Key topics: careers, community journalism, computer-assisted reporting, current issues, database searching, desktop journalism, economic models, ethics, features, future trends, information access, information retrieval, legal issues, media writing, minority issues, online newspapers, online magazines, personalized news services, push technologies, reporting skills, story strategies, webcasting

Site name: Columbia Journalism Review
URL: http://www.cjr.org/
Why is it R.E.A.L.? Current and past issue are available online, also resources organized by subject, updated information on past issues, journalists email addresses and resource guides.

Key topics: careers, community journalism, computer-assisted reporting, current issues, database searching, desktop journalism, economic models, ethics, features, future trends, information access, information retrieval, legal issues, media writing, minority issues, online newspapers, online magazines, peronalized news services, push technologies, reporting, skills, story strategies, webcasting

Site name: Editor and Publisher
URL: http://www.mediainfo.com/
Why is it R.E.A.L.? Daily headline stories, weekly columns, archived stories, contest winners and conference information is available.
Key topics: advertising, careers, community journalism, computer-assisted reporting, current issues, database searching, demographics, desktop journalism, economic models, ethics, features, future trends, information access, information retrieval, legal issues, marketing, media writing, minority issues, online newspapers, personalized news services, push technologies, reporting, skills, story strategies, webcasting

section 4

A New Wild West: Where's the law? Whose ethics?

Key Points

- Become familiar with the key ethical and legal issues framing the debate about the Internet and online journalism, including copyright, privacy and libel.

- Know the key components of the First Amendment and the Communications Decency Act.

- Explore your own thoughts about journalistic ethics and the law. Think about what it means to be an ethical reporter. Think about what it means to be a responsible publisher.

> " 'It's really the Wild West out there,' says one New York advertising executive. 'I don't have to really worry about truth in advertising on the Internet. I just have to worry about kiddie porn.' "
> —Christopher Harper

WiseGuide Intro

The First Amendment to the U.S. Constitution is the basic source of rights for journalism in the United States. Journalists working in the electronic arena have to be aware of these rights. They also have to be aware of the limitations of these same rights in order to avoid running afoul of the law. The articles in this section examine these rights as well as related ethical and professional issues. These readings examine freedom of speech, accuracy, copyright, privacy, libel, fair use and pornography.

The Internet is an international medium. Discussions are presently underway to develop worldwide rules and standards for the Internet. These rules and standards will be debated for sometime. Meanwhile, online journalists need to be aware of U.S. rules and regulations that apply to U.S. citizens. Local standards, especially when dealing with pornography, also apply creating a legal climate that varies from jurisdiction to jurisdiction.

Free speech guidelines established under the First Amendment cover e-mail and online discussions. The rules against libel, usage of inaccurate information and invasion of privacy still prevail.

Online journalists also need to consider the question of libel. An individual can be just as easily defamed online as in print. At what point an online contributor crosses the line from private individual to public figure is the topic of yet another debate and is subject to case-by-case interpretation. The courts are struggling with these issues as case law winds its way through the legal system.

Meanwhile, freelancers have taken publishers to task for distributing their material on Web sites without additional compensation. This issue goes to the heart of discussions about copyright. Other copyright issues include the collecting and bundling of previously published material on listservs or newsgroups without appropriate permission and the downloading of art and graphics for reproduction on other sites.

The bottom line, of course, is that the online arena is not that different from its print counterpart. Journalists who operate in an ethical manner don't have to worry about libel, invasion of privacy and problems with accuracy. Thus, the first defense against unethical, inaccurate or unfair journalism starts with the individual reporter.

Questions

1. The Communications Decency Act has stirred controversy since its inception and will continue to do so. What are your thoughts about the recent revisions to this bill? How would you like to see your rights protected in this area? (Watch for updates on the CDA at the CourseLinks Web site.)

2. Although the case continues to be made that the same laws that apply to traditional journalism apply to online work as well, are there exceptions? In what areas? How should the ethical reporter navigate exceptions to the rule?

3. What steps do you need to take to protect your freelance writing? How is your work protected if you are a salaried employee of a publisher? How do you think freelancers who develop online content (text, photos, art) should be compensated?

Although the U.S. Surpreme Court has overturned the Communications Decency Act, the following article by Amy Harmon raises interesting questions still to be resolved. The article dissects the issues in light of the global nature of the Internet. Can the Internet be controlled? What steps are being taken by other countries to try to control online information? What impact has the Memphis obscenity case had regarding control? Will encryption become the next Internet battlefield?

Internet Tests Boundaries of Decency—And Nations

Amy Harmon
Times Staff Writer

Computers: Cyberspace may be making laws of any one country irrelevant, shifting power from governments.

When the Supreme Court hears arguments today on the Communications Decency Act, some people think the justices will be mostly wasting their time. That's because national law is increasingly irrelevant when it comes to governing the Internet.

The global computer network is blind to the terrestrial boundaries that have traditionally dictated legal jurisdiction—and there's nothing resembling consensus among the nations of the world on what can properly flow across them.

An eclectic collection of legal scholars, libertarians, crypto-anarchists and ordinary Internet users is predicting that cyberspace will ultimately render the nation-state as we know it irrelevant, with law rooted in physical control of geographic territory giving way to new forms of governance springing from online communities.

"Activity in cyberspace ultimately forecasts the end of national control," said David Post, visiting associate professor of law at Georgetown University. "People will still sell shoes and send their kids to school. But there will be an enormous upheaval in the status quo."

Regulation of indecent communications and other forms of speech is only the beginning when it comes to earthbound laws being subverted by the cyberspace sprawl. States are now struggling to assert their authority over online gambling. The federal government remains mired in a largely futile effort to control the use of encryption technology in the name of national security.

The growth of online commerce and development of "digital cash" systems, moreover, promise to strike at the heart of government power: the ability to levy and collect taxes.

The challenge to the age-old notion of geographically based political power springs, first of all, from the simple fact that in cyberspace, there is no distance between two points. From Los Angeles, it takes about as long to look at a picture stored on a computer in China as it does to view one housed in Santa Barbara.

Therefore, if the CDA—which prohibits placing indecent material on computer networks where children might find it—is upheld, Americans who want unrestricted access to indecent material can simply point their World

From Amy Harmon, "Internet Tests Boundaries of Decency—And Nation" in *Los Angeles Times Business & Technology,* March 19, 1997. Copyright 1997, Los Angeles Times. Reprinted by permission.

Wide Web browsers to Finland, or to any other country where such information is unregulated.

And those who want to distribute indecent items can—albeit not without a certain degree of hassle—find citizens of other nations willing to rent out computer space to house the material.

The American Civil Liberties Union is leading a broad coalition—which includes the American Library Assn., the Newspaper Assn. of America and Microsoft Corp.—in challenging the CDA, whose enforcement has thus far been blocked by lower courts.

The plaintiffs' case focuses mainly on the arguments that the CDA bans constitutionally protected adult communications in the guise of protecting children, and the term "indecent" is so ill-defined that it could include everything from AIDS pamphlets to hard-core pornography. They also argue, though, that because about 40% of the "indecent" material on the Internet is located outside the United States, the law is unconstitutional because it won't achieve its goals.

In principle, of course, it is possible to control the Internet by controlling the physical infrastructure: Authoritarian governments in China, Singapore and Vietnam do just that to maintain restrictions on political speech.

Short of such draconian measures, though—which would be all but unthinkable in the United States—governments must resort to the strictures of law. And that's already proving ineffective.

Last year, Germany ordered Internet service providers to block access to a site in the Netherlands that carried a left-wing magazine called Radikal, which is banned in Germany. The site, XS4ALL, simply rotated its Internet address continuously, thwarting many of the automated blocking efforts.

Similarly, when the German government banned a Holocaust revisionist site, Internet activists created multiple "mirror" sites—in California, among other places—where the same information could be obtained.

As a recent report prepared for the European Parliament notes: "Where certain acts are punishable under the criminal law of one member state but not in others, practical difficulties of enforcing the law may arise."

"These laws tend to reflect their own national customs and national interests," said Barry Steinhardt, associate director of the ACLU. "I suspect that in the end there will have to be international treaties, and the only effective controls are likely to be on things where there is broad international acceptance that content should be illegal."

This broadening of jurisdictions forced by the Internet doesn't necessarily mean that laws will become more liberal. In the United States, the Supreme Court decreed in a 1973 case that obscenity should be defined locally by applying "contemporary community standards" to a particular form of media. Thus a pornographic movie could be banned in Memphis, Tenn., but freely screened in Los Angeles.

But in writing the CDA, Congress said in a conference report that its intention was to create a "uniform national standard of content regulation." And most experts agree it is likely that the standards of the most conservative communities would prevail on a national level.

The one precedent—set before the CDA was passed—is the case of Robert and Carleen Thomas, a California couple who were convicted of 11 counts of obscenity in Memphis because an undercover postal inspector there downloaded sexually explicit images from their Milpitas-based bulletin board.

As states pass their own versions of the CDA—at least 11, including California, have done so—sticky questions of jurisdiction get even more complex. An Internet message posted in New York and retrieved by readers in Georgia and Connecticut might well be illegal for different reasons in each state.

The ACLU has challenged New York's law on the grounds that it violates the interstate commerce clause, which states that only Congress has the right to issue laws having to do with things that are interstate in nature.

Meanwhile, jurisdictional disputes are beginning to crop up in other areas. A Minnesota state judge ruled in December that Minnesota could block a Las Vegas corporation, Granite Gate Resorts, from soliciting gambling business in the state via the Internet. But the issue is sure to be broached elsewhere as the online gambling business grows—and even Minnesota might be out of luck if Granite Gate were to, say, move its gambling site to the Cayman Islands.

Many believe the advent of digital cash systems, which in their most sophisticated form enable people to move money over computer networks with complete anonymity, will deal another big blow to traditional government by making tax evasion and money laundering far easier.

"The supranational nature of electronic payment mechanisms may be a primary factor in the nation-state becoming a fleeting footnote in social history," said Roger Clarke, a visiting fellow in computer science at Australian National University. "In the near future, not only wealthy corporations but also ordinary individuals will utilize opportunities to place monetary flows, profits and assets beyond the grasp of national taxation agencies."

Perhaps the most dramatic face-off between national sovereigns and the electronic frontier centers on encryption, the ability to encode data so that law enforcement officials can't get at it. The U.S. government has launched a global—and so far unsuccessful—campaign to unify the world around a plan to allow law enforcement officials with legitimate warrants access to the keys to every user's code.

The plan has drawn ferocious opposition from "netizens" and civil libertarians, who say encryption is the only way that individuals will be able to protect their privacy in the Digital Age.

Some legal scholars argue that no matter what governments do, cyberspace will ultimately be governed by the architecture of the Internet. If privacy is to be protected, for example, it cannot be legislated but must be built into software code—as in Netscape Communication's recent decision to allow users of its Web software the option of disabling a feature that corporations use to track Web-surfing habits. "Law is becoming irrelevant," said Lawrence Lessig, a law professor at the University of Chicago. "The real locus of regulation is going to be [computer] code."

David Post and David Johnson, co-directors of the Cyberspace Law Institute, propose an explicit rejection of the view—first formalized by philosopher John Locke in the 17th century—that political power in modern society derives from the state's ability to impose physical punishment.

They say cyberspace should be treated as a legal jurisdiction unto itself, subject to laws and regulations that are created and enforced by members of individual online communities. Rather than the use of physical force, banishment could become the most effective way to handle criminals.

If, as German social theorist Max Weber put it, "the state is a human community that successfully claims the monopoly of the legitimate use of physical force within a given territory," then cyberspace is a voluntary human community where "netizens" join based on common interests and rules are imposed as a condition of membership.

As one Clinton administration official responsible for information technology policy puts it: "Government is formed because there's a community of allegiance people have based on language and territory. So as communities begin to form in cyberspace that are not based on territory, the question becomes 'What is government?'"

Article Review Form at end of book.

The Communications Decency Act, rejected by the U.S. Supreme Court in 1997, posed challenges to schools, universities and libraries. Those challenges remain. Christopher Harper examines the impact CDA had on society even as it was argued in court. Do you think there should be controls on what can be read or seen on the Internet? What do you think about the decision by the University of Oklahoma to suspend sexually explict discussion groups? Should librarians act as censors? What is your reaction to the governor of South Dakota's decision to block protestors' e-mail?

Bad Law, Tough Issues

The Internet, free speech and the CDA

Christopher Harper

It is quite possibly the only time that talk radio host Rush Limbaugh and Clinton advisor Ira Magaziner have ever agreed on an issue. That issue: the Communications Decency Act, which was argued this week before the U.S. Supreme Court. Both Limbaugh and Magaziner think the CDA is a bad law.

The law basically prohibits adults from using a computer to send pornography to a child and imposes fines and prison sentences for doing so. But opponents argue that the law is too general and poses a challenge to the right of free speech. Existing statutes already prohibit the giving of pornographic or "obscene" materials to those under the age of 18. "Obscene," a term based on local standards as defined by law, means the material depicts individuals engaged in sexual acts in a manner that offends local moral standards and has no artistic value.

Limbaugh said in an interview that "a law that is not enforceable is a worthless law. Politicians were making a statement that they were anti-porn. The people who don't want to be part of those (pornographic) conversations will ignore them."

Clinton's New Guru

Magaziner, who has become the Clinton Administration's point man on the Internet, said in an interview that he opposed the law. He agreed to the interview by stating he was only expressing his personal beliefs—not the policy of the Clinton Administration. Nevertheless, Magaziner said: "I don't think government should get into censoring the Internet. As a parent I can understand why you want to restrict access to pornography. That should be a decision that each household makes."

Both Limbaugh and Magaziner endorse so-called "filtering" systems that prevent children from accessing pornographic sites on the Internet.

"Really the Wild West"

So far, CDA is really only one of few federal laws specific to the Internet—it's unclear what other laws cover the new medium. "It's really the Wild West out there," says one New York advertising executive. "I don't really have to worry about truth in advertising on the Internet. I just have to worry about kiddie porn."

For the most part, the advertising executive is correct. It is the Wild West. While many analysts and attorneys think existing laws will apply to the Internet, there are a number of sticky new issues

From Christopher Harper, "Bad Law, Tough Issues" in *E&P Interactive,* March 18, 1997. Reprinted by permission of Christopher Harper.

emerging that require some tough calls. Consider, for instance, barring access to public discussion groups, pressing librarians into service as community censors, and silencing citizens who criticize government officials via e-mail.

Barring Access to Newsgroups

The University of Oklahoma recently suspended access to sexually explicit discussion groups—called newsgroups—to ensure that students under the age of 18 could not access the information. The university established two separate routes of access to the Internet—one that refused access to the sexual sites, the second that allowed it.

Federal Court Judge Wayne E. Alley determined that the university did not violate the First Amendment. "The result of this policy is to allow recreational use of Internet services on the 'A' server, but to restrict the use of certain newsgroups to academic and research purposes," Alley wrote in a seven-page decision. "A university is by its nature dedicated to research and academic purposes. The limitation of OU [University of Oklahoma] Internet services to research and academic purposes on the 'B' server is not a violation of the First Amendment, in that those purposes are the very ones for which the system was purchased."

University President David Boren, a former United States senator, said he was pleased by the judge's decision. "The university did its best to strike a very careful balance in order to protect legitimate academic and intellectual freedom while at the same time assuring that the University does not act as a distributor of obscene materials which is not protected by the First Amendment," he said.

Librarians as Cyber Censors

At many libraries throughout the United States, *The New York Times* reports that librarians are playing a role they would rather not play—censor. The Austin Public Libraries have installed software to block users' access to potentially objectionable sites on the Internet. Library director Brenda Branch said she believed she had no choice but to install the programs after receiving reports of patrons using library computers to view sexually explicit material on the Internet. In one case, a library user was seen viewing images of young children engaged in sex. "No professional librarian ever wants to compromise intellectual freedom in any way," says Branch. "But the only way I can put it is that I am trying to balance a lot of different needs here. I am trying, in addition to supporting the First Amendment, to deal with the legal, ethical and moral issues arising because of some of the kinds of things that are available on the Internet and out of my control."

Librarians throughout the country are trying to decide whether they should offer the Internet to their patrons uncensored. In Boston, Mayor Thomas M. Menino ordered that filtering software be installed on all city-controlled computers to which children have access. Menino acted after a local city councilwoman complained that children in her district could view pornography in a local public library. Patrons of the Los Angeles public library system, with 66 branches and a main library, find quite a different attitude. A notice on the library's own Web site informs users, "The library has no control over the information on the Internet, and cannot be held responsible for its content."

Opposed to Censoring Library Access

The American Library Association opposes the use of filtering software in public libraries. One reason is that the technology often lumps innocent sites in with lists of banned material. For example, American Online banned the use of the word "breast" at one point. That eliminated steamy chatroom conversation about breasts, but it also prevented "breast" cancer from being discussed. AOL changed its position.

Silencing Citizens' Criticism of Government

How will the doctrine of free speech be treated online? Last December, the governor of South Dakota ordered a small Michigan-based Internet service provider to block the account of one of its users. The governor faced an electronic mail campaign from a woman who used Technology Dimensions Inc. The customer, a digital artist and Native American named Ishgooda, organized a protest against what she described as the governor's plan to prohibit Native Americans in groups larger than 40 people from holding ceremonies on state land.

Ishgooda, which means "dabble with fire," is a member of the American Indian Movement's Cyber-Support chapter. Electronic mail attacking the governor's position quickly started streaming in from around the world. Ishgooda forwarded the e-mail to the lieutenant governor, the parks and recreation office, the Wildlife Division and the South Dakota state office of information services. Each organization received more than 300 pieces of mail. Officials in the governor's office, annoyed at the volume of mail, instructed the bureau of information and telecommunications to call the service provider stop the campaign by pulling the plug on Ishgooda's account from which she forwarded most of the electronic mail.

Tim Gossiaux, the company's service manager, said he asked "if the messages stated any harm for anybody or were they vulgar." When the state officials replied that no threats or vulgarity were included in the messages, Gossiaux told the governor's office the messages were "perfectly legal."

The governor's office ordered the state's webmaster to warn Gossiaux: Stop the e-mail or the webmaster would block all traffic coming from his Internet service. Gossiaux contacted Ishgooda about the matter but stopped short of turning off her account. Subsequently, Gossiaux' service was cut off from sending messages to the governor's web site. The governor's office defends its action by calling the e-mail protests nothing but "junk mail" and equates the blockade with telling the post office to stop delivering it.

There are a lot of tough calls out there with a new medium. The U.S. Supreme Court began deliberating the first tough call this week on the Communications Decency Act. It is unlikely this argument will be the last.

Article Review Form at end of book.

Although it might appear that all information available on the Internet is free, it is not. Don Labriola examines copyright issues in the following article and offers tips on how to avoid violations. Can you recognize a copyright notice? What do you do if you want to use material you find on the Web? How can you decide if material is in the public domain?

Getting Through the Maze

Don Labriola

It should have been your finest hour. Armed with an expensive new multimedia computer, you gave the mother of all presentations, packed with flashy effects like a Jurassic Park video clip, excerpts from old Beatles songs, an animated Superman flying around the screen and even a shot of Sports Illustrated's swimsuit cover girl. Just as you'd planned, the entire audience was charmed by your wit and dazzled by the technology—but there was one fly in the ointment: the half-dozen lawsuits that were waiting on your desk the next morning.

Your mistake—and it's a common one—was thinking that you could use other people's creative properties without first asking permission. Composers, authors and artists who spent a lot of time and money developing marketable properties expect to be compensated when someone else benefits from their work. But this can be a problem if you simply want to spice up a business presentation, software demo or interactive tutorial with recognizable music and visuals. In many cases, it's not even clear who, if anyone, owns the rights to specific properties.

One alternative is simply to stick with royalty-free "clip media." Collections of photos, music and video clips that can be incorporated into a presentation or multimedia production without any additional payment are widely available, usually on CD-ROM. But what if there's other, existing material—whether it's Mickey Mouse or the Apollo moon landing—that you just have to use?

The first step is to determine whether it's actually necessary to obtain permission to use the properties you're interested in. When a copyright expires, the work is said to enter the public domain; it can then be used by anyone without restriction. But it's not always simple to tell when copyrights expire (see "Public Domain," page 000*). Furthermore, some media—such as film or recorded music—may be protected by multiple copyrights that expire at different times.

Name That Tune

When you determine that you'll need permission to use a property, the toughest part of the task may be tracking down the owners. If you're interested in a popular song, for example, you'll need to identify the music publisher (usually listed in album liner notes or on sheet music) and then contact either BMI (Broadcast Music Inc.) or ASCAP (the American Society of Composers, Authors & Publishers), which can help you identify and contact the copyright holder. If the publisher is willing to let you use the music, you may wind up paying a flat rate, a per-unit royalty or some combination of the two, depending on the nature of your usage.

If you want access to a specific recording, you'll need to negotiate with the record label, and you may also have to obtain permission from the performers and arrangers (although in many cases the record label will represent the primary artist).

If you want to use a MIDI song file, you'll also need a so-called MIDI license. Most MIDI files contain contact information for the MIDI arranger or performer either in a bundled README file or embedded into the MIDI sequence itself.

To secure rights to published photographs or artwork, you'll first have to determine where the image came from—just because it

*Not included in this publication.

Reprinted with permission from the September 1994 issue of *Presentations* magazine. Copyright 1994, Lakewood Publications. 800.707.7749, www.presentations.com.

appeared in a particular magazine doesn't necessarily mean that it originated there. A product shot that accompanies a software review, for example, could be the property of the vendor. Current events photographs may have been licensed from a news service like United Press International or the Associated Press. A piece of graphic art, depending on the artist's contract, may belong either to the artist or to the publication in which it appears.

The name of the copyright holder often appears in small print next to the image, but if this isn't the case, the magazine may own the image or it could be in the public domain. If it looks like you'll need to contact a publisher for licensing information, check the masthead for a phone number. You'll find that many periodicals have formed in-house photo services to manage the licensing of images they print.

Another thing to keep in mind is that the content of an image may force you to obtain additional releases. Celebrities and private individuals, whether alive or dead, retain varying degrees of control over how their likenesses are used. Furthermore, if a photograph depicts personal property, such as a private home, you may also need permission from the owner.

Using reproductions of fine art involves many of the same issues: Although Claude Monet obviously holds no copyright on his century-old Water Lilies triptych, you'll need permission from New York's Museum of Modern Art—which owns and displays the paintings—to use photographs of them. These types of situations usually call for professional representation; not only can it be difficult to track down the various property owners, but in many cases you'll need help from someone familiar with the subtleties of copyright law.

The Silver Screen

Obtaining film and television rights can be especially complex and expensive. Not only will you have to track down and negotiate with the studio or network that owns the property, but you'll also need permission from every performer involved in the sequence you're interested in, and may have to pay fees to writers', directors', or screen actors' guilds, as well as to other types of trade unions.

Characters from comic books, such as Spider-Man or Wonder Woman, are usually owned by comic-book publishers like Marvel Entertainment Group or DC Comics, although some artists and writers retain copyrights to the characters they create. Check the comic's indicia—usually located on the first page or inside front cover—for definitive copyright and contact information.

Comic strip characters like Blondie are owned either by the syndicates that distribute them, such as King Features Syndication, or, rarely, by the cartoonists who created them. To determine ownership, look for a copyright notice on or adjacent to the strip in your local newspaper. If all else fails, a quick call to the paper may net you a cooperative editor willing to provide more detailed contact information.

Obtaining rights to animated cartoon characters combines the complexities of both motion-picture and comics licensing. To use a Beavis and Butthead clip, for example, you'd need rights not only to the characters themselves, but also to the actual footage.

Let a Pro Do It

By now, it should be obvious that rights negotiation is no task for a novice. If you'll be using copyrighted materials on a regular basis, or want to incorporate them into a major promotional effort, plan on retaining the services of an attorney specializing in copyright and contract law.

If you're new to the field, or are having trouble identifying copyright holders, it can pay to hire a rights-clearance service, such as BZ/Rights and Permissions. Such agencies specialize in locating copyright owners and negotiating pricing on your behalf. They can also provide a variety of other services—BZ, for example, offers free initial consultations at which they discuss how much a particular property will probably cost and what your chances are of securing rights. Other agencies like Thompson & Thompson provide special services like guaranteed same-day identification of copyright owners.

If your needs are more modest, you might want to work with the U.S. Copyright Office of the Library of Congress. For a relatively low hourly fee, they'll identify the owners of any copyrighted work, and can help determine if a property is in the public domain. This can be a good option if you don't have a big budget, but it's not for anyone on a tight schedule—a Copyright Office search can sometimes take weeks or months.

Another way to locate photographs and movie footage is through stock houses, which manage the rights to huge collections that they license to clients in a variety of ways. Although you may not wind up with the precise image you wanted, licensing properties from a stock house can save you a great deal of time and money.

Going Online

If you have a computer and modem, an even better alternative may be to dial into an electronic stock service. These operations let you browse online through the inventories of dozens of stock houses, news agencies and archival photo services. One of the first such services was PressLink, which specializes in current events photos and text aimed at newspaper publishers. PressLink provides online access to more than 150,000 online photographs from sources like Reuters and The New York Times, and also includes suppliers like ABC television, making it a good resource for stills from TV shows like Roseanne and NYPD Blue.

But although PressLink provides the tools to locate and download images, it doesn't get involved in licensing. If you don't already have an account with the owner of an image, it usually takes a phone call to set one up and negotiate pricing.

The Kodak Picture Exchange offers similar services, but is oriented more toward general stock photo audiences than newspaper editors, who require quick turnaround, but aren't as concerned with high-resolution reproduction. It provides access to more than 20 stock photo agencies, and even lets users order images electronically by filling out an on-screen form. Lower-resolution proof images—which often provide acceptable results for the computer screen—may be downloaded as soon as a price is negotiated, but high-quality film transparencies require at least 24 hours for courier delivery.

Although online services aren't for everyone, they can be ideal for multimedia applications. They free you from having to hunt down copyright owners for specific photographs and text, and provide access to a far greater selection of images than you would get from a single news agency or stock house. Newer services, like Picture Network International's Seymour, are also adding time-saving features like a natural-language interface that lets you search for images by describing them in plain English.

An even simpler and less expensive way to access copyrighted photographs, video clips and sound recordings is to purchase them in clip media collections, which automatically grant you a liberal set of usage rights. There are a variety of sources for clip libraries: graphic packages like Asymetrix Compel and CorelDRAW include large selections of clip media, and an increasing number of stock photo shops have begun to offer collections on CD-ROM. Some of the earlier CD photo libraries suffered from uneven image quality, scanning problems and color imbalances, but most newer products contain top-quality reproductions.

Digital Stock Inc., for example, markets a line of $249 Digital Stock Professional Photo CDs that each contain 100 24-bit Photo CD images at resolutions up to 3,072 × 2,048—good enough to be printed at 150 lpi in an 8- × 10-inch format. The original photographs are scanned with a special algorithm

---

Public Domain

If you don't want to hassle with identifying copyright owners and negotiating rights, public domain properties may be your best bet. Determining if a work is actually in the public domain, though, can be tricky. Further complicating matters is the fact that copyright law has changed several times in the past few decades, so even the date that a work was first published can make a difference. You'll often need an attorney or rights-clearance agency to make a definitive decision about a specific property, but here are some general guidelines that can be helpful in less ambiguous situations.

- Materials produced entirely by the Federal government are in the public domain. This doesn't, however, imply that every component of any government publication can be used without permission; sometimes a work will contain materials that have been licensed from other sources.

- Any copyrighted property published more than 75 years ago is in the public domain. Copyrights expire on the first day of the year, so that means during 1994 anything published before January 1, 1919 can be used without permission.

- Work published before January 1, 1964 is in the public domain if its copyright has not been renewed. Copyrights that originated prior to 1964 normally ran 28 years but could be renewed for a second 28-year term. Works created between January 1, 1964 and December 31, 1977 are automatically protected for a period of 75 years.

- Material published on or after January 1, 1978 is protected by copyright until 50 years after the death of the last surviving author. If it's not possible to identify individuals as copyright holders—such as when a corporation owns a property—the work enters the public domain 75 years after the year of first publication or 100 years after its creation, whichever comes first.

co-developed by Digital Stock and Kodak to produce images balanced for both RGB monitor presentations and CMYK film separations.

PhotoDisc also markets a stunning line of CD photo collections, but computerized presenters will be most interested in their $199 ClipPix product, a two-disc set that contains 500 photos optimized for use with Mac or PC presentation software, computer monitors and LCD projection panels. Multiple versions of each image offer users their choice of 640 × 480 or 1,024 × 768 resolutions, 8-bit or 24-bit color and BMP, PICT or JPEG file formats.

An even less expensive option is Corel's line of Professional Photos CD-ROMs, which the company has been aggressively marketing to the multimedia community: More than 200 titles are already shipping at a street price of about $30 per disc. Like the Digital Stock products, Corel's discs each contain 100 pro-quality Photo CD-resolution images, but because the discs themselves aren't in Photo CD format, they don't require a CD-ROM XA-compliant drive.

There are also dozens of vendors who market collections of other types of media, including celebrity film clips (The Movie BBS' The Actor and Actress Collections), MIDI arrangements of well-known songs (Voyetra Technologies' Music Clips collections) and digitized sound effects (B&B Soundworks' Sound Resource Libraries). One particularly impressive product designed specifically for multimedia applications is Cambium Development's line of Sound Choice discs, which contain CD audio, WAV and MIDI versions of classical music and original pop/jazz compositions.

There are no straightforward procedures for obtaining rights to multimedia properties. The process is often expensive and complicated enough to justify hiring an attorney and clearance house, but if your needs are flexible, you may do as well with a stock shop, online service or clip media collection.

Article Review Form at end of book.

Knowing what can be republished on the Internet and what cannot can prove tricky. News, information, graphics, audio and video are readily available. In the following article, Robert Penchina makes the point that copyright law applies to cyberspace in much the same way it does elsewhere. How do publishers avoid copyright violations? What limits and/or policies are needed? What tools are available to journalists and editors to help them avoid violations?

Venturing Online

Protecting you and your product in cyberspace

Robert Penchina

Penchina is a lawyer specializing in copyright and First Amendment law with the New York City and Washington law firm of Rogers & Wells.

When publishers enter cyberspace, media law issues take on a new dimension.

It's not that the types of legal issues change because the information sources and the publication medium are electronic. Reporters must still respect copyrights, and publishers must designate all intended uses in their license agreements. Yet, the very accessibility of online services and the extraordinary research and dissemination opportunities they provide may escalate the risks of copyright and contractual violations. Publishers must be extra vigilant in ensuring that their rights and others' are preserved when they depart from the printed page.

What materials can you republish from the Internet?

The Internet and commercial online services deliver, with a few strokes on the keyboard, late-breaking news, breathtaking photos and features of every description—all of which can easily be downloaded and stored. Tempting though it may be, journalists must purposely avoid using this material without permission.

Copyright laws apply to materials published electronically just as they do to printed works. Unauthorized reproduction and distribution of materials found online may subject a publisher to liability for infringement.

Importantly, the lack of a copyright notice does not signify that online materials are in the public domain. Under current law, the placement of a copyright notice is strictly optional and a work is fully protected by law—even in the absence of such a notice. Moreover, journalists cannot claim innocent intent as a defense to copyright infringement. Under copyright law, you may be found to have infringed even if you honestly believed you were free to copy.

Cyberspace offers plentiful sources for journalists to investigate news topics. As a general rule, however, materials found there should be treated no differently than materials published in rival newspapers: do not republish without express permission of the copyright owner.

What materials can a publisher post on the Internet?

Though a publisher may have diligently secured the right to publish each and every item appearing in its newspaper, it does not necessarily have the right to publish the same items in electronic form.

Where a publisher owns the copyright in a particular item outright, it is free to post that item online. Posting a newspaper in its entirety, however, may run afoul of wire service agreements, syndication agreements or contracts with advertising agencies. Even items written exclusively for the

---

From Robert Penchina, "Venturing Online: Protecting You and Your Product in Cyberspace" in *Editor & Publisher,* June 24, 1995. Reprinted by permission of Robert Penchina.

newspaper by a freelancer are not necessarily available for electronic publication by the publisher.

The same may be true for photos and graphics provided by stringers and outside agencies. If materials appearing in a newspaper are merely licensed to the publisher, the license agreement must be closely scrutinized to determine whether it covers electronic publication.

Going forward, publishers can obtain all of the rights they might need by utilizing license agreements that spell out all of the potential desired uses, including electronic publication.

How can publishers protect electronic products?

Once a publisher has obtained rights to distribute material electronically, it should actively protect its electronic product.

Although use of a copyright notice is not required by law, prominently displaying a copyright notice and a statement reserving the publisher's rights in the electronic product sends a strong message. The electronic community will be alerted that the publisher is serious about enforcing its rights.

In addition, online service subscription agreements provide a vehicle for the publisher to set the terms and conditions for accessing its electronic product. Here, the publisher can specify that works may be accessed only for the subscriber's personal, noncommercial use and may not be republished without the publisher's prior consent

The electronic medium itself also provides tools for protecting published materials. Publishers can electronically post the terms and conditions under which access will be granted to their materials. Access can then be denied to any users who refuse to give their electronic consent to those terms. Thus, publishers will have contractual rights as well as copyrights to enforce in the event they must resort to legal action to halt the misuse of their product.

The electronic medium provides important opportunities for publishers to expand and improve their services. Yet, in many ways, media law has not yet kept pace with online technology. Publishers can safely venture forward in this climate by considering their rights, remedies and potential liabilities before going online and taking protective steps in advance.

Article Review Form at end of book.

Freelancers are waging a battle to retain the electronic rights to their articles. And, although the defendants in the *Tasini vs. New York Times* suit prevailed, freelancers are still searching for a solution to the controversy. Nan Levinson and Donna Demac examine the issues in the following article. When a freelancer sells an article to a newspaper or magazine, should the publication retain rights to republish the article online without additional compensation? Or is the online version just a continuation of the print version?

The Cutting Edge

New media bring new problems to copyright arena; publishing: A civil war is brewing over compensation for electronic use of print material

Nan Levinson and Donna Demac

Special to the Times; *Donna Demac is an attorney in New York.*

When Therese Iknoian learned that the sports and fitness column she wrote for the San Jose Mercury News was being reproduced on the paper's World Wide Web site, she was more angered than flattered.

As a freelance contributor, she assumed she had granted the Mercury News only "first serial rights," the standard for print publication. But the Mercury News, following the policy of its parent company, Knight-Ridder, wanted her to sign a contract turning over the right to use her work in all electronic media.

For months, Iknoian negotiated without success. "In March of this year," she recounts, "they told me to sign it or get lost, so I quit writing for the paper."

Tales like Iknoian's are becoming common as individual creators of words, sound and images—content providers, in online parlance—lock horns with the corporations that assemble their output into CD-ROMs, Web pages, online services and other electronic media.

At issue ultimately is the status of intellectual property in the electronic marketplace. More immediately, disagreement over compensation for electronic use of material originally created for print is turning into a publishing civil war.

"These are complicated issues," says David Yarnold, the editor involved in the negotiations with Iknoian and now editorial director for new media at Knight-Ridder. "And everyone ought to be thinking about fairness for everyone involved."

That's not so easy. Newspapers and magazines usually own the <u>copyright</u> for the material their employees create on the job. But many freelancers, who get few of the benefits of employees, have traditionally sold only one-time print rights and retained full ownership of their work for subsequent sales.

Now a growing number of publishers, scrambling to be a part of the new-media world, are insisting that creators explicitly turn over control of electronic rights without additional compensation. Others are asking freelancers to sign work-for-hire

From Nan Levinson and Donna Demac, "The Cutting Edge" in *Los Angeles Times Electronic Library,* September 2, 1996. Copyright 1996 Los Angeles Times. Reprinted by permission.

agreements, thereby relinquishing **copyright** and all other rights—including the right to revise their work—to the publisher. These latter rights, known in legalese as "moral rights," are particularly vulnerable since malleability is a defining characteristic of digital media.

This newspaper, for instance, has issued contracts in which freelancers grant the paper nonexclusive rights to use the material "in any format or media whether now known or later devised."

The publishing rights conflict involves some of the biggest names in the business, from the glossy magazines of the Hearst empire (Redbook, Good Housekeeping, etc.) to educational publishing giant Scholastic Inc. to wire service Associated Press, which recently began requiring freelance photographers to sign contracts granting all rights to their work.

Publishers say their motives for developing the new contracts are practical as much as financial. Bob Simon, legal counsel for KRI/Knight-Ridder, says: "Publishers want the ability to disseminate by any means available. It's not practical for authors to retain rights to approve or disapprove, so the ultimate solution will give all rights to the publisher and cover even technologies not yet invented."

The biggest e-rights battle began last summer, when the New York Times instituted a policy of assuming the rights to freelance work in all formats for all time without additional payment. Alarmed that the Times contract would set a nationwide precedent, the Authors Guild, the National Writers Union and the American Society of Journalists and Authors formed an unusual alliance to protest the policy through old media and new.

This May, when the Boston Globe, a New York Times subsidiary, sent similar work-for-hire contracts to its freelancers, Robert Jordan, a Globe columnist and president of the Boston Globe Employees Assn., sent a letter to the paper's managing editor protesting the policy—apparently the first time an employee group at a newspaper has backed freelancers on the issue. Jordan warned that where electronic rights are concerned, "we would also voice strong objections to any similar language that would surrender to the Globe the complete ownership of all [bargaining] unit employee writings. . . ."

The controversy is expected to come to a head late this fall when a federal judge in New York rules in *Tasini vs. New York Times* on whether **freelance writers** retain their **copyright** on works reused for electronic databases.

In December 1993, 11 freelancers, led by National Writers Union President Jonathan Tasini, sued the publishers of the New York Times; Newsday (owned by Times Mirror Co., parent company of the Los Angeles Times); Sports Illustrated (Time Inc.); and the Atlantic, along with Nexis and UMI, for the unauthorized sale of their articles in online databases and CD-ROM compilations.

"The suit has the potential to totally reshape the area of writers' rights," says Tasini. "If we win, we'll have the opportunity for unprecedented leverage with the industry."

But Bruce Keller, lead attorney for the defendants, insists that the issue is much narrower, turning on a single provision of the **copyright** act.

Using the New York Times as his example, he says: "The question is, does the publisher have the right to take today's issue of the New York Times and put it in a database so it can be retrieved electronically? Our position is that there is no difference between the print edition of the New York Times and the electronic edition of the New York Times. We're not talking about the right of freelancers to control their work in a whole host of other media."

Behind all the bad blood is a mix of confusion, panic and hype as the electronic market explodes. Newspapers and magazines are racing to open sites on the World Wide Web; many appear on commercial services, such as CompuServe and America Online; and a growing number are joining forces with online archival services, such as Nexis and Magazine Database, that provide the text of old articles to professional researchers at a hefty price.

Meanwhile, periodical publishers, looking to cut costs, are turning more to freelancers, as freelancers, also eager to benefit from technological advances, are counting on secondary electronic sales to augment their incomes.

To a great extent, fortunes made from the Web are still more potential than real. Time's popular Pathfinder site, for instance, brought in just $2 million in advertising in 1995; industry estimates put its start-up cost at about $3 million. "There's no pot of gold here yet," says Paul Sagan, president and editor of new media at Time.

Other parts of the digital universe are already generating large revenue streams, however. Karen Burka of Simba Information, a market research firm in Connecticut, estimates that the market for online services in 1995 was about $15.7 billion. Though she doesn't break that into categories, writers' advocates say the sale of full-text articles from newspapers and magazines is already a multibillion-dollar business.

"Freelancers' work is being distributed via online databases that can cost $90 an hour to access and via CD-ROMs that sell for thousands of dollars a copy," says writers union Vice President Philip Mattera. "Print publishers may have entered into lousy deals with the electronic services, but that's no reason to deprive writers of their fair share of what appears to be a substantial amount of money."

John R. (Rick) MacArthur, publisher of Harper's and a writer himself, sees something in both perspectives. In February, Harper's became the first major publication to announce that it would share royalties—past, present and future—from electronic uses with its freelancers, even though MacArthur thinks the issue is somewhat tangential.

"It's chump change all around," he says. "I can't understand why the publishers are trying so zealously to screw the writers."

Most publishers are waiting to see how the Tasini case is resolved, but some are moving ahead with writer-friendly policies on electronic rights. Publishers Weekly and the Nation have followed Harper's lead on sharing royalties with freelancers, and other magazines, such as Woman's Day and Sierra, routinely pay a separate fee for electronic republishing. K-III, owner of New York and other titles, recently sent checks to freelancers for past electronic uses, and the Washington Post has reimbursed individual freelancers who complained about unauthorized use.

Realizing that there is no one-size-fits-all solution, writers organizations hope to build an infrastructure to make payment for electronic use of freelance work feasible.

Last year, the Authors Guild and ASJA spearheaded the Authors Registry, an entity now involving dozens of writers organizations and literary agencies, through which publishers, including Harper's and the Nation, will make rights payments to freelancers.

The Publication Rights Clearinghouse, a project of the National Writers Union, is working with Uncover, a hybrid online-fax document delivery service owned by CARL Corp., a subsidiary of Knight-Ridder. Through the Clearinghouse, **copyright** fees collected from Uncover's customers will go directly to freelancers rather than to publishers, as in the past.

The granddaddy of royalty distribution systems is the American Society of Composers, Authors and Publishers, founded in 1914. But ASCAP-like schemes that monitor use as a basis for payment can be cumbersome online, so the National Writers Union is advocating a system in which print publishers pay freelancers an additional flat fee for a finite period for each electronic usage.

David Goodman, a Vermont writer, helped negotiate such an arrangement in which all freelancers writing for SkiNet, a new online service owned by Times Mirror, receive a 10% fee for electronic reuse of their work for one year.

Says Goodman, who is optimistic about the arrangement: "Publishers who deal with their writers in good faith will come up with lots of models."

Article Review Form at end of book.

Fred Mann raises challenging and provocative questions in the following article about online journalism. They go to the heart of issues editors struggle with as they develop policies for their online publications. Try answering the questions he poses: What are newspapers doing online? How important are journalistic ethics on an online publication? Who determines the content for an online publication? What are the boundaries relating to content?

Moving Beyond 'Code First, Ask Questions Later'

Fred Mann

Fred Mann is general manager of Philadelphia Online.

While Web publishing offers tantalizing possibilities, your reputation is paramount; retain it by tackling hard ethical questions now, before they're so sticky.

It is said, probably correctly, that the only people making money on the Internet are the folks who run the endless streams of seminars and conferences to talk about making money on the Internet.

At the online newspaper conferences, the topics are pretty much the same: technology breakthroughs, advertising models, marketing tips, cool interactive content. Everything except journalism and the values behind it.

Maybe there's no need to talk about ethics and values. It's probably a no-brainer: if you're an online journalist, you're still a journalist. The same sensibilities apply.

But do they? And are you the same journalist with a mouse that you were with a pica pole? See what you think about the next four questions:

What Are You Trying to Prove by Going Online?

Your newspaper is probably online for the same reason the others are: they are afraid not to be. No one really knows if there is big money to be made on the Internet. No one can say for sure that being online will build circulation for the paper. (Indeed, it might even cost ink-on-paper circulation.)

Maybe being online is preparing your company for the future. But just maybe it's like investing in eight-track stereo . . . or Earthshoes.

The only real reason to be out there today is to protect your franchise.

Now that you are in charge of this new, exciting online venture, are you sure what your goals are?

Do you want to be another distribution channel for the newspaper, or do you want to be more than that?

Do you know who your target audience is? Who your advertisers might be?

Are you a free service, or will you charge for your content?

Does your online image reflect the image of your paper: responsible, authoritative, trustworthy? Or are you trying to be a tad cooler with your online version? Can you be both authoritative and cool? (Your parents couldn't.)

Are you expected to be a profit center, or are you a value-added service that can lose some dollars while making the larger company look more appealing to advertisers and readers?

Once you answer these questions, think about how journalistic values and ethics fit in. Are these goals—of presenting information with balance, fairness, wholeness, accuracy, authenticity, credibility and strong news judgment—relevant for this new world?

From Fred Mann, "Moving Beyond 'Code First, Ask Questions Later'" in *The American Editor,* November 1996. Reprinted by permission.

How Important Are Journalistic Ethics Now That You're a Business Person?

Just as a newspaper has to establish a new identity on the Internet, so too does the manager of that project. For most of us, it means leaving a secure career in the newsroom for the unknown world of the entrepreneur.

All of a sudden, you are a businessman or woman, worrying about advertising rates, subscriber revenue, bandwidth and marketing. You don't have the resources to keep up with everyone else on the Web, though former newsroom colleagues tell you in the cafeteria that you represent the company's future.

Who's got time to think of values—or journalism for that matter? You've got a business to run, dammit.

But say that you do get a chance to reflect on the values and ethics that served you as a reporter and editor:

How do they relate to what you're doing now?

Do you have the same commitment to them outside the newsroom?

Is your news judgment affected by your closer relationship with advertisers and your marching orders to make a profit? Running a negative story about an advertiser used to be the publisher's problem. Are you really going to play up that piece that makes the local Realtor look bad when he represents 50 percent of your advertising?

If you expect to make money, you probably will put ads on your home page. What does that do to your credibility?

When you're trying to compete in an "instant" medium, do you really have time to insist on "journalistic wholeness" and "authenticity"? What is "accuracy" anyway when you're updating your site every eight minutes and can clarify and correct mistakes before most anyone sees them?

Don't you need attitude online? Are you going to be as gray and boring as your newspaper? How do you speak to the hip online generation—and make them love you—when you're hung up on "balance" and "fairness"?

Who's in Control?

It used to be pretty clear: newspapers made editorial decisions that guided their coverage and set the agenda for public debate, and public journalism advocates favored giving more control to readers.

Online, there are many levels to the debate—each one as cloudy as the next. Who calls the shots—and why—bears on how we do our jobs and which values lose their special status when others set priorities for us.

- **Newspapers vs. The Online Audience:** Online users are much more involved than newspaper readers. With today's relatively small online populations, each user represents a larger share of audience than does one reader to the newspaper. Plus, online users demand—and get—a host of interactive services, from chat rooms to consumer purchases to interactive games and puzzles.

Those who read the news online are often given many paths and sidebar-type detours to choose from. With all this power in the hands of the customer, how can a newspaper online exert leadership?

- **Newspapers vs. Their Corporate Parents:** Given the high cost of staffing and dealing with new technology, plus the uncertain future of publishing on the Internet, newspaper groups are trying to hold down costs and standardize purchases. Some are building content networks and making group purchases of outside content. Does meeting corporate expectations jeopardize the quality of our journalism—or the values behind it?

- **Newspapers vs. The Barbarians:** Microsoft. America Online. AT&T. The cable companies. The competition online is unlike anything newspaper companies have seen in generations. If ever. Newspaper groups are banding together with CareerPath and New Century Network and other industry creations.

They may save the classified markets, but are they good for the values of journalism? Are our users and our communities best served when newspapers circle the wagons?

Where Are the Boundaries?

And then there are boundaries. Where are the boundaries of taste? Of responsibility? Between privacy and openness? Between editorial and advertising? When your most important asset is credibility and the reputation of the newspaper that spawned you, you've got some decisions to make.

- Presumably, you'd protect the privacy of a rape victim, just as you would in print. In an interactive medium, you might create a forum or chat session on date rape. That helps focus the community debate. But your attorney says you'd better not moderate or censor those forums because it leaves you open to legal problems. And some bozos are writing some pretty nasty stuff about the date rape victim in your forum. What to do?

- You've developed a great popular music page on your Web site. To increase diversity and unpredictability, you link to the home page of a 13-year-old girl who has built a Web site listing her favorite new music. Her list includes a link to a rap music bulletin board featuring lyrics that would instantly put your newspaper editor into a coma. The girl has already been covered in her junior high school newspaper and wants to know why you want to break the link. So does her principal—who accuses you of racism. What's your call?

- You are a journalist—a serious journalist. You believe that your Internet site ought to reflect the separation of news and advertising. Then an advertiser asks you to create an interactive game based on the news of the day and put it at the top of your home page. To enter and win prizes, the user has to download something from the advertiser's Web site. Oh yes, and the advertiser promises to pay half of your monthly advertising revenue goal.

We all have standards, but shouldn't we be a little flexible in this new world? Besides, where's the line between editorial content and sponsored entertainment anyway?

They may not be as cutting-edge or easy to discuss as business models or bandwidth problems, but journalism values deserve to be front and center in every discussion of the new media. For the medium may be new, but the ethical dilemmas stubbornly stay the same.

Article Review Form at end of book.

WiseGuide Wrap-Up

The U.S. Constitution originally contained no special provisions for the freedom of the press. Those rights did not appear until two years later, with the adoption of the Bill of Rights. The First Amendment was controversial when initially adopted. Some early Americans were fearful this amendment provided the press with too much range. But advocates of a free and unfettered press prevailed.

Discussions about controlling the Internet mirror these earlier debates. Many people view the Internet as a free and independent entity, not owned by any one individual or organization and not confined by tradition. While the basic belief is true—no one entity owns the Internet—the laws of society still prevail. Reporters can be sued for libel. Reporters have to honor existing privacy laws. Reporters have to deal with copyright issues.

Just as the right to a free press has existed in this country for over 200 years, so also have the rights of individuals been protected. This wonderfully complex relationship works because the right of one serves as a check against excessiveness by the other. By recognizing and respecting this balance, online journalists will keep themselves free of legal problems while working in the new Wild West.

R.E.A.L. Sites

The adjacent list provides a print preview of typical CourseWise R.E.A.L. Sites. (There are over 100 such sites at the CourseLink™ Site.) The danger in printing URLs is that Web sites can change overnight. As we went to press, these sites were functional using the URL provided. If you come across one that isn't, please let us know via email at webmaster@coursewise.com. Use your Passport to access the most current list of R.E.A.L. sites at the CourseLinks™ Site.

Site name: The Free Expression Clearinghouse
URL: http//www.freeexpression.org/info/site.html
Why is it R.E.A.L.? More than 30 groups created the clearinghouse, which offers action alerts, legislative updates, legal briefings and news on local censorship cases. This site will keep you current on legal happenings.
Key topics: access, copyright, current issues, decency issues, ethics, freelance issues, information access, legal issues, pornography, online journalism, regulation, research

Site name: National Writers Union
URL: http://www.nwu.org/nwu/
Why is it R.E.A.L.? Offered your first freelance contract? curious about your online rights? This site covers the legal issues and current topics of interest to freelance writers. You can find sample contracts, information on the Publishing Rights Clearinghouse, job resources and a general store.
Key topics: careers, copyright, freelance issues, legal issues, skills, webcasting

Site name: Student Press Law Center
URL: http:www.splc.org:80/
Why is it R.E.A.L.? The rules affecting campus publications may not be what you think they are. Check this site for the latest, most accurate information. Includes guides to student press law and updates on pending cases. Legal help to student journalists is available via the site.
Key topics: access, copyright, current issues, research, legal issues, regulation

Site name: Meta-index for Legal Research
URL: gsulaw.gsu.edu/metaindex
Why is it R.E.A.L.? What could be more real than a massive listing of legal cases? Covered are judicial rulings, legislative information, federal law and a legal "people-searching" site.
Key topics: copyright, decency issues, legal issues, multimedia issues, pornography, regulation

Site name: Society of Professional Journalists Freedom of Information site
URL: http://spj.org/FOIA
Why is it R.E.A.L.? FOIA affects all journalists, including those on campus. This site offers stories relating to freedom of information issues, guides for filing under the FOIA, the history of FOIA and a state-by-state breakdown of laws.
Key topics: access, current issues, legal issues, online access, regulation

section 5

Digging Behind the Screen: Two cases

WiseGuide Intro

When President Theodore Roosevelt labeled journalists "muckrakers" he meant it as an insult. Journalists, however, wore the label like a badge of honor. (Raking the muck implies a willingness to look into things, often unattractive, that others choose to ignore.) The term goes to the heart of investigative reporters' efforts to write about complicated issues, to challenge the deeds of people in power and to examine news events in the face of controversy.

American journalism has a long history of controversy. From John Peter Zenger's defiance of Colonial rule to the publication of John Steinbeck's *Grapes of Wrath,* journalists have exposed society's warts. *Washington Post* reporters Bob Woodward and Carl Bernstein took investigative reporting to even higher levels. Their Watergate reporting led to the resignation of President Richard Nixon and a renewed interest in investigative reporting.

The following articles deal with controversies surrounding investigative journalism online. Raised are questions about ethics, propriety and the role of online journalism in a digital age. In dealing with these issues, journalists have to consider what is good journalism, how to prevent online news publications from falling into the tabloid mold, and how business decisions impact editorial decisions. Of importance, too, are the challenges journalists face with the acceleration from daily to immediate deadlines.

This section's readings address these issues head on. They reflect problems inherent in online journalism. The *San Jose Mercury News* series and *The Dallas Morning News* controversy garnered attention not only because of their content but because of the fact that the Internet spread that content.

It's rare when reporters at other newspapers set out to debunk an investigative series published by a major daily. It's even more rare when the publisher backs off from its own story. After reexamining the stories and supplemental material, and listening to the critics, the *Mercury News* did just that. The Internet had given the story unusual exposure and, eventually, that exposure turned it upside down.

The decision by *The Dallas Morning News* to publish Timothy McVeigh's alleged confession on its Web site before print publication became controversial, because it involved the Oklahoma City bombing. It is not unusual for newspapers to post material on a Web site before print publication. Generally, Web publication occurs in the wee hours of

Key Points

- Develop an understanding of and appreciation for editorial decision making. Understand the ramifications of "running the story" and the role that courts, attorneys and the law play in these cases.

- Think about the implications of online investigative reporting—and how it differs from print and broadcast.

"Every news organization ought to be digging beneath surface events on local, national and international issues. Some never do. Others do it occasionally."
—Steve Weinberg

the morning and is seen only by a few late-night Web surfers and the competition. Its decision illustrated that a Web site can combine the best of print and television news: immediate news with the textual background of print and the visual quality of broadcast. As computer usage grows, we can expect more news to be delivered in this fashion.

Questions

1. How did the Internet impact the *San Jose Mercury News* series? If you were the editor, how would you have handled this controversy?

2. What were the key reasons *The Dallas Morning News* decided to publish the McVeigh "confession" online prior to publishing in print? What are the advantages and disadvantages of the online scoop?

3. Do you see controversies brewing in today's news that are similar to the three presented in this section?

Case 1: *The San Jose Mercury News*

The *San Jose Mercury News* published a highly respected online news service. And so, at first there was nothing unusual about the paper's decision to post on site a series linking inner-city drug sales and the contras with the CIA. Support for the series was so strong that supplemental material, including audio recordings of hearings and hypertext supporting documents, were posted on the site. But, when professionals from other media organizations began examining the documents and researching the story, the series became the focus of controversy and criticism nationwide. The following three article discuss the series and its aftermath. Do you think the series would have garnered as much attention if it had not been posted on the Web site? What if the series had appeared without the supporting documents? Did Gary Webb's editors fail to do their job before publication? What do you think of the role taken by the other media organizations? Do you agree or disagree with Steve Weinberg's conclusions?

Reading 34: Hunkel, P. "Soul Searching" *Columbia Journalism Review*, July/August 1997, pp. 38–43.

Reading 35: Kornbluh, P. "The Storm over 'Dark Alliance'" *Columbia Journalism Review*, Jan./Feb. 1997, pp. 32–39.

Reading 36: Weinberg, S. "Drawing Conclusions from Investigative Reporting" *The IRE Journal*, Nov./Dec. 1996, pp. 4–7.

Soul Searching in San Jose

How the *Mercury News* painfully distanced itself from a big but flawed story

Pia Hinckle

Pia Hinckle, a 1996–97 Knight-Bagehot Fellow at Columbia's Graduate School of Journalism, is a former managing editor of The San Francisco Bay Guardian.

The events that preceded the publication of the "Dark Alliance" series in the *San Jose Mercury News* last August and that led up to executive editor Jerry Ceppos's unusual mea culpa column about it this May have the elements of a pretty good newspaper movie. There is the aggressive lone-wolf investigative reporter who may or may not have fallen down a reportorial rabbit hole; the young Latina city editor, newly promoted and protective of her star reporter; the thoughtful executive editor struggling with his conscience as parts of a huge "holy shit!" story seem to unravel before his eyes; the racial and social undertones of newsroom politics; plus tales of personal tragedies and professional laxity. The backdrop is the CIA's history and dirty laundry, angry mistrust among some African-Americans about their government, about the injustices of the drug war, and the devastation of inner-city communities from crack.

The movie would be about a newspaper slowly and painfully distancing itself from what it once had seen as one of the bigger and better stories it had done. But getting the plot just right would be tough. The details are difficult to put together, partly because after much grandstanding about healthy public debate and openness with readers, the *Mercury News* has gone silent. Ceppos and the editors involved in the con-

Reprinted from *Columbia Journalism Review*, July/August 1997. Copyright © 1997 by Columbia Journalism Review.

tentious story and its internal review all declined to be interviewed. The only person directly involved in the making of it who spoke freely and on the record is Gary Webb, the embattled author.

From another perspective, maybe the story is too mundane for a movie. What happened inside the *Mercury News* during this last year is something like what can and does happen in any number of newsrooms—writers misjudging or exaggerating the portent of their reporting; editors failing to inspect the undergirding of a story's logic; busy executives getting distracted; editorial systems breaking down. Except that what went wrong in San Jose was so much more damaging, inside and outside the newsroom. And thus worth trying to understand.

The series certainly invited scrutiny. (See "The Furor Over 'Dark Alliance,'" CJR, January/February.) Right in its opening sentences it made inflammatory charges:

For the better part of a decade, a Bay Area drug ring sold tons of cocaine to the Crips and Bloods street gangs of Los Angeles and funneled millions in drug profits to a Latin American guerrilla army run by the U.S. Central Intelligence Agency, a *Mercury News* investigation has found. This drug network opened the first pipeline between Colombia's cocaine cartels and the black neighborhoods of Los Angeles, a city now known as the "crack" capital of the world. The cocaine that flooded in helped spark a crack explosion in urban America . . . and provided the cash and connections for L.A.'s gangs to buy automatic weapons.

Similar allegations of contra involvement with inner-city drug dealing had been reported for years. But this was the first time that a major daily had found a small chain of named individuals—three drug dealers, two of them connected to the contras—and drawn such horrifying conclusions.

The reaction in the black neighborhoods of South Central Los Angeles was intense and immediate. On August 30, 1996, Maxine Waters, the U.S. congresswoman, wrote Attorney General Janet Reno demanding an investigation so that her crack-ravaged community might "get answers to the many questions that have been raised by the *San Jose Mercury News* expose." In a highly unusual move, CIA Director John Deutch held a community meeting in Watts in November to try to defuse the anger. Debate over the series built up, fanned by attention on the Internet and on talk radio.

On October 4, *The Washington Post* slammed the series in a page-one news piece. On October 13, in reaction to the *Post's* article, Webb's fellow *Mercury News* investigative reporter, Pete Carey, dissected the series in the pages of the *Merc*. Carey's article confirmed charges raised by critics that Webb had left out some evidence that contradicted one of the story's key sources.

After *The New York Times* and the *Los Angeles Times* also ran page-one stories alleging major inaccuracies in the series, Ceppos wrote a lengthy article in November defending it. Staff meetings were held to address newsroom tension. And a steady flow of memos concerning questions about the series' reporting flew back and forth between San Jose and Sacramento, where Webb lives and works, from winter into spring.

At one point, in February, Webb was summoned to San Jose to meet with top *Mercury News* editors to talk once again, "I thought we were finally going to discuss the follow-up," Webb says. "Instead, I got told that we still needed to settle the issues about the series. I said, 'What issues? I thought we already did that.'"

In his celebrated May 11 column, Jerry Ceppos explained to readers that the paper still supports what he sees as the core of the series—that "a drug ring associated with the Contras sold large quantities of cocaine in inner-city Los Angeles in the 1980s at the time of the crack explosion there" and that "some of the drug profits from those sales went to the Contras."

But, he went on: "After spending months reexamining our effort with the help of seven other reporters and editors, I have concluded that the series did not meet our standards in four areas."

- The *Mercury News* "presented only one interpretation of complicated, sometimes-conflicting pieces of evidence."

- "We made our best estimate of how much money was involved, but we failed to label it as an estimate."

- The paper "oversimplified the complex issue of how the crack epidemic in America grew."

- And finally, the *Mercury News* "through imprecise language and graphics," created "impressions that were open to misinterpretation."

One such "impression" was the strong implication that the Central Intelligence Agency knew about the drug dealing. Webb argues that the series never actually says that the CIA knew about that. The paper's own editorial department had the impression that it did. Its editorial on the series was headlined ANOTHER CIA DISGRACE: HELPING THE CRACK FLOW.

In his column, Ceppos conceded: "Although members of the drug ring met with Contra leaders paid by the CIA, I feel that we did not have proof that top CIA officials knew of the relationship. I believe that part of our contract with readers is to be as clear about what we don't know as what we do know." He noted that reporter Webb does not agree with his conclusions about the series.

Webb was surprised and angered by the column—"I told them, everyone who wants this story to die will read this as a retraction." *The Washington Post* and *The New York Times* both ran front-page stories covering the *Merc's* second thoughts, as well as editorials that praised Ceppos for "repudiating" the series, as the *Post* editorial put it.

Ceppos's column may have little effect on anti-government sentiment in segments of the black community. "There is a lot of suspicion that there is some truth associated with the claims in the story," Los Angeles city councilman Mark Ridley-Thomas told *Time*, "Frankly, these suspicions will not go away."

The CIA said its own investigation of the charges would be completed by the end of the year. The Justice Department and two congressional committees have also said they would look into the charges.

If Webb was surprised by Ceppos's column, many of his colleagues were not. Inside the San Jose newsroom, Webb's series had become controversial soon after he filed it, in March 1996. Word got around about "Gary's cocaine story" after several reporters sneaked unauthorized reads of it from the central computer system.

Some thought it might give the *Merc* a chance at its third Pulitzer, but many others could not believe the paper would publish something that they thought read like a conspiracy manifesto.

It didn't help Webb's case in the newsroom that quite a few reporters and editors at the *Mercury News* see him as an arrogant reporter who is given too much freedom by management despite "problems" with his stories. In one such problem, according to *The New York Times*, the *Mercury News* assigned a second reporter to check out Webb's 1994 series about the alleged failures of Tandem Computers, Inc. to modernize state motor vehicle computers. The reporter wrote in a memo that Webb's series was, "in all its major elements, incorrect." But others at the *Merc* say at least some of the disputed elements of that story were seen, in time, as on target. The paper never ran a correction.

Not many journalists at the *Mercury News* really know Webb, who works out of his home in Sacramento and the *Merc's* three-person bureau there, a two-and-a-half-hour drive from San Jose. In his nearly ten years at the paper he has had minimal contact with San Jose.

He had a similar investigative position at *The Plain Dealer* in Cleveland before being recruited by Jonathan Krim, the *Mercury News's* assistant managing editor for projects, in 1988. As *The New York Times* reported, Webb was sued for libel three times at *The Plain Dealer*. One suit was dismissed. The paper settled the other two.

Over the years he has won more than two dozen journalism awards, including the 1996 Journalist of the Year award from the Society of Professional Journalists Northern California Chapter for his work on "Dark Alliance," and the 1994 H.L. Mencken award from the Free Press Association for his series on drug forfeiture laws. He was also part of the six-person *Mercury News* team that won a 1990 Pulitzer for its coverage of the 1989 San Francisco earthquake.

And he has his backers. "I'm seeing Gary being made out to be a pariah and I just don't get it," says Tim Graham, editor of *The Oakland Tribune*, who has known Webb for nineteen years. "He is one of the finest and most aggressive reporters around and he is also always in need of a strong editor—what's wrong with that? The editors are supposed to be the gatekeepers."

According to Webb and other *Mercury News* reporters, the normal editing process for an investigative project requires a reporter to work closely with an assistant city editor who then turns over the story to a senior editor, usually projects editor Krim, for a second read and edit. Once these three people have all signed off on the story, it goes to the managing editor or executive editor for final approval and then to lawyers if the subject matter warrants. "Dark Alliance" followed a somewhat different route.

Webb's frontline editor and main San Jose contact is city editor Dawn Garcia. She had come south in 1993 from the rival *San Francisco Chronicle*, where she covered city politics, after a stint as a John S. Knight fellow at Stanford. Garcia rose quickly at the *Merc*, moving from state editor to city editor in May 1996. Some saw her as having bypassed a more experienced editor, a white male, and thus something of an affirmative-action-backlash cloud hung over

Timeline

1996

March Webb files "Dark Alliance series with editor Dawn Garcia. Managing editor David Yarnold oversees project.

July Yarnold leaves *Mercury News*. Assistant managing editor Paul Van Slambrouck takes over.

August 18-20 *Mercury News* publishes the series, followed by an editorial: "Another CIA Disgrace: Helping the Crack Flow."

August–September Paper publicizes series on Web site and through Webb's media interviews. Senators Boxer, Feinstein, Representative Waters call for government investigations.

October 4 *The Washington Post* runs piece slamming "Dark Alliance."

October 10 Ceppos's memo criticizes in-house "Dark Alliance" critics for gloating over *Post* story.

October 13 *Mercury News* publishes reporter Pete Carey's analysis of the *Post*'s attack.

October 14 First staff meeting on "Dark Alliance."

October 18 *Mercury News* publishes Ceppos's letter to *The Washington Post* in strong defense of the series. The *Post* had refused to print it.

October 20-22 The *Los Angeles Times* publishes three-part series highly critical of "Dark Alliance."

October 21 *The New York Times* publishes its critique of "Dark Alliance."

October Committee forms to examine editing procedures.

October 29–November 8 Webb goes to Central America to investigate "Dark Alliance" leads.

November 3 *Mercury News* publishes article by Ceppos discussing the media controversy. He still defends the series.

1997

January–February Webb files four follow-up stories; none run.

February Webb attends three meetings with editors in San Jose concerning "Dark Alliance." He is allowed to keep working on the story.

March Webb goes to Nicaragua on vacation time.

May Staff meets to discuss Ceppos's coming column.

May 11 *Mercury News* runs Ceppos's mea culpa.

June 5 Webb is transferred from the investigative beat to spot news.

---

the internal debate on "Dark Alliance."

Webb's next line of editing on the series came from David Yarnold, a *Mercury News* veteran who rose from the graphics department to become managing editor when Ceppos was promoted to executive editor in 1995. Several staff members note that projects editor Krim, who has a reputation as a tough and thorough editor, particularly on investigative projects, would normally oversee a complicated series like "Dark Alliance." But for reasons not altogether clear, Krim was not involved in the editing. Insiders say that management seemed to want to spread the chance to work on major projects to other top editors. In any event, Yarnold took an interest in "Dark Alliance," and it was soon known as "Yarnold's baby."

For four months, Garcia and Yarnold worked on shaping Webb's long and complex stories into a series. Then, about a month before publication, Yarnold left the paper to go to corporate parent Knight-Ridder's new-media department in San Jose. He would return to his position at the *Mercury News* in April 1997, eight months after "Dark Alliance" was published. Paul Van Slambrouck, assistant managing editor for news, stepped in to fill Yarnold's shoes both as acting managing editor and senior "Dark Alliance" editor. Van Slambrouck decided to re-edit the entire series. He later told staff members that he "toned it down."

How much sustained attention the people responsible for "Dark Alliance" were actually able to give it is open to question. Garcia's promotion meant that she was supervising about forty reporters instead of seven. She was also struggling with a recently reorganized metro section that left fewer reporters to fill the same space. Yarnold, criticized behind his back for his background in graphics but respected as a good administrator, was managing editor for a newsroom of about three hundred people, as was Van Slambrouck when he filled Yarnold's shoes.

Much was happening during the editing in the personal lives of some of the players as well. Garcia was going through a divorce. Ceppos was quietly getting medical tests that would confirm that he had prostate cancer.

Webb says he doesn't know whether the story went to the papers' lawyers. And whether Ceppos read it before publication is also unclear. Webb, again, says he doesn't know. Sources close to management say that if the managing editor has already read a series, then Ceppos might not read it himself if he is too busy.

As Webb sees it, the editing process was "more intense than what I usually get. It basically got edited twice," going from four parts to three, then back to four, then back to three. He argues that the criticisms of the 400-inch series that are warranted stem from a lack of space. "We didn't detail some stuff very well," he admits, "specifically regarding the money trail and specifically regarding the genesis of the crack market in LA." He says that when he raised that concern, his editors told him that he had made his case.

When the series finally saw ink last August, the newsroom divided roughly into two camps: those who believed that regardless of its flaws, the series was significant, and those who thought it was a one-sided conspiracy theory from a cowboy reporter. To some extent the split fell along lines of who tended to be critical of management and who didn't, but it also tended to break along ethnic and gender lines. "The 'supporters,' the people who believed aspects of the theories, were mostly women and ethnic minorities, while the opposition was led by what I guess you could call the 'angry white guys,'" says Ricardo Sandoval, Mexico correspondent for the *Mercury News,* who was in the San Jose newsroom through most of the controversy. "It really reflected the division in the public at large." Several other staffers also confirmed this characterization.

When the *Washington Post* story ran October 4, the level of gloating by what some staff members were calling the "Dark Alliance Nazis" got so high that executive editor Ceppos wrote a two-page memo October 10 calling for dialogue and inviting everyone to a "brown-bag" to talk the situation over. The memo said:

Everybody: Many of you have been talking about the Washington Post's reporting on our 'Dark Alliance' series. A copy of the letter that I've written to the Post is attached. In brief, it says that no one—including the Post—has proven that our conclusions were wrong. It says that we strongly support the conclusions that the series drew—and will until someone proves them wrong. . . . There are papers famous for their back-stabbing environment (when Woodward and Bernstein first broke Watergate, the Post newsroom sounded much like ours does now, only worse). I tell applicants that, at the Mercury News, our goal is to become famous for dealing with tough situations in a much healthier fashion.

Ceppos is big on dialogue, and he got it. At staff meetings in October and again in May, some employees expressed deep frustration and anger. "If I had done what Gary did I would be fired," one staffer said during the May meeting. "Why is he still working here?" Another said that the series had "shamed" everyone at the paper.

Ceppos announced in October that Jonathan Krim would be heading a "projects committee" to scrutinize the editorial process and make recommendations for improvements in handling special projects. The goal, says committee member Stephen Buel, an assistant editor and an outspoken critic of "Dark Alliance," "was to make sure that something like this doesn't happen again." Other committee members concur.

In a preliminary five-page memo, the committee concluded that "We believe the newspaper needs a more formal process for vetting projects—at the idea stage and at the editing stage." The committee's recommendations, written by Krim, include a much more formal review of special projects from beginning to end.

Once a project has been edited . . . at least three other people will formally review the story. These three will be the AME Projects or AME News; a reporter or editor who knows something about the subject area, and the ME or EE. . . . Stories whose original editor is one of the people involved in the process still will be reviewed by three other people.

That is still fewer people than at some papers. "The stuff that happened in San Jose would never happen here," says Jim Mulvaney, speaking as projects editor at *The Orange County Register.* "There are always reporters who push the envelope and it is the editors' jobs to pull them back." Mulvaney, who moved in June to the New York *Daily News,* says the *Register* has at least five editors read any major investigation, at least one of whom comes to the story cold.

In his May 11 column, Ceppos said "Dark Alliance" would be edited differently today: "It would state fewer conclusions as certainties, and be clearer in examining why, given the thicket of sometimes conflicting evidence . . . we drew the conclusions that we did."

While the projects committee was at work, another committee was doing its own assessment of "Dark Alliance," one that would lead to Ceppos's May 11 column. Meanwhile, Webb and two other experienced reporters were working on follow-up stories to the series.

Back in October, Webb says, he was offered three book deals and one movie deal for the series. But he contends Ceppos told him he couldn't do those projects and still follow the story for the *Mercury News,* which, Webb says, Ceppos wanted him to do. In late October and early November, "I went down to Central America to follow up the CIA and the money angles." He worked with a Managua-based free-lance journalist, Georg Hodel, who has helped Webb with his Central America reporting. "We came up with some great stuff," he says. "If anything, I feel better about the series now than when we ran it. We didn't know how right we were."

In January, Webb claims, management seemed eager to get these stories into the paper, "because they wanted to shut *The Washington Post* up." Webb says he filed four stories in January and February, one 130 inches long, another 220 inches, and two 50 to 60 inches. None of the follow-ups ever ran.

Sources close to management say that the four stories have indeed been filed, but that they are not the nails in the CIA's coffin that Webb sometimes makes them out to be. According to one person who read them, they have some very promising information, most of which is buried deep in long, rambling articles that need lots of editing. During one March meeting Webb attended with top editors, he says, Ceppos told him that they were not going to run his stories. "I got very agitated. I said, 'This is outrageous.'" But Webb claims that Garcia later told him that it was her intention to make sure they got into the paper.

Earlier in March, Webb had gone to interview another source in Florida and then took vacation time to go to Managua, Nicaragua, for more interviews with people allegedly familiar with contra drug deals—despite having been told by Paul Van Slambrouck to come back to "settle this other stuff first," meaning the questions still open about his series. Webb says the trip resulted in "some amazing interviews with these people, but nobody was very interested. They never asked for notes or anything."

In late May, Webb told CJR that he had had no communication with anyone in San Jose except Garcia since March: "Total silence." He said that no one had given him a copy of the projects memo yet and wasn't sure how or if he would be affected by it. He said he would keep researching his leads to follow-up "Dark Alliance" until somebody in San Jose told him to stop.

On Wednesday, June 4, somebody did. Ceppos called Webb and took him off the story. Webb said he was invited to drive to San Jose the next day to "discuss my future at the paper." There, Ceppos told him that he would be transferred from the state capital to Cupertino, and out of investigative work. Webb said he would fight his job change through the Guild. Yarnold and Garcia remain in the same positions; Van Slambrouck was promoted June 11 to deputy managing editor.

Ceppos also told Webb that another reporter would follow-up "Dark Alliance" for the *Mercury News*, Webb says, but he isn't holding his breath. "I think that Ceppos's column is the last time that this story will ever go in the *Mercury*. I mean, when they put it up in the Web site as an 'epilogue,' that's a pretty clear sign."

Article Review Form at end of book.

Case 1: *The San Jose Mercury News* continued

The Storm Over "Dark Alliance"

Crack, the Contras, and the CIA

Peter Kornbluh

Peter Kornbluh is senior analyst at the National Security Archive, a public-interest documentation center in Washington, and co-author of The Iran-Contra Scandal: A Declassified History.

After Gary Webb spent more than a year of intense investigative reporting and weeks of drafting, his editors at the *San Jose Mercury News* decided to run his three-part series late last August, when the nation's focus was divided between politics and vacation. The series, DARK ALLIANCE: THE STORY BEHIND THE CRACK EXPLOSION, initially "sank between the Republican and Democratic Conventions," Webb recalls. "I was very surprised at how little attention it generated."

Webb needn't have worried. His story subsequently became the most talked-about piece of journalism in 1996 and arguably the most famous—some would say infamous—set of articles of the decade. Indeed, in the five months since its publication, "Dark Alliance" has been transformed into what *New York Times* reporter Tim Weiner calls a "metastory"—a phenomenon of public outcry, conspiracy theory, and media reaction that has transcended the original series itself.

The series, and the response to it, have raised a number of fundamental journalistic questions. The original reporting—on the links between a gang of Nicaraguan drug dealers, CIA-backed counterrevolutionaries, and the spread of crack in California—has drawn unparalleled criticism from *The Washington Post, The New York Times,* and the *Los Angeles Times.* Their editorial decision to assault, rather than advance, the *Mercury News* story has, in turn, sparked critical commentary on the priorities of those pillars of the mainstream press.

Yet in spite of the mainstream media, the allegations generated by the *Mercury News* continue to swirl, particularly through communities of color. Citizens and journalists alike are left to weigh the significant flaws of the piece against the value of putting a serious matter, one the press has failed to fully explore, back on the national agenda.

Drugs and Contras Redux

Although many readers of the *Mercury News* articles may not have known it, "Dark Alliance" is not the first reported link between the contra war and drug smuggling. More than a decade ago, allegations surfaced that contra forces, organized by the CIA to overthrow the Sandinista government in Nicaragua, were consorting with drug smugglers with the knowledge of U.S. officials.

The Associated Press broke the first such story on December 20, 1985. The AP's Robert Parry and Brian Barger reported that three contra groups "have engaged in cocaine trafficking, in part to help finance their war against Nicaragua." Dramatic as it was, that story almost didn't run, because of pressure by Reagan administration officials (see "Narco-Terrorism: A Tale of Two Stories," CJR, September/October, 1986). Indeed, the White House waged a concerted behind-the-scenes campaign to besmirch the professionalism of Parry and Barger and to discredit all reporting on the contras and drugs.

Whether the campaign was the cause or not, coverage was minimal. While regional papers like the *San Francisco Examiner*—which ran a June 23, 1986 front-page exposé on Norvin Meneses, a central figure in the *Mercury News* series—broke significant ground on contra-drug connections, the larger papers and networks (with

Reprinted from *Columbia Journalism Review,* January/February 1997. © 1997 by Columbia Journalism Review.

the exception of CBS) devoted few resources to the issue. The attitude of the mainstream press was typified during the November 1987 press conference held to release the final report of the Congressional Joint Iran-Contra Committees. When an investigative reporter rose to ask the lead counsel of the committees whether the lawmakers had come across any connection between the contras and drug-smuggling, a *New York Times* correspondent screamed derisively at him from across the aisle: "Why don't you ask a serious question?"

Even when a special Senate subcommittee on Terrorism, Narcotics, and International Operations, chaired by Senator John Kerry, released its long-awaited report, *Drugs, Law Enforcement and Foreign Policy,* big-media coverage constituted little more than a collective yawn. The 1,166-page report—it covered not only the covert operations against Nicaragua, but also relations with Panama, Haiti, the Bahamas, and other countries involved in the drug trade—was the first to document U.S. knowledge of, and tolerance for, drug smuggling under the guise of national security. "In the name of supporting the contras," the Kerry Committee concluded in a sad but stunning indictment, officials "abandoned the responsibility our government has for protecting our citizens from all threats to their security and well-being."

Yet when the report was released on April 13, 1989, coverage was buried in the back pages of the major newspapers and all but ignored by the three major networks. *The Washington Post* ran a short article on page A20 that focused as much on the infighting within the committee as on its findings; *The New York Times* ran a short piece on A8; the *Los Angeles Times* ran a 589-word story on A11. (All of this was in sharp contrast to those newspapers' lengthy rebuttals to the *Mercury News* series seven years later—collectively totalling over 30,000 words.) ABC's *Nightline* chose not to cover the release of the report.

Consequently, the Kerry Committee report was relegated to oblivion; and opportunities were lost to pursue leads, address the obstruction from the CIA and the Justice Department that Senate investigators say they encountered, and both inform the public and lay the issue to rest. The story, concedes Doyle McManus, the Washington bureau chief of the *Los Angeles Times*, "did not get the coverage that it deserved."

Evolution of a Metastory

The *Mercury News* series "touched a raw nerve in the way our stories hadn't," observes Robert Parry. One reason is that Parry and Barger's stories had focused on the more antiseptic smuggling side of drug trafficking in far-off Central America. Webb's tale brought the story home, focusing on what he identified as the distribution network and its target, the inner cities of California. Particularly among African-American communities, devastated by the scourge of crack and desperate for information and answers, Webb's reporting found ready constituencies. From Farrakhan followers to the most moderate of black commentators, the story reverberated. "If this is true, then millions of black lives have been ruined and America's jails and prisons are now clogged with young African-Americans because of a cynical plot by a CIA that historically has operated in contempt of the law," wrote Carl T. Rowan, the syndicated columnist.

The wildfire-like sweep of "Dark Alliance" was all the more remarkable because it took place without the tinder of the mainstream press. Instead, the story roared through the new communications media of the Internet and black talk radio—two distinct, but in this case somewhat symbiotic, information channels.

With the Internet, as Webb put it, "you don't have to be *The New York Times* or *The Washington Post* to bust a national story anymore." Understanding this media reality, Mercury Center, the *Mercury News's* sophisticated online service, devoted considerable staff time to preparing for simultaneous online publishing of the "Dark Alliance" stories on the World Wide Web. In the online version, many of the documents cited in the stories were posted on the Mercury Center site, hyperlinked to the story; audio recordings from wiretaps and hearings, follow-up articles from the *Mercury News* and elsewhere, and, for a time, even Gary Webb's media schedule were also posted.

As Webb began giving out his story's Mercury Center website address (*http://www.sjmercury.com/drugs/*) on radio shows in early September, the number of hits to the Center's site escalated dramatically, some days reaching as high as 1.3 million. Over all, Bob Ryan, who heads Mercury Center, estimates a 15% visitor increase since the stories appeared. "For us," he says, "it has certainly answered the question: Is there anyone out there listening?"

The demographics of Web traffic are unknown, but some media specialists believe that the rising numbers at Mercury Center in part reflect what the *Chicago*

Tribune syndicated columnist Clarence Page calls an emerging "black cyber-consciousness." Online newsletters and other Net services made the series readily available to African-American students, newspapers, radio stations, and community organizations. Patricia Turner, author of *I Heard it Through the Grapevine,* the definitive study on how information travels through black America, suggests that this marked the "first time the Internet has electrified African-Americans" in this way. "The 'black telegraph,'" noted Jack White, a *Time* magazine columnist, referring to the informal word-of-mouth network used since the days of slavery, "has moved into cyberspace."

Black-oriented radio talk shows boosted this phenomenon by giving out the Web site address. At the same time, the call-in programs themselves became a focal point of information and debate. African-American talk-show hosts used their programs to address the allegations of CIA complicity in the crack epidemic, and the public response was forceful. The power of talk radio was demonstrated when Congresswoman Maxine Waters was a guest on WOL's Lisa Mitchell show in Baltimore on September 10, and announced that the Congressional Black Caucus meeting that week would address the issues raised by "Dark Alliance." Two hundred people were expected; nearly two thousand attended.

Political pressure, organized at the grassroots level around the country and channeled through the Black Caucus in Washington, pushed both the CIA and the Justice Department to initiate internal investigations into the charges of government complicity in the crack trade. In November, John Deutch, then the director of the CIA, even left the secure confines of Langley headquarters to travel to Watts and address a town meeting of concerned citizens on the *Mercury News* allegations—an unprecedented event.

By then, the "Dark Alliance" series had become the journalistic *Twister* of 1996, with information, misinformation, allegations, and speculations hurtling across the airwaves day after day. A common charge emerged on black talk-radio programs: the U.S. government had conspired to use the crack trade to deliberately harm the African-American community. "CIA" now meant "Crack in America," or as Rep. Cynthia McKinney stated on the floor of Congress, "Central Intoxication Agency." Thousands of copies of "Dark Alliance" were handed out at town meetings across the country, playing "into the deepest fears—sometimes plunging into paranoia—that have haunted the subject of race in America," *The Boston Globe* editorialized in October. "We've always speculated about this," said Joe Madison, a Washington talk-show host, who along with the activist Dick Gregory was arrested in front of the CIA in mid-September in an act of civil disobedience. "Now we have proof."

The Stories Themselves

In the very first *Washington Post* treatment of the *San Jose Mercury News* phenomenon—appearing in the Style section on October 2—media reporter Howard Kurtz noted "just one problem" with the controversy: despite broad hints, Gary Webb's stories never "actually say the CIA knew about the drug trafficking." In an interview with Kurtz, Webb stated that his story "doesn't prove the CIA targeted black communities. It doesn't say this was ordered by the CIA."

What did the *Mercury News* stories actually say? The long three-part series covered the lives and connections of three career criminals: "Freeway" Ricky Ross, perhaps L.A.'s most renowned crack dealer in the 1980s; Oscar Danilo Blandon Reyes, a right-wing Nicaraguan expatriate, described by one U.S. assistant district attorney as "the biggest Nicaraguan cocaine dealer in the United States"; and Juan Norvin (Norwin in some documents) Meneses Cantarero, a friend of the fallen dictator Anastasio Somoza, who allegedly brought Blandon into the drug business to support the contras and supplied him, for an uncertain amount of time, with significant quantities of cocaine.

The first installment of the series, headlined 'CRACK' PLAGUE'S ROOTS ARE IN NICARAGUAN WAR, opened with two dramatic statements:

For the better part of a decade, a San Francisco Bay Area drug ring sold tons of cocaine to the Crips and Bloods street gangs of Los Angeles and funnelled millions in drug profits to a Latin American guerrilla army run by the U.S. Central Intelligence Agency.

The second paragraph, which captured even more public attention, read:

This drug network opened the first pipeline between Colombia's cocaine cartels and the black neighborhoods of Los Angeles, a city now known as the 'crack' capital of the world.

The rest of the article attempted to flesh out those assertions and explain "how a cocaine-for-weapons trade supported U.S. policy and undermined black America."

The second installment, entitled ODD TRIO CREATED MASS MARKET

FOR 'CRACK,' provided far more detail on the alliance between Ross, Blandon, and Meneses and their role in the crack explosion. Part three, WAR ON DRUGS' UNEQUAL IMPACT ON U.S. BLACKS, focused on an issue that outrages many in the African-American community: sentencing discrepancies between blacks and whites for cocaine trafficking, as illustrated by the case of Blandon and Ross. Ross received a life sentence without the possibility of parole; Blandon served twenty-eight months and became a highly paid government informant.

In a defense of Webb's work published in the Baltimore *Sun*, Steve Weinberg, a former executive director of Investigative Reporters & Editors (and a CJR contributing editor), argues that the reporter

> took the story where it seemed to lead—to the door of U.S. national security and drug enforcement agencies. Even if Webb overreached in a few paragraphs—based on my careful reading, I would say his overreaching was limited, if it occurred at all—he still had a compelling, significant investigation to publish.

Indeed, the series did provide a groundbreaking and dramatic story of two right-wing Nicaraguans with clear—although not necessarily strong—connections to the FDN "freedom fighters," who became major drug dealers, inexplicably escaped prosecution, and made a significant contribution to the thousands of kilos of coke that flowed into the inner cities of California. "They pay cash," a wiretapped audio on the Web site records Blandon as telling an associate who complained he didn't "like niggers." Blandon continues: "I don't deal with anybody else. They buy all the time. They buy all the time." Blandon's grand jury and trial testimony—which Webb often over-dramatically sources as "court records"—along with a 1986 sheriff's department search warrant and affidavit and a 1992 Probation and Parole Department report, documented that an undetermined amount of drug funds was going into the contra coffers, possibly as late as 1986.

Far less compelling was the evidence the *Mercury News* presented to tie the Nicaraguans to the CIA itself. But not for lack of trying. Speculative passages like "Freeway Rick had no idea just how 'plugged' his erudite cocaine broker [Blandon] was. He didn't know about Norwin Meneses or the CIA," were clearly intended to imply CIA involvement. As implied evidence of CIA knowledge of and participation in the drug trade, the articles emphasized the meetings between Blandon and Meneses (identified without supporting evidence as FDN officials) and FDN leaders Adolfo Calero (identified without corroboration as "a longtime CIA operative") and Enrique Bermudez (identified as a "CIA agent"). To be sure, the FDN was, as the articles described it, the "CIA's army"—a paramilitary force created, trained, financed, equipped, and largely directed by the CIA. Nevertheless, the articles failed to distinguish between CIA officers who ran the contra war—none of whom are identified or quoted in the articles—and Nicaraguan "agents" or "operatives" such as Calero and Bermudez, who were put on the CIA payroll for purposes of control, support, and/or information. While to some this may seem a trivial distinction—"It doesn't make any difference whether [the CIA] delivered the kilo themselves, or they turned their heads while somebody else delivered it, they are just as guilty," Representative Maxine Waters said in one L.A. forum— the articles did not even address the likelihood that CIA officials in charge would have known about these drug operations.

Moreover, a critical passage Webb wrote to suggest that Blandon himself had CIA connections that the government was trying to cover up, quoted court documents out of context. Webb reported that "federal prosecutors obtained a court order preventing [Ross's] defense lawyers from delving into [Blandon's] ties to the CIA." He then quoted this motion to suppress as stating that Blandon "will admit that he was a large-scale dealer in cocaine, and there is no additional benefit to any defendant to inquire as to the Central Intelligence Agency." But Webb omitted another part of that sentence, which reads, "the threat to so inquire is simply a gambit," as well as the opening paragraph of the motion, which states:

> The United States believes that such allegations are not true, and that the threat to make such allegations is solely intended to dissuade the United States from going forward with the prosecution....

These omissions left the impression that Assistant U.S. Attorney L. J. O'Neale was attempting to conceal a CIA connection, when a reading of the full motion showed that his stated purpose was to keep Ricky Ross's defense lawyer from sidetracking the prosecution.

Blandon, according to Webb's story, implied CIA approval for the cocaine trafficking when he told a federal grand jury in San Francisco that after the contras started receiving official CIA funds, the agency no longer needed drug money. "When Mr. Reagan get in the power, we start receiving a lot of money," he stated. "And the people that was in charge, it was the, the CIA, so they didn't want to raise any [drug] money because they have, they had the money that they wanted." At that point, he said, "we started doing business by ourselves."

Intriguing as that statement is, neither Webb nor his editors appear to have noticed that it contradicted the thrust of "Dark Alliance." Ronald Reagan came to power in 1981; the CIA received its seed authorization of $19.9 million later that year to organize the covert war against Nicaragua. If Blandon and Meneses stopped supporting the FDN at that point, it could not be true that "for the better part of a decade" drug profits in the millions were channeled to the contras. Nor, then, could it be true that this dark alliance with the contras was responsible for the crack epidemic in California in the early 1980s.

This inconsistency demonstrates the overarching problem in the series: the difficulty in using Blandon's grand jury and court testimony, which is often imprecise—Blandon at one point appeared to date Reagan's rise to power in 1983—and contradictory. Particularly regarding the timeline of when he met Meneses, supported the contras, broke with Meneses, and became Ricky Ross's mentor and supplier—a series of dates critical to the central allegation, that this Nicaraguan drug ring opened the inner city market to the crack trade to finance the contra war—Blandon's testimony and other documents are vague or inconsistent or both.

In an unusual follow-up evaluating the controversy over "Dark Alliance," thirty-year *Mercury News* veteran Pete Carey reviewed the discrepancies in Blandon's testimony and other records. Webb, according to Carey, acknowledged that it would be damaging to the series "if you looked only at the [Blandon] testimony. But we didn't. We looked at other sources." The other evidence, Carey pointed out, included the 1986 L.A. County Sheriff's affidavit for searching the homes of Blandon in which "three confidential informants said that Blandon was still sending money to the contras." While Carey laid out all the differing evidence "for the readers to make up their own mind," he says, the original series did not. That omission left the series wide open to attack.

The Media Response

Initially the national media greeted the series with a deafening silence. No in-depth articles were published in the major papers in the month of September on the growing controversy. The networks were similarly silent that month, with the exception of CNN, which ran several pieces, and NBC, which did an in-depth *Nightly News* report on September 27. Despite pressure from some staffers and outsiders, Ted Koppel's *Nightline* did nothing until November 15, when CIA Director Deutch held his town meeting in Watts; PBS's *NewsHour with Jim Lehrer* also used the Deutch peg for its first piece on the subject, on November 18.

In some cases, the absence or delay of coverage reflected the deep-rooted skepticism of veteran reporters who had covered the contra war. One newspaper reporter who has written on intelligence for a decade compared the articles to "a crime scene that has been tampered with," rendering the true story difficult to obtain. "Dark Alliance," he suggested, was "a stew of hard fact, supposition, and wild guesswork." For David Corn of *The Nation*, Webb's "claims were not well substantiated; that was pretty obvious from reading the story." *The New York Times's* Weiner agreed that the opening declaration that millions in drug funds had been kicked back to the contras "was unsupported in the body of the story." Upon first read, the *Los Angeles Times's* Washington bureau chief, Doyle McManus, thought "Dark Alliance" was "a hell of a story"; after further review, he concluded that "most of the things that are new aren't true, and most of the things that are true aren't new." Of all the contra-war journalists polled, only the one who originally broke the contra/drug story, Robert Parry, felt "Dark Alliance" was credible. "It didn't strike me as 'Oh wow, that's outlandish.'"

It was public pressure that essentially forced the media to address Webb's allegations. *The Washington Post,* after an internal debate on how to handle the story, weighed in first on October 4 with THE CIA AND CRACK: EVIDENCE IS LACKING OF ALLEGED PLOT, a lengthy—and harsh—report written by Roberto Suro and Walter Pincus. "A *Washington Post* investigation," the article declared, had determined that "available information does not support the conclusion that the CIA-backed contras—or Nicaraguans in general—played a major role in the emergence of crack as a narcotic in widespread use across the United States"—an odd argument since "Dark Alliance" had focused mostly on the rise of crack in California. The article emphasized parts of Blandon's court testimony, where he limited the time he was connected to the contras to 1981–82, but failed to mention, let alone evaluate, contradictory evidence that Blandon's drug money was being laundered through a Miami bank for contra arms purchases possibly into 1986. The Suro/Pincus dismissal of the series, combined with a companion piece on the black community's susceptibility to conspiracy theories, only served to stir the controversy.

On October 21, *The New York Times* covered the same ground as the *Post*—finding "scant proof" for the *Mercury News's* contentions—but with a more measured approach. A lengthy article by Tim Golden, THOUGH EVIDENCE IS THIN, TALE OF CIA AND DRUGS HAS LIFE OF ITS OWN, examined how and why "Dark Alliance" had resounded throughout African-American communities, the problems with the evidence, and the politics surrounding the issue.

Long as it was, the Golden piece was overshadowed by a massive three-part rebuttal in the *Los Angeles Times* that began on October 20. Unlike the East Coast papers, the *Los Angeles Times* had been scooped in its own backyard about events that took place in its own city. "When I first saw the series," Leo Wolinsky, Metro editor for the *Times* told *L.A. Weekly*, "it put a big lump in my stomach." Still, it took almost a month for editors (who blame vacation plans and the conventions for the delay) to begin to focus on how to follow up on the *Mercury News*. A query to the Washington bureau for direction and advice brought a substantive memo, written by McManus, that made three points:

- The Washington bureau had no expertise on the history of crack in California; the L.A. desk would have to take up that issue on its own.

- There had been earlier reporting on the contras and drugs, including in California—most notably by Seth Rosenfeld of the *San Francisco Examiner* in 1986. Although the lead allegation of "millions" in drug revenues going to the contras was not substantiated, "There is something there."

- The allegations of government protection of Meneses and Blandon from prosecution were the "most convincing and troubling" part of the *Mercury News* exposé and fertile ground for further investigation. On that, the memo recommended a full-court press.

As McManus characterized his response, "I said: 'This goddamn thing is full of holes. There is no sourcing or terribly weak sourcing in the story. There is phraseology in here that is dishonest. But it is obviously worth going back and seeing what we can establish.'"

Both McManus and Wolinsky deny that the *Times* response was ever intended, as Wolinsky put it, "as a knockdown of the *Mercury News* series." But one *Times* reporter characterized himself as being "assigned to the 'get Gary Webb team'" and another was heard to say "We're going to take away that guy's Pulitzer." The opening "About this series" teaser made it clear that the *Times* pieces would explicitly address, and deny, the validity of all the main assertions in "Dark Alliance."

For all the effort spent trying to highlight the shortcomings of the *Mercury News*, however, the *Times* stumbled into some of the same problems of hyperbole, selectivity, and credibility that it was attempting to expose. For example, the first installment highlighted many of the dealers who had played a role in the advent of crack in L.A. The point was to show that Ricky Ross may have been a *big* player, but was not *the* player, as Webb had suggested, in the arrival of crack into the black neighborhoods of L.A. "The story of crack's genesis and evolution . . . is filled with a cast of interchangeable characters, from ruthless billionaires to strung-out curb dealers, none of whom is central to the drama," Jesse Katz wrote, based on his reporting and that of six other *Times* reporters. "Even on the best day Ricky Ross had, there was way more crack cocaine out there than he could ever control," Katz quoted a San Fernando narcotics detective as stating, and then noted: "How the crack epidemic reached that extreme, on some level, had nothing to do with Ross. Before, during, and after his reign, a bewildering roster of other dealers and suppliers helped fuel the crisis."

Less than two years earlier, however, the same Jesse Katz had described Ross as the veritable Dr. Moriarty of crack. Katz's December 20, 1994 article, DEPOSED KING OF CRACK, opened with this dramatic statement:

If there was an eye to the storm, if there was a criminal mastermind behind crack's decade-long reign, if there was one outlaw capitalist most responsible for flooding Los Angeles streets with mass-marketed cocaine, his name was Freeway Rick. . . . Ricky Donnell Ross did more than anyone else to democratize [crack], boosting volume, slashing prices, and spreading disease on a scale never before conceived.

Either Katz was guilty of vast exaggeration in 1994 or of playing down evidence that he had in 1996. If Ross was "key to the drug's spread in L.A.," as the

Times said in 1994, then his key supplier, Blandon, bore at least some of the responsibility for the "democratization" of crack that Gary Webb ascribed to him.

The second installment, written by McManus, drew on three unnamed associates of Blandon and Meneses, who denied that the two had sent "millions" to the contras; they believed the figure closer to $50,000, because the drug smugglers were awash in debt, not profit, in the early years. Perhaps more importantly, the *Los Angeles Times* obtained an admission from Dawn Garcia, who edited the piece at the *Mercury News*, that the "millions" figure was an extrapolation, based on the amount of coke Blandon and Meneses had sold between 1981 and 1986 combined with Blandon's testimony that everything went to the contras.

But the *Times*, like the *Post*, drew on the pieces of Blandon's court testimony in which he confined his contra drug dealings to a short period in 1981 and 1982—using the same kind of selectivity in highlighting evidence as the *Mercury News*, but to arrive at opposite conclusions, and failing to pursue leads in the other contradictory testimony and documents that Webb had used to present his case.

At the same time as it sought to undermine the specifics of "Dark Alliance," the McManus piece actually advanced its contra/crack connection thesis. To the two Nicaraguan drug dealers that Webb had written about, the *Times* added two more members of that ring: Meneses's nephew, Jairo Morales Meneses, and Renato Peña Cabrera. Both were arrested on cocaine charges in November, 1984. Unlike Blandon and Norvin Meneses, whose depiction in Webb's series as FDN officials was challenged by critics, Peña had a verifiable role, having served as an FDN press secretary in California.

The McManus piece credulously painted a portrait of the CIA as a law-abiding, conscientious agency. It included an abundance of denials from prominent CIA and Justice Department officials—while failing to inform readers of their roles in some of the scandals of the contra war—that the CIA would ever tolerate drug smuggling or that there had ever been any government interference with prosecuting drug smugglers connected to the contras. This despite documentation to the contrary.

Indeed, all three papers ignored evidence from declassified National Security Council e-mail messages and *The New York Times* and *The Washington Post* ignored evidence, from Oliver North's notebooks, which lend support to the underlying premise of the *Mercury News* series—that U.S. officials would both condone and protect drug traffickers if doing so advanced the contra cause. The October 21 *New York Times* piece didn't even mention the Kerry Committee report. "A decade ago, the national media low-balled the contra-drug story," David Corn observed in *The Nation*. "Now it's, Been there, done that."

In the Aftermath

On October 23, the Senate Select Committee on Intelligence held its first hearing on the controversy surrounding contra-drug allegations. Jack Blum, the former lead investigator for the Kerry committee, was the lead witness. Blum testified that his investigators had found no evidence whatsoever that the African-American community was a particular target of a plot to sell crack cocaine or that high U.S. officials had a policy of supporting the contras through drug sales. But, he testified further, "if you ask whether the United States government ignored the drug problem and subverted law enforcement to prevent embarrassment and to reward our allies in the contra war, the answer is yes." In a long session, he also detailed the Reagan Administration's obstruction of the Kerry investigation.

A story on ABC's *World News Tonight* about the hearing led with Blum's "no evidence" statement but excluded any reference to the rest of his testimony. *The New York Times* ran an AP story on the hearing but cut references to Blum's testimony. The *Los Angeles Times* covered the hearing but failed even to mention the lead witness or his testimony.

For conspiracy buffs, this non-coverage raised the specter of a government/media collaboration to bury the contra-cocaine story. That is farfetched. Yet the furor over "Dark Alliance" and the mainstream media's response to it dramatically raise the issue of responsible and irresponsible journalism—particularly in an era of growing public cynicism toward both government and the institutional press.

For many in the media, Webb's reporting remains at the core of the debate over journalistic responsibility. One veteran TV producer decried the impact of "Dark Alliance" on the profession: "Those stories have cheapened the coin of the realm." Another veteran reporter asks, "Can anyone doubt that Gary Webb added two plus two and came out with twenty-two?" At The Washington Post, senior management, led by Stephen Rosenfeld, deputy editorial-page editor, even refused to print a letter to the editor written by Jerry Ceppos, the Mercury News's executive editor, regarding the Post's critique of the series. Although Ceppos had redrafted the letter several times at the demand of the Post, Rosenfeld disparaged it as "misinformation."

In her November 10 column, the Post's own ombudsman, Geneva Overholser, objected to that decision, as well as to the Post's response to "Dark Alliance." "There is another appropriate response, a more important one, and that is: 'Is there anything to the very serious question the series raised?'"

Overholser's point resonated inside the Post. "There was a lot of unhappiness," says one editor. "A lot of frustration. Why pick on the Mercury News? There was a recognition that it would be appropriate to do something else." That recognition led to the publication of a follow-up piece headlined CIA, CONTRAS AND DRUGS: QUESTIONS ON LINKS LINGER. It reported that in 1984 the CIA had authorized a contra group in Costa Rica to take planes and cash from a prominent Colombian drug dealer then under indictment in the U.S. The planes, according to the drug dealers, were used to ferry arms to the contras and then drugs to the United States.

Clearly, there was room to advance the contra/drug/CIA story rather than simply denounce it. Indeed, at the Post, The New York Times, the Los Angeles Times, and other major oracles, the course of responsible journalism could have taken a number of avenues, among them: a historical treatment of drug smuggling as part of CIA covert operations in Indochina, Afghanistan, and Central America; an investigation into the alleged obstruction, by the Justice Department and the CIA, of the Kerry Committee's inquiry in the late 1980s; an evaluation of Oliver North's mendacious insistence, after the Mercury News series was published, that "no U.S. government official" ever "tolerated" drug smuggling as part of the contra war; and a follow-up on the various intriguing leads in "Dark Alliance." "The big question is still hanging out there," said one Los Angeles Times reporter who disagreed with his editors' decision to simply trash "Dark Alliance." "What did the government know and when did they know it? This story is not put to rest by a long shot."

To be sure, the "Dark Alliance" series was an overwritten and problematically sourced piece of reporting. It repeatedly promised evidence that, on close reading, it did not deliver. In so doing, the Mercury News bears part of the responsibility for the sometimes distorted public furor the stories generated. (A thorough editing job might have spared the Mercury News such responsibility and still resulted in a major exposé.) "Webb has convinced thousands of people of assertions that are not yet true or not yet supported," McManus points out. "That pollutes the public debate."

Yet the Mercury News was single-handedly responsible for stimulating this debate. This regional paper accomplished something that neither the Los Angeles Times, The Washington Post, nor The New York Times had been willing or able to do—revisit a significant story that had been inexplicably abandoned by the mainstream press, report a new dimension to it, and thus put it back on the national agenda where it belongs. "We have advanced a ten-year story that is clearly of great interest to the American public," Ceppos could rightfully claim.

The unacknowledged negligence of the mainstream press made that possible. Indeed, if the major media had devoted the same energy and ink to investigating the contra drug scandal in the 1980s as they did to attacking the Mercury News in 1996, Gary Webb might never have had his scoop.

And having shown itself still unwilling to follow the leads and lay the story to rest, the press faces a challenge in the contra-cocaine matter not unlike the government's: restoring its credibility in the face of public distrust over its perceived role in the handling of these events. "A principal responsibility of the press is to protect the people from government excesses," Overholser pointed out. "The Post (and others) showed more energy for protecting the CIA from someone else's journalistic excesses." The mainstream press shirked its larger duty; thus it bears the larger burden.

Article Review Form at end of book.

Case 1: *The San Jose Mercury News* continued

Drawing Conclusions from Investigative Reporting

Where should journalists draw the line?

Steve Weinberg
Editor, the IRE Journal

When Gary Webb started writing what became "Dark Alliance: The Story Behind the Crack Explosion," an investigative project for the *San Jose Mercury News*, he was pretty sure he had something that would attract attention outside his newspaper's circulation area.

An experienced investigative reporter at the *Cleveland Plain Dealer* before joining the *Mercury News*, Webb knew something about attracting controversy as a result of his work.

But little did Webb suspect that the project, about possible Central Intelligence Agency involvement in crack cocaine sales, would attract the kind of attention—both the lavish praise and the severe criticism—it has.

Lavish Praise, Severe Criticism The controversies surrounding the San Jose, ABC and Philadelphia projects are about the soul of journalism in the 1990s.

Since the series appeared (Aug. 18–20, 1996, plus follow-ups), praise has come from countless readers, many fellow journalists and some politicians, especially those already suspicious of CIA activities in the United States and other nations. But Webb and his editors have also become the center of unexpected criticism, as skeptical journalists, outraged politicians and accused bureaucrats have questioned their motives, reporting techniques, editing, presentation (especially on the newspaper's Internet site) and the series' conclusions.

Within the *Mercury News'* own newsroom, there was some grumbling about the content and presentation of the series. *The Baltimore Sun* raised questions about Webb's reporting in a Sept. 27, 1996, article on page 2 by a national staff writer. *The Washington Post* published a front-page story (on Oct. 4), reported by four people, and a separate piece (Oct. 2) by its media writer suggesting that Webb's series might be misleading. *The Mercury News'* top editor replied to the newspaper's internal critics by memo and in meetings. He replied to the *Post* findings in a detailed letter, then took the unusual step of assigning a top investigative reporter from within the *Mercury News* to re-report the Webb series. Pete Carey's findings, mostly supportive but partly critical, ran in the *Mercury News* on Oct. 13.

That did not stem the tide of outside scrutiny. *The Los Angeles Times* published a three-part series (Oct. 20–22) by a ten-person team finding fault with Webb's work. *The New York Times* published a front-page article (Oct. 21) that was partly critical. Some journalism commentators—in magazines, syndicated columns, op-ed pieces and on the air—outside those big three newspapers have joined in the criticism. The Central Intelligence Agency has issued denials.

Reprinted with permission from Steve Weinberg and Investigative Reports & Editors.

Putting Journalists on the Defensive

The specific controversy over Webb's work is interesting in its own right. But its significance transcends one reporter and his newspaper, especially when considered in conjunction with other controversial investigative projects disseminated during the 1990s. Among the most prominent of those projects are "Smokescreen," the ABC News investigation led by Walt Bogdanich into tobacco company use of nicotine, as well as three series by James Steele and Donald Barlett at the *Philadelphia Inquirer* that blame the legislative and executive branches of the federal government, working closely with multinational corporations, for sabotaging the standard of living for millions of U.S. citizens.

Critics of these and other ambitious investigative projects have tried to place dedicated, talented journalists on the defensive. The debate centers on these questions:

Have the reporters and editors behind the projects:

1. begun their work with suppositions that skewed the findings?
2. drawn conclusions that go beyond whatever expertise they may have developed?
3. caused the credibility of all journalists to decline?

Although it sounds melodramatic, the controversies surrounding the San Jose, ABC and Philadelphia projects are about the soul of journalism in the 1990s. As a result of the attacks on their credibility, the investigative reporters and editors involved have arrived at a watershed: Will they pull back from piecing together hard-to-gather information from a variety of sources on sensitive topics? Will they stop short of drawing conclusions and proposing solutions?

Looked at another way, does Webb, do Barlett and Steele and Bogdanich have an obligation to practice what I like to call "expert journalism," or do they have an obligation to eschew expert journalism and all that term implies?

The Genesis of Dark Alliance

The genesis of Webb's revelations, like the genesis of many journalistic blockbusters, is grounded in an experienced investigative reporter with a prepared mind. The way Webb came to his topic demonstrates, once again, that there might be lucky reporters, but there are no lazy, lucky reporters.

In 1993, the *Mercury News* published Webb's series "The Forfeiture Racket." While reporting that series, Webb ran across the case of a convicted Los Angeles drug dealer, "Freeway Rick" Ross, whose assets had been seized by law enforcement officers. Webb found the Ross case interesting, but could not make room for it in the series.

In June 1995, the U.S. Justice Department released a policy memo on asset forfeiture. Because the policy seemed to conflict with federal court decisions, Webb wrote a story. A woman in Oakland, Calif., saw the story and called Webb. Her boyfriend, a Nicaraguan national, was incarcerated and had been victimized by the local asset forfeiture policy, she said. Webb replied that he appreciated the call, but simply could not write up every forfeiture case that came to his attention.

The woman was insistent. By the way, she mentioned, drug running and U.S. intelligence agencies had inexplicably been mentioned in her boyfriend's case. What was that all about? She said she had a partially redacted federal grand jury transcript about the case. Did Webb want to look at it? Webb, curiosity piqued, said he would meet the woman.

The transcript introduced Webb to Oscar Danilo Blandon Reyes, a Nicaraguan national who had been a cocaine seller in the United States before turning informant for the U.S. Drug Enforcement Administration. Blandon was telling the grand jury what he knew about the Nicaraguans under investigation, including the boyfriend of the woman who had called Webb. Blandon testified that some of his knowledge about Nicaraguans running drugs in the United States came from Norwin Meneses Cantarero, a higher-up in the drug chain. Blandon and Meneses had been unknown to Webb, but he was interested in learning more.

About that time, a judge hearing the case of the incarcerated Nicaraguans ordered disclosure of the grand jury transcript, so that the defendants could learn more about Blandon, their accuser. The U.S. attorney opposed the judge's disclosure order, saying national security was involved. How about if the government just set aside Blandon's testimony? Then there would be no need to delve into his background or credibility.

Now Webb was really interested. As he called around looking for more information about Blandon and Meneses, he talked to a San Diego lawyer who mentioned a possible link between Blandon and Freeway Rick Ross. Webb could sense his separate pieces of string balling together, as sometimes happens when the pursuit of a story is going well.

Webb wrote Ross in prison. Did he know Blandon? Sure, Ross replied; Blandon was a big supplier of crack cocaine when Ross was selling the substance to Los Angeles' inner-city blacks. Wow, Webb thought. It appeared Blandon has drug connections, national security connections, and connections to the Contras, the CIA-endorsed army that fought Nicaragua's socialist government.

With help from a reporter in Managua, Webb made contact with Meneses, who had escaped prosecution for his drug running in the United States but run afoul of the Nicaraguan authorities. Meneses agreed to talk, partly, Webb suspects, because he felt betrayed by the U.S. Drug Enforcement Administration.

Webb slowly realized what he was uncovering might be linked to the Iran-Contra political scandal during the Ronald Reagan-George Bush administrations. Webb reviewed a 1988 report issued by the U.S. Senate subcommittee on terrorism, narcotics and international operations, chaired by John Kerry, D-Mass. There it was. The committee report said, in part, "It is clear that individuals who provided support for the Contras were involved in drug trafficking, the supply network of the Contras was used by drug trafficking organizations, and elements of the Contras themselves knowingly received financial and material assistance from drug traffickers. In each case, one or another agency of the U.S. government had information regarding the involvement either while it was occurring, or immediately thereafter."

"Dark Alliance" was coming together. As published, the day one headline said: "America's Crack Plague Has Roots in Nicaragua War/Columbia-San Francisco Bay Area Drug Pipeline Helped Finance CIA-backed Contras."

Key Findings

The day one lead said: "For the better part of a decade, a San Francisco Bay Area drug ring sold tons of cocaine to the Crips and Bloods street gangs of Los Angeles and funneled millions in drug profits to a Latin American guerilla army run by the U.S. Central Intelligence Agency, a *Mercury News* investigations has found."

Key day one findings:

Blandon and Meneses, the Nicaraguan men supplying cocaine to Ross, the Los Angeles dealer, for resale "met with CIA agents both before and during the time they were selling the drugs in L.A. . ."

A result of the Nicaraguan-Californian connection was "the first pipeline between Columbia's cocaine cartels and the black neighborhoods of Los Angeles," providing availability of a narcotic "virtually unobtainable in black neighborhoods before members of the CIA's army started bringing it into South-Central in the 1980s at bargain-basement prices."

The pipeline provided "the case and connections needed for L.A.'s gangs to buy automatic weapons," and eventually "helped spark a crack explosion" in other U.S. cities.

Meneses, the Nicaraguan supervisor of the cocaine sales in the United States, was known to law enforcement authorities, but "the CIA or unnamed national security interests" hampered prosecution, according to sources cited by Webb.

The articles that criticize Webb's work use sources no more reliable—and, in some cases, perhaps less reliable—than his own sources.

As for foreign policy implications, Meneses and Blandon used cash from sales to Ross "to buy weapons and equipment for a guerrilla army" in Nicaragua that was "the largest of several anti-communist groups commonly called the Contras." The CIA and other elements of the U.S. government hoped the Contras would help overthrow the Nicaraguan socialists who had come to power during 1979.

On the newspaper's Internet site, Webb supplied the text of documents he relied upon, including grand jury proceedings, sworn court testimony, Congressional hearings and investigative files from law enforcement agencies.

The Big Question

Despite the voluminous documentation, or perhaps because of it, much of the controversy over "Dark Alliance" revolves around this question:

Does the *Mercury News* series say outright that the CIA knowingly sponsored the California-based Nicaraguans in the crack cocaine sales business? Not really, though Webb certainly serves up tantalizing, apparently credible evidence. Consider:

He quotes a federal public defender in Los Angeles as saying police believed the CIA compromised the investigation of one of two key Nicaraguan drug dealers in California.

The same dealer is quoted by Webb as implying, during testimony to a federal grand jury in San Francisco, "that his cocaine sales were, for a time, CIA-approved."

The statement of the lawyer for that dealer is portrayed like this by Webb: "Blandon's lawyer,

Brunon, said in an interview that his client never told him directly that he was selling cocaine for the CIA, but the prominent Los Angeles defense attorney drew his own conclusions from the 'atmosphere of CIA and clandestine activities' that surrounded Blandon and his Nicaraguan friends. 'Was he involved with the CIA? Probably. Was he involved with drugs? Most definitely. Were those two things involved with each other? They've never said that, obviously. They've never admitted that. But I don't know where these guys get these big aircraft . . .'"

Reactions from Journalists

The reactions from experienced investigative journalists have been all over the lot. Here is a sampling:

In *Newsweek*, Sept. 30, 1996, reporters Gregory L. Vistica and Vern E. Smith said "Webb . . . suggests that the CIA must have been aware of the Nicaraguan connection . . . But that is just his supposition—Webb does not say anyone in the CIA actually knew about the Nicaraguans' cocaine trafficking or that any CIA operative actually took part."

In *Time*, Sept. 30, 1996, columnist Jack E. White gave Webb some credit for good work, then quoted colleague/author Elaine Shannon, "who has covered the war on drugs for so long that she know as much about it as any narc," as saying "Even sources who are routinely skeptical of the official line on the Contras agree that the idea that the agency was behind drug smuggling by the Contras is fantasy . . ."

On CNN Today, Sept. 20, 1996, Webb and Ron Kessler debated the story, with host Lou Waters moderating. Kessler, a former *Washington Post* and *Wall Street Journal* reporter who has written books about national security topics, slammed Webb's series. Kessler accused Webb of lacking documentation for the gist of the series. Webb shot back that Kessler obviously had failed to do his homework, because the documentation was voluminous.

For what it is worth, I am impressed with Webb's reporting—even after carefully considering the criticisms by fellow investigative journalists I respect.

The newspapers, magazines and broadcast outlets examining the series should be congratulated for their efforts at media criticism. I started publishing media criticism in 1975, with an article in *Columbia Journalism Review*. I am a contributing editor there now. I have also scrutinized the work of fellow journalists in *The Quill*, *American Journalism Review*, the American Society of Newspaper Editors' magazine, *Mother Jones* magazine, numerous book review pages and many other forums. It is prickly work, and certainly no way to make friends in newsrooms.

So while I praise the efforts of those examining Webb's reporting, I found them largely unconvincing. Webb found himself with an important story building after learning the connection between Nicaraguan drug sellers and a Los Angeles customer. He took the story where it seemed to lead—to the door of U.S. national security and drug enforcement agencies. Even if Webb overreached in a few paragraphs—based on my careful reading, I would say his overreaching was limited, if it occurred at all—he still had a compelling, significant investigation to publish.

It looks to me as if many critics of Webb are holding him to a higher standard of evidence than they usually insist upon for their own stories. Their articles that criticize his work rely on sources no more reliable—and, in some cases, perhaps less reliable—than Webb's own sources. Webb's sources were almost all men and women with something to gain or lose by telling less than the whole truth. But the same was true for some of the sources—a few of them unnamed—quoted by the *Washington Post*, *Los Angeles Times* and *New York Times* reporters.

That is why Webb relied so heavily on documents and sworn testimony. What else could he do? Would it have been realistic for him to expect prosecutors, DEA agents and CIA officials to admit their complicity? Of course not. Would it have been realistic for Webb to expect the drug dealers, Nicaraguan or Angelino variety, to tell the whole truth? Of course not.

Webb attempted an investigation with a high degree of difficulty. He uncovered revelatory connections between government national security considerations (which I consider to be overblown, if not entirely manufactured) and the failure to prosecute dangerous drug dealers. Even it turns out the CIA had no direct complicity, those connections are an important story. In parts two and three of the series, Webb presents the connections compellingly. (My opinion of the presentation in part one is much lower. I had to read it three times to understand it.) Perhaps most important from my perch, Webb and his editors put a great deal of documentation on the newspaper's Internet site, for any reader to evaluate.

Later findings might erase my praise; I certainly cannot totally discount the skepticism of so many talented colleagues. But I think Webb should receive an "A" for effort, and—until I see convincing evidence to the contrary—an A-minus for execution.

If Webb's work turns out to be shoddy, will that chill investigative reporting across the board, as I have heard some journalists worry? It shouldn't. Every news organization ought to be digging beneath surface events on local, national and international issues. Some never do. Others do it only occasionally. They cannot be chilled because there is little or nothing to chill.

On the other hand, a minority—but nonetheless impressive number—of news organizations do practice investigative journalism regularly. They have withstood many predictions of a chilling effect, most recently during 1995 when ABC News settled a lawsuit brought by Philip Morris tobacco company concerning the "Smokescreen" investigation mentioned earlier in this article. They are unlikely to cut back on investigative reporting because of one series undergoing scrutiny. One interpretation, mine as it happens, is that it is actually encouraging to see the impact of the *Mercury News* series.

The *Mercury News* series drew few outright conclusions, leaving readers to draw their own. The ABC News "Smokescreen" investigation openly came to a few conclusions, which seemed richly justified by the evidence gathered. The three *Philadelphia Inquirer* series by Barlett and Steele mentioned earlier drew lots of conclusions, as well as suggesting solutions.

Is it warranted for investigative journalists to draw conclusions, to hold themselves out as experts? Sometimes yes. I know of many instances where after a year or more of work, journalists know as much as any source. Furthermore, those sources—no matter how well-intended—usually have hidden agendas and conflicts of interests. Talented investigative journalists generally have no hidden agendas and no conflicts of interests. So who better to act as experts?

Given the knowledge Webb accumulated, I think he had an obligation to practice expert journalism at some level, which is exactly what he tried to do.

What do you think? We at *The IRE Journal* want to hear your thoughts. But, please, contact us only if you have carefully read and analyzed the original *San Jose Mercury News* series.

Article Review Form at end of book.

READING 37

Case 2: Timothy McVeigh and *The Dallas Morning News*

When *The Dallas Morning News* broke the story of Oklahoma City bombing defendant Timothy McVeigh's alleged confession online, it marked the first time a major newspaper let its Web site scoop its print publication. Digital journalists praised the move, citing the Internet's ability to move information quickly. Many traditional journalists questioned the motives of the *Morning News*'s editors.

In the first of the following articles, Ralph Langer, editor of The Morning News, discusses the decision-making process. In the second article, Paul Buser compares the Morning News case to other highly publicized legal cases. What conclusion did Langer reach about the decision to publish on the paper's Web site first? What conclusion did Buser come to regarding the Morning News case? The other articles raise additional questions. Do you feel the Morning News acted appropriately? What difference did it make that the story appeared online before print publication? What impact did it have on the legal process? Do you think that if the story had appeared only in the print version it would have garnered as much attention? How will this case impact publishers' decisions about using Web sites to break stories?

Reading 37: Langer, R. "Our Story, Our Process: Correct" *Quill*, April 1997.

Reading 38: Buser, P. J. "Fair Trial vs. Free Press" *Quill*, April 1997.

Reading 39: Sanford, B. "Openness Benefits All" *Quill*, April 1997.

Reading 40: Buser, P. J. "Legal Ethics Issues" *Quill*, April 1997.

Reading 41: Steele, B. "Until We Know, Let Us Challenge" *Quill*, April 1997.

Our Story, Process Correct

Public discourse diverted by series of allegations

Ralph Langer
Ralph Langer is executive vice president and editor of The Dallas Morning News.

The discussion took place over parts of several days before we decided to publish a story that said Timothy McVeigh acknowledged to his defense team that he bombed the federal building in Oklahoma City and that the hour chosen for the explosion was designed to maximize the body count.

Even as the material itself was being assessed and a possible story drafted, senior editors at The Dallas Morning News, sometimes with our lead First Amendment attorney, discussed the important, threshold question: whether or not to publish.

"At least a few critics have suggested that The News gave no thought whatever to the effect on the trial. We had concern about the trial but, ultimately, came to believe that the information in that part of the material was of national importance and that we were obligated to publish it."

We had already determined that the material was valid.

Our attorney's opinion, later publicly stated as well, was that the information was legally obtained.

The decision process covered—multiple times and from

First published in *Quill* Magazine, April, 1997. Reprinted by permission of Ralph Langer.

several perspectives—the basic questions concerning use of material from the defense files and the possible impact on the trial.

At least a few critics have suggested that The News gave no thought whatever to the effect on the trial. We had concern about the trial but, ultimately, came to believe that the information in that part of the material was of national importance and that we were obligated to publish it.

We believe that the courts—in particular the federal courts—have many tools available to ensure that a fair jury is empaneled. There are other means available to the judge to conduct the trial in a fair way even under the intense news coverage that this trial would certainly generate.

We concluded that the court could and would oversee a proper trial. U.S. District Judge Richard P. Matsch agreed with that conclusion and so have the defense attorney (off and on) and the prosecutors.

It's worth noting that many aspects of the evidentiary case against Timothy McVeigh have been reported over the intervening two years. This includes detailed telephone records; allegations that McVeigh's fingerprint is on a receipt for fertilizer chemically identical to the bomb; witnesses to rental of the Ryder truck which carried the bomb; and other parts of the case.

Because of inaccurate accusations by lead defense attorney Stephen Jones, we were forced to respond publicly. This caused the furor to grow and to continue long past the time it probably otherwise would have died down.

Jones' charges were quite successful in focusing attention more on the messenger and less on the message.

Almost immediately, Jones alleged that we had given him the name of our source. Several days later he repeated the charge, that time suggesting that it might have been a "Freudian slip."

The News never gave Jones a name or a hint or a description of any source in this case. He may have been attempting to smoke out anyone who had provided information to us.

He also alleged that The News had stolen the information and had "hacked" into his computer files.

Also totally untrue.

After several days of changing responses from Jones, The News published a graphic showing how his positions had changed during the first three days.

For example, on the first day the defense said no such document existed in their files. They said they had the electronic ability to quickly check that. Attorney Jones said he would know if such document or documents existed in the files and they did not.

At the same time, he said we may have "stolen" the documents which he said didn't exist.

He suggested that we may have been "hoaxed" by an individual he named who, he said, had ill-will toward The News.

Within a short time, he indirectly acknowledged that the documents existed but blended the two accusations by saying that the documents were present in defense materials but claiming that he knew they were "hoaxed" because the defense had fabricated them. He said this was part of a sting operation against neo-Nazis or Middle East terrorist sources or others who might be tricked into talking to the defense if they thought they were not targets of an investigation since McVeigh had already acknowledged doing the bombing.

Eventually he said his staff researched faking a defense document and concluded it is "ethical and proper."

The last word on this subject came days later when the investigator whose name is on the defense reports said he never falsified anything, that he only wrote down whatever the defendant told him and that he sent the material directly to Stephen Jones, the attorney.

Deciding to publish was not a short discussion, and a legitimate debate over that decision is both inevitable and healthy. I believe the discussion needs to be separated from the diversionary and inaccurate charges that encrusted the public conversation in the first week after publication.

Article Review Form at end of book.

Case 2: Timothy McVeigh and *The Dallas Morning News* continued

Fair Trial vs. Free Press

Media today face complex legal questions

Paul J. Buser

It was 1954, and one of the most highly publicized criminal trials of this century was underway. The site was a Cleveland courthouse, a block from Lake Erie. The suspect, Dr. Sam Sheppard, was convicted of the murder of his wife Marilyn.

After more than a decade of appeals, the U.S. Supreme Court resoundingly reversed Sheppard's conviction, and the case went into journalism textbooks.

The reasoning in 1966: The enormity of prejudicial publicity before and during the trial. The court said the trial was carried out in a "carnival atmosphere" not unlike a "Roman holiday." One newspaper, The Cleveland Press, during the trial declared Sheppard's guilt in an editorial on its front page.

Now it's 1997, and coverage of the trial of Timothy McVeigh has raised once again discussions about "fair trial" and "free press."

And, another newspaper, The Dallas Morning News, has found itself the subject of much scrutiny because it published on its Web site a story about McVeigh's supposed confession.

Are the cases similar or are there other issues that make them different?

In the Sheppard reversal, the U.S. Supreme Court said the trial judge should have taken more care to manage his courtroom and the trial so the jury would not be swayed by media reports of virtually every fact and allegation.

The Supreme Court said that to prevent undue bias on the jury panel, the trial judge could—with the prosecution and defense actively taking part in jury questioning at the outset—sequester witnesses, sequester the jury, change venue, delay the trial until emotions settled and calmer minds were ready to listen and deliberate.

Those preventive measures sound good in theory, but when applied to the McVeigh case, the reality and practicality are very different. The Morning News story about McVeigh became worldwide news just as the McVeigh court had sent out pre-trial questionnaires to hundreds of prospective jurors. Is it possible to question effectively hundreds of jurors, much less responsibly delve into the subject of bias?

The McVeigh trial already had been moved from Oklahoma City to Denver. However, changing venue is a moot point because the case will be covered closely by the media in every detail whether the court sits in Alaska, Hawaii, northern Maine, Texas, or on a U.S. island in the South Pacific.

Soon after the venue change to Denver, Judge Richard Matsch issued a gag order to prevent the attorneys from talking about anything other than the "dry facts" of the case. But, the situation changed after The Morning News story. The defense demanded that Judge Matsch immediately modify his gag order so they could respond to the story. The judge complied.

While we don't yet know all the evidence against McVeigh—nor do we know all the circumstances surrounding The Morning News decision—we can look at some of the considerations that enter into situations like these.

One caveat: The law at trial is subject to interpretation by lawyers, judges and juries. Some issues we will explore may never be raised in a courtroom. Questions we've overlooked may

---

From Paul J. Buser, "Fair Trial vs. Free Press" in *Quill,* April, 1997. Reprinted by permission of Paul J. Buser, Board Member and Legal Counsel, Cleveland, OH. Professional Chapter of the Society of Professional Journalists.

be asked. It is impossible at this point to render judgment on Timothy McVeigh or the actions of The Dallas Morning News. But, it is possible to broaden our understanding of the complexities of "fair trial-free press."

How did McVeigh's supposed confession get away from the custody and control of his defense attorney's team? We don't know. But, the myriad of ways in which this kind of situation might occur requires any news organization to make difficult and deliberate decisions.

Even if someone on the inside of a team, an undercover reporter or one of the defense team members, offers material, there could be criminal liability for any media outlet that publishes that material.

All the privileged discussions and documents prepared by a defense team are called "work product," a form of intellectual property. Work product has value. Taking work product without consent and with the intent to use it can be more than civil conversion of property rights. A crime could be charged.

Accepting work product from a source who obtained it unlawfully can be a problem. Receiving stolen property or being an accomplice or accessory after the fact to the commission of a crime in some states is called "facilitating a crime."

Let's hypothesize that a media outlet wants to review and publish a portion of the work product of an attorney who is defending an individual at a criminal trial or who is representing a client in highly public negotiations, for example a corporate acquisition of one company by another.

It is easy to sketch a scenario: The media organization works with someone on the inside to obtain confidential documents from "unidentified sources," "reliable sources," "sources close to."

But the plan goes awry. The media organization cannot get the documents it wanted. The law says that planning and intent to steal private property, though never accomplished, can be considered a crime in itself.

In fact, depending on what state you live in, two crimes might be considered. One would be attempted theft, the other criminal conspiracy. The former is a "specific intent" crime in which there is intention to take intellectual property owned by another and steps are undertaken. It doesn't matter whether the plan succeeds. Criminal conspiracy is the combination or concert of action of two or more persons to accomplish a criminal or unlawful purpose—or some purpose not unlawful or criminal in itself but accomplished by criminal or unlawful means. Even if the taking of property is never accomplished as planned, the crime of conspiracy has occurred.

Reporters and editors should ask themselves where they have a lawful right to be when gathering news. Entry on a private or public premises with the intent to steal, or to commit another felony, is a crime. News organizations must be clear about the lines between investigative journalism and stealth.

But, there is no theft when the owner of the property consents to the taking or receipt of the property. A media outlet that has received private property voluntarily from a defense team (or the prosecution—as the case may be) cannot be charged with theft because any claim of privileged information has been waived.

Who is the real owner of attorney work product in a highly publicized criminal case such as McVeigh's? Does McVeigh own the truth of the bombing? The "black letter law" is that the work product privilege can be waived only by the defendant—not by the attorney or any member of the defense team.

Consequently, unless a media organization receives the intellectual property—the work product—from the defendant, there still is a risk of liability.

Media organizations also can be held liable in a civil or common law sense for use of intellectual property without permission of the owner. What if the information eventually were to be part of a book written by a defendant, an attorney, or both?

If a news organization uses this information without permission, it could be liable for civil damages for "loss of prospective business advantage" (the adverse effect on the publishing of the book and sales gained from it), for "tortious interference with business relationship" (where a contract for profit already has been struck or is in the planning stages and a third person, outside the contract, prevents its success or accomplishment) or for both.

Finally, if a news organization used attorney work product for its own sales, books or circulation, the intellectual property information has been converted or misappropriated and the owner has been denied a right of publicity or other business opportunity.

Remember the bombing in Atlanta during the Olympics?

Remember Richard Jewell? He has been visiting the executive suites of media companies, seeking damages for his loss suffered during the weeks when he was the prime suspect in the bombing.

Though not the stuff of everyday media analysis, what Jewell is seeking is compensation for damage to his reputation and for invasion of his privacy. The type of claims he is liable to make include:

- being put in a "false light," similar to a defamation suit;

- the publication of true but private facts about his life that would be "highly offensive" to a reasonable person similarly situated;

- intrusion into his private life, with the standard again being the question of whether this would be highly offensive to a reasonable person similarly situated;

- publication of unauthorized biography of a non-public figure, with false or misleading information.

A false-light or defamation suit brought when a media organization is just plain wrong is likely to turn to a question of damages. "Reckless disregard of the truth" would be likely to increase damage awards. "Negligence" in the research process before publication would be likely to bring lesser damages.

Let's examine the possibility of Timothy McVeigh bringing a false-light, defamation suit.

First, has McVeigh been "defamed" in the legal sense? This is coverage of the trial of someone accused of the worst act of terrorism in this country. Doesn't the media have a right to cover this event if for no other purpose than

"Truth is the only weapon for a defendant who hopes to be a plaintiff against a news organization. McVeigh would have to be found not guilty to have even a hope of pursuing a defamation claim against a media organization."

to fulfill the public's right to know all the pretrial investigative facts?

Defamation is generically defined as a false publication causing injury to a person's reputation, or exposing the defendant to public hatred, contempt, ridicule, shame or disgrace, or otherwise adversely affecting the defendant; for example, in trade or business or employment opportunities. In McVeigh's situation—even before the publication of the alleged confession—wasn't the defendant already scorned by many, that is, not given the benefit of the doubt nor the Constitutional presumption of innocence by the reading and viewing public?

Second, assuming McVeigh could prove the legal elements of the defamation claim, there still is a question of whether McVeigh—a defendant charged with a crime that killed or injured hundreds of people—is a "public figure" or a "private person" in the context of a damage suit.

If a criminal defendant is later found innocent, is he a "public figure" who should be denied damages because of the newsworthiness of the event and because of the worldwide publicity stemming from the charges against him?

Truth is the only weapon for a defendant who hopes to be a plaintiff against a news organization. McVeigh would have to be found not guilty to have even a hope of pursuing a defamation claim against a media organization.

The Sheppard case is going back to court because DNA testing has shown that blood at the scene of the murder apparently has been proven not to be that of Sheppard. Even though the Supreme Court's decision in 1966 paved the way for Sheppard's eventual freedom, his son now wants to sue the State of Ohio for false imprisonment of his father.

Earlier we talked about criminal conspiracy and its implications to the aggressive investigative reporter. There is another issue—civil conspiracy damages. An injured defendant could sue a media organization and the unidentified source for planning to conspire to damage reputation and to usurp business opportunities.

Or, a criminal complaint might be filed by an individual against a media organization for criminal conspiracy to pirate and use intellectual property—work product. The prosecution could offer a deal: tell us the source and we will drop the charges against you.

An offer like that puts the media organization between Scylla and Charybdis. To cooperate with the prosecution means criminal liability is avoided. Cooperation, however, also means being subject to civil liability to the unidentified source. In 1991, the Supreme Court held that a reporter can be sued for damages by an unidentified source for disclosing the name of the confidential source.

There is no right answer and there has been none over the past three centuries of American press law on what "liberty of the press" means.

In 1769, the noted English legal scholar Sir William Blackstone said the "liberty of the press [consists] in laying no previous restraints upon publications, and not in freedom from censure for criminal matters when published."

In 1927, in Whitney v. California, Supreme Court Justice Louis Brandeis observed, "[t]hose who won our independence . . . valued liberty both as an end and as a means."

While the First Amendment's freedom of the press is the Constitution's "most majestic guarantee," says Constitutional law scholar Lawrence Tribe, the central question still remains and may never be answered to any one person's satisfaction:

"Is freedom of speech to be regarded only as some means to some further end—like successful self-government or social stability, or the discovery and dissemination of truth—or is freedom of speech in part also an end in itself, an expression of the sort of society we wish to become and the sort of persons we wish to be?"

Article Review Form at end of book.

Case 2: Timothy McVeigh and *The Dallas Morning News* continued

Openness Benefits All

Criminal defense lawyers can't have it both ways

Bruce W. Sanford

Bruce W. Sanford serves as counsel to the Society of Professional Journalists and numerous news organizations in Washington, D.C. This commentary first appeared in the Rocky Mountain News, March 19, 1997.

Talk shows, editorial columns and Internet home pages have been clobbering The Dallas Morning News for publishing information about Timothy McVeigh's supposed confession to the 1995 Oklahoma City bombing.

Much of the "piling on" has come from criminal defense lawyers who have complained bitterly about prejudice to McVeigh's Sixth Amendment right to a fair trial. These lions of the defense bar charge that pretrial publicity that reveals inadmissible evidence poisons the prospective jury pool in Denver.

This chorus of whining is not just unadulterated bunk, it's also hypocritical. The criminal defense bar wants it both ways. They huff and puff about the danger to the rights of their clients just as they use selective leaks and their own "spin" on pretrial news stories to manipulate the media for the benefit of their clients.

After more than 30 years of celebrated criminal trials, we have learned two facts about pretrial publicity that ought to be indisputable:

1. Judges can impanel a fair and impartial jury despite massive pretrial publicity.

Believe it or not, average citizens actually keep their sworn oath to decide a criminal case just on the evidence presented in court, not on extraneous noise. Time and time again, famous defendants have won acquittals after a saturation of adverse publicity before trial. Former Texas Gov. John Connally beat the rap in the Watergate-era "milk-fund" prosecution. Legendary Washington, D.C. Mayor Marion Barry was acquitted of felony charges despite television's repetitive use of the videotape showing him smoking crack cocaine. And need we even mention the O. J. Simpson case?

History tells us that judges can in fact sort out and excuse potential jurors who have been hopelessly handicapped by pretrial publicity. As the U.S. Supreme Court recognized in a 1976 ruling which broadly prohibited "gag" orders against pretrial coverage by the media, courts have a wide array of techniques available to them to ferret out jurors who are not up to the task. In Nebraska Press Association vs. Stuart the high court wrote: "Pretrial publicity even if pervasive and concentrated, can not be regarded as leading automatically and in every kind of criminal case to an unfair trial."

2. Trials don't seek the truth, but journalism does.

Criminal trials have a singular, express purpose: to ascertain if the evidence can prove guilt beyond a reasonable doubt. If the truth emerges, so much the better. But we have all seen instances where truth was a casualty of litigation. Journalism, on the other hand, has as its chief purpose the pursuit of truth. Certainly, most news reports, including the one in The Dallas Morning News, just deal in the currency of accurate facts, not ultimate truth. But at least they aspire in the right direction.

In the months since a bomb exploded in front of the Alfred P. Murrah federal building in Oklahoma City, killing 168 people and injuring another 500, the print and electronic media have pursued thousands of tips. The result-

From Bruce W. Sanford, "Openness Benefits All" in *Quill*, April 1997. Reprinted by permission of Bruce W. Sanford.

ing news reports have compelled McVeigh's lead attorney Stephen Jones to claim that his client could not get a fair trial, and to threaten that he would seek a federal investigation and a delay of the trial. As the case has evolved, Jones has used the media for his own purposes, calling into question key prosecution evidence. Yet, when the news isn't favorable, Jones readily telephones reporters to argue that press coverage will taint the jury pool. He also proceeds to muddy the waters by putting out his own spin on the evidence, whether it's admissible or not.

After posturing, Jones acknowledged that The Morning News story will not jeopardize a fair trial and agreed that it could start as scheduled. Such a concession reiterates the fact that there was no legal justification preventing The Morning News from publishing its story.

The logical conclusion to be drawn from the criticism of the press by Jones and other criminal defense attorneys would be adoption of a rule similar to that in England, where the media can report little on court proceedings until a verdict is issued. Such prior restraint, fortunately, is not part of the American grain. Instead, our traditions of openness benefit both the public—which receives abundant information about its criminal justice system—and criminal defense attorneys, who are increasingly turning their defense of high-profile criminals into lucrative second careers on the speaking and book circuits.

Article Review Form at end of book.

Case 2: Timothy McVeigh and *The Dallas Morning News* continued

Legal Ethics Issues

What guides conduct of attorneys?

Paul J. Buser

Paul J. Buser, a practicing attorney, is legal counsel to and a board member of the SPJ professional chapter in Cleveland. He based this article on legal ethical standards generally supported by the American Bar Association, the nation's largest professional and legal organization, and by the Colorado Code of Professional Responsibility.

The prosecutor's primary role in any criminal law case is to seek justice, not to convict. The prosecutor must disclose in timely fashion to the criminal defense team all evidence and information that tends to negate the guilt of the accused or to mitigate the degree of the defense. Lack of such disclosure is grounds for reversal of a conviction.

In the Oklahoma City bombing case, Timothy McVeigh's lawyers have received thousands of pages of FBI investigative files in the pretrial discovery stages.

A prosecutor may discuss publicly the basic facts leading to an indictment or criminal complaint. Beyond that, no member of the prosecution's team—lawyers, investigators, police, employees and others assisting in the preparation and presentation of the government's case—may make out-of-court statements that have a "substantial likelihood of heightening public condemnation of the accused."

The government attorneys and their staffs in the Oklahoma City trial have not, as of this writing, been under scrutiny for withholding evidence or criticized for purposely "poisoning the well" of public opinion before trial. This clearly has not been a problem because of all the disclosure from investigative journalism efforts of the media and because of the far-reaching public statements of the defendant's legal team.

What the legal defense team usually can say about a pending criminal case is limited to the "dry facts" concerning the charge, who is involved, what is on the public record, what the procedures for court will be.

This rule applies to the entire defense team, not just to the lawyers who are responsible for the team of associate attorneys, investigators, jury consultants, and arguably, for lay and expert witnesses who will provide evidence on behalf of the defendant.

One exception permits the defense lawyer to make a public statement when a "reasonable attorney would believe [he/she] is required to protect a client from the substantial undue prejudicial effect of recent publicity not initiated by the lawyer or the lawyer's client."

In applying this exception to the rule, called "the right of the reply," to the McVeigh case, how the purported confession was obtained becomes an important question.

When the case was moved to Denver from Oklahoma City, U.S. District Judge Richard Matsch issued a "gag order" for both the prosecution and defense. The teams were instructed not to discuss with the media the merits and the intricacies of evidence and legal theories in the case.

As soon as The Dallas Morning News article appeared on the World Wide Web, the lawyers on both sides went into conference with Judge Matsch.

Within hours, the defense team came back with a public attack on the newspaper. The lead defense attorney charged The Morning News with a crime of theft, and both the defense attorney and the defense investigator made what appeared to be contradictory public statements about what was done and not done pertaining to the development of the confession.

At this point, the usual rules of legal ethics and trial publicity

From Paul J. Buser, "Legal Ethics Issues" in *Quill,* April 1997. Reprinted by permission of Paul J. Buser, Board Member and Legal Counsel, Cleveland, OH. Professional Chapter of the Society of Professional Journalists.

created by a participant, in this case the defense team, were on the edge of professional responsibility in advocacy of a client's case.

The prosecution, on the other hand, at the time of this writing, needs no "right of reply" exception. It is sitting back, watching the defense team squirm. The prosecution will be at risk in this particular public debate involving legal ethics only if the defense team diverts attention from itself to charge that the prosecution team was responsible for the leak to The Morning News.

For every first-year law student studying "professional responsibility," there are basic foundations, building blocks that an attorney must understand and practice for successful client representation. These same standards are the guideposts for lawyers in the real world.

The primary guidepost is that an attorney must zealously advocate a client's cause within the bounds of the law.

Should the defendant's lead defense attorney—in a ploy to bring forward "people representing the most extreme wing of political thought" who the defense team believes were responsible for the crime—be able to rely on this standard for fabricating the false confession?

Within a week after The Morning News story, the attorney was widely quoted as saying, "We were not investigating a white-collar crime here. We used every means available to us. I offer no apology for that."

Legal ethicists scoff at this "anything goes" attitude, which is the banner cry of criminal defense lawyers in the higher-profile cases. Before the McVeigh case, planting of false information was used by the defense team in the O. J. Simpson murder trial to find out what member of the defense team was leaking defense background information to the media.

A broad-based "anything goes" philosophy for the defense flies in the face of several composite legal ethical standards.

The first is that a lawyer must avoid even the appearance of impropriety.

McVeigh's lead lawyer has said the false confession was the brainchild of one of his own defense team, that it was stolen by a reputable and well-known daily newspaper, that the legal ruse was "no more of a deception than the tactics law enforcement officers and investigators use every day to solve crimes."

Maybe so, but the lawyer here surely has not escaped the appearance of impropriety.

The second standard is that a lawyer must undertake representation of the client with the utmost trust, allegiance and fiduciary duty toward the client.

This standard means protecting the secrets and property of the client, including the information developed from the special confidential relationship known as attorney-client privilege. Only the client, not the attorney, can waive or consent to releasing information that comes under the umbrellas of this privilege.

In the McVeigh case, whether the purported confession was intentionally or negligently released to the media by a member of the defense team does not matter from the legal ethicist's point of view. The damage is still done to the defendant.

Fiduciary means of the trustee type the parlance of the law of professional responsibility, it has been considered of highest order. From what appears in the media reports regarding the conflicting responses of the defense team, the public is left to wonder who is in charge and what is the real truth about the confession, its purpose and method of release.

A third standard is that a lawyer should do nothing to adversely affect [his/her] independent, competent, professional judgment on behalf of a client.

Included in this standard is a subset ethical guideline that no lawyer shall become a trial witness to the client's cause. The purpose is to prevent the client's defense from being undermined at trial.

When the jury hears a lawyer testify, is the lawyer advocating the client's case, with an expected slant of facts for the benefit of the defendant's position, or is the lawyer just presenting the facts? The roles of witness and advocate are confused; they merge and tend to overlap. The lawyer must avoid a dual role as trial counsel and trial witness.

Still, this question remains: Was the confession a hoax or not? Will this be answered at trial? Will the lawyer be called by the judge, the prosecutor or by himself to present evidence to the jury about the confession document? If by himself, is the lead defense lawyer or his chief investigator who was said by the attorney to have developed the hoax strategy, going to be a credible witness when questioned by another member of the defense team?

Both the American Bar Association Code of Professional Conduct and the more resent ABA Model Rules emphasize that a lawyer is trained to be a partisan advocate. If the lawyer takes the stand as a witness, then the lawyer's own credibility is at stake. This obviously lessens the credibility of the client's case if the lawyer is not believed by the jury.

Another concern with a dual role of attorney and witness is that the attorney may be a fantastic trial attorney, a "golden throat" the jury loves to hear orate, a latter-day Clarence Darrow. That quality of advocacy may make the lawyer even more believable as a witness.

When a defense lawyer takes the stand, the prosecution in cross-examination of the lawyer—in the McVeigh case, this might be on the truth or falsity of the confession document—may "ease up" on the questioning so as not to offend the jury by "hurting" a witness the jury likes or for whom it may have developed an empathy. The consequence is that the truth may not be known, and the prosecutor's role of finding justice, mentioned first in this commentary, never will be achieved.

With this immense ethical and judicial dilemma in the McVeigh case, the lead defense team attorney or lead investigator or both clearly are potential witnesses. But will the public be denied an explanation of this ethical dilemma because of the judge's gag order?

The ABA is a voluntary organization. Its rules do not apply unless the state where the lawyer practices has adopted one of these rules. One state, such as Colorado, which has adopted many of the ABA principles, may be more restrictive than another.

Both the ABA and the Colorado Code of Professional Responsibility for lawyers, applicable to the McVeigh trial, limit an attorney's conduct as trial lawyer and witness.

The Colorado Code says when an attorney learns that he/she or a firm member may be required to give testimony prejudicial to the client, the attorney must cease representing the client because the attorney's ability to champion the client's cause becomes substantially impaired.

In 1987 and 1994 Colorado federal court cases, it was held that an attorney has a mandatory duty to withdraw if (a) independent professional judgment indicates that lawyer's testimony is "relevant, material, and unobtainable elsewhere."

With this ethical provision looming over the trial, should any lawyer for the defendant be permitted to testify about the alleged false confession? Should the prosecution bring this issue before the jury? Is the jury, the finder of fact, entitled to hear evidence that was published on the Web?

All of these questions must be preceded by other questions concerning the law of evidence, not the law of professional ethics of lawyers.

Judge Matsch is in a difficult position. Though he may not be happy with the defense team's tactics, if the confession truly is false, he also may be concerned about how to keep the confession (if proven outside the jury to be false) from the jury as part of the prosecution's case. With a publication on the Web and throughout the print and other electronic media, this well could be impossible, even with a jury pool of hundreds.

If the confession is proven false before the trial begins, Judge Matsch may have to instruct the jury, at the beginning of the case, to disregard any publication of it. The result then may be that the defense need not be called as a witness by anyone.

But is that a good enough remedy for the defendant? Should his defense team still be allowed, from a professional ethics standpoint, to continue the defendant's representation? If the defense team's ethics are at issue, and the jury knows it, can the defendant, regardless of the actual trial competence of his attorneys, get a fair trial?

The answer goes back to the lawyer's fiduciary duty to the client. The scope of the ABA ethics code and similar state codes accentuate the never-ending theme not to do harm to one's own client.

If his defense team is even potentially prejudicial to McVeigh receiving a fair trial, by the ABA way of thinking, the defense lawyer should withdraw. The "anything goes" defense approach would keep the trial attorney in the middle, including continued use of the media for the defense team's purposes until the judge again tightens the gag order.

Both the ABA Code and the ABA Model Rules of professional legal conduct say a lawyer is subject to discipline for offering evidence that the lawyer knows is false. But these rules are meant to apply to judicial proceedings. The Dallas Morning News is not a judicial forum. It is one of the public's many forums of fact and opinion.

The published confession may never end up as evidence in Denver. That does not mean the existence of this out-of-court evidence is not "prejudicial to the administration of justice" or that the defense team's conduct in creating the false confession—if it is false—does not show "dishonesty or untrustworthiness" on the part of the defense.

There is a sub rosa trial going on in the McVeigh situation. It will affect the case's outcome.

Article Review Form at end of book.

Case 2: Timothy McVeigh and *The Dallas Morning News* continued

Until We Know, Let Us Challenge

Questions of journalism, ethics

Bob Steele

Bob Steele is director of the ethics program at The Poynter Institute in St. Petersburg, Florida. He is co-author of Doing Ethics In Journalism: A Handbook with Case Studies, published for SPJ.

The publication in The Dallas Morning News of the purported confession of Timothy McVeigh offers a classic case in journalism ethics. Just as importantly, it offers a significant case study in the process of ethical decision-making.

At its core, this case is about competing principles and conflicting values. It is about tension between the First and Sixth Amendments. It is about duty and responsibility, about consequences and alternatives. It is about fairness to the accused, concern for the families of victims and respect for the judicial process. It is also a case about public service, journalistic independence and competitive instincts.

Clearly there are legal issues, but why, when, and how to publish are essentially ethical decisions. While ethics is about right and wrong, it is prudent to resist the temptation to cast a thumbs up or thumbs down on The News actions. Ethical decision-making is more complex than that.

Additionally, we are missing pieces of the puzzle necessary to evaluate the newspaper's decisions. We have not seen the documents The Morning News used as the basis for its story. Nor were we in the newsroom to observe and to hear the deliberations on the decision to publish.

Dallas Morning News Editor Ralph Langer said the paper had an obligation to publish the story about McVeigh's alleged confession because "the information in that part of the material was of national importance and . . . we were obligated to publish it."

Since the public did not have the same access to the documents as The Morning News, Langer is asking us to make a considerable leap of faith in accepting the reasons. It is appropriate, therefore, to be more detailed in explaining how it reached its decision. We want to know why the paper decided to publish that story on that weekend. And, it's very important to understand to what degree they considered the interest of the victims and the victims' families.

Until the time when we know more, it is best to hold The Morning News accountable by challenging rather than cheering or condemning. That accountability might be structured around some key questions related to various journalistic and ethical elements of this case—questions that newsroom decision makers should ask. Obviously the progression of questions depends on the answers to previous questions.

Newsgathering Issues

- Why did we get the documents?
- Is this information we want to have?
- Where and how did we get the documents?
- Did we steal them?
- Did someone else steal them?
- If so, did they do so at our urging With our knowledge?
- Is there a risk to others in our having these documents?
- Was there another way to obtain the same documents in a less intrusive manner That creates less legal liability for others and ourselves? That does not violate other ethical principle?
- Can we properly secure the documents once we have them to protect our source and guard sensitive information?

From Bob Steele, "Until We Know, Let Us Challenge" in *Quill*, April 1997.

- If we don't want to use the documents what do we do with them?

Source Issues

If the documents came from a source

- Who is our source?
- What is our contractual understanding with the source?
- How many of us know the identity of the source so we can ensure independent judgment?
- Do we have a high level of confidence in this source and what the source is telling us?
- Are we prepared to protect our source if we are ordered in court to reveal the source's identity?
- What are the source's motives for giving us the documents?
- Even if those motives are questionable, does the importance of the documents necessitate publishing them?

Authenticity of Documents

- Do we believe these documents are authentic?
- Do we believe the information in the documents to be factually accurate?
- Are the documents what we think they are? Do we know the context surrounding their creation and their use?
- How can we verify our beliefs?

Fairness Issues

- How can we fairly treat the stakeholders in this case?
- Are we being fair to Timothy McVeigh? What if the "confession" turns out to be erroneous or a hoax? What if McVeigh is acquitted?
- Are we being considerate of the rights of the victims' families who are eager for the trial to proceed properly?
- Have we given reasonable opportunity for response to those most affected by what we plan to publish?
- At what point do we need to ask questions directly of McVeigh and his attorney? Of the prosecutors?
- Are we being fair to potential jurors?

Consequences Issues

If we publish the supposed confession and other information from the documents:

- What impact might it have on the judicial process?
- How might it affect the selection of a jury?
- How might it affect McVeigh's Sixth Amendment rights?
- How might it affect the government's ability to prosecute the case on behalf of the public?
- What benefit will there be to the public to know about the documents and McVeigh's admission that he did the bombing?
- What impact might our publishing have on our newspaper? On our credibility? On our ability to continue to report on this story?
- What is the impact on McVeigh if he is found not guilty in the trial?

If we don't publish the supposed confession:

- Will the public be disserved by the absence of that information?
- Will we fail to fulfill our journalistic duty? Would that jeopardize our credibility?

Independence Issues

- Why are we doing what we plan to do?
- To whom do we owe ultimate loyalty in this case?
- Are we overly influenced by our own self-interest? By economic considerations? Competitive pressures? By deadlines?
- Are we being manipulated by our sources? By powerful people? By special interests?
- Are we being overly cautious in fear of legal action against us?

Publishing Issues

- Why would the public need to know the information contained in these documents? Is there an issue of national or personal security? Is there an issue of system failure? Is there essential information that the public must know to understand the legal process? Is there essential information of great value to the families of the victims of the bombing?
- Is there a real need to know or a legitimate right to know? Does it go beyond a mere want to know?
- If we publish a story, *what* does the public need to know?
- *When* does the public need to know the information?

- Can we delay publishing to minimize the negative consequences? What is the downside of that delay?
- Do other news organizations have these same documents or might they get them? How might that affect our decisions?
- Are we giving appropriate weight to any competition factors that are part of this equation?
- Is it possible that parties involved in the trial might release the documents themselves?
- Is it possible that parties involved in the trial might attempt to prevent our publishing the documents?
- What is the benefit of first publishing this story on our Internet site? What is the downside?

Process Issues

- Have we devoted enough time

"While ethics is about right and wrong, it is prudent to resist the temptation to cast a thumbs up or thumbs down on The News actions. Ethical decision-making is more complex than that."

and attention to the decision-making?
- Have we included the right people in the process?
- Have we sought contrarian positions to challenge our notions and prevent group think?
- Have we sought outside advice to pose different types of questions, challenge any tunnel vision and offer particular expertise regarding both ethical decision-making and the specific issues of this case?
- Have we resisted the tendency to see this decision as an "either/or" dilemma?
- Have we explored a range of alternative courses of action?

Accountability Issues

- What must we do to publicly explain our decision and justify our actions?
- What should we reveal about how we obtained the documents?
- How much information can we reveal regarding sources for the documents without compromising that relationship?
- How much information should we reveal about additional content of the documents?
- How much information should we reveal about our decision-making process?
- How can we be as forthcoming as possible in the same way we would expect of other organizations if we were questioning their decisions and actions?

This case has high stakes on many levels for all of the affected parties. The editors of The Dallas Morning News still need to tell us more about their decision-making process. That public accountability will help all of us judge whether the newspaper responsibly fulfilled its journalistic obligation.

Article Review Form at end of book.

WiseGuide Wrap-Up

Computers in the newsroom have altered the work of investigative reporters. No longer are investigative reporters limited by time and energy to manually recording and reviewing records. Computers make it possible to conduct sophisticated analyses of records in much shorter time periods. Reporters also can draw conclusions from the data and not rely on official interpretations. Additionally, given the advantages of online searching, news stories can be written with more detailed information drawn from wider-ranging sources. Such capabilities can impact the content of stories by creating additional context. But there are dangers in relying on computers too much. Computers cannot think. They perform functions as directed. The existence of incomplete or inaccurate data only clouds the results and can lead to misinformed conclusions. Computers are only a tool in the arsenal of a good reporter.

Teddy Roosevelt probably wouldn't like the modern breed of investigative reporter any more than he liked the journalists of his day. But the job of a good reporter is not to please those in power, but to serve those who have no power. This creed works for print, broadcast and online reporting.

R.E.A.L. Sites

The adjacent list provides a print preview of typical CourseWise R.E.A.L. Sites. (There are over 100 such sites at the CourseLink™ Site.) The danger in printing URLs is that Web sites can change overnight. As we went to press, these sites were functional using the URL provided. If you come across one that isn't, please let us know via email at webmaster@coursewise.com. Use your Passport to access the most current list of R.E.A.L. sites at the CourseLinks™ Site.

Site name: San Jose Mercury News
URL: http://www.sjmercury.com
Why is it R.E.A.L.? You've read the articles about the controversy, now take a look at the paper. See what the Mercury News is cooking up today. This site provides a look at the paper behind the controversy.
Key topics: current issues

Site name: Dallas Morning News
URL: http://www.dallasnews.com
Why is it R.E.A.L.? You've read about the Dallas Morning News' Web site scoop. Take a look at what is posted today. A look at the online newspaper behind the controversy.
Key topics: current issues

Site name: Poynter Center for Media Studies
URL: http:www.poynter.org
Why is it R.E.A.L.? Poynter is the premier training ground for journalists. This site offers articles, research and conference summaries on issues affecting journalists. Maybe you'll find a seminar just for you.
Key topics: computer-assisted reporting, current issues, ethics, journalism administration, legal issues, media writing, online journalism, online newspapers, research, reporting, story strategies, skills, webcasting

Site name: Freedom Forum
URL: www.freedomforum.org
Why is it R.E.A.L.? This nonpartisan international foundation offers articles on current media issues, a look at the Newsmuseum outside Washington, D.C., and a taste of the professional world.
Key topics: current issues, ethics, legal issues, media writing, online journalism, online newspapers, research, reporting, webcasting

Site name: Foundation for American Communications
URL: http://www.fasnet.org/
Why is it R.E.A.L.? Aimed at journalists and scholars, the site offers a look at the top issues of the day, the AP digest, Internet resources, reporting tools and online sources.
Key topics: current issues, ethics, legal issues, media writing, online journalism, online newspapers, research, reporting, webcasting

Index

A

ABC News, online offerings described, 27-28
Abrams, Bill, on ABC online news, 27, 28
Access, to government records, 82-87
Access Atlanta, features of, 91
Adams, Henry, 3
AdOne Classified Network, 40
Advertising, online, 18, 38
    approaches to, 91
    audience for, 52-53
    classifieds, 39-40
    lack of separation from news, 16
    response rates, 53
    revenues, 38, 40, 53-54
    user tolerance for, 50
African-Americans, response to "Dark Alliance" story, 167-68, 173, 174
Age, as factor in Internet usage, 45
Agnew, Beth, on writing, 33
Allen, Robert, 29
Alley, Wayne E., decision on University of Oklahoma case, 148
Alliance for Education, and *Dayton Daily News* project, 132
AllPolitics, 15
Amazon.com, success of, 51
Ambrose, Stephen, 3
American Bar Association, ethical guidelines for lawyers, 194-95
American Civil Liberties Union, 145
American Cybercast, 49
American Society of Composers, Authors & Publishers, and music copyright, 150
American Society of Journalists and Authors, and freelance rights, 157
America Online
    advertising on, 50
    online databases of, 80
    software conflict with CNN news service, 25
America's Choice Mall, 51
Anderson, Kurt, on quality of Web pages, 37
Andreesson, Marc, 5, 8
Arizona Daily Star
    approach to online journalism, 91
    online offerings of, 33-34
Armao, Rosemary, on computer-assisted reporting, 67
Art, online copyright for, 150-51, 155
Artist, and writing, 33
Asians, use of Internet by, 44, 47
Assessment data, and public records policies, 83
Associated Press (AP)
    birth of, 33
    coverage of Contra drug smuggling, 172
    training in computer-assisted reporting, 67, 68
AT&T split, online coverage of, 29
The Atlantic Monthly, online offerings of, 13
Atlantic Unbound, 13
Attorney-client privilege, and McVeigh bombing case, 194
Attorneys, duties in criminal cases, 193-95
Audience
    expectations of, 58
    influence on online news, 160
    interacting with, 126, 131-32
    for online vs. traditional content, 53-54
    profile on *Chicago Tribune* online, 115
Audience response
    and Nando online news service, 106-7
    as part of online journalism, 101, 131-32
Authors Guild, and freelance rights, 157
Authors Registry, and freelance rights, 158
Auto-by-Tel, 39

B

Baker, Brent, on online journalism, 119-20
Baker, Tom, on Wall Street Journal Interactive Edition, 90
Baltimore Sun, use of custom databases, 77
Banners, as online advertising form, 53
Barger, Brian, coverage of Contra drug smuggling, 172
Barlett, Donald, and investigative reporting, 181
Barry, Marion, 191
Bartel, Marsha, on limitations of databases, 81
Bartley, Brad, 20, 21, 23
Bass, Bill
    on expectations for Internet, 49-50
    on online classifieds, 40
Bayers, Chip, on HotWired, 135
Bender, Walter, on future online news, 60-61
Bergen, Annie, and Bloomberg services, 137
Bermudez, Enrique, in "Dark Alliance" story, 175
Berners-Lee, Tim, 5-9
Biggs, Brooke S., on need for gatekeepers, 37
Blacks, use of Internet by, 44, 47
Black Sun Interactive, 50
Blake, Mary Kay, on new journalism job skills, 98
Blandon Reyes, Oscar Danilo
    investigation of, 181-82
    subject of "Dark Alliance" story, 174-76, 177, 178
Blatt, Les, on broadcast news online, 26
Bloomberg, Michael, 136-39
Blum, Jack, on "Dark Alliance" story allegations, 178
Bogdanich, Walter, tobacco company investigation, 181
Bond system story, use of computer-assisted reporting, 109
Boren, David, on University of Oklahoma case, 148
Borowski, Neill A., on computer-assisted reporting, 65, 74
boston.com, 12, 88-89
Boston Globe,
    approach to online publishing, 88-89
    and freelance rights, 157
    size of online audience, 90
Boundaries, for online journalism, 160-61
Branch, Brenda, on librarians as online censors, 148
Brew, Tom, on move to online journalism, 124
Brisco, Robert, on online competition for newspapers, 40
Broadcast Music, Inc., and music copyright, 150
Broadcast news, online versions, 25-29
Broadhurst, Michael, online news responsibilities, 123
Brown, Jim, on data specialists, 108
Brown, Merrill, on MSNBC, 125-26
Budde, Neil
    on electronic media, 36
    on online service profitability, 50
    on Wall Street Journal Interactive Edition, 90
Budget analysis program, for computer-assisted reporting, 73
Buel, Stephen, and "Dark Alliance" story, 170
Buffalo News, use of custom databases, 77
Bulletin boards. *See* Electronic bulletin boards
Buser, Paul J., 187, 193
Bush, Vannevar, proposal of hypertext, 6
Business news, online coverage of, 12, 136-39
Business Week Online, 12
Bylines, crediting data person in, 70
Bylines (online story-marketing service), 99
BZ/Rights and Permissions, 151

Entries in boldface type indicate Reading's authors and pages on which their pieces appear.

C

Cafe Los Negroes, 44, 47
Cailliau, Robert, on shortcomings of World Wide Web, 7-8
Calero, Adolfo, in "Dark Alliance" story, 175
California demographics story, use of computer-assisted reporting, 109
Cancel, Luis, 47, 48
CareerPath, 40
Careers in online journalism, 95-96, 97-102, 118-23
Carey, Pete, review of "Dark Alliance" story, 167, 176
CARnet, at *The Raleigh News & Observer*, 105
Cartoons, online publication of, 98, 151
Caruso, Denise, 17
Cause and effect, identifying with computers, 110
Cauthorn, Bob
   on newspaper profits, 40
   on online journalism, 91
CBS SportsLine, 13
CD-Now, 51
Cekay, Thomas, on online journalism, 113
Census data, in digital form, 109
Central Intelligence Agency, and "Dark Alliance" story, 166, 167, 168, 170, 174, 175-76
Ceppos, Jerry, and "Dark Alliance" story, 166, 167, 169, 170, 171, 179
CERN, 6, 7
Channel A, 47
Chesnais, Pascal, 20, 21
Chicago Bulls, online reporting about, 115
ChicagoLand TV, 116
Chicago Tribune, online version, 12, 112-17
China, online coverage of floods, 22
Ciotta, Rose, 65
City guides
   Access Atlanta, 91
   Microsoft Sidewalk project, 42-43
   as part of online journalism, 116
Civil War, use of telegraph in, 3, 4
Clarke, Roger, on electronic payment systems, 145-46
Classified advertising, online competition for, 39-40
Click-through rates, for online advertising, 53
Clip media, and copyright issues, 150, 152-53
CNET: The Computer Network, 13
CNNfn, online offerings of, 12
CNN Interactive, 11, 25, 26-27
Colorado Code of Professional Responsibility, 195
Column, in spreadsheet, 74
Comic book characters, permission to use, 151
Commercial database services, 80, 110
Commercialism, on the Internet, 50-51
Communication, computer-mediated, 30-34
Communications Decency Act, 52, 144-46, 147-49
Communication Technology Update, 63
Community-assisted reporting, and online journalism, 131
Community journalism, online journalism as, 102
Competition, effect on decision to publish, 197
CompuServe
   financial losses of, 49
   journalism forum, 63
   online databases of, 80
Computer-assisted reporting (CAR)
   building databases for, 76-78
   challenges to acceptance, 69
   defined, 74
   everyday use of, 71-75, 103-7
   examples of, 65-70, 76, 108-11
   limitations of, 79-81
   software examples, 73
   use at *Dayton Daily News*, 129-33
Computer-mediated communication, 30-34
Computers
   changes to traditional journalism, 33, 129-33
   online ratings of, 12, 13
   public-access terminals, 85
   and public record keeping, 83
   use in reporting, 65-70, 110-11. See also Computer-assisted reporting
   use in research, 32, 58. See also Technology
Computer skills, journalists' need for, 98
Confidential sources, and pretrial publicity issues, 188
Connally, John, 191
Conspiracy, and pretrial publicity, 189
Consumers, as information gatekeepers, 36-37. See also Audience
Contras, and drug trafficking, 167, 182. See also "Dark Alliance" story
Control, issues in online journalism, 160
Copyright
   enforcing online, 154-55
   for repurposed print material, 156-58
   securing permissions, 150-53
Corel, 153
Corn, David, on "Dark Alliance" story, 176
Cox, Alan, use of computer-assisted reporting by, 71, 73
Cox Interactive Media
   approach to online journalism, 91
   online offerings of, 35, 39
Cox Newspapers, and computer-assisted reporting, 68
Credibility, in online journalism, 16
Crime stories, interest in, 45
Criminal cases, prosecutor's duties, 193
Crooke, Robert, on high-speed telephone lines, 139
Curran, Tom, on computer-assisted reporting, 66
Customized news services
   advantages and disadvantages, 20-23
   development of, 20-21
   features of, 21-22
   listed, 24
Cybertimes, 11, 119

D

The Dallas Morning News,
   editor's defense of McVeigh confession story, 185-86
   ethics of McVeigh story, 196-98
   and McVeigh pretrial publicity, 187, 191
   World Wide Web publication of McVeigh story, 90
Dangling links, and hypertext, 6-7
Daniels, Franklin III, on benefits of digital information, 104, 107
Danko, Pete, move to online journalism, 134
"Dark Alliance" story, 11
   and investigative reporting, 180-84
   publication of, 166-71
   reaction of other journalists, 183-84
   responses to, 172-79
   World Wide Web publication, 120, 169, 173
Data
   encryption of, 146
   sources of, 67, 110
Database editors, at *The Raleigh News & Observer*, 104
Database management software, 110
Databases
   commercial online, 80, 110
   and computer-assisted reporting, 71, 73, 74
   creating, 76-78
   defined, 74
   limitations of, 79-81
   at *The Raleigh News & Observer*, 104
   use in computer-assisted reporting, 130-31
Data sharing, of government information, 86
Dateline, feature on dangerous roads, 10
Davis, Allison, and broadcast news online, 25, 27
Davis, Jefferson, 4
Davis, Lynn, on limitations of databases, 80, 81
Davis, Mickey, on public journalism, 131
DeBrosse, Jim, and *Dayton Daily News* education project, 132
Decency, enforcing online, 144-46, 147-49
Dedman, Bill, on computer-assisted reporting, 68
Defamation, and pretrial publicity, 189
Dell Computer, online marketing of, 51
Demac, Donna, 156
Democratic convention, online coverage of, 113
Demographic data, online collection of, 50
Deutch, John, and "Dark Alliance" story, 167, 174
DeVigal, Andrew, on online journalism, 115
Dial-in computer access, to government records, 85
Dialog (database service), 80
Diamond, Edwin, on ease of use, 45
Digital Cities, 12, 116
Digital Ink, 98-99
Digital Stock Inc., 152-53
Digital telephone lines, 139
Digital World conference, 63
Disintermediation, the Internet and, 36
DO CENSUS, 71, 72-73
Documents, authenticity of, 197
Doig, Stephen K., 70
Dow Jones, news service of, 80, 90, 139

Drug smuggling, and "Dark Alliance" story, 166-71, 172-79
Duffy, Brian, on computer-assisted reporting, 67

E

E-beat, required skills for, 58-59
Edelman, Vladimir, on online journalism, 118-19, 120
Editor & Publisher, Web award, 89
Editors, role in electronic age, 21, 23, 36-37
Effron, Seth, on hiring for online news, 119
Eldridge, Emily, work with MSN, 126
Electronic bulletin boards
  journalistic limitations of, 15
  as online databases, 80
  and online news, 28
Electronic database libraries
  building, 77-78
  commercial database services, 80
  limitations of, 79-81
  at *The Raleigh News & Observer*, 104
  use in computer-assisted reporting, 76-78
Electronic mail
  importance of, 61
  journalistic limitations of, 15
  popularity of, 31
Electronic payment systems, 144, 145-46
Electronic rights, ownership of, 156-58
Electronic Yellow Pages, proposed, 91
Encoding, influence of telegraph on, 4
Encryption, and government access to data, 146
Enquire, as forerunner of World Wide Web, 6, 7
Entertainment and recreation guides, online, 38
Equipment, for online news reporters, 116
Erickson, John, on computer-assisted reporting, 130
Espionage, influence of telegraph on, 4
ESPN SportsZone, 50
  extent of audience for, 53-54
  offerings of, 13
Estes, Ben, on multimedia reporting, 106
Ethics
  and online journalism, 160-61
  of pretrial publicity, 196-98
Ewing, Jack, use of computer-assisted reporting, 109
Excite, 39
Expert journalism, 181
Extras, and online journalism, 36

F

False-light suits, and pretrial publicity, 189
Fax, and computer-assisted reporting, 74
Fear, as motive for online journalism, 17-19
Fidler, Roger, on future of journalism, 62-64
Field, Emily, and online writing, 119
Field, in database, 74
Film, permission to use, 151
Filtering software, 148
Filters, news organizations as, 21, 23, 36-37, 61
Financial news, Bloomberg services, 136-39

Fisher, Dan, move to online journalism, 127
FishWrap, 20-23
Fixmer, Rob, on online writing, 119
Flinn, Kathleen, on print vs. computer jargon, 127
Focus groups, use in newsgathering, 131
Forbes, Steve, 10
FoxPro, 110
Frammolino, Ralph, use of computer-assisted reporting, 72
Frankel, Max, on future of newspapers, 32
Franklin, Jon
  developing World Wide Web service, 97
  move to online journalism, 99
  on new journalism job skills, 100
Freedom Forum Media Studies Center, 63
Freelancers, and electronic rights, 156-58
Fresno Bee, use of custom databases, 77
Frischling, Bill, online news responsibilities, 120-21
Fulton, Katherine, 60

G

Gag order, in McVeigh bombing case, 187, 193
Garcia, Dawn, role in "Dark Alliance" story, 168, 178
Gatekeepers, news professionals as, 21, 23, 36-37
Gegax, T. Trent, online news responsibilities, 122
Gentry, Leah, on online journalism, 23, 113
Geographical information systems, 110-11
Gersh, Ruth, on new media job skills, 97-98
Gilder, George, on newspapers and computers, 33
Glover, Dick, on online service profitability, 50
Goff, Russ, on access to public records, 84
Golden, Tim, review of "Dark Alliance" story, 177
Goodman, David, on freelance rights, 158
Gordon, Mike, on print vs. computer jargon, 128
Gossiaux, Tim, and e-mail censorship, 149
Government, regulation of online services by, 52-53
Government records, access vs. privacy issues, 82-87
Government stories, audience interest in, 46
Graham, Tim, on "Dark Alliance" reporter Gary Webb, 168
Grand Forks Herald, online offerings of, 132
Graphical user interfaces, for World Wide Web, 7
Greaves, McClean, on minority use of Internet, 44, 47, 48
Green, Lisa, on computer-assisted reporting, 70
Grouping, with database program, 110
Grover, Joel, on computer-assisted reporting, 67
Groves, Miles E., on online classifieds, 40
Grumman, Cornelia, 112, 113
  on online reporting equipment, 116
  on writing online news, 114
Guilbault, David, on print vs. computer jargon, 128

Gunther, Marc, 25
Gutfreund, John, 136
Gwertzman, Bernard
  on New York Times on the Web, 89
  on online audience, 52

H

Hamilton, Andrea, move to online journalism, 127
Hanchette, John, on limitations of databases, 79-80
Harbut, Marcy, online news responsibilities, 121-22
Hardin, Arzie, 44
Harmon, Amy, 144
Harper, Christopher, 20, 44, 112, 147
Heaven's Gate suicides, 11
Helms, Jesse, 104
Henderson, Stephen, on online reporting, 113, 114
Hendricks, Christian, on online journalism, 91
Henzey, Debra, on open access to public records, 87
Hickey, Claire, 137-38
Higgins, Pete, on newspapers and Internet, 40
Himowitz, Mike, on using custom databases, 78
Hinckle, Pia, 166
Hispanics, use of Internet by, 44, 47
Hits, online audience measurement by, 52
Hockenberry, John, and live chat controversy, 28
Hodel, Georg, role in "Dark Alliance" story, 170, 171
Holbrook, Bill, online cartoon publishing, 98
Hooker, Michael, on future of newspapers, 31
Horton, Sherry L., 82
HotWired, 13, 134, 135
Houston, Brant, on computer-assisted reporting, 66, 67, 72, 109
The Houston Chronicle
  approach to online journalism, 91-92
  online classified advertising, 39
Hull, Mark, online news responsibilities, 120
Hume, Ellen, on online news, 28
Hypermedia, 7, 63
Hypertext
  application to journalism, 62-64
  Berners-Lee application of, 6-7
  importance to online news, 33
Hypertext markup language (HTML), creation of, 7
Hypertext software, at *The Raleigh News & Observer*, 104
Hypertext transfer protocol (HTTP), creation of, 7

I

Ianzito, Christina, 118
Iknoian, Therese, on freelance rights, 156
Immediacy, of online news, 18
Income level, of Internet users, 44
Inflation rate, calculating on computer, 73

Index **203**

InfoDial, 51
InfoLatino, 47
Ingle, Bob, on online advertising, 53
Ingrassia, Paul, on Dow Jones information services, 139
Interactive Media Writers Association, 119
Interactivity
    as goal of online journalism, 126
    journalistic limitations of, 15
Internet
    access to databases via, 77
    advantages for news presentation, 114
    application of World Wide Web to, 7
    controlling distribution of information on, 145
    copyright enforcement on, 150-55
    and future of online journalism, 10-14, 30-31
    growth rate of, 58
    legislating content of, 144-46, 147-49
    marketing on, 51
    as medium for updating news, 36
    minority use of, 44-46
    online publishing approaches via, 88-92
    restricting access to, 147-49
    standards for content, 142
    as threat to traditional media, 35-40
    See also World Wide Web
Inverted pyramid, alternatives to, 132-33
Investigative journalism
    and "Dark Alliance" story, 166-71, 180-84
    exposure online, 164
Investigative Reporters & Editors, training at conferences, 63
Investigative reporting
    debate over techniques of, 180-84
    effect of "Dark Alliance" story on, 184
Ishgooda, use of e-mail for political protest, 148-49
Italiano, Laura, move from online to print, 119

J

Jargon, print vs. computer, 127
Jaspin, Elliot, and computer-assisted reporting, 68, 108, 111, 130
Jefferson, Thomas, 3
Jennings, Max, on changes in journalism, 129, 132, 133
Jewell, Richard, and Atlanta bombing, 189
Jobs, in online journalism, 118-23
John S. and James L. Knight Foundation, 131
Johnson, David, on regulation in cyberspace, 146
Johnson, J. T., on importance of research, 32
Jones, Stephen, on McVeigh pretrial publicity, 186, 192
Jordan, Robert, on freelance rights, 157
Journalism
    and the digital revolution, 60-64
    ethical questions, 196-98
    general influence of technology on, 129-33
    investigative (*see* Investigative journalism)
    new online careers in, 95-96, 97-102
    online (*see* Online journalism)
    roots of reporting in literature, 33
    See also Computer-assisted reporting (CAR); Newspapers; Writing
Juries, fairness of, 191

K

Kann, Peter, and Wall Street Journal Interactive Edition, 90
Kaplan, Sheila, move to online journalism, 127
Katz, Jesse, criticism of "Dark Alliance" story, 177
Katz, Jon
    on computer bulletin boards, 61
    on online newspapers, 31
Keller, Bruce, on debate over electronic rights, 157
Kerry, John, and Kerry Committee report, 173
Kerry Committee
    influence on "Dark Alliance" story, 182
    media coverage of report, 173
Kessler, Ron, attack on "Dark Alliance" story, 183
Kettering Foundation, 131
Key word searching, 80, 81
King, Maxwell, E. P., on computer-assisted reporting, 67
Kinsley, Michael, 13, 50, 122
Knight-Ridder, and computer-assisted reporting, 68
Koch, Tom, on influence of technology, 106
Kodak Picture Exchange, 152
Kohut, Andrew, on online news, 29
Koppel, Ted
    and "Dark Alliance" story, 176
    on personalizing news delivery, 29
Kornbluh, Peter, 172
Krim, Jonathan
    on computer-assisted reporting, 66
    and "Dark Alliance" story, 170
    recruitment of Gary Webb, 168
Krohn, Cyrus, online news responsibilities, 122
Kurtz, Howard, on "Dark Alliance" story, 174

L

Labriola, Don, 150
LaFleur, Jennifer, on computer-assisted reporting, 69, 76-77
Landau, George, 108
    on computer-assisted reporting, 69
    on database building, 77, 78
Langer, Ralph, and McVeigh confession story, **185,** 196
Lapham, Chris, 30
Law, applying to Internet, 144-46
Lawrance, Sharon, on Bloomberg services, 139
Layering, writing style for online news, 114
Legal ethics, and McVeigh bombing case, 193-95
Lehoullier, Norman, on Internet challenge to newspapers, 38
Leonard, Teresa, on news research department, 104, 105
Lessig, Lawrence, on online regulation, 146
Levin, Alan, on use of custom databases, 77, 78
Levinson, Nan, 156
Lexis/Nexis, 80
Liability, and pretrial publicity, 188
Libel, on Internet, 142
Librarians, censoring online materials, 148
Limbaugh, Rush, opposition to Communications Decency Act, 147
Lincoln, Abraham, 4
Links, dangling, 6-7
Listing Link, 40
Little, Darnell, and online journalism, 113-14
Loeb, Penny, and computer-assisted reporting, 67
Los Angeles earthquake, online news of, 28
The Los Angeles Times,
    attack on "Dark Alliance" story, 167, 177, 179, 180
    extent of online audience, 53
    online classified advertising, 39
    size of online audience, 90
Lucasville prison riot story, 133
Lux, John, on new journalism job skills, 98, 100

M

MacArthur, John R., on freelance rights, 158
Macedo, Ed, on MSNBC, 125
Macintosh, and computer-assisted reporting, 73
Magaziner, Ira, opposition to Communications Decency Act, 147
Magazines, online, 98
Maniscalco, Gina, on boston.com, 89
Mann, Fred, 159
Many-to-many communication model, 31
Mapping software, 74-75
Marketing, on the Internet, 51
Massachusetts Institute of Technology, Media Lab, 20
Mathews, David, and Kettering Foundation, 131
Matsch, Richard P., role in McVeigh trial, 186, 187, 193, 195
Mattera, Philip, on freelance rights, 157-58
McAdams, Melinda, 23
McCarty, Mary, on Ohio prison riot story, 133
McDonald, Lany, 104
McKenna, Chris, 16
McLeod, Ramon G., use of computer-assisted reporting, 109
McLuhan, Marshall, 31, 33, 35
McManus, Doyle
    attack on "Dark Alliance" story, 176, 177, 178, 179
    on Kerry Committee report, 173
McVeigh, Timothy
    attorneys' duties, 193-95
    bombing confession story, 185-86

pretrial publicity about, 185-98
Meeker, Mary, on online advertising, 52
Meeks, Brock, on online newspapers, 36, 88
Mendels, Pamela, 47
Meneses Cantarero, Juan Norvin
    investigation of, 181-82
    subject of "Dark Alliance" story, 172, 174-75, 176, 178
Menino, Thomas M., and library Internet access, 148
Mercury Center
    features of, 11-12
    publication of "Dark Alliance" story, 173
Mercury Mail, personal news features of, 22
Metastory, "Dark Alliance" story as, 172
Metropolitan news, audience interest in, 46
Meyer, Philip, on computer-assisted reporting, 70, 105, 106, 110
Microsoft
    cuts in online services, 49
    office environment at, 125
    online news venture, 124-28
    Sidewalk news project, 12, 42-43, 127
Microsoft Access, 72, 77
Microsoft SQL Server software, 77
Microsoft Visual FoxPro, 77
Microsoft Windows, 73
Microspeak, 127-28
MIDI license, and music copyright, 150
Miller, Judy, use of computer-assisted reporting, 109
Miller, Stephen C., on online journalism skills, 95
Milliron, David A., and computer-assisted reporting, 68
Millstein, Lincoln
    on boston.com, 89
    on TV influence on newspapers, 38
Minorities, use of Internet by, 44-46, 47-48
Missouri Institute for Computer-Assisted Reporting, 108, 111
Mitchell, Lisa, 174
Modems, 110
Moeller, Philip, 103
Money Machine, 105
Money magazine, Money Online, 10
Morales Meneses, Jairo, and "Dark Alliance" story followup, 178
Morris, Dwight L., on computer-assisted reporting, 70
Morse, Samuel, 3-4
Mosley, Jim, on computer-assisted reporting, 67
MSNBC
    approach to newsgathering, 124-28
    and *Dateline* feature on dangerous roads, 10
    jobs with, 118-19
    recruiting of print journalists by, 124
    story rating gimmick, 15
Muckrakers, 164
Multimedia
    in education, 61-62
    influence on new journalism skills, 99-100
    in Internet Tribune, 115
    at *The Raleigh News & Observer*, 104
    reporting requirements of, 106

Mulvaney, Jim, on reviewing investigative stories, 170
Music, permission to use, 150
Myhrvold, Nathan, on charging for access to Slate, 50

N

Nando, 106-7
Nando Land, 107
Nando.net, 99
The Nando Times, features of, 12, 91
Napolitano, Carol, on computer-assisted reporting, 69
National Institute for Advanced Reporting, 108, 111
National Institute for Computer-Assisted Reporting, 66, 67, 72
National news, online examples, 11
National Writers Union, and freelance rights, 157
NBC, online news venture with Microsoft, 27, 124
NBC Desktop Video, 26
Negroponte, Nicholas, 20
Nelson, Ted, and Xanadu concept, 7
The Netizen, in HotWired, 135
The Netly News, offerings of, 13
Netscape, World Wide Web site visits to, 54
The Newark Star-Ledger, and computer-assisted reporting, 66
New Century Network, 116
New Jersey Online, reporter's experience with, 121
Newman, Heather, use of computer-assisted reporting by, 74
New media, careers in, 95-96, 97-102
News
    audience interest by category, 45
    availability online, 10-14
    costs of producing, 18
    evolution of, in digital age, 60-64
    See also Journalism; Online journalism
Newshour with Jim Lehrer, and "Dark Alliance" story, 176
News libraries, at *The Raleigh News & Observer*, 105
Newspapers
    advantages of, 36, 37
    advertising revenues of, 38-39
    approaches to online publishing, 88-92
    evolution of, 30-34, 35-40
    growth of online offerings, 134-35
    online copyright issues, 154-55
    reasons for going online, 159
NEWSpot, 22
News Research Department, at *The Raleigh News & Observer*, 105
Newsrooms, reorganizing, 130
New York Online, 47
The New York Times
    accessing through Nexis, 80
    approach to online publishing, 88, 89-90
    coverage of digital issues, 63
    criticism of "Dark Alliance" story, 167, 177, 179, 180
    and debate over electronic rights, 157
    online version, 88, 89-90, 119

size of online readership, 90
Nightline, and "Dark Alliance" story, 176
NineTrack Express, 111
Nine-track tape, 75
Norfolk Virginian-Pilot, use of computer-assisted reporting by, 69
"North Carolina Discoveries," 106
North Carolina Public Records Act, 82-83
North Carolina Technological Information Study, 83-84
Novak, Tim, 108

O

Objectivity, in reporting, advent of, 33
Obscenity
    defining, 145
    regulating online, 144-46, 147-49
Oklahoma City bombing, suspect confession story, 185-86
Older, Susan, on new journalism job skills, 99, 100, 101
Olsen, Lise, on computer-assisted reporting, 70
O'Neale, L. J., in "Dark Alliance" story, 175
One-to-many communication model, 31
Ong, W., 30
Online access to copyrighted materials, 155
Online advertising, 53
Online commerce, effect on taxation, 144, 145-46
Online communities, vs. online news, 18
Online journalism
    accuracy in, 37
    advantages and disadvantages, 1, 15-16, 125
    audience profile, 44-46, 119
    audience response to, 101, 131-32
    broadcast news and, 25-29
    careers in, 95-96, 97-102, 118-23
    customized news services, 20-23
    described, 58
    differences from newspapers, 114-15
    ethics and, 160-61
    evolution of, 1, 14
    future of, 10-14, 40
    hypertext in, 62-64
    Microsoft's projected role, 42-43
    need for gatekeepers, 36-37
    revenues and expenditures, 17-19, 40
    staffing for, 112-17, 124-28
    technical problems with, 26
    and updating stories, 36
Online publishing, varied approaches to, 88-92
Online services
    commercial, 110
    revenues from, 157
Online shopping, 39-40, 51
Oracle software, 77
Overholser, Geneva, critique of press attacks on "Dark Alliance" story, 179

P

Page views, online audience measurement by, 52
Paid links, on World Wide Web, 18

Parry, Robert
 on Contra drug smuggling, 172, 173
 on "Dark Alliance" story, 176
Pathfinder
 described, 28
 features of, 135
 personal news service of, 22
Paul, Nora
 on computer-assisted reporting, 66
 on role of news libraries, 105
Pauley, Jane, show on MSNBC, 126
Pavlik, John V., 10
Pawlosky, Mark, move to online journalism, 126-27
Pellet, Charlie, and Bloomberg services, 138
Pena Cabrera, Renato, and "Dark Alliance" story followup, 178
Penchina, Robert, 154
Percentage change, calculating on computer, 73
Personal computers, utility of, 108-10
Personal News Page, 22
Personal news services, 20-23
Petersen, Laurie, on new journalism job skills, 100, 101
Petrovich, Jon, and broadcast news online, 26
Philadelphia Inquirer, training in computer-assisted reporting, 74
Phillips, Cheryl, use of computer-assisted reporting by, 68
PhotoBubble, 115
PhotoDisc, 153
Photographs, permission to use, 150-51, 155
Photojournalism, on the World Wide Web, 11
Pincus, Mark, on new vs. old media, 37
Pincus, Walter, criticism of "Dark Alliance" story, 176
Pisani, Francis, 61
Platform for Internet Content Selection, 6
PLUM, feature of FishWrap program, 22
Pogash, Carol, 134
PointCast, 22
Politics Now, 49
Polzin, Ken Jr., online coverage of JonBenet Ramsay murder, 16
Port, Bob, 68
Post, David
 on Internet's effect on government, 144
 on regulation in cyberspace, 146
Powell, Adam Clayton III, on minority use of the Internet, 45
Powers, Julie Ann, on multimedia reporting, 106
Poynter Institute for Media Studies, 63
PressLink, 152
Pretrial publicity
 attorneys' duties, 193-95
 effect on trials, 185-86, 191-92
 ethical questions, 196-98
 Sheppard and McVeigh trials, 187-90
Privacy
 and access to public records, 82-87
 and online communications, 146
Privitera, Deborah, and computer-assisted reporting, 71
Profits, of online services, 49-50

Programs, for computer-assisted reporting, 73, 104, 110-11
Project on Public Life and the Press, 131-32
Prosecutor, duties in criminal cases, 193
Public-access terminals, for government records, 85
Publication Rights Clearinghouse, and electronic rights for freelance works, 158
Public journalism, and computer-assisted reporting, 67
Public records, access vs. privacy issues, 82-87
Public vs. private figure, and McVeigh pretrial publicity, 189
Pull technology, in online news, 22
Push technology, 8, 12, 22

Q

Quittner, Josh, and The Netly News, 13

R

The Raleigh News & Observer
 approach to online journalism, 12, 91, 104, 106-7
 quality of research, 32-33
 use of electronic tools at, 70, 103-7
Ramsay, JonBenet, online coverage of murder, 16
Readers, online communication with, 101, 106-7
RealAudio
 for sound transmissions on World Wide Web, 89
 use by Internet Tribune, 115
R.E.A.L. sites
 American Journalism Review, 140
 Computer-Assisted Research, 93
 Dallas Morning News, 199
 Digital Direct Marketing, 141
 Driving a newspaper on the data highway, 57
 Editor and Publisher, 140
 Federal government information, 94, 141
 Foundation for American Communications, 200
 Freedom Forum, 199
 The Free Expression Clearinghouse, 162
 Investigative Reporters and Editors Inc., 93
 The Media in Cyberspace III, 56
 Meta-Index for Legal Research, 163
 National Institute for Computer-Assisted Reporting, 93
 National Writers Union, R.E.A.L. sites, 162
 Net Gain, 56
 Poynter Center for Media Studies, 199
 San Jose Mercury News, 199
 A seat at the table, 57
 Society of Professional Journalists, 140
 Society of Professional Journalists Freedom of Information, 163
 StudentPress, 94
 Student Press Law Center, 162
 A tour of our uncertain future, 56

Record, in computer program, 75
Records (personal), creating personal databases, 76-78
Records (public), access vs. privacy issues, 82-87
Reed, Cheryl, use of computers in reporting, 130-31
Regional news, online coverage of, 11-12
Regulation, of online services, 52-53
Reilley, Mike, on online journalism, 115
Reisner, Neil H., 71
Reitz, Stephanie, on computer-assisted reporting, 69-70
Reporters
 for online services, 112-17
 online vs. print, 116-17
 role in electronic age, 36-37, 106
 training in digital skills, 63
 use of computers by, 58, 65-70
Reporting
 objectivity in, 33
 for online news, 116
 roots in literature, 33
Research
 computer-assisted, 58
 importance to reporting, 32
Researchers, professional, 80
Retailers, online marketing by, 51
Reuter, 139
Revenues, in online services, 17-19, 49-50, 91, 115-16
Rheingold, Howard
 on communication revolution, 31
 on need for gatekeepers, 36-37
Ridley-Thomas, Mark, on "Dark Alliance" story, 168
Right of the reply, in McVeigh case, 193
Rights-clearance services, 151
Riley, Steve, on use of database in reporting, 105
Roberts, Gene, on computer-assisted reporting, 67, 70
Robinson, Ray, on computer-assisted reporting, 69
Rodgers, George, Bylines developer, 97, 99
Rodman, Dennis, 115
Rollins, Ron, on Ohio prison riot story, 133
Rosati, Allison, on limitations of databases, 79
Rose, Charlie, and Bloomberg services, 138
Rosen, Jay, on public journalism, 131
Rosenfeld, Stephen, and "Dark Alliance" story, 178-79
Ross, "Freeway" Ricky, subject of "Dark Alliance" story, 174-75, 177, 181-82
Ross, Steven S., on computer-assisted reporting, 68
Row, in spreadsheet, 75
Rowan, Carl T., on "Dark Alliance" story, 173
Royko, Mike, memorialized in online *Chicago Tribune,* 12
Rutkowski, A., 31
Ryan, Bob, on "Dark Alliance" story, 173
Rykiel, Boots, on extent of online audience, 52-53

S

Sagan, Paul
  on online journalism, 135
  on online profits, 157
St. Louis Post-Dispatch, computer-assisted reporting by, 77
Salinger, Pierre, and TWA Flight 800 rumor, 37
Salomon Bros., Bloomberg service with, 136
Salon, 13, 100
Sandoval, Ricardo, on internal reaction to "Dark Alliance" story, 169-70
Sanford, Bruce W., 191
The San Jose Mercury News,
  and computer-assisted reporting, 66
  "Dark Alliance" story explained, 166-71
  "Dark Alliance" story online, 120, 169, 173
  and debate over electronic rights, 156
  online version, 11-12
Saul, Anne, on computer-assisted reporting, 67-68
Schoenfeld, Adam, on broadcast news online, 26
Schreiner, Jim, use of computer-assisted reporting, 109
Schwadron, Terry, on Internet challenge to newspapers, 38
Search engines, advertising revenues of, 54
Searching, with database program, 110
Security, for Internet commercial transactions, 51-52
Senate Select Committee on Intelligence, and "Dark Alliance" story, 178
Sensationalism, 38
Server, World Wide Web, 7
Shannon, Elaine, on "Dark Alliance" story, 183
Shaw, David, 49, 88
Shepard, Alicia C., 124
Shepard, Charles
  move to online journalism, 99
  on new journalism job skills, 100, 101
Sheppard, Sam, 187
Shopping, online, 39-40, 51
Siceloff, Bruce, on requirements of online journalism, 107
Sidewalk, 12, 42-43, 127
Sidlo, Steve, on changes in journalism, 129
Silberman, Michael, on MSNBC, 125, 126
Simon, Bob, and debate over electronic rights, 157
Simons, David, on online journalism, 135
Simpson, O. J.
  trial reported online, 38
  use of CAR in trial coverage, 72
Singer, Jane, on online journalism skills, 95
Singer, Rena, 65
SI Online, 13
Slate
  charging for access to, 50
  online offerings of, 13
  staff member's duties, 122
Small, Biggie, murder story online, 44

Smith, Trisha, on online journalism, 121
Smith, Vern E., on "Dark Alliance" story, 183
Society for Displaced Journalists, 128
Software
  for computer-assisted reporting, 110-11
  database, 71, 73, 74, 77
Sorting, with database program, 110
Sources, questioning authenticity of, 197
South Dakota e-mail censorship incident, 148-49
South Hackensack corruption story, 71
Sparkman, Robin, move to online journalism, 118, 120
Spartanburg Herald-Journal, computer programs developed by, 73
Special requests, for public records, 86
Sports, audience interest in, 46
Sports Illustrated, online offerings of, 13
The Sports Network, 13
Sports news, online coverage of, 13
Spreadsheets, and computer-assisted reporting, 71, 73, 74, 75
Stahlman, Mark, on online journalism, 119
StarNet, 33-34
The Star Tribune, use of custom databases, 77
Statistical software programs, 110
Statistics, as reporting skill, 70
Steele, Bob, 196
Steele, James, and investigative reporting, 181
Steffens, Martha, on community-assisted reporting, 131, 132
Steiger, Paul
  on newspapers vs. electronic media, 35
  on Wall Street Journal Interactive Edition, 90
Steinhardt, Barry, on legislating Internet content, 145
Stepp, Carl Sessions, 97
Stevens, Hugh, on access to public records, 86
Stevens, Richard, on public access to Wake County (NC) data, 86
Stith, Pat, on computer-assisted reporting, 70, 104
Stock houses, 151-52
Story boards, use in online reporting, 114
Strauss, Trip, on Bloomberg services, 139
Structured query language (SQL), 110
Sullivan, Drew, 68, 76
Supernet, 25
Suro, Robert, criticism of "Dark Alliance" story, 176
Swann, John, and *Dayton Daily News* education project, 132
Sybase software, 77

T

Talbot, David, move to online publishing, 100
Talk radio, and "Dark Alliance" story, 173, 174

Tasini, Jonathan, and freelance rights, 157
Taxation, and online commerce, 144, 145-46
Tax records, and public records policies, 83
Team journalism, and computer use, 103
Technical standards, for World Wide Web, 6
Technology
  advances in, 3-4, 30
  and changes to traditional journalism, 129-33
Technology news, online examples, 13
Telegraph, social impact of, 3-4
Television
  advertising revenues vs. online, 54
  influence on newspapers, 37-38
  similarity to online content development, 126
Television news
  and computer-assisted reporting, 67, 73
  development of online versions, 25-29
Television programs, permission to use, 151
Text, online vs. print, 100-101
Thomas, Robert and Carleen, obscenity conviction, 145
Thompson & Thompson, rights-clearance service, 151
Tillson, Brad, and *Dayton Daily News* education project, 132
Time Inc., cost of online offerings, 18
Time Online, coverage of Heaven's Gate suicides, 11
Times Mirror, and online real estate site, 40
Time Warner, revenue losses of Pathfinder, 49
Todd, Rusty, on Bloomberg service, 137
Torok, Tom, creation of CAR database, 69
Train, social impact of, 4
Training, in computer-assisted reporting, 63, 66-68, 70
Tribe, Lawrence, on freedom of press, 190
Tribune Co., ownership in online businesses, 116
Tucher, Andie, 15
Turner, Patricia, on "Dark Alliance" story response, 174
Turow, Scott, and Bloomberg services, 137
TWA Flight 800, electronic misinformation about, 37

U

Unabomber, online publication of manifesto, 28
Unique users, measuring online audience by, 52
Universal resource locator (URL), creation of, 7
University of Oklahoma, cutting access to sexually explicit newsgroups, 148
Urban directories, 42-43
USA Today, online marketing service, 51
U. S. Copyright Office, and obtaining reproduction rights, 151

V

Values, for online journalism, 159-61
Van Slambrouck, Paul, role in "Dark Alliance" story, 169, 171
Virtual Melanin, 44, 47
Virtual Voyager, 92
Vistica, Gregory L., on "Dark Alliance" story, 183
Vote fraud story, use of computer-assisted reporting, 108-9

W

Wake County, NC, public records policies, 82-87
Walker, James, on limitations of databases, 79, 80, 81
The Wall Street Journal, approach to online publishing, 22, 90-91
Wannamaker, John, 52
War, use of telegraph in, 3-4
The Washington Post,
    criticism of "Dark Alliance" story, 167, 176-77, 179, 180
    online version, 11, 121
Washingtonpost.com, audience figures, 121
Wasow, Omar, 47, 48
Waters, Charlie, and writers' bill of rights, 133
Waters, Maxine, and "Dark Alliance" story, 167, 174, 175
Webb, Gary, and "Dark Alliance" story, 167, 168, 169, 170, 171, 172, 174, 180, 181-84
Web browsers
    development of, 6, 8
    use with custom databases, 78
Weeks, Linton, 136
Weights-and-measures conversion program, 73
Weinberg, Steve, on "Dark Alliance" story, 175
Weiner, Tim, on "Dark Alliance" story, 172, 176
Weir, David
    on accuracy in online journalism, 37
    and HotWired journalism, 135
The WELL, 33
Wendland, Mike, on computer-assisted reporting, 67
Werner, Dan, on broadcast news online, 26
Wheeler, Michael, on broadcast news online, 26, 29
White, Jack, on "Dark Alliance" story response, 174
Whites, use of Internet by, 44
Whitt, Toni, on computer-assisted reporting, 70
Wiesner, Jerome, 20
Williams, Penny, 79
Williamson, Laura, move into online publishing, 101
Winkler, Matthew, and Bloomberg services, 138
Winter, Peter
    on online revenues, 91
    on the role of the Internet, 35
The Wire, 12
Wired magazine, 63
Woelfel, Scott, on CNN online news, 27, 28
Wolfe, Buster, use of computer-assisted reporting by, 68
Wolinsky, Leo, on "Dark Alliance" story, 177
Woods, Dan, work at *The Raleigh News & Observer,* 104
Work product, misappropriation of, 188
World Wide Web
    advertising on, 18, 52-53
    creators' disappointments with, 7-8
    HotWired coverage of, 135
    invention and development of, 5-9
    online publishing approaches via, 88-92
    role in delivery of communications, 33
    story of McVeigh confession on, 193, 195
    use by *The Raleigh News & Observer,* 107
    use of RealAudio on, 89
    See also Internet
World Wide Web Consortium, 5, 6
Wright, Robert, 5
WriterL, 99
Writers' bill of rights, 133
Writing
    effect of new approaches on, 132-33
    electronic rights to, 156-58
    for online vs. print news, 100, 119, 124

X

Xanadu, 7
Xenia, OH, *Dayton Daily News* project, 132

Y

Yahoo!, 39
Yang, Jeffrey, 47, 48
Yarnold, David
    and debate over electronic rights, 156
    role in "Dark Alliance" story, 169
Yellow Pages, electronic, 91
Young, Allegra, on extent of online audience, 53
Youngman, Owe
    on online journalism, 112-13, 115, 116
    on technology and newspapers, 36
Youth violence, *Dayton Daily News* project, 131

Z

ZDNet, 13
Ziff Davis, online offerings of, 13
Zoghlin, Malia, on equipment glitches, 116

Putting it in Perspective
-Review Form-

Your name:_____   Date:_____

Reading title:_____

Summarize: provide a one sentence summary of this reading: _____
_____
_____
_____

Follow the Thinking: how does the author back the main premise of the reading? Are the facts/opinions appropriately supported by research or available data? Is the author's thinking logical?

_____
_____
_____
_____
_____
_____
_____

Develop a Context: answer one or both questions: how does this reading contrast or compliment your professor's lecture treatment of the subject matter? How does this reading compare to your textbook's coverage?

_____
_____
_____
_____
_____
_____
_____

Question Authority: explain why you agree/disagree with the author's main premise?

_____
_____
_____
_____
_____
_____
_____

COPY ME! Copy this form as needed. This form is also available at http://www.courselinks.com Click on: "Putting it in Perspective"